This is the last page.

In keeping with the original Japanese comic format, this book reads from right to left—so action, sound effects, and word balloons are completely reversed. This preserves the orientation of the original artwork—plus, it's fun! Check out the diagram shown here to get the hang of things, and then turn to the other side of the book to get started!

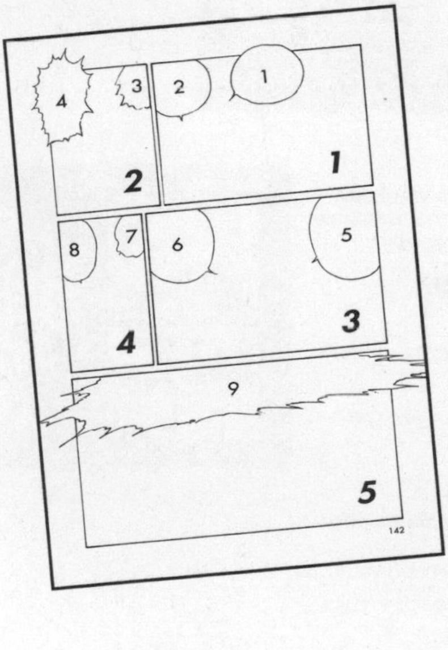
1
2
1
3
4
2
5
6
3
7
8
4
9
5
142

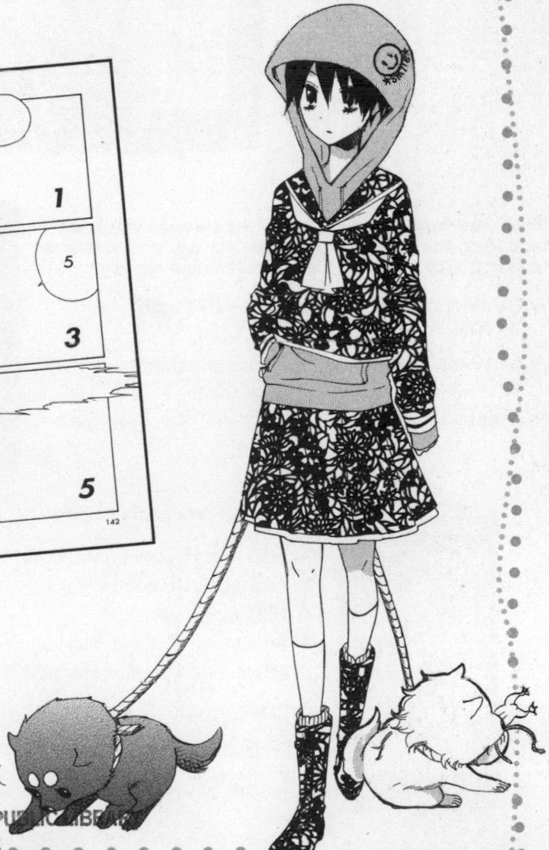

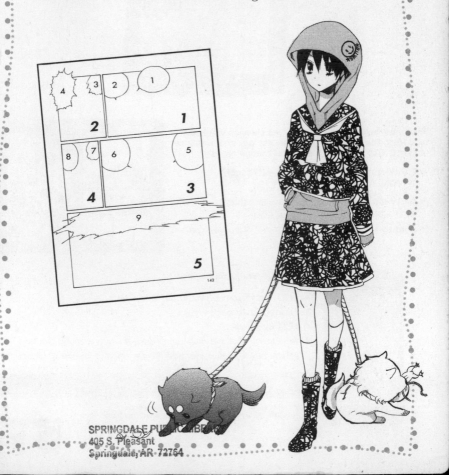

Jiu Jiu

Vol. 5

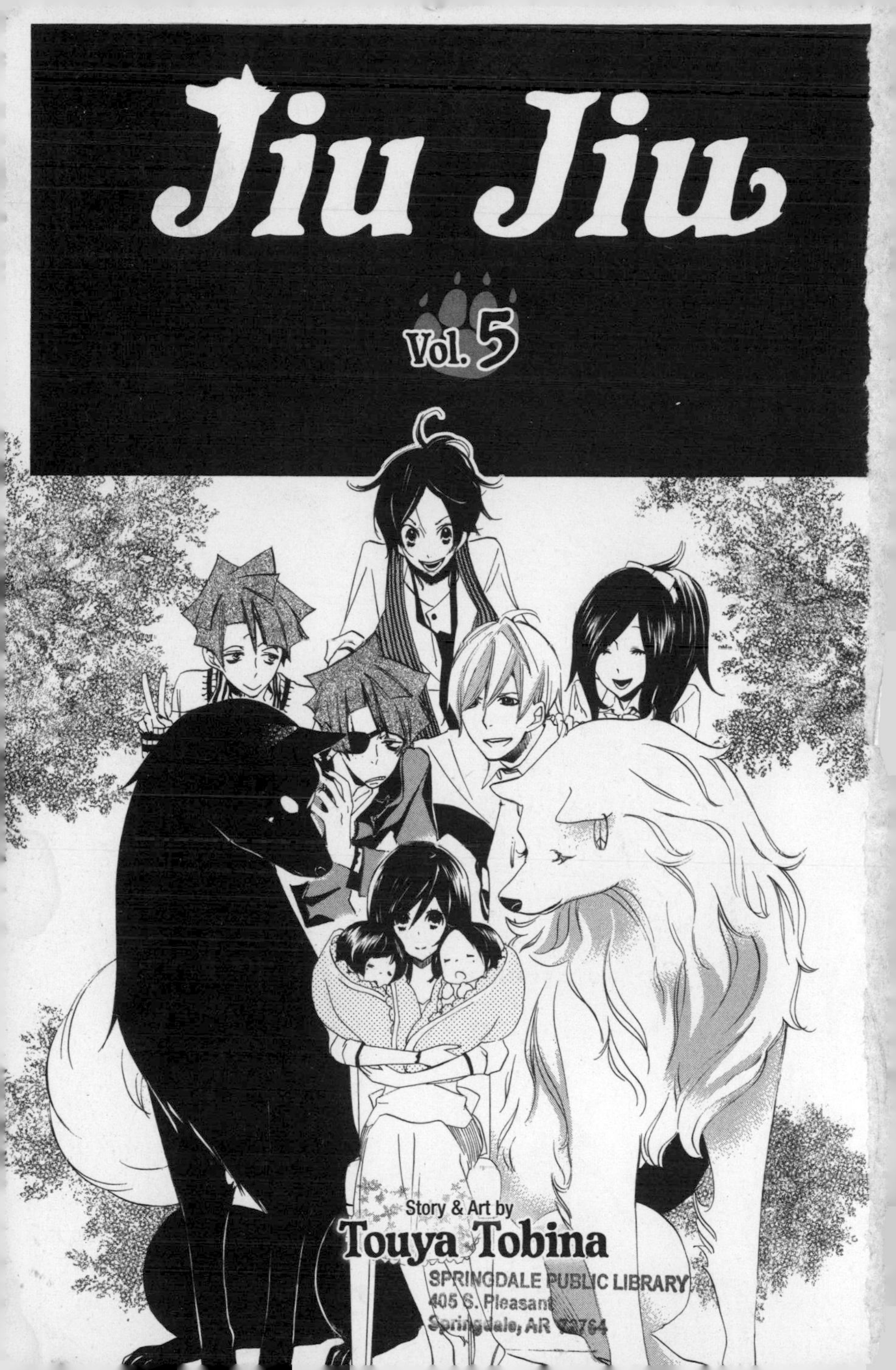

Story & Art by
Touya Tobina

JIUJIU 5

Contents

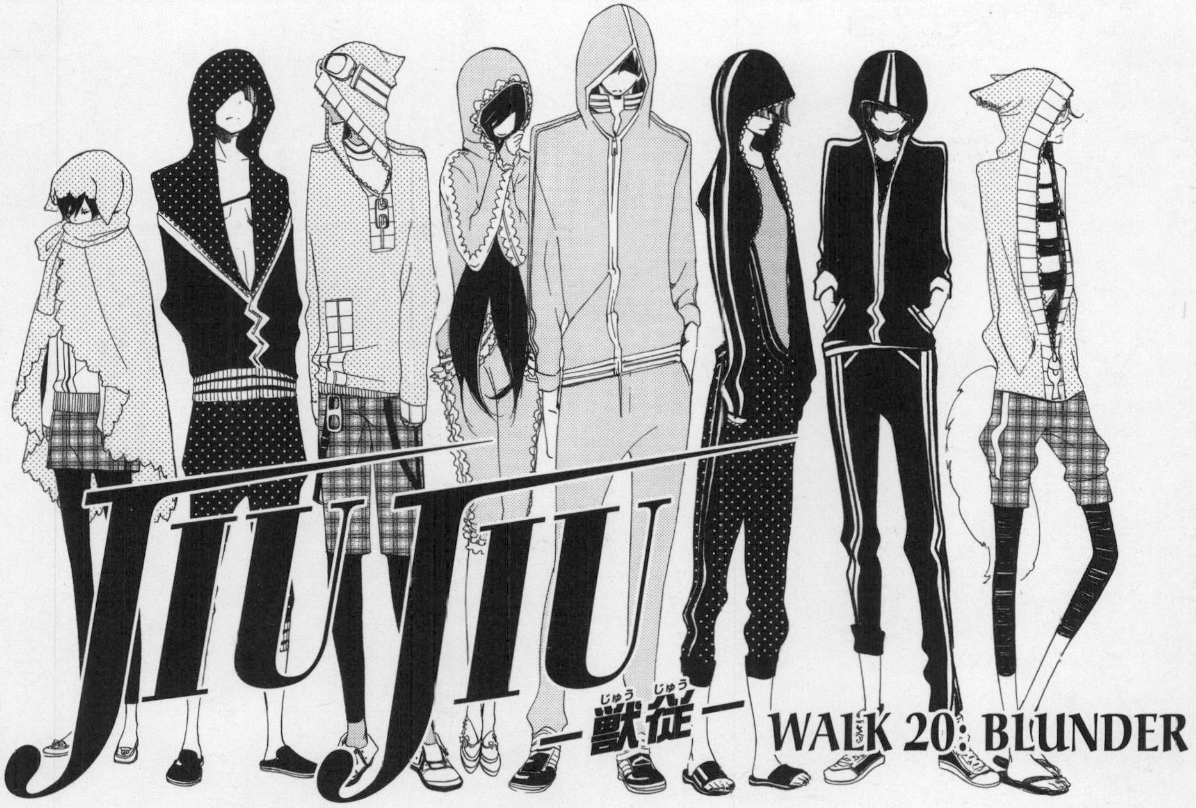
JIUJIU
—獣従—
WALK 20: BLUNDER

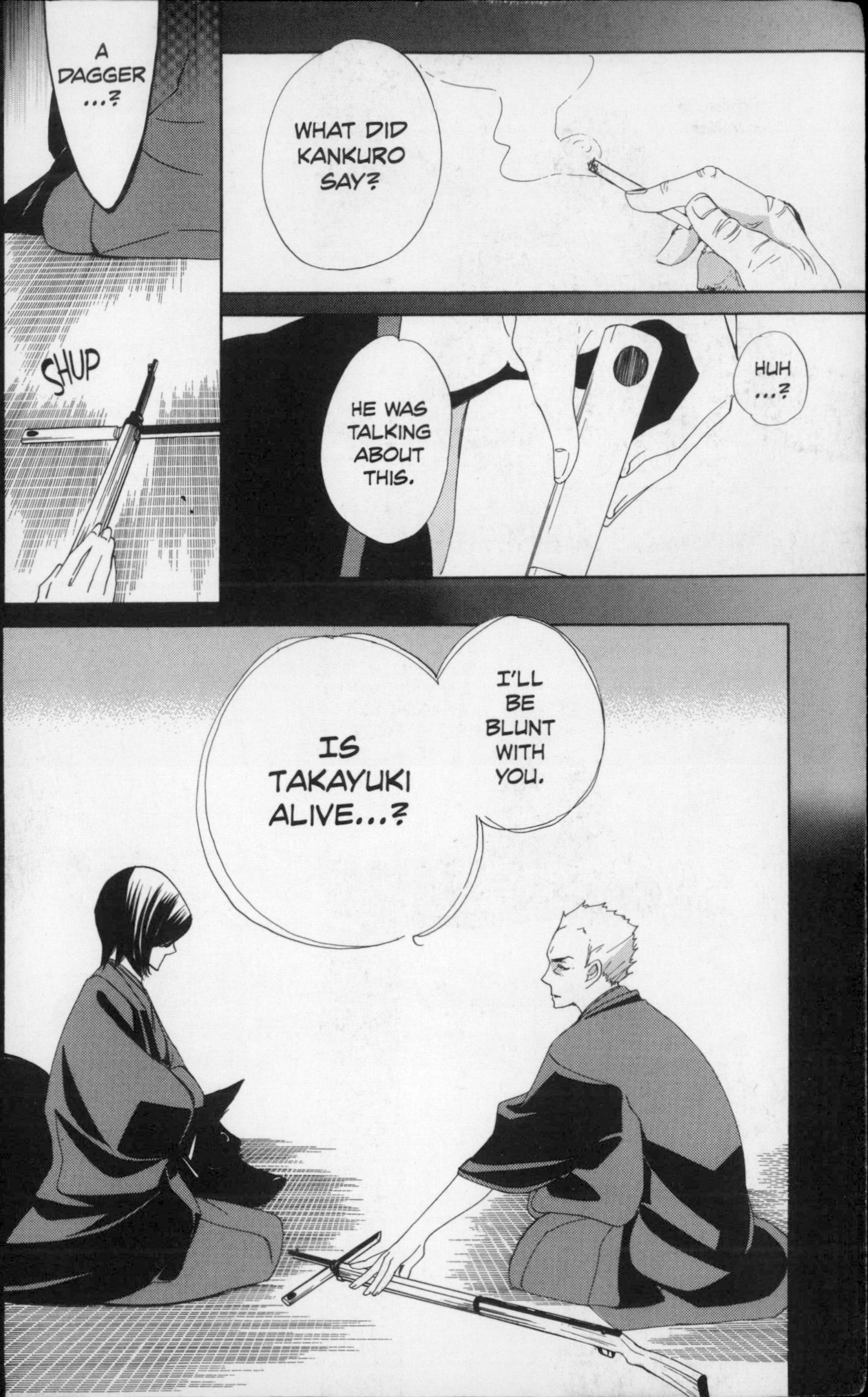
WHAT DID KANKURO SAY?
A DAGGER ...?
HUH ...?
HE WAS TALKING ABOUT THIS.
SHUP
I'LL BE BLUNT WITH YOU.
IS TAKAYUKI ALIVE...?

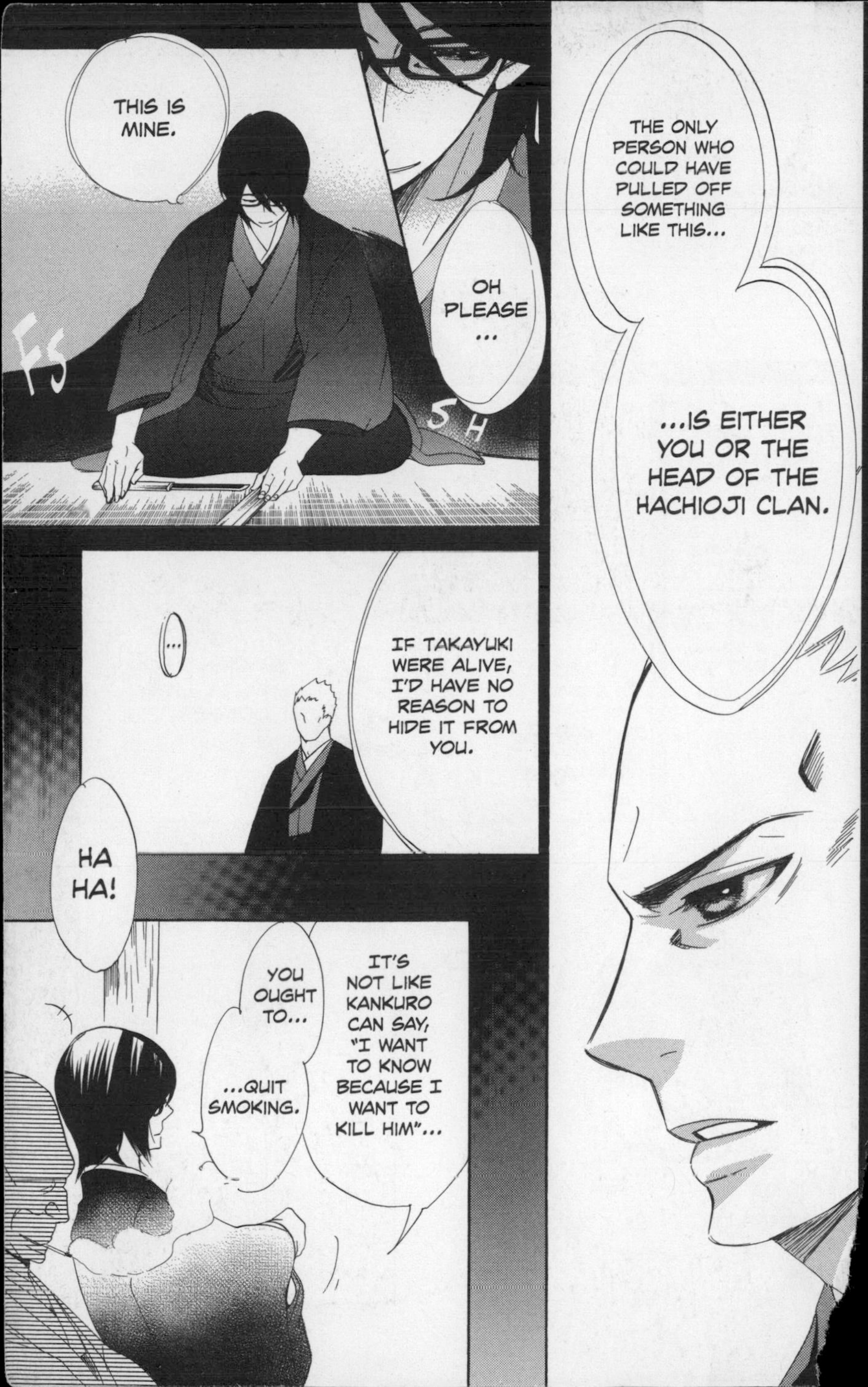
THE ONLY PERSON WHO COULD HAVE PULLED OFF SOMETHING LIKE THIS...
...IS EITHER YOU OR THE HEAD OF THE HACHIOJI CLAN.
THIS IS MINE.
OH PLEASE ...
SH
FS
IF TAKAYUKI WERE ALIVE, I'D HAVE NO REASON TO HIDE IT FROM YOU.
...
HA HA!
IT'S NOT LIKE KANKURO CAN SAY, "I WANT TO KNOW BECAUSE I WANT TO KILL HIM"...
YOU OUGHT TO...
...QUIT SMOKING.

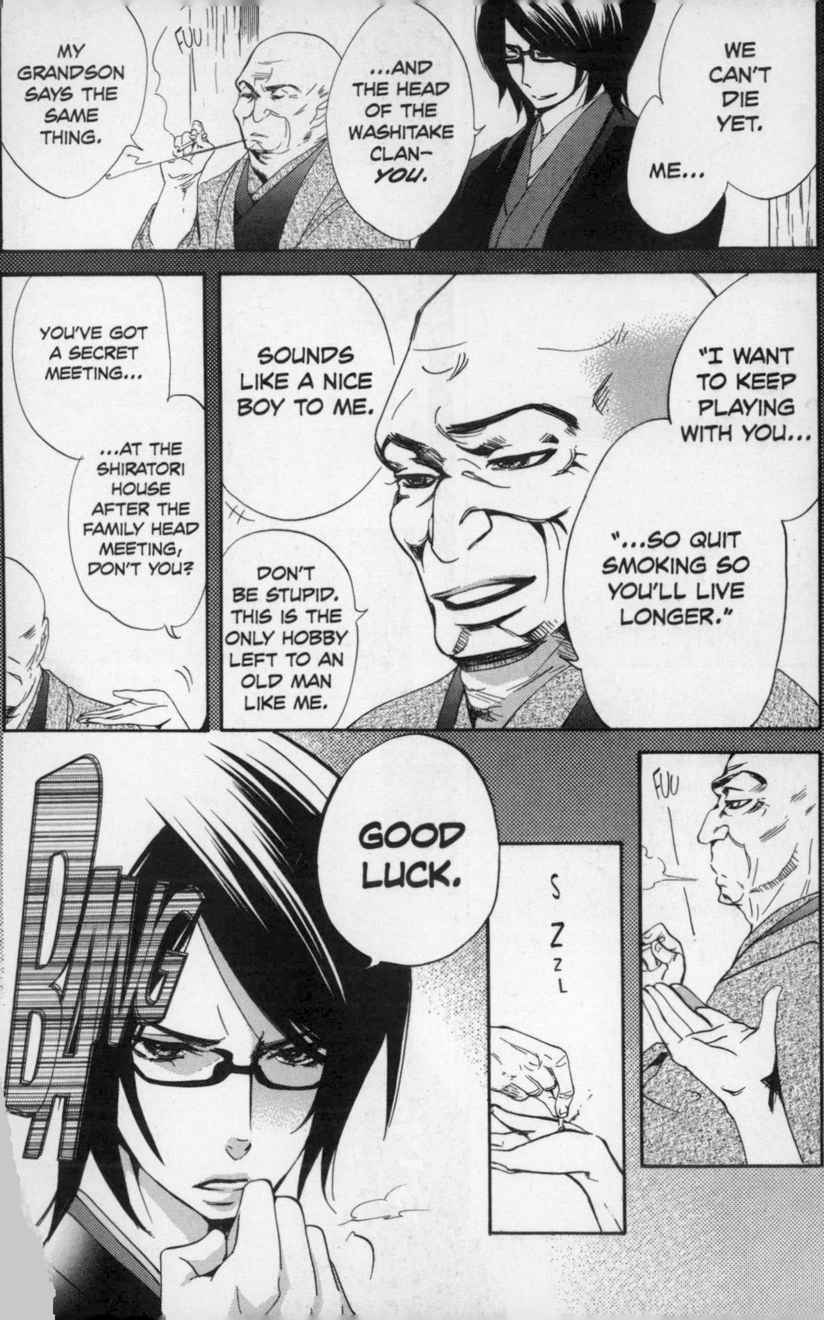
WE CAN'T DIE YET.
ME...
...AND THE HEAD OF THE WASHITAKE CLAN—YOU.
FUU
MY GRANDSON SAYS THE SAME THING.
"I WANT TO KEEP PLAYING WITH YOU...
"...SO QUIT SMOKING SO YOU'LL LIVE LONGER."
SOUNDS LIKE A NICE BOY TO ME.
DON'T BE STUPID. THIS IS THE ONLY HOBBY LEFT TO AN OLD MAN LIKE ME.
YOU'VE GOT A SECRET MEETING...
...AT THE SHIRATORI HOUSE AFTER THE FAMILY HEAD MEETING, DON'T YOU?
FUU
SZZL
GOOD LUCK.

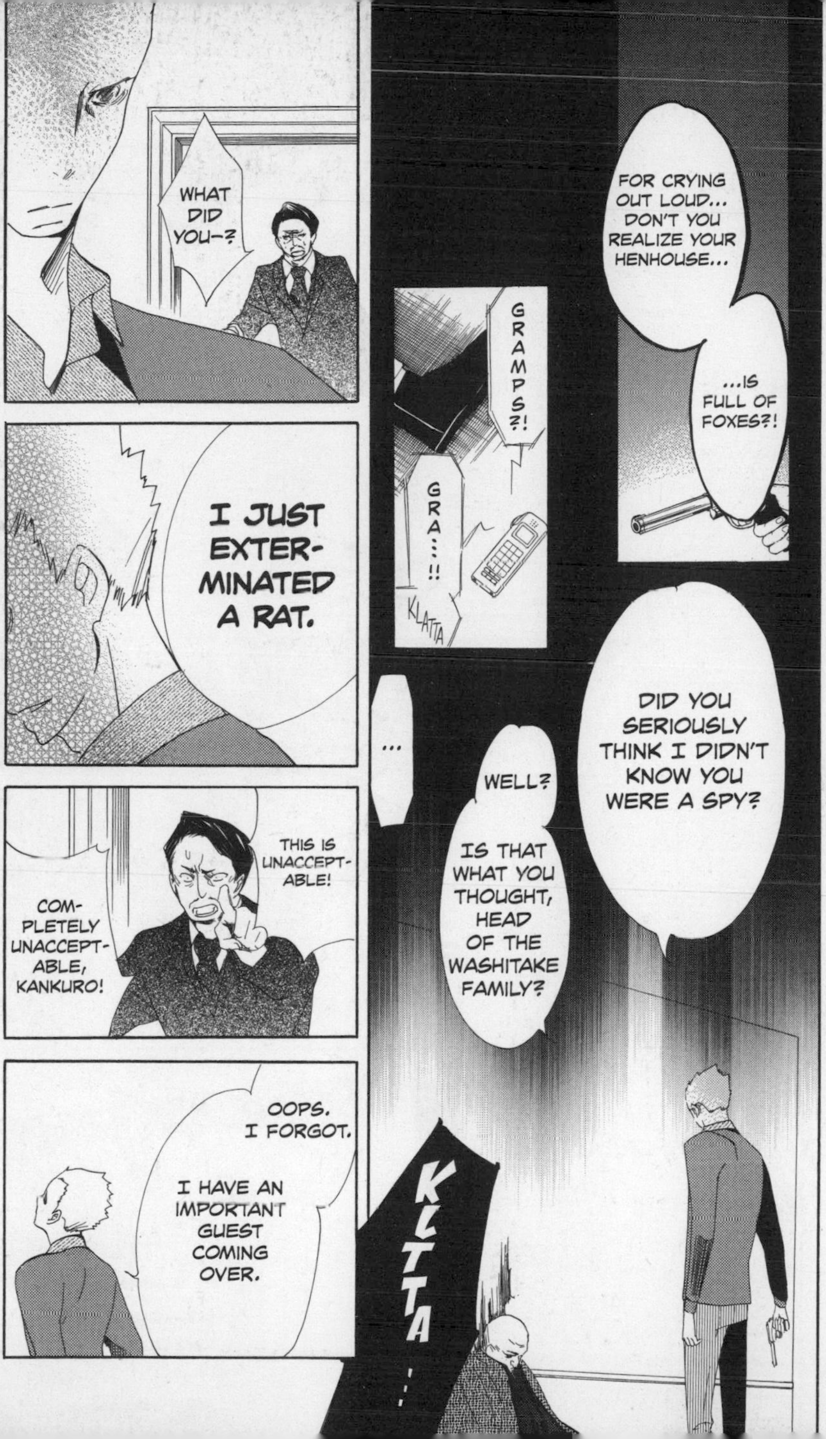
FOR CRYING OUT LOUD... DON'T YOU REALIZE YOUR HENHOUSE...
...IS FULL OF FOXES?!
GRAMPS?!
GRA...!!
KLATTA
DID YOU SERIOUSLY THINK I DIDN'T KNOW YOU WERE A SPY?
WELL?
IS THAT WHAT YOU THOUGHT, HEAD OF THE WASHITAKE FAMILY?
...
KLTTA!!
WHAT DID YOU-?
I JUST EXTERMINATED A RAT.
THIS IS UNACCEPTABLE!
COMPLETELY UNACCEPTABLE, KANKURO!
OOPS. I FORGOT.
I HAVE AN IMPORTANT GUEST COMING OVER.

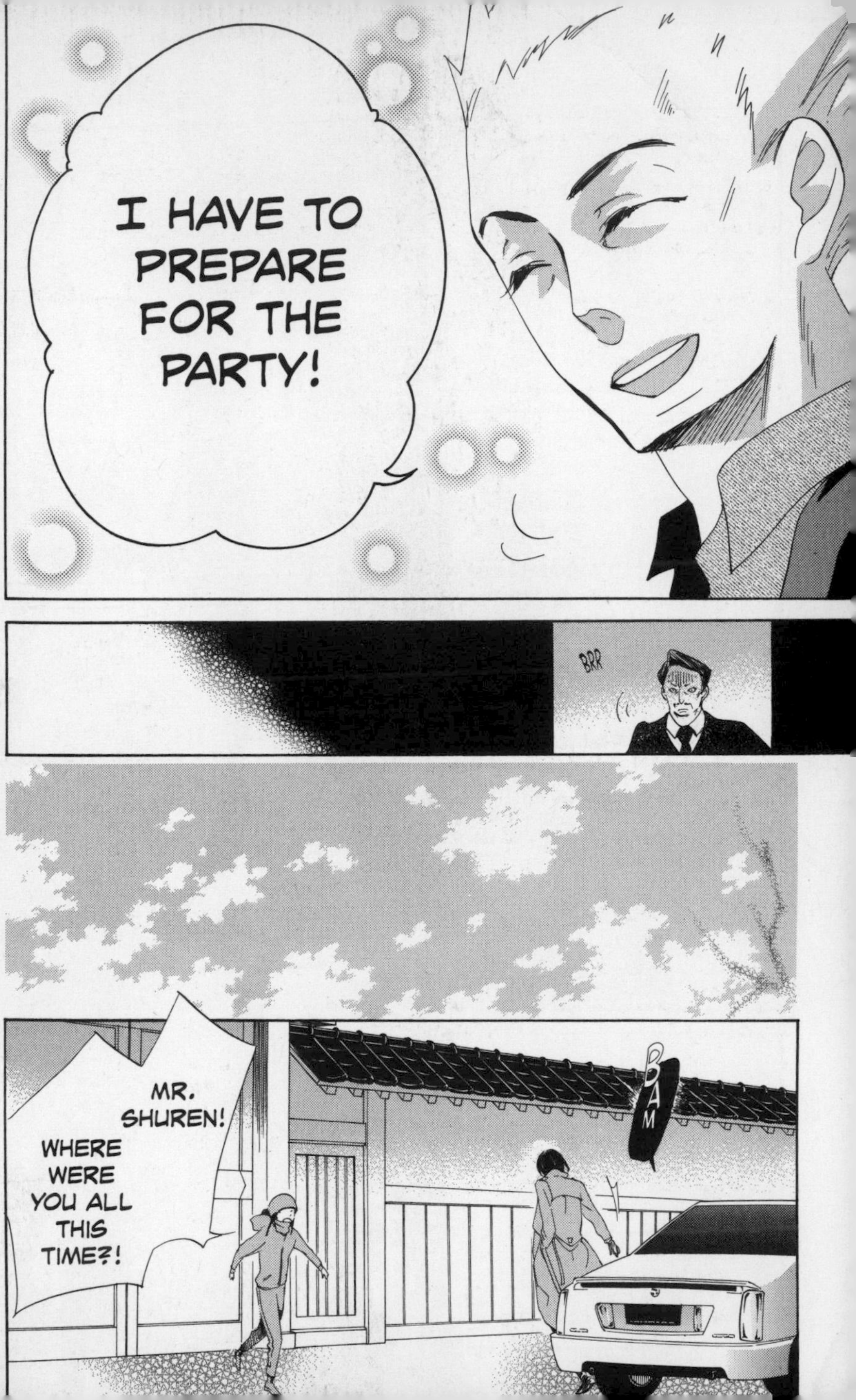
I HAVE TO PREPARE FOR THE PARTY!
BRR
BAM
MR. SHUREN!
WHERE WERE YOU ALL THIS TIME?!

Kanawaga Prefecture: Y-sama

Q: What dialect does Mika speak?

A: Mika dialect. And White speaks White dialect.

Q2: Where is Takamichi's mother?

A: I guess you could say I'm Takamichi's mother in a way...

Q3: Night is wearing earrings too, isn't he?

A: Oh! You're right!!

Q4: Volume 3, chapter 15. Re: The scene with Kankuro and Miku fighting. Takamichi was wearing shoes in the beginning, but she's barefoot later on. When did she take her shoes off?

A: Er... Well, I popped out of nowhere like *swish* and took her shoes off like *swish*... You know how that goes...

Tottori Prefecture: Tobunki-sama

Q1: Who is your favorite manga artist and what is your favorite manga?

A: I have lots.

Q2: Do you have any good manga artist friends?

A: I would never be able to get over it if they said, "I'm not friends with that Tobi-whatcha-macallit!" So it's a secret.

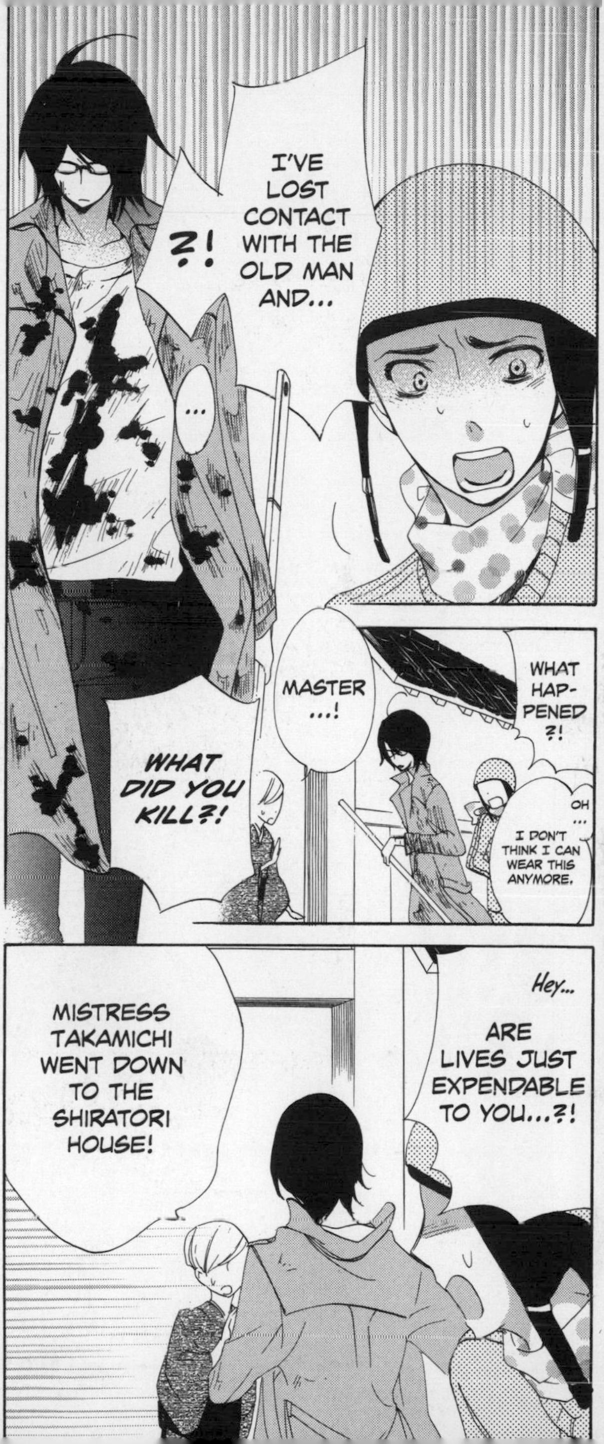
I'VE LOST CONTACT WITH THE OLD MAN AND...
WHAT HAPPENED?!
MASTER...!
OH... I DON'T THINK I CAN WEAR THIS ANYMORE.
?!
...
WHAT DID YOU KILL?!
Hey...
ARE LIVES JUST EXPENDABLE TO YOU...?!
MISTRESS TAKAMICHI WENT DOWN TO THE SHIRATORI HOUSE!

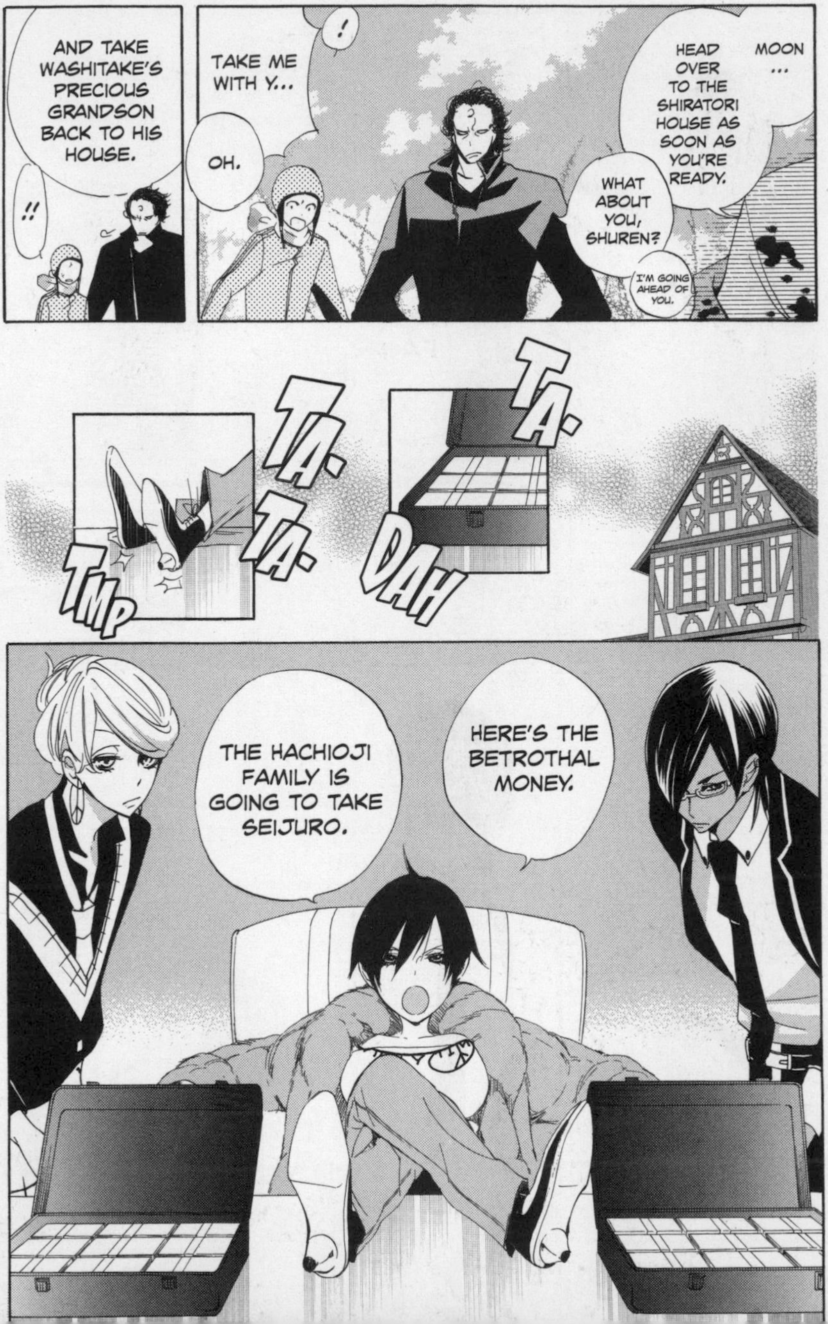
MOON ...
HEAD OVER TO THE SHIRATORI HOUSE AS SOON AS YOU'RE READY.
WHAT ABOUT YOU, SHUREN?
I'M GOING AHEAD OF YOU.
!
TAKE ME WITH Y...
OH.
AND TAKE WASHITAKE'S PRECIOUS GRANDSON BACK TO HIS HOUSE.
!!
TA-
TA-
TA-
DAH
TMP
HERE'S THE BETROTHAL MONEY.
THE HACHIOJI FAMILY IS GOING TO TAKE SEIJURO.

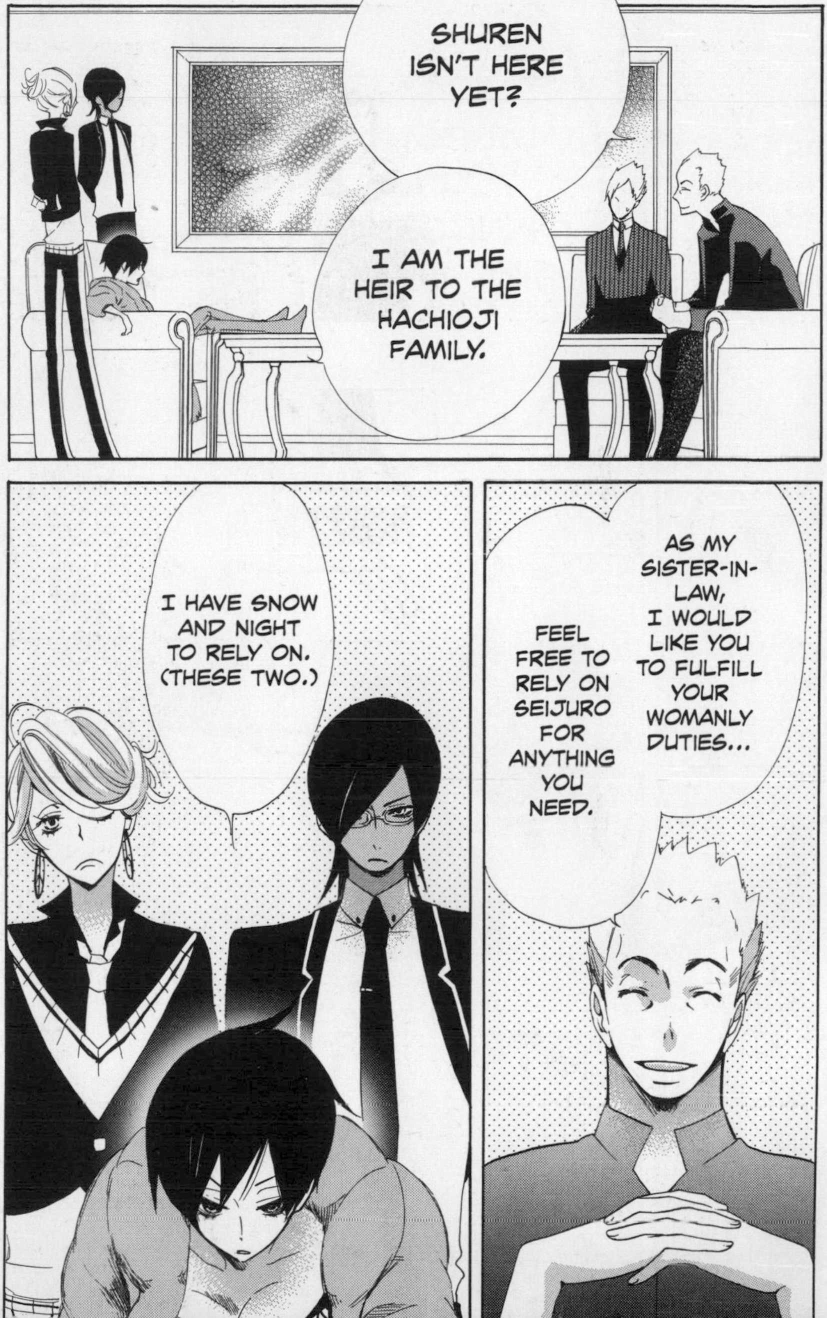
SHUREN ISN'T HERE YET?
I AM THE HEIR TO THE HACHIOJI FAMILY.
AS MY SISTER-IN-LAW, I WOULD LIKE YOU TO FULFILL YOUR WOMANLY DUTIES...
FEEL FREE TO RELY ON SEIJURO FOR ANYTHING YOU NEED.
I HAVE SNOW AND NIGHT TO RELY ON. (THESE TWO.)

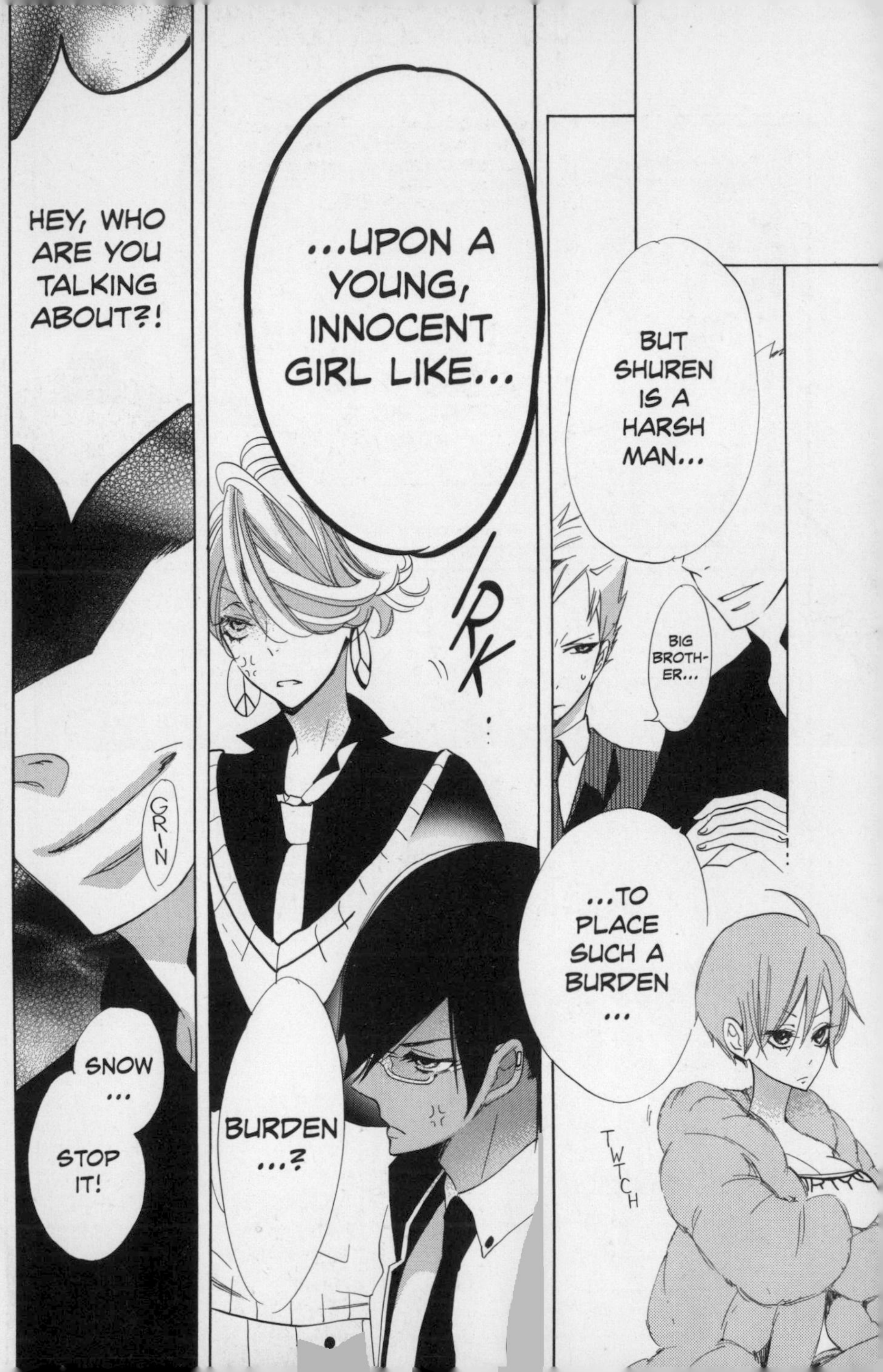
BUT SHUREN IS A HARSH MAN...
BIG BROTHER...
...TO PLACE SUCH A BURDEN ...
TWTCH
...UPON A YOUNG, INNOCENT GIRL LIKE...
IRK
BURDEN ...?
HEY, WHO ARE YOU TALKING ABOUT?!
GRIN
SNOW ... STOP IT!

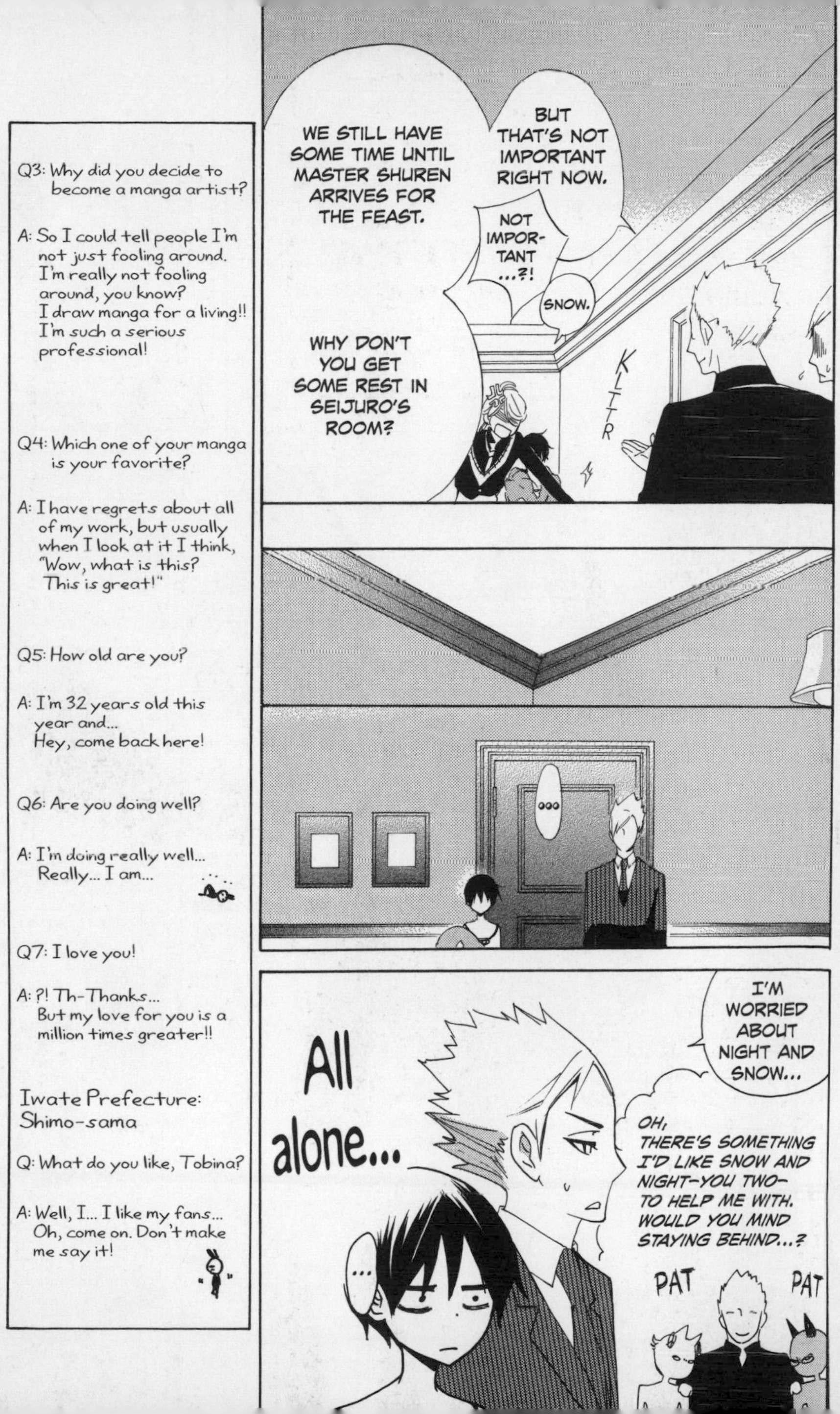
WE STILL HAVE SOME TIME UNTIL MASTER SHUREN ARRIVES FOR THE FEAST.
BUT THAT'S NOT IMPORTANT RIGHT NOW.
NOT IMPORTANT ...?!
SNOW.
KLTTR
WHY DON'T YOU GET SOME REST IN SEIJURO'S ROOM?
...
I'M WORRIED ABOUT NIGHT AND SNOW...
OH, THERE'S SOMETHING I'D LIKE SNOW AND NIGHT—YOU TWO—TO HELP ME WITH. WOULD YOU MIND STAYING BEHIND...?
PAT
PAT
All alone...
...

Q3: Why did you decide to become a manga artist?

A: So I could tell people I'm not just fooling around. I'm really not fooling around, you know? I draw manga for a living!! I'm *such* a serious professional!

Q4: Which one of your manga is your favorite?

A: I have regrets about all of my work, but usually when I look at it I think, "Wow, what is this? This is great!"

Q5: How old are you?

A: I'm 32 years old this year and... Hey, come back here!

Q6: Are you doing well?

A: I'm doing really well... Really... I am...

Q7: I love you!

A: ?! Th-Thanks... But my love for you is a million times greater!!

Iwate Prefecture:
Shimo-sama

Q: What do you like, Tobina?

A: Well, I... I like my fans... Oh, come on. Don't make me say it!

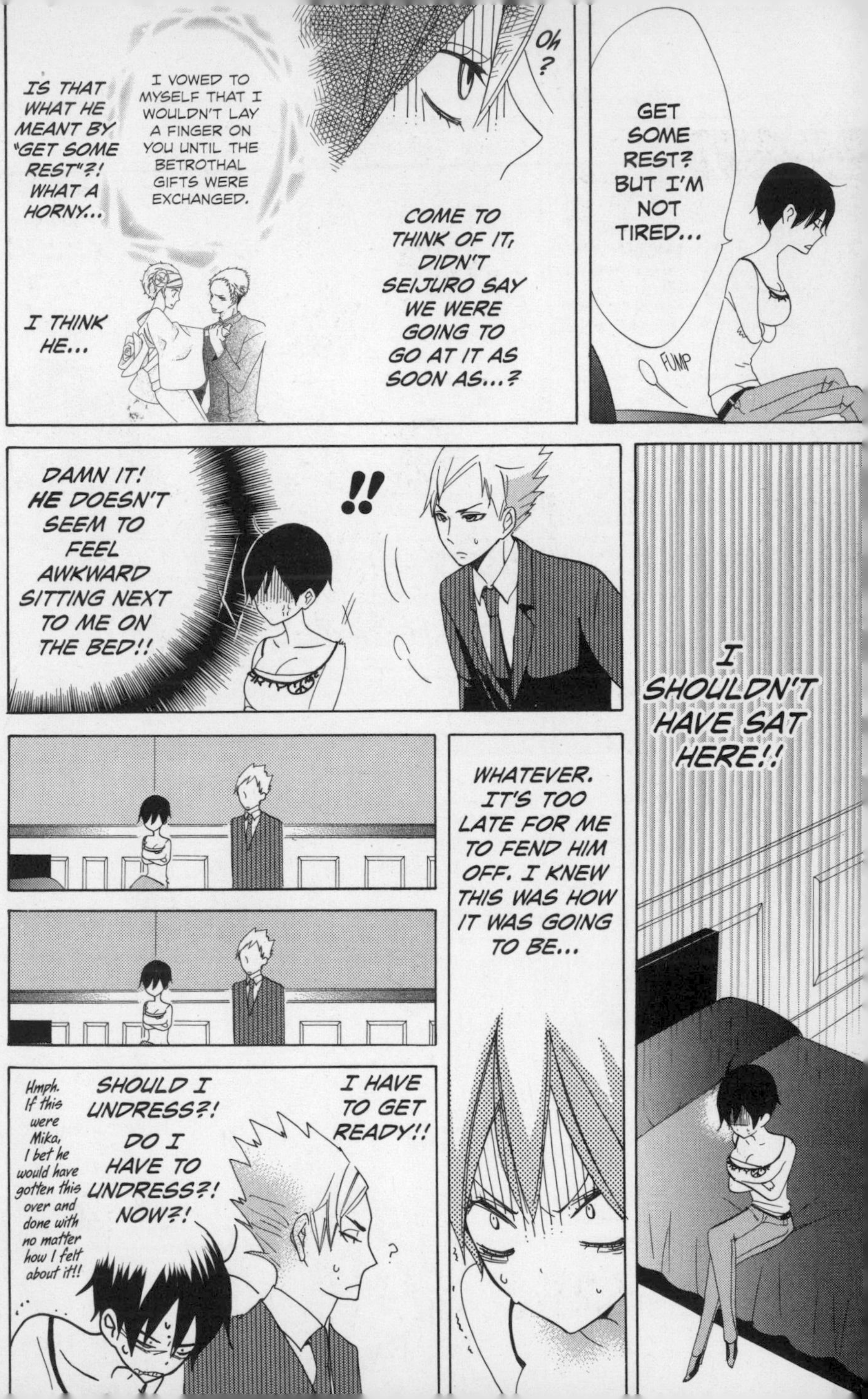
GET SOME REST? BUT I'M NOT TIRED...
FUMP
Oh?
COME TO THINK OF IT, DIDN'T SEIJURO SAY WE WERE GOING TO GO AT IT AS SOON AS...?
I VOWED TO MYSELF THAT I WOULDN'T LAY A FINGER ON YOU UNTIL THE BETROTHAL GIFTS WERE EXCHANGED.
IS THAT WHAT HE MEANT BY "GET SOME REST"?! WHAT A HORNY...
I THINK HE...
I SHOULDN'T HAVE SAT HERE!!
!!
DAMN IT! HE DOESN'T SEEM TO FEEL AWKWARD SITTING NEXT TO ME ON THE BED!!
WHATEVER. IT'S TOO LATE FOR ME TO FEND HIM OFF. I KNEW THIS WAS HOW IT WAS GOING TO BE...
I HAVE TO GET READY!!
SHOULD I UNDRESS?!
DO I HAVE TO UNDRESS?! NOW?!
Hmph. If this were Mika, I bet he would have gotten this over and done with no matter how I felt about it!!
?

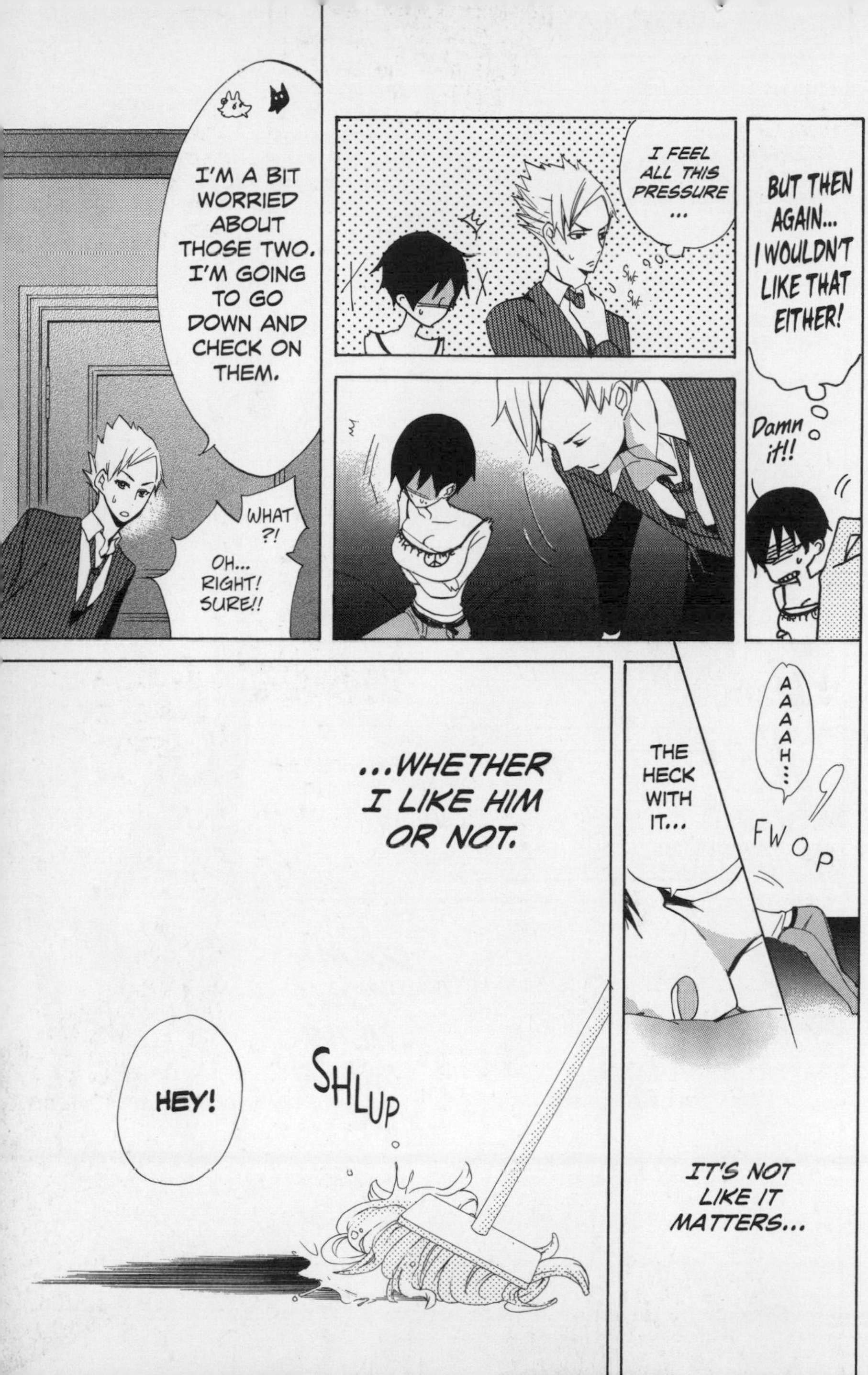
BUT THEN AGAIN... I WOULDN'T LIKE THAT EITHER!
Damn it!!
I FEEL ALL THIS PRESSURE ...
SWF SWF
I'M A BIT WORRIED ABOUT THOSE TWO. I'M GOING TO GO DOWN AND CHECK ON THEM.
WHAT?!
OH... RIGHT! SURE!!
AAAAH...
FWOP
THE HECK WITH IT...
IT'S NOT LIKE IT MATTERS...
...WHETHER I LIKE HIM OR NOT.
SHLUP
HEY!

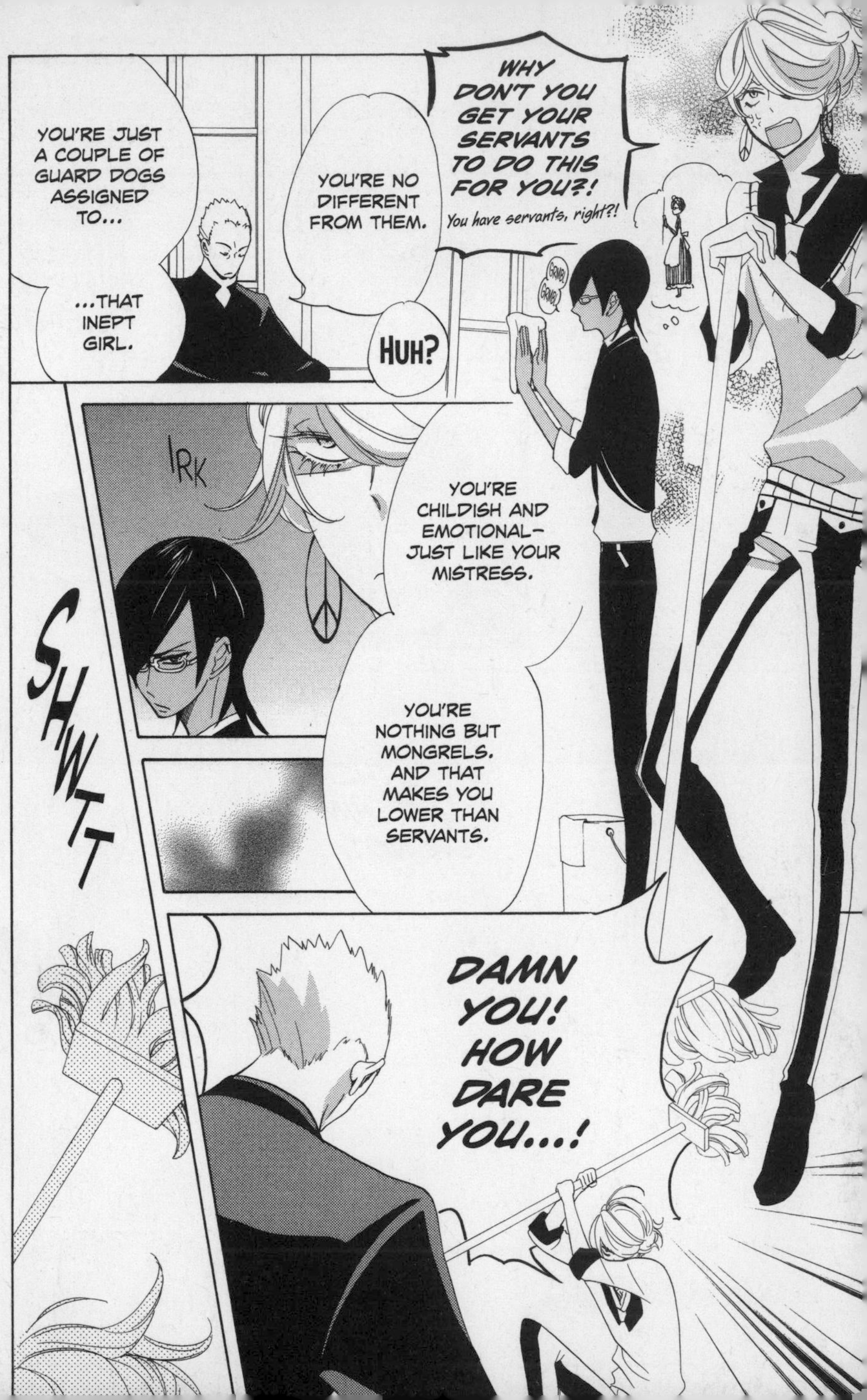
WHY DON'T YOU GET YOUR SERVANTS TO DO THIS FOR YOU?!
You have servants, right?!
GRMBL GRMBL
HUH?
YOU'RE NO DIFFERENT FROM THEM.
YOU'RE JUST A COUPLE OF GUARD DOGS ASSIGNED TO...
...THAT INEPT GIRL.
IRK
YOU'RE CHILDISH AND EMOTIONAL— JUST LIKE YOUR MISTRESS.
YOU'RE NOTHING BUT MONGRELS. AND THAT MAKES YOU LOWER THAN SERVANTS.
SHWTT
DAMN YOU! HOW DARE YOU...!

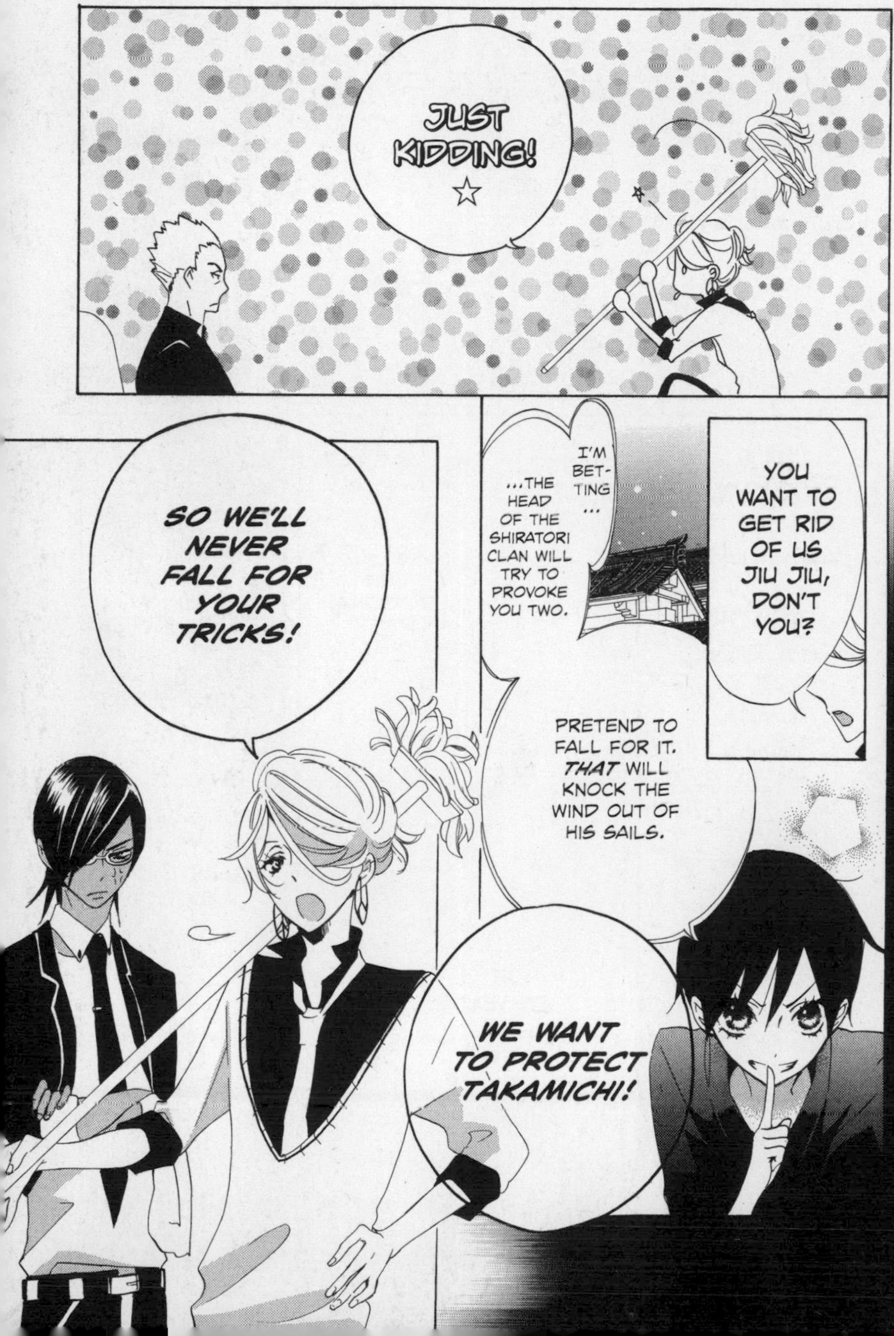
JUST KIDDING! ☆
YOU WANT TO GET RID OF US JIU JIU, DON'T YOU?
I'M BETTING...
...THE HEAD OF THE SHIRATORI CLAN WILL TRY TO PROVOKE YOU TWO.
PRETEND TO FALL FOR IT. *THAT* WILL KNOCK THE WIND OUT OF HIS SAILS.
SO WE'LL NEVER FALL FOR YOUR TRICKS!
WE WANT TO PROTECT TAKAMICHI!

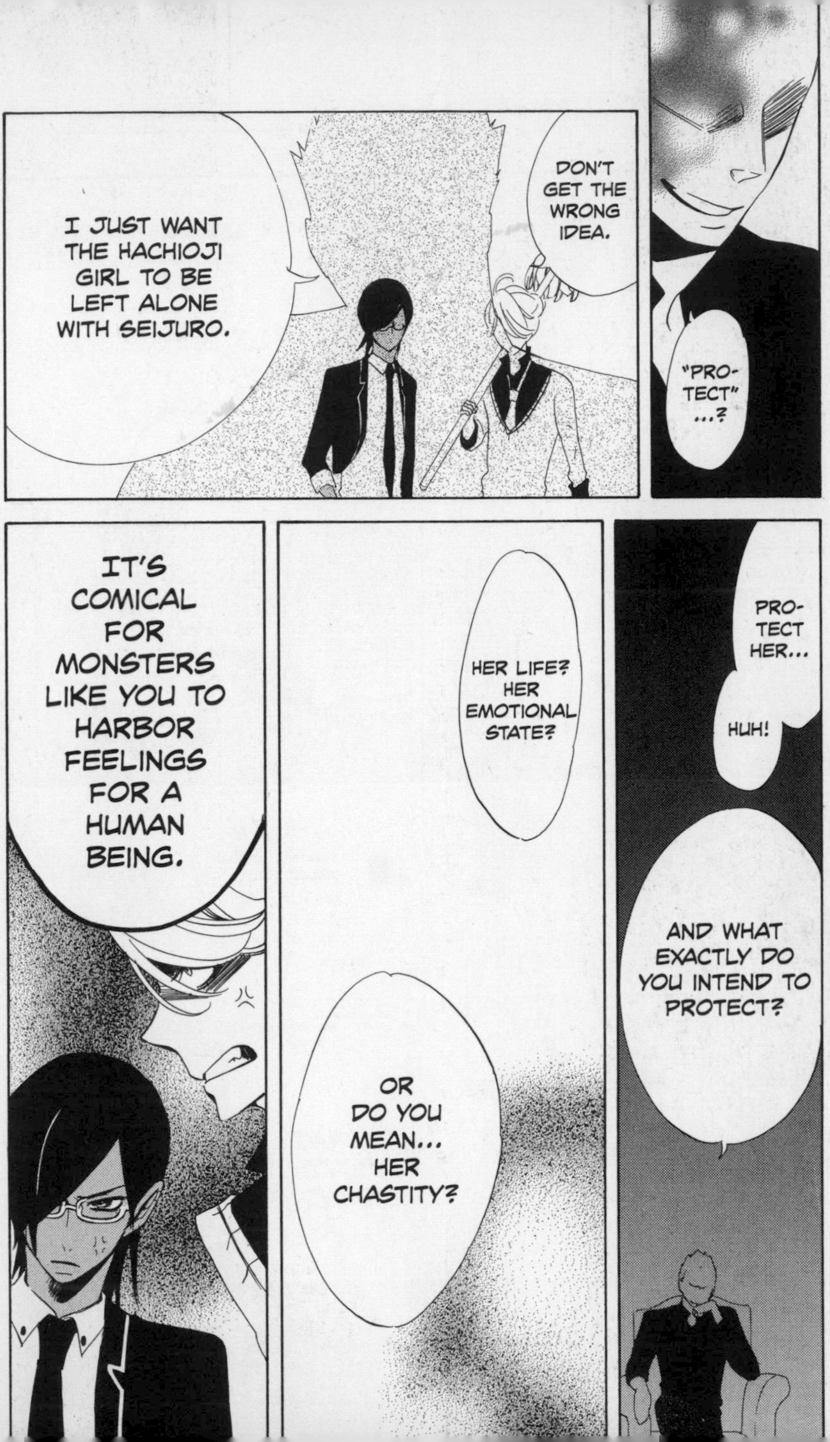
"PRO-TECT"...?
DON'T GET THE WRONG IDEA.
I JUST WANT THE HACHIOJI GIRL TO BE LEFT ALONE WITH SEIJURO.
PRO-TECT HER...
HUH!
AND WHAT EXACTLY DO YOU INTEND TO PROTECT?
HER LIFE? HER EMOTIONAL STATE?
OR DO YOU MEAN... HER CHASTITY?
IT'S COMICAL FOR MONSTERS LIKE YOU TO HARBOR FEELINGS FOR A HUMAN BEING.

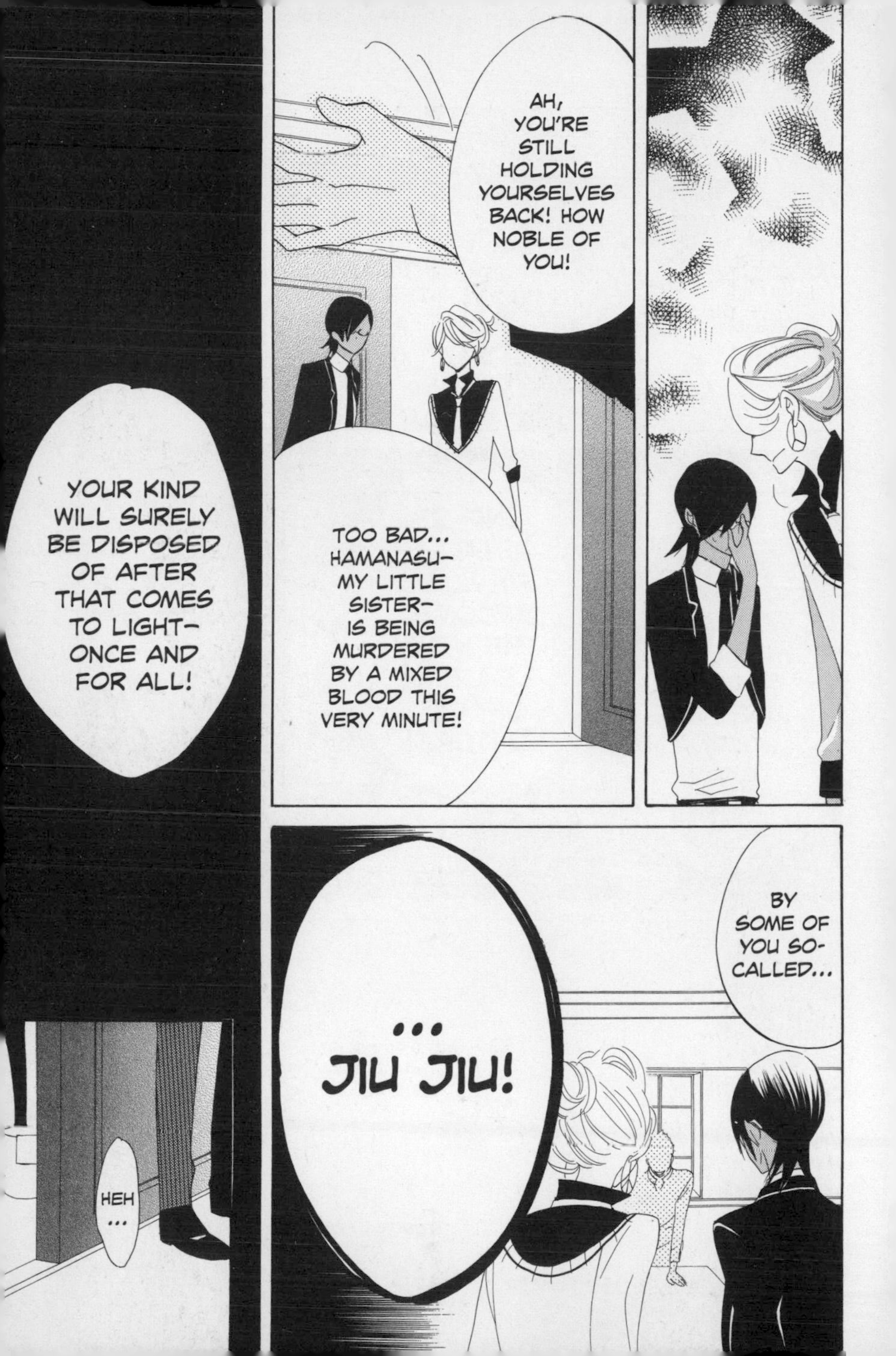
AH, YOU'RE STILL HOLDING YOURSELVES BACK! HOW NOBLE OF YOU!
TOO BAD... HAMANASU— MY LITTLE SISTER— IS BEING MURDERED BY A MIXED BLOOD THIS VERY MINUTE!
BY SOME OF YOU SO-CALLED...
...JIU JIU!
YOUR KIND WILL SURELY BE DISPOSED OF AFTER THAT COMES TO LIGHT— ONCE AND FOR ALL!
HEH...

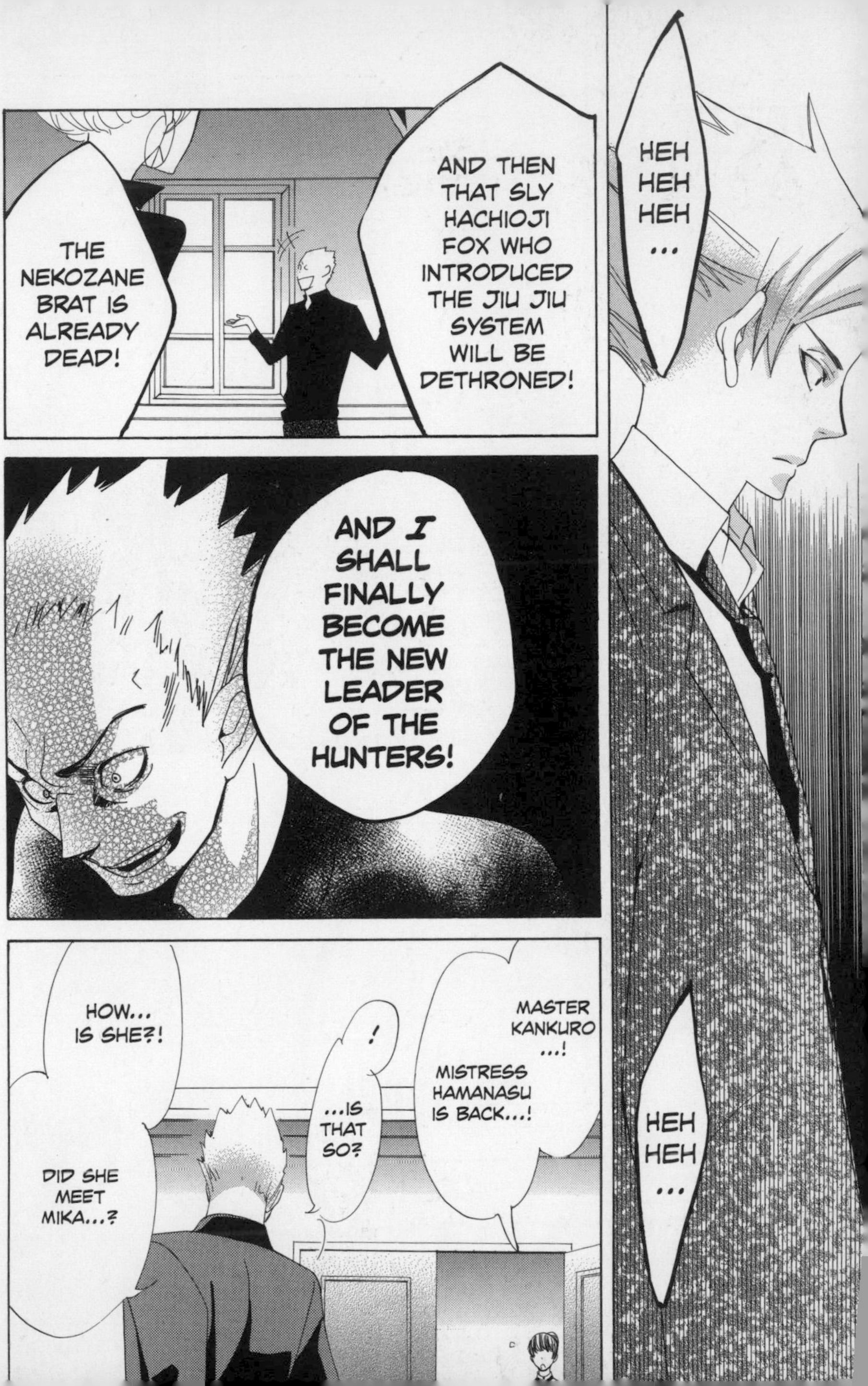
HEH HEH HEH ...
HEH HEH ...
AND THEN THAT SLY HACHIOJI FOX WHO INTRODUCED THE JIU JIU SYSTEM WILL BE DETHRONED!
THE NEKOZANE BRAT IS ALREADY DEAD!
AND I SHALL FINALLY BECOME THE NEW LEADER OF THE HUNTERS!
MASTER KANKURO ...!
MISTRESS HAMANASU IS BACK...!
!
...IS THAT SO?
HOW... IS SHE?!
DID SHE MEET MIKA...?

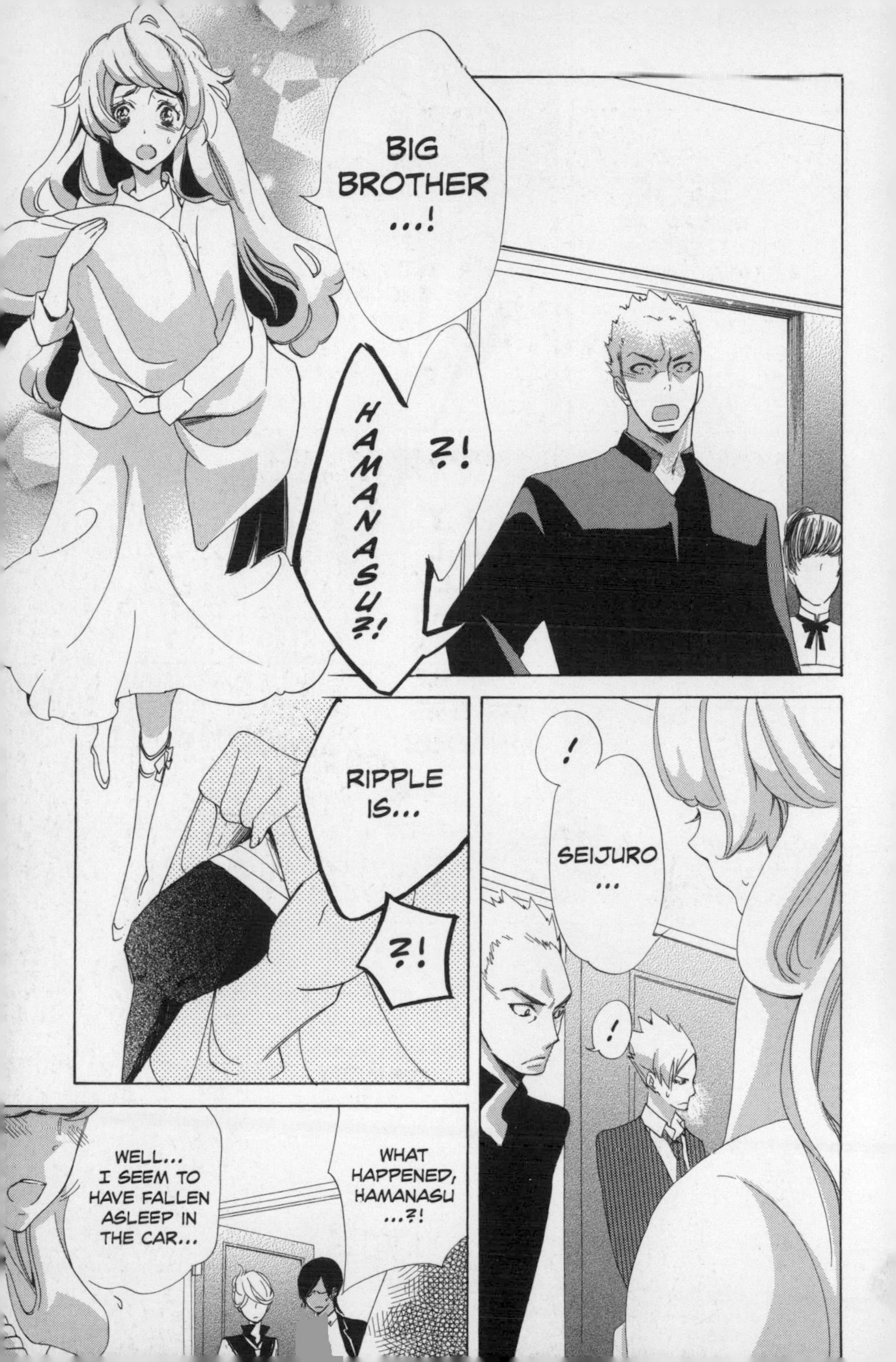
BIG BROTHER ...!
?!
HAMANASU?!
!
SEIJURO ...
!
RIPPLE IS...
?!
WHAT HAPPENED, HAMANASU ...?!
WELL... I SEEM TO HAVE FALLEN ASLEEP IN THE CAR...

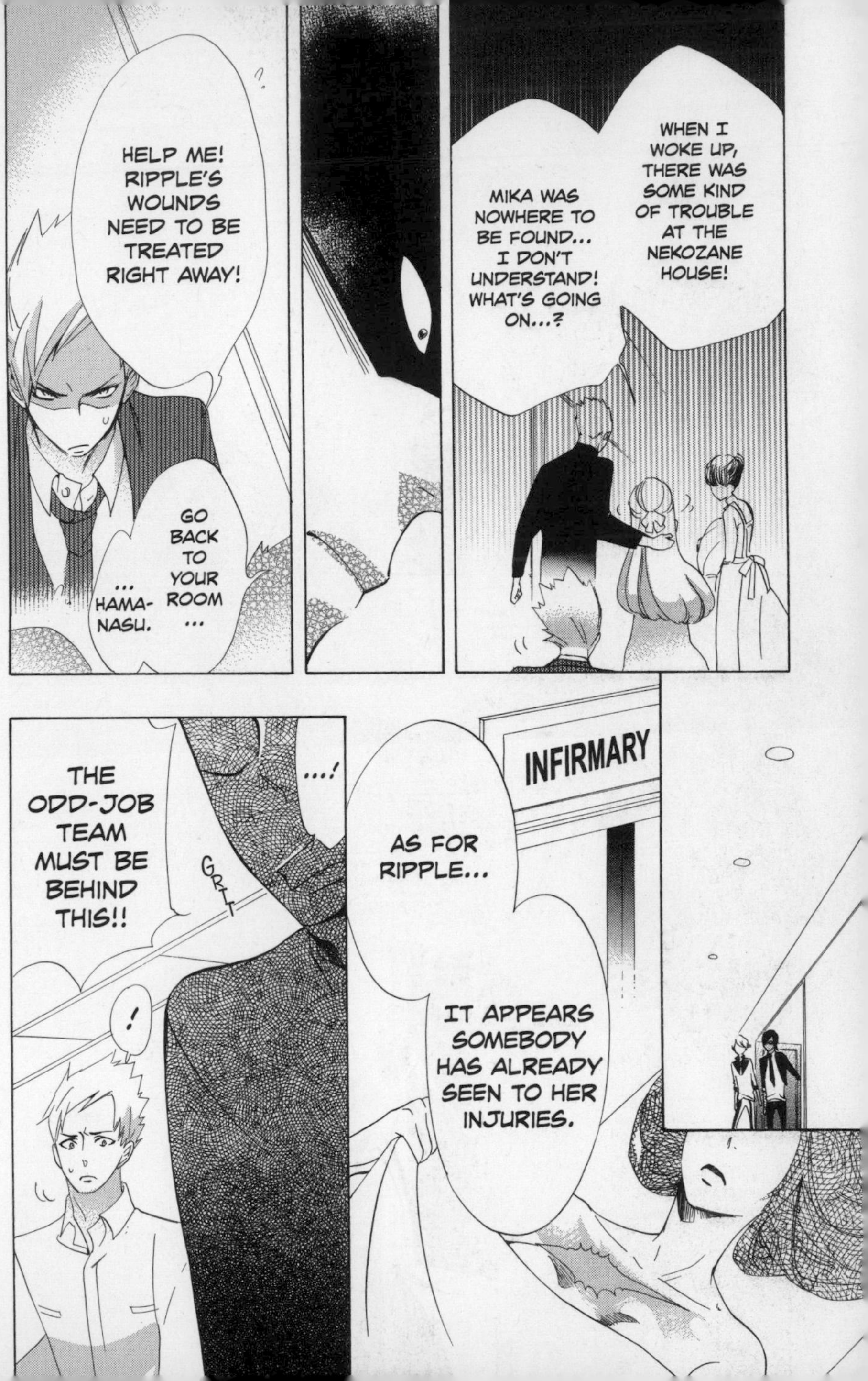
WHEN I WOKE UP, THERE WAS SOME KIND OF TROUBLE AT THE NEKOZANE HOUSE!
MIKA WAS NOWHERE TO BE FOUND... I DON'T UNDERSTAND! WHAT'S GOING ON...?
?
HELP ME! RIPPLE'S WOUNDS NEED TO BE TREATED RIGHT AWAY!
GO BACK TO YOUR ROOM ...
... HAMA-NASU.
INFIRMARY
AS FOR RIPPLE...
IT APPEARS SOMEBODY HAS ALREADY SEEN TO HER INJURIES.
!!
...!
THE ODD-JOB TEAM MUST BE BEHIND THIS!!
GRIT
!

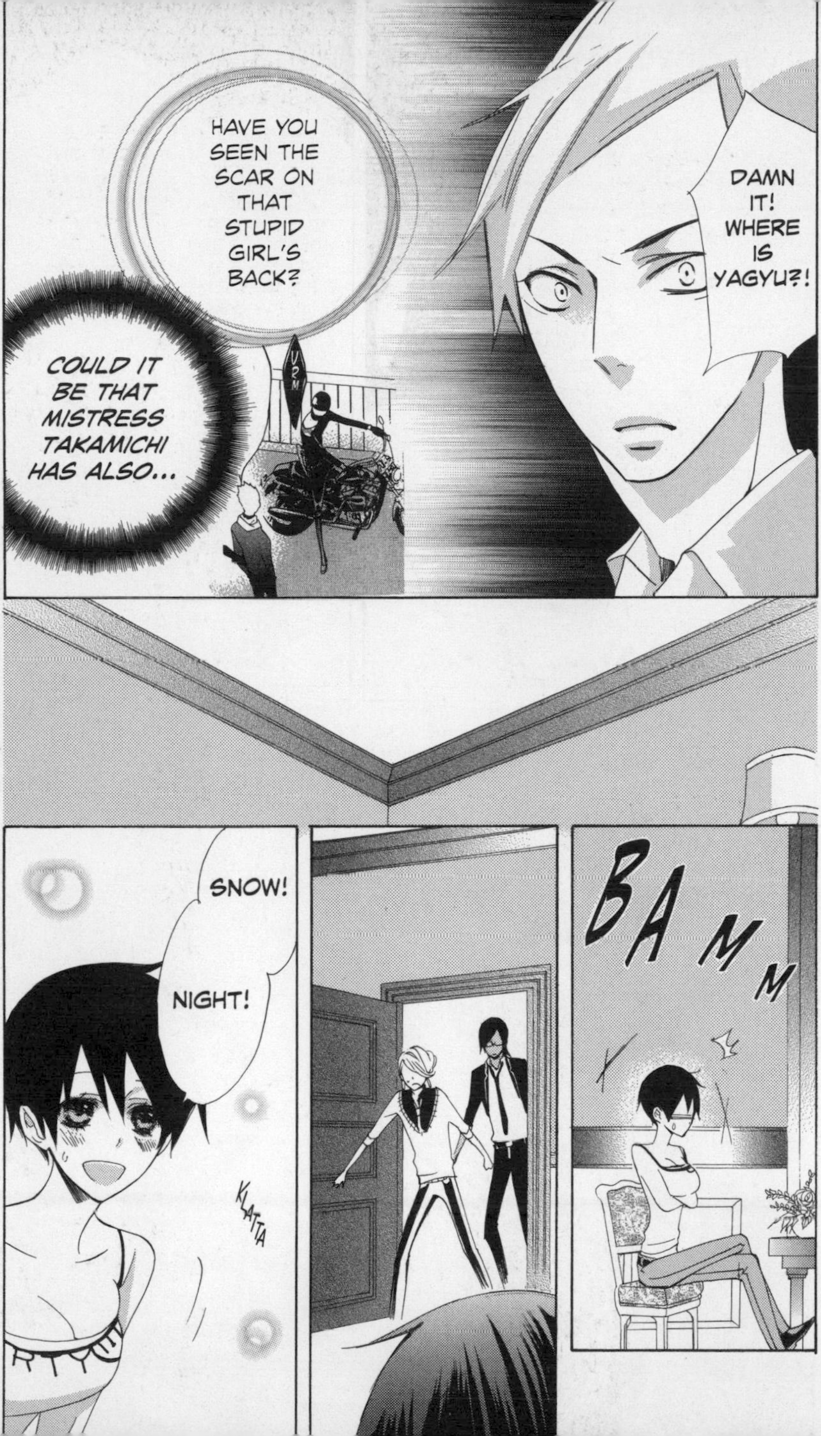
DAMN IT! WHERE IS YAGYU?!
HAVE YOU SEEN THE SCAR ON THAT STUPID GIRL'S BACK?
COULD IT BE THAT MISTRESS TAKAMICHI HAS ALSO...
BAMM
SNOW!
NIGHT!
KLATTA

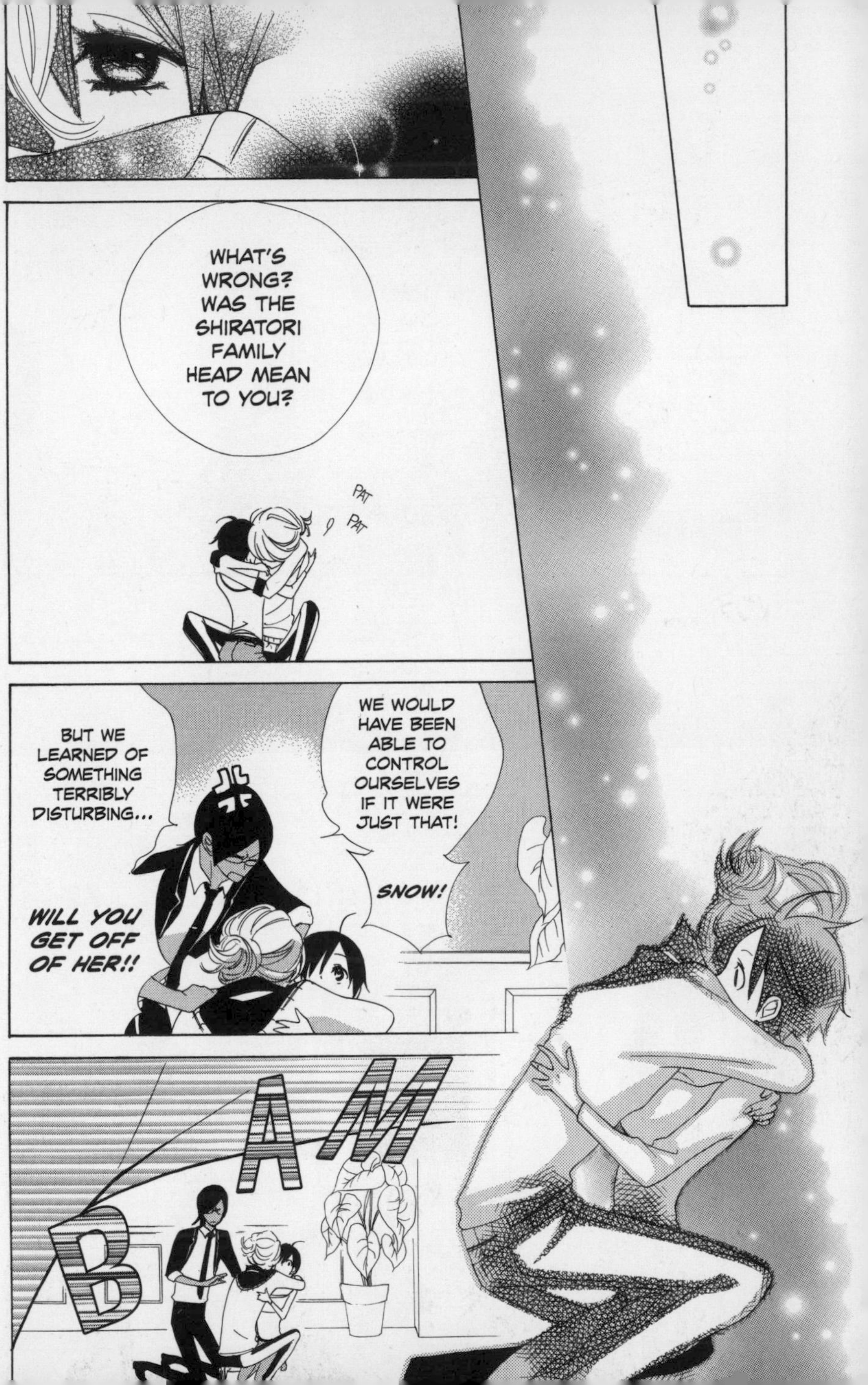
WHAT'S WRONG? WAS THE SHIRATORI FAMILY HEAD MEAN TO YOU?
PAT PAT
WE WOULD HAVE BEEN ABLE TO CONTROL OURSELVES IF IT WERE JUST THAT!
BUT WE LEARNED OF SOMETHING TERRIBLY DISTURBING...
SNOW!
WILL YOU GET OFF OF HER!!
BAM

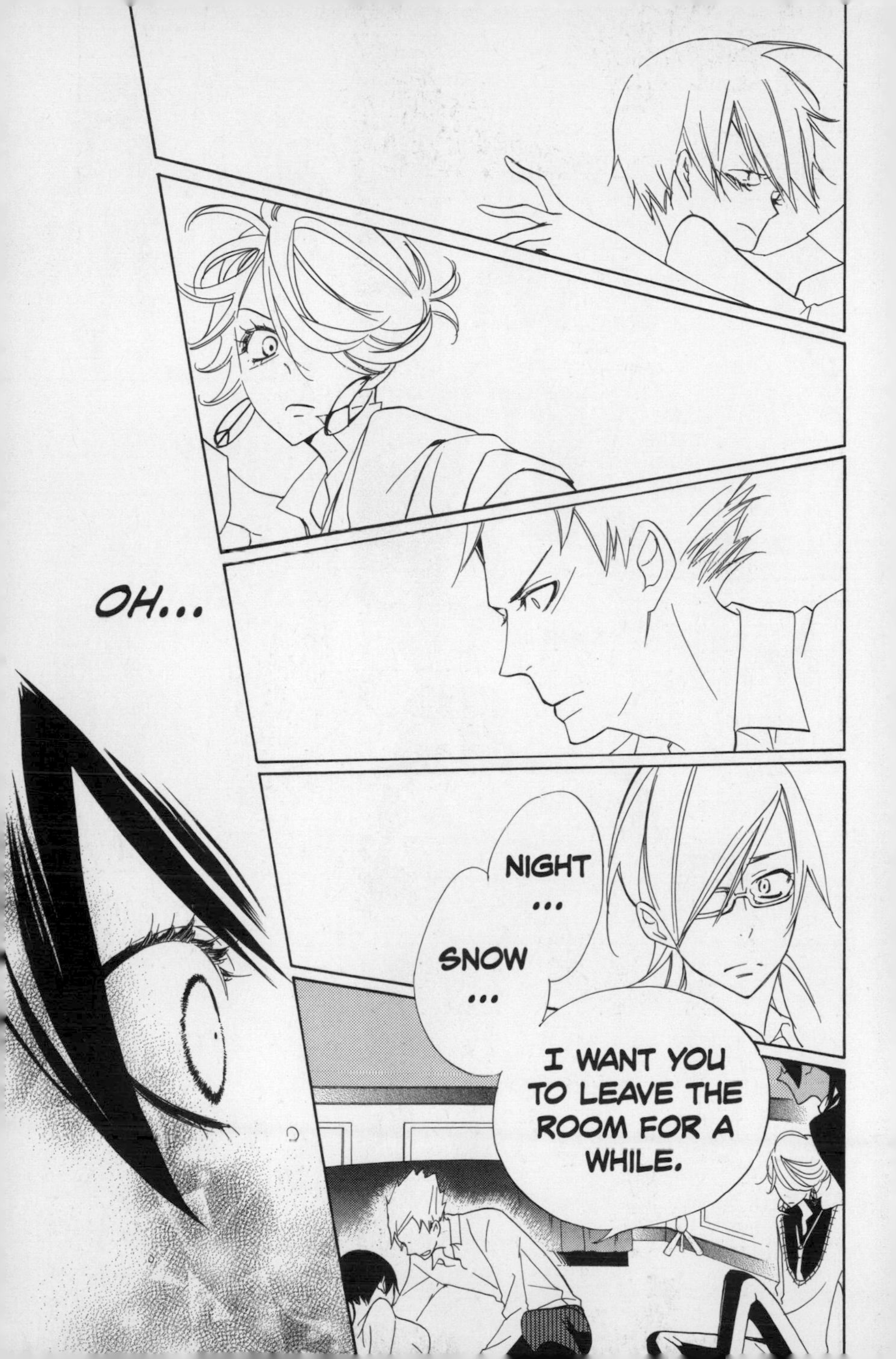
NIGHT ...
SNOW ...
I WANT YOU TO LEAVE THE ROOM FOR A WHILE.
OH...

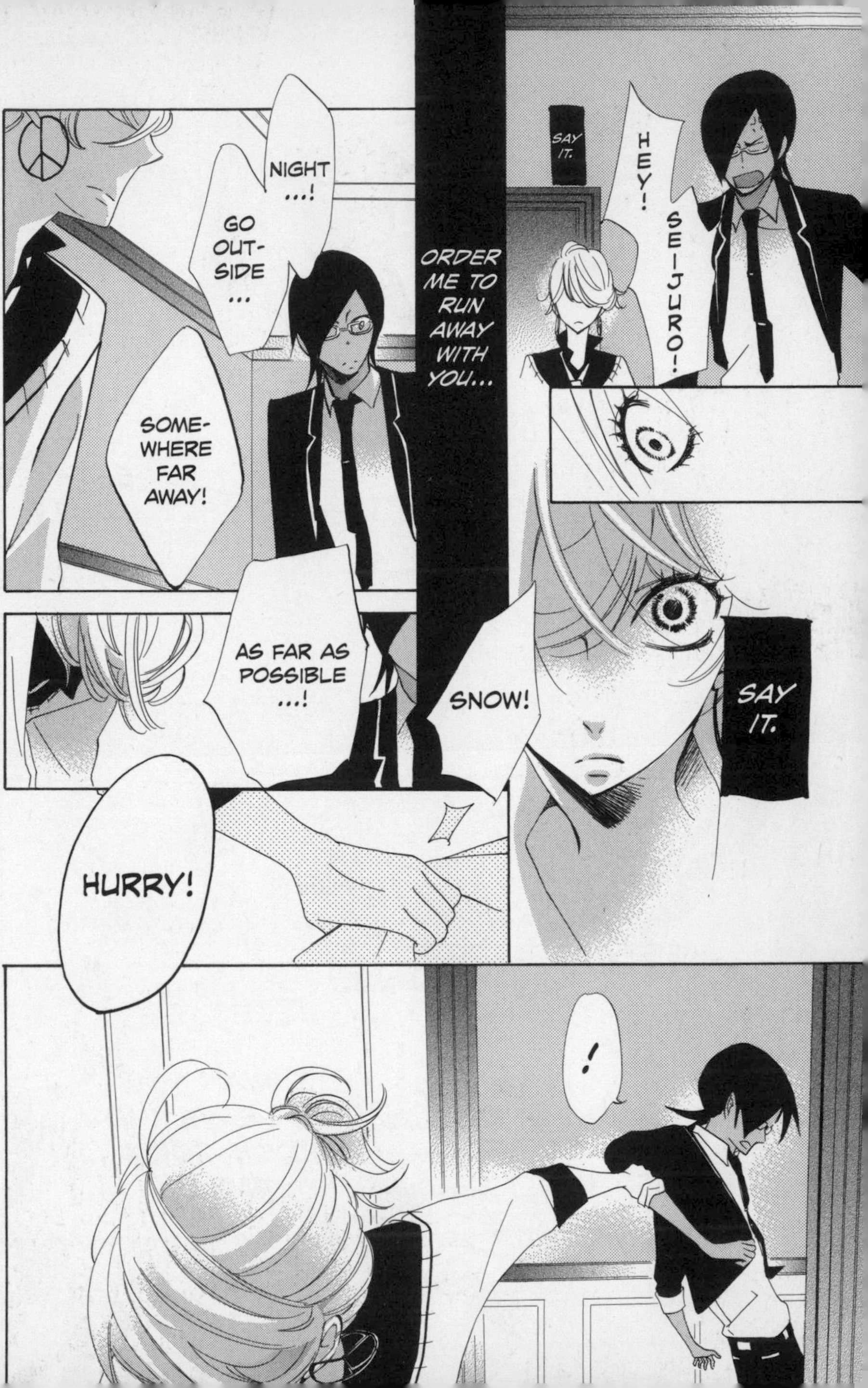
SAY IT.
HEY! SEIJURO!
ORDER ME TO RUN AWAY WITH YOU...
SAY IT.
SNOW!
NIGHT ...!
GO OUT-SIDE ...
SOME-WHERE FAR AWAY!
AS FAR AS POSSIBLE ...!
HURRY!
!

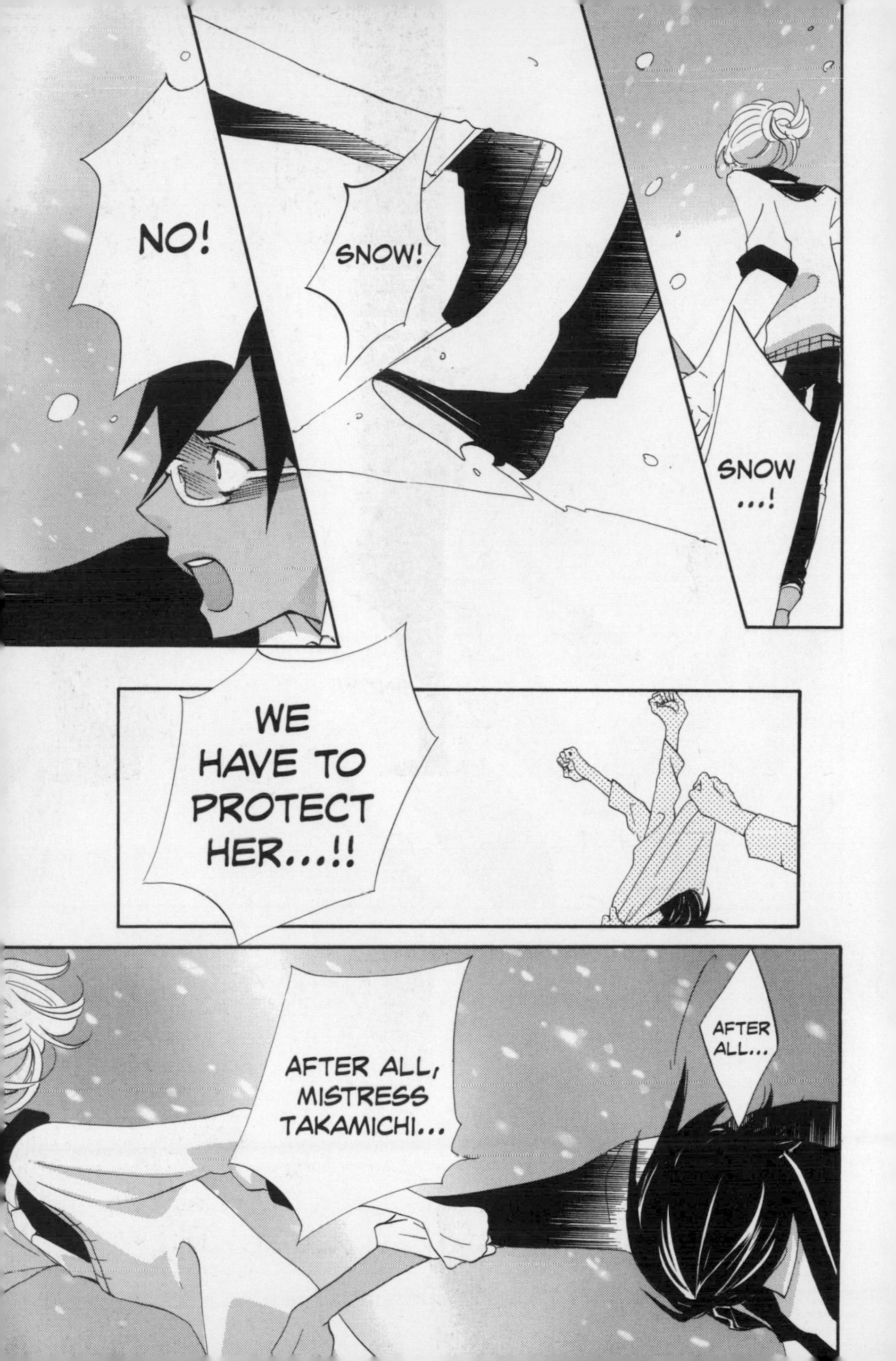
SNOW ...!
SNOW!
NO!
WE HAVE TO PROTECT HER...!!
AFTER ALL...
AFTER ALL, MISTRESS TAKAMICHI...

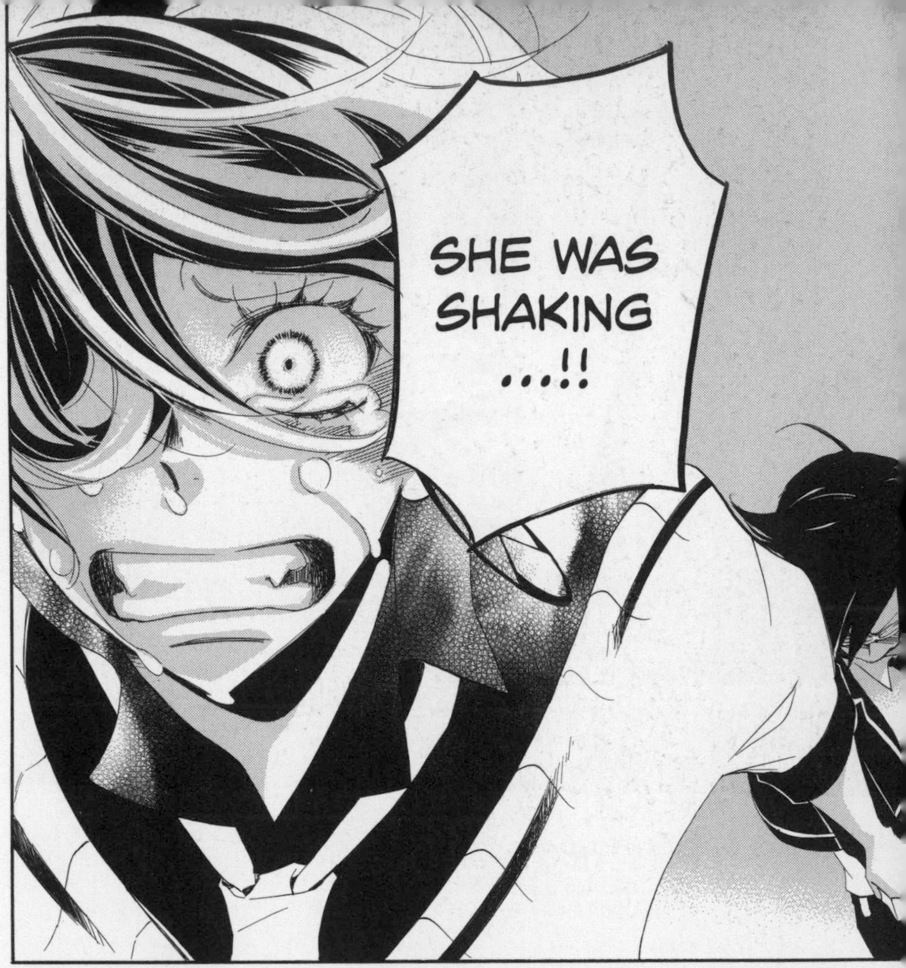
SHE WAS SHAKING ...!!
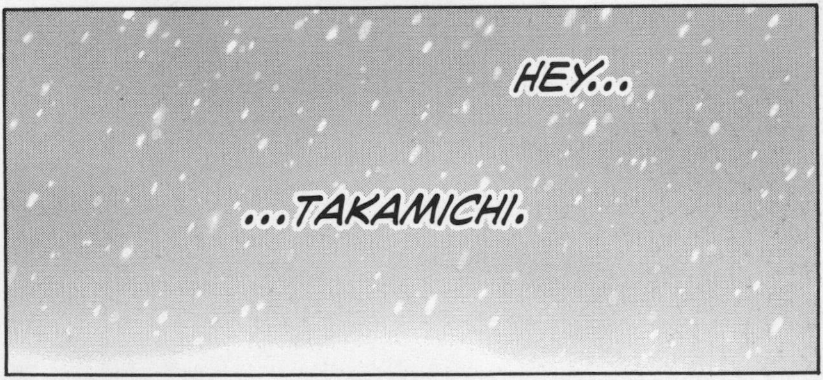
HEY...
...TAKAMICHI.

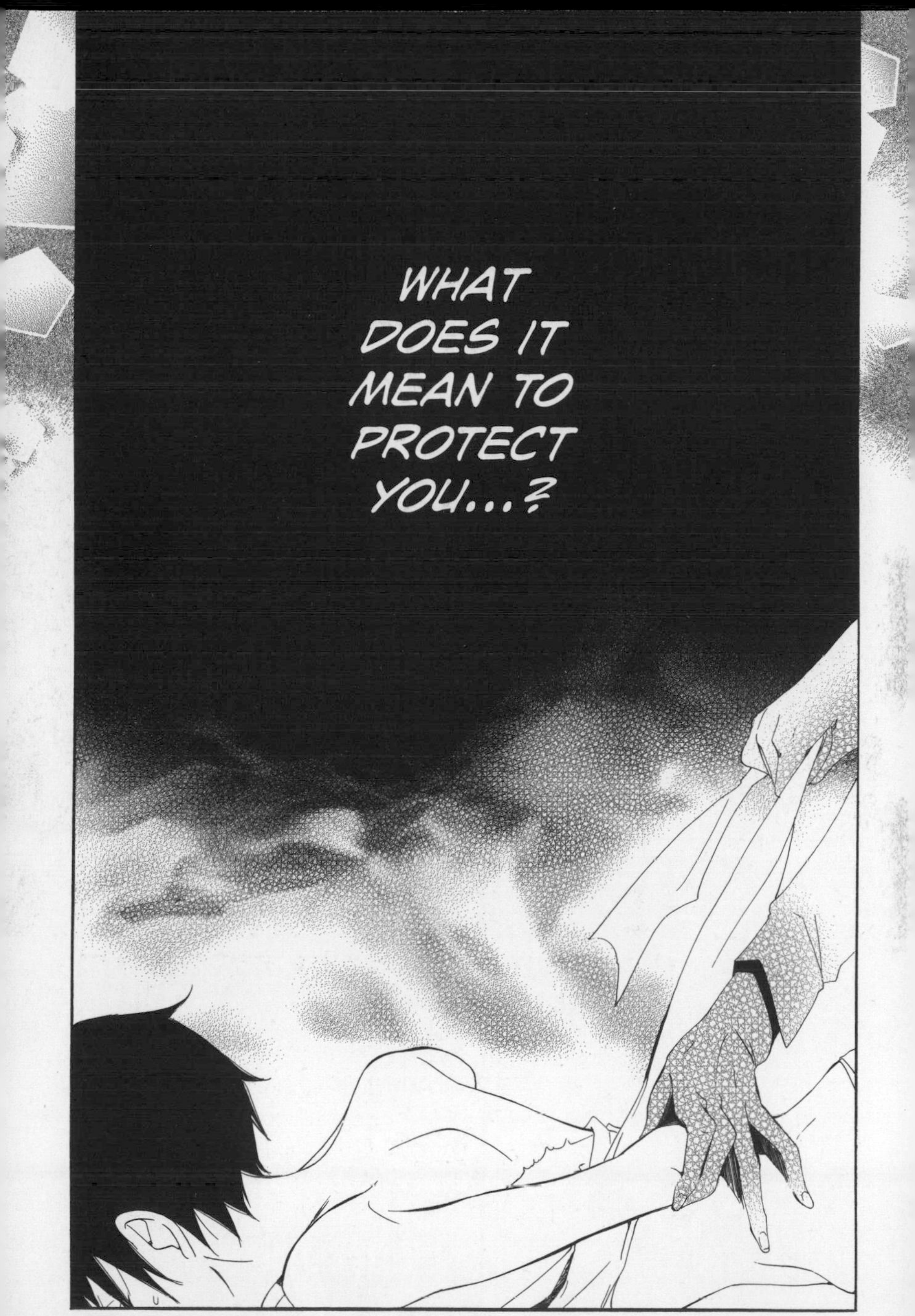
WHAT DOES IT MEAN TO PROTECT YOU...?

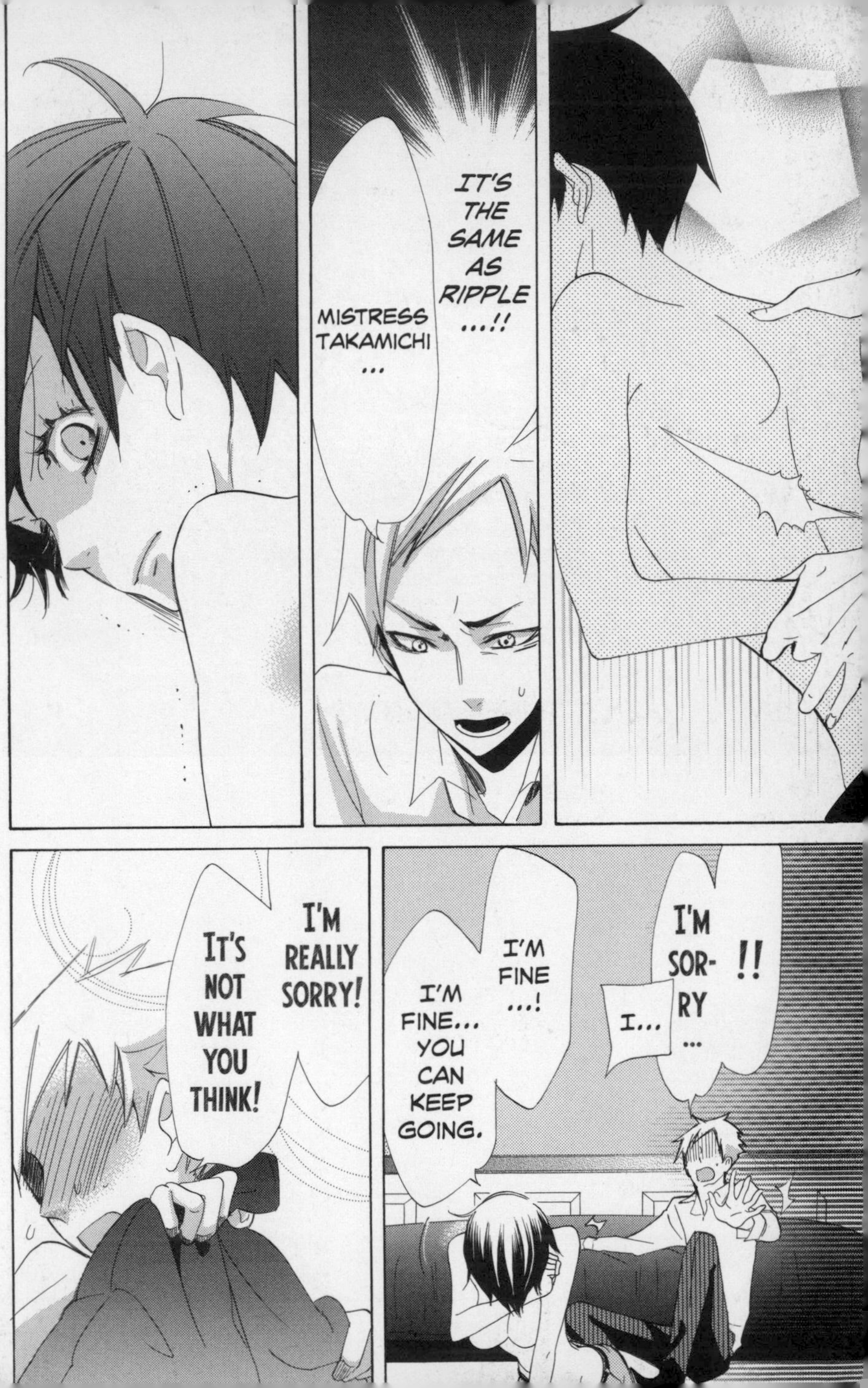
IT'S THE SAME AS RIPPLE ...!!
MISTRESS TAKAMICHI ...
I'M SOR-RY ...
!!
I...
I'M FINE ...!
I'M FINE... YOU CAN KEEP GOING.
I'M REALLY SORRY!
IT'S NOT WHAT YOU THINK!

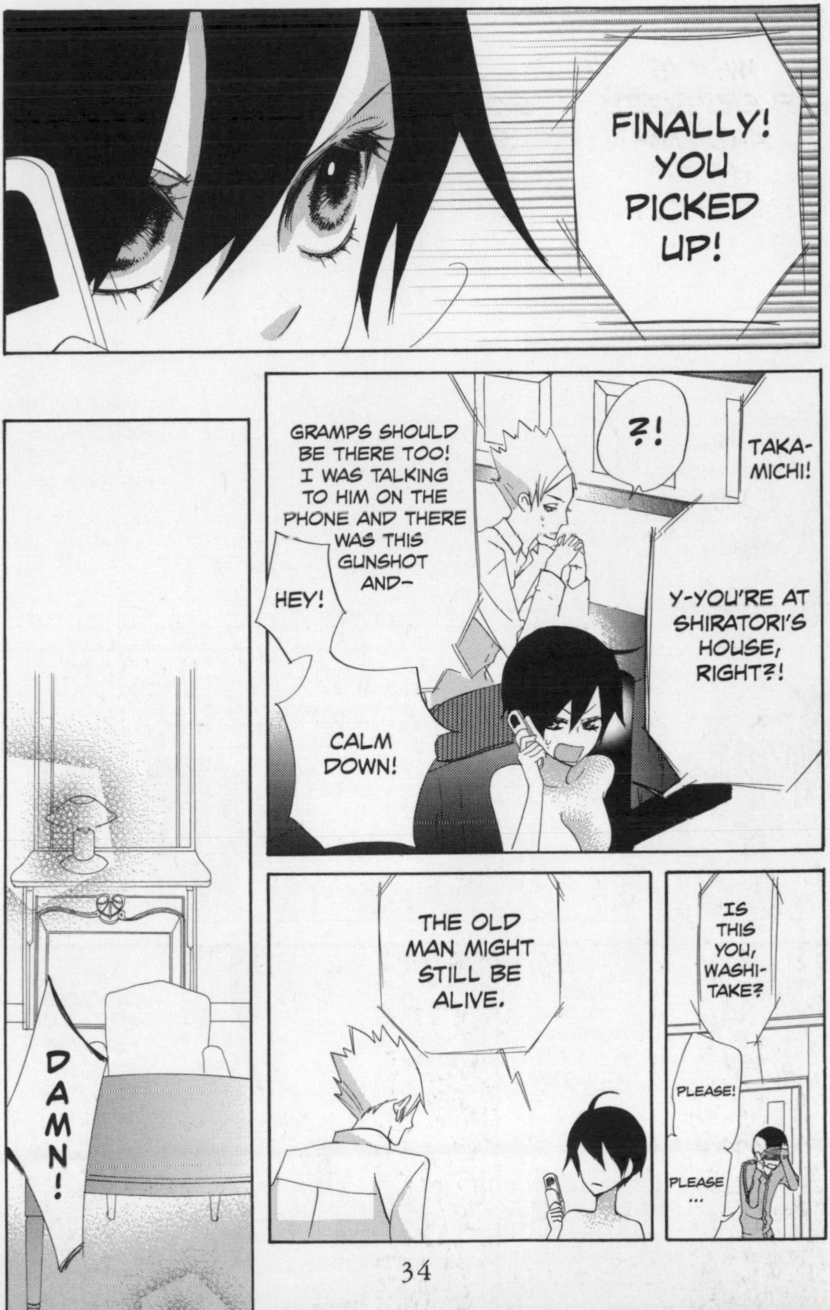
FINALLY! YOU PICKED UP!
TAKA-MICHI!
?!
Y-YOU'RE AT SHIRATORI'S HOUSE, RIGHT?!
GRAMPS SHOULD BE THERE TOO! I WAS TALKING TO HIM ON THE PHONE AND THERE WAS THIS GUNSHOT AND—
HEY!
CALM DOWN!
IS THIS YOU, WASHI-TAKE?
PLEASE!
PLEASE ...
THE OLD MAN MIGHT STILL BE ALIVE.
DAMN!

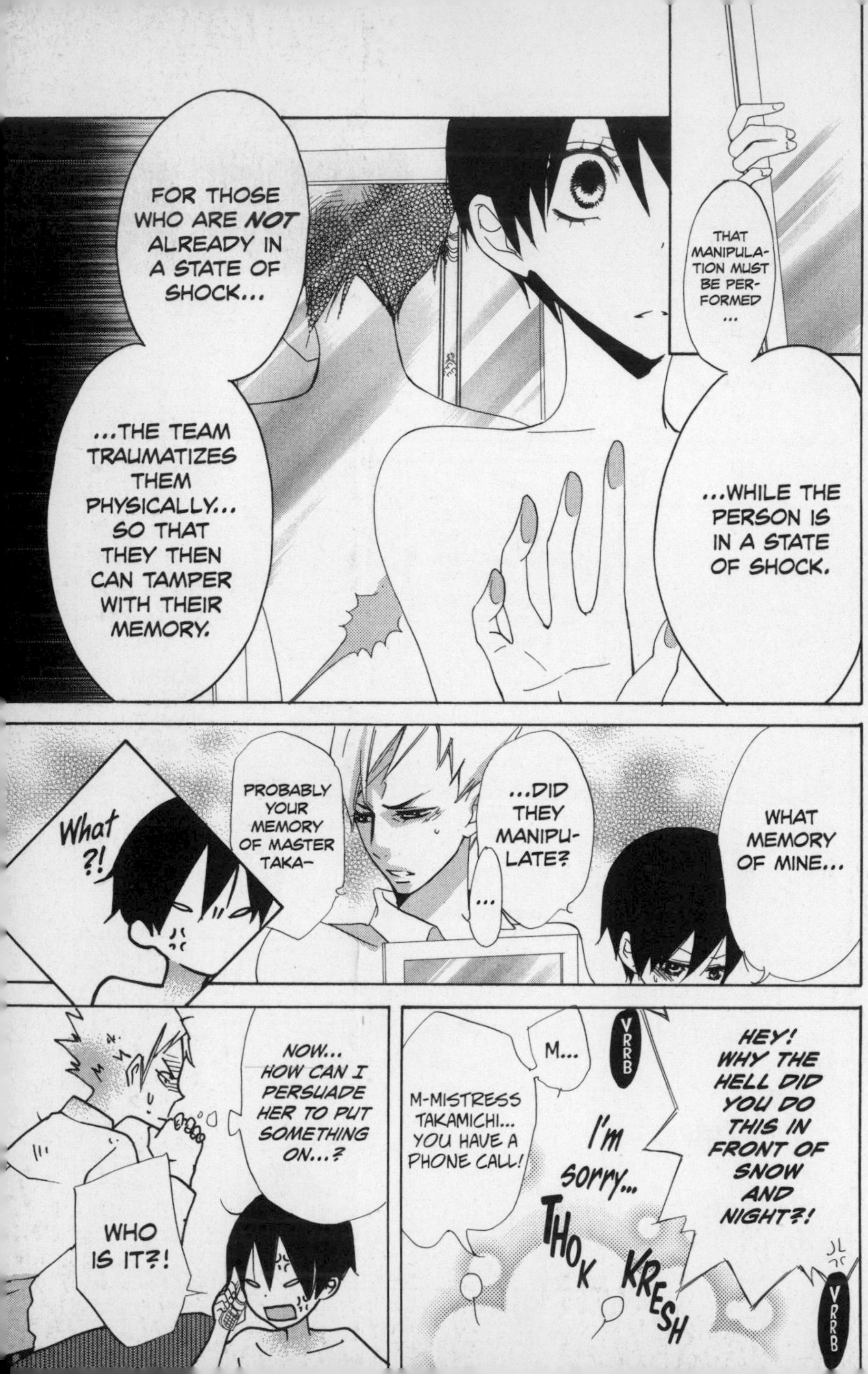
THAT MANIPULATION MUST BE PERFORMED...
...WHILE THE PERSON IS IN A STATE OF SHOCK.
FOR THOSE WHO ARE *NOT* ALREADY IN A STATE OF SHOCK...
...THE TEAM TRAUMATIZES THEM PHYSICALLY... SO THAT THEY THEN CAN TAMPER WITH THEIR MEMORY.
WHAT MEMORY OF MINE...
...DID THEY MANIPULATE?
...
PROBABLY YOUR MEMORY OF MASTER TAKA-
What?!
HEY! WHY THE HELL DID YOU DO THIS IN FRONT OF SNOW AND NIGHT?!
VRRB
M...
VRRB
I'm sorry...
THOK
KRESH
M-MISTRESS TAKAMICHI... YOU HAVE A PHONE CALL!
NOW... HOW CAN I PERSUADE HER TO PUT SOMETHING ON...?
WHO IS IT?!

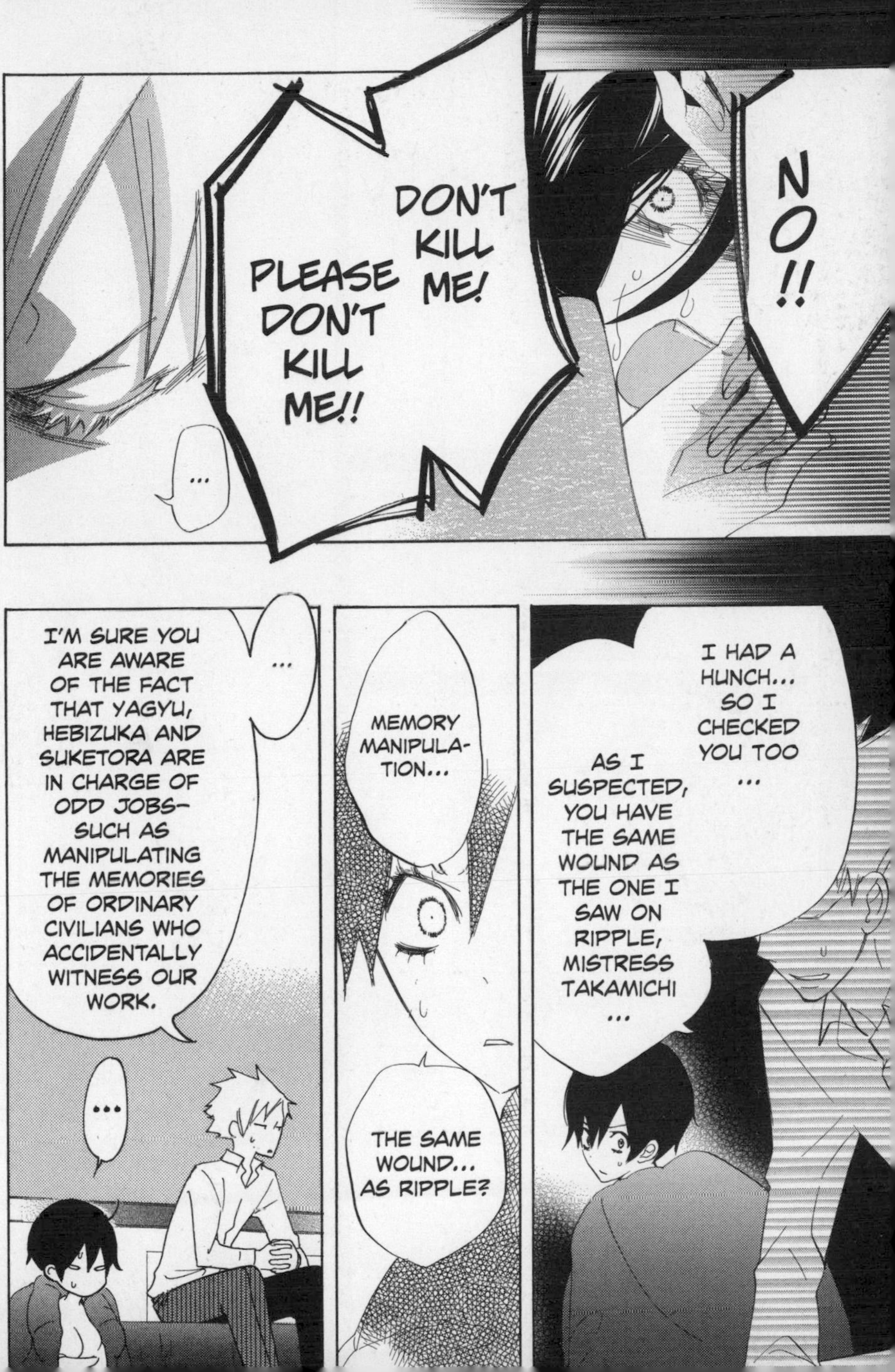
NO!!
DON'T KILL ME! PLEASE DON'T KILL ME!!
...
I HAD A HUNCH... SO I CHECKED YOU TOO ...
AS I SUSPECTED, YOU HAVE THE SAME WOUND AS THE ONE I SAW ON RIPPLE, MISTRESS TAKAMICHI ...
MEMORY MANIPULATION...
THE SAME WOUND... AS RIPPLE?
...
I'M SURE YOU ARE AWARE OF THE FACT THAT YAGYU, HEBIZUKA AND SUKETORA ARE IN CHARGE OF ODD JOBS-SUCH AS MANIPULATING THE MEMORIES OF ORDINARY CIVILIANS WHO ACCIDENTALLY WITNESS OUR WORK.
...

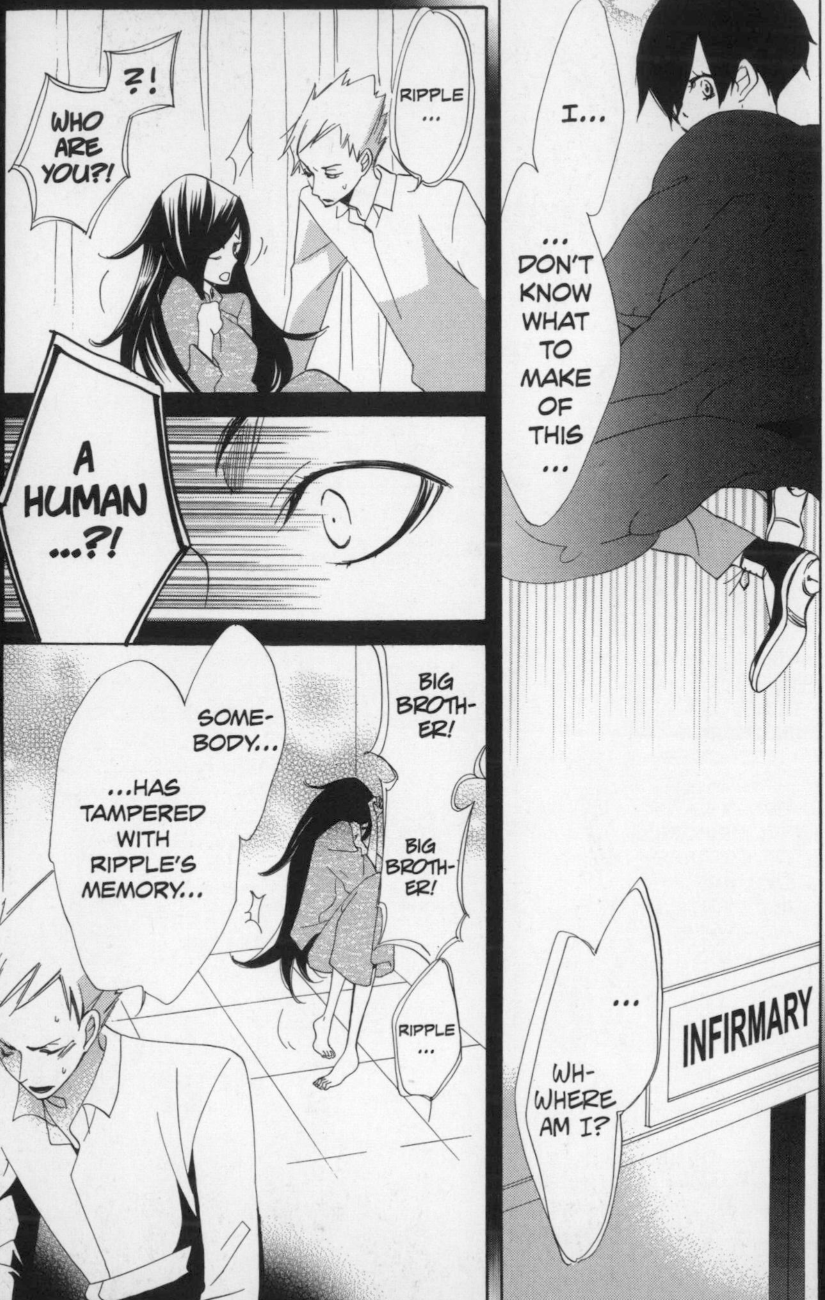
I...
...DON'T KNOW WHAT TO MAKE OF THIS...
INFIRMARY
...
WH-WHERE AM I?
RIPPLE...
?! WHO ARE YOU?!
A HUMAN...?!
BIG BROTHER!
BIG BROTHER!
SOME-BODY...
...HAS TAMPERED WITH RIPPLE'S MEMORY...
RIPPLE...

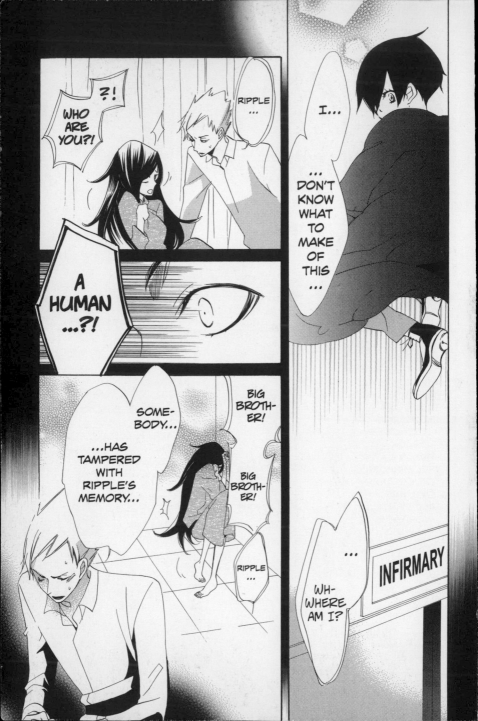

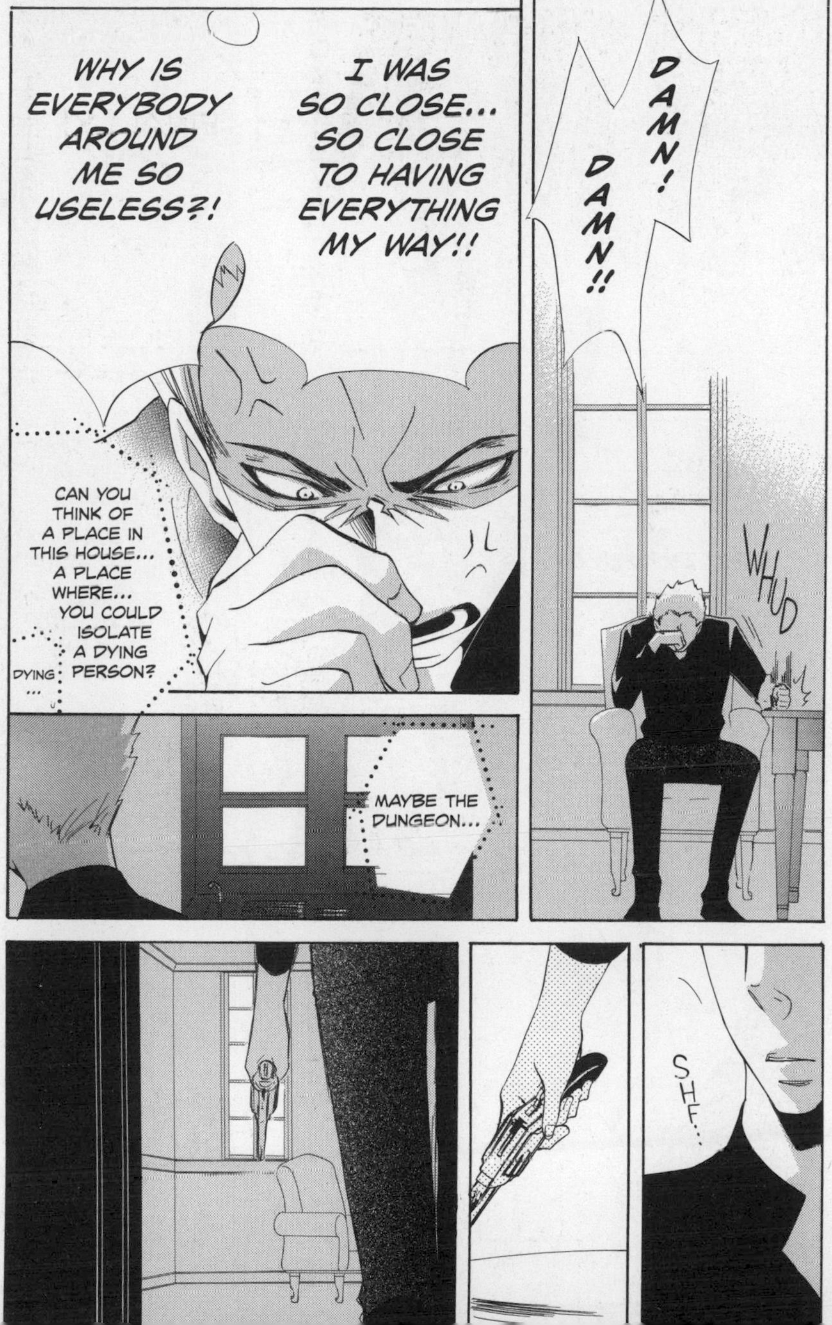

DAMN! DAMN!!
WHUD
I WAS SO CLOSE... SO CLOSE TO HAVING EVERYTHING MY WAY!!
WHY IS EVERYBODY AROUND ME SO USELESS?!
CAN YOU THINK OF A PLACE IN THIS HOUSE... A PLACE WHERE... YOU COULD ISOLATE A DYING PERSON?
DYING...
MAYBE THE DUNGEON...
SHF...

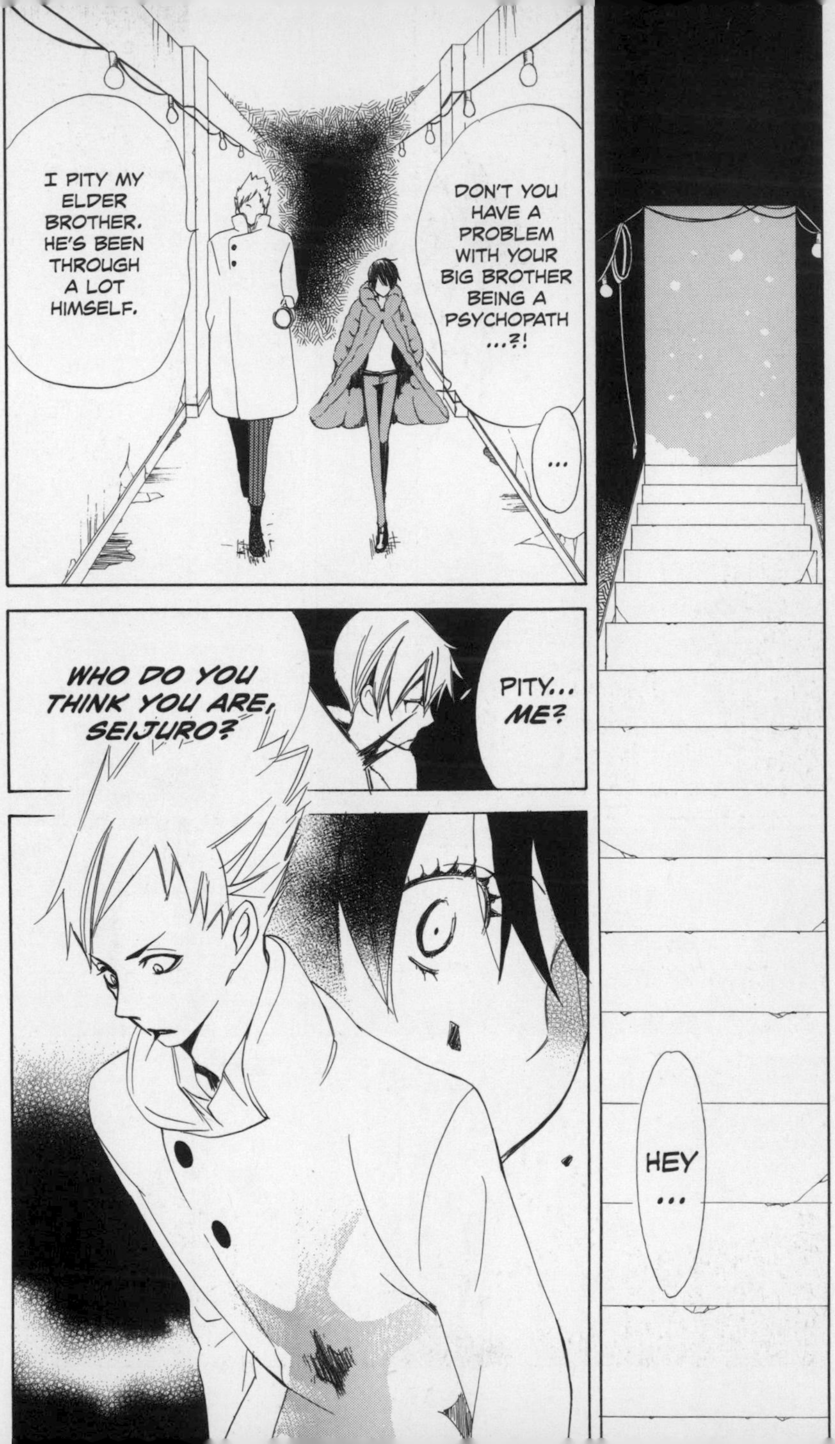
HEY ...
DON'T YOU HAVE A PROBLEM WITH YOUR BIG BROTHER BEING A PSYCHOPATH ...?!
...
I PITY MY ELDER BROTHER. HE'S BEEN THROUGH A LOT HIMSELF.
PITY... ME?
WHO DO YOU THINK YOU ARE, SEIJURO?

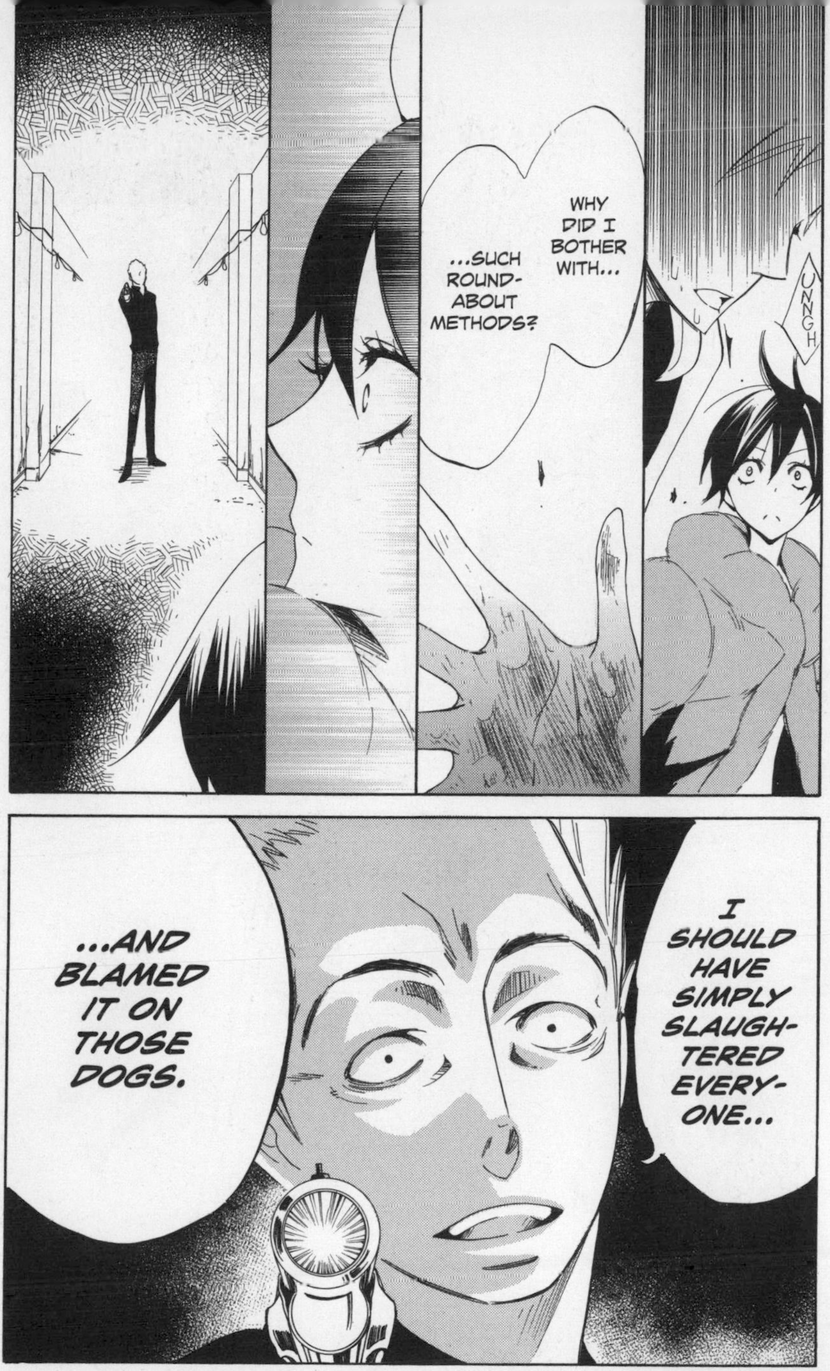
UNNGH
WHY DID I BOTHER WITH...
...SUCH ROUND-ABOUT METHODS?
I SHOULD HAVE SIMPLY SLAUGH-TERED EVERY-ONE...
...AND BLAMED IT ON THOSE DOGS.

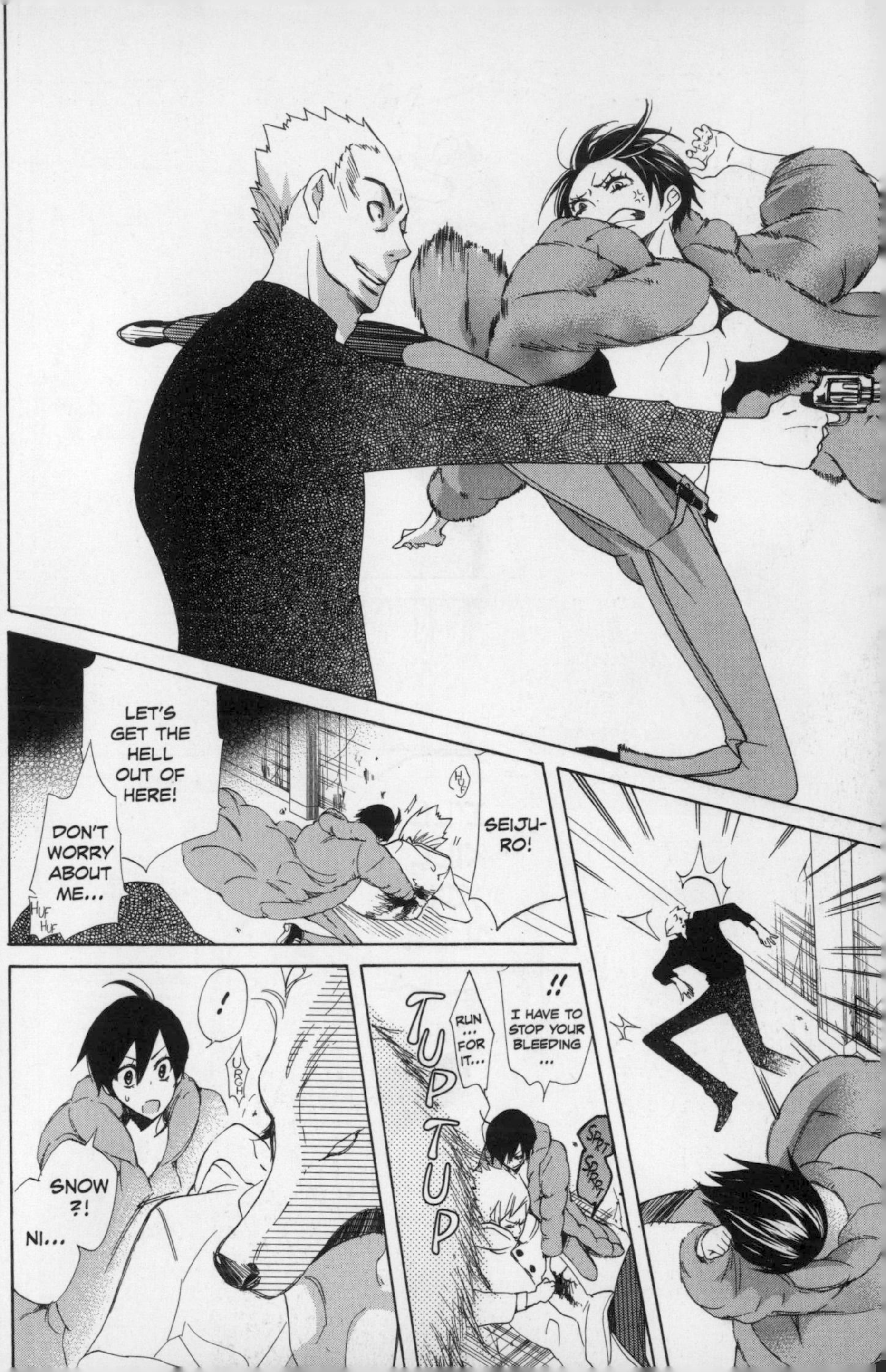
SEIJU-RO!
HUF
LET'S GET THE HELL OUT OF HERE!
DON'T WORRY ABOUT ME...
HUF HUF
!!
I HAVE TO STOP YOUR BLEEDING ...
RUN ... FOR IT...
TUP TUP
SPRT SPRRT
!
URGH
SNOW ?!
NI...

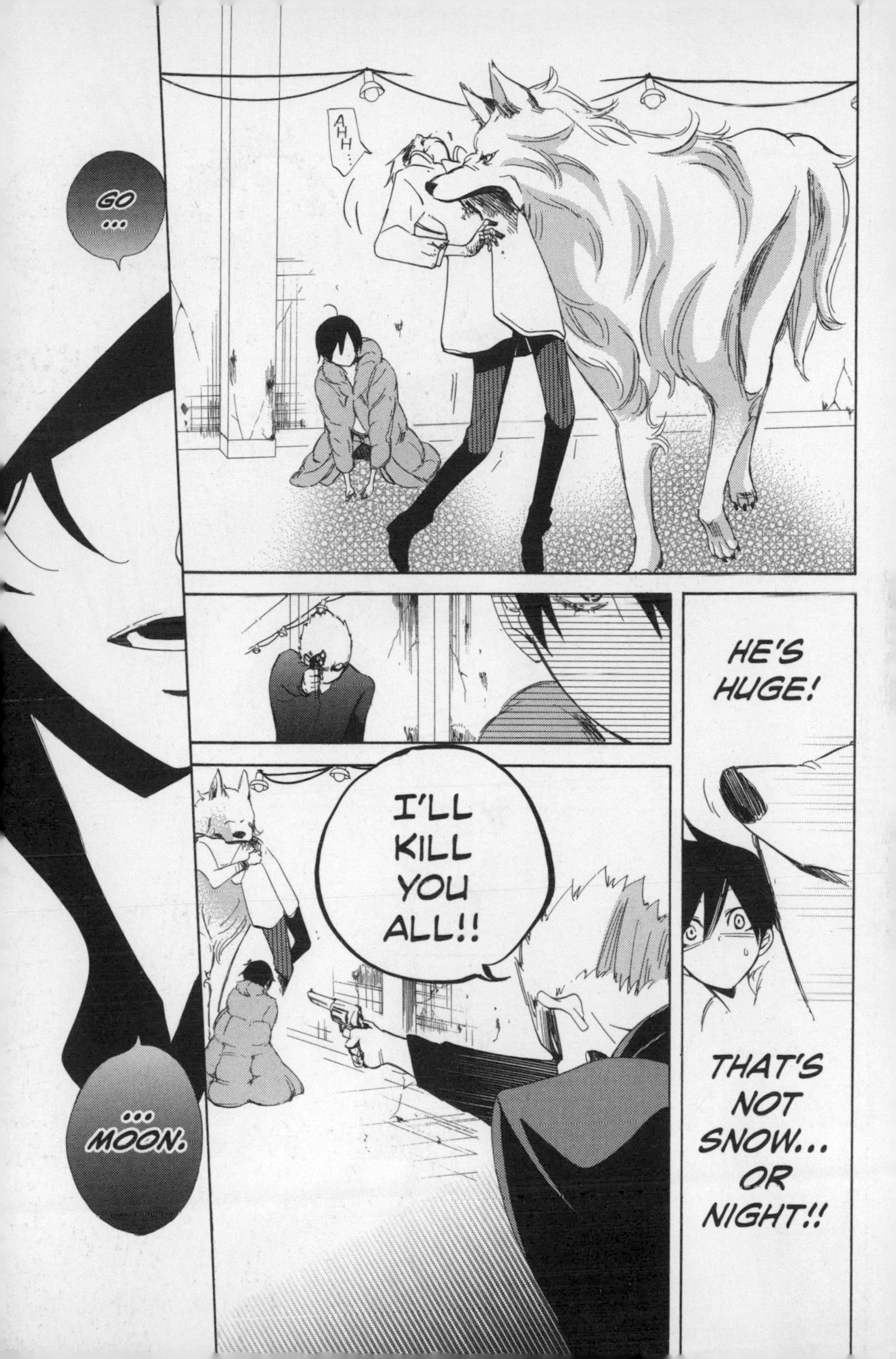
AHH...
HE'S HUGE!
THAT'S NOT SNOW... OR NIGHT!!
I'LL KILL YOU ALL!!
GO...
...MOON.

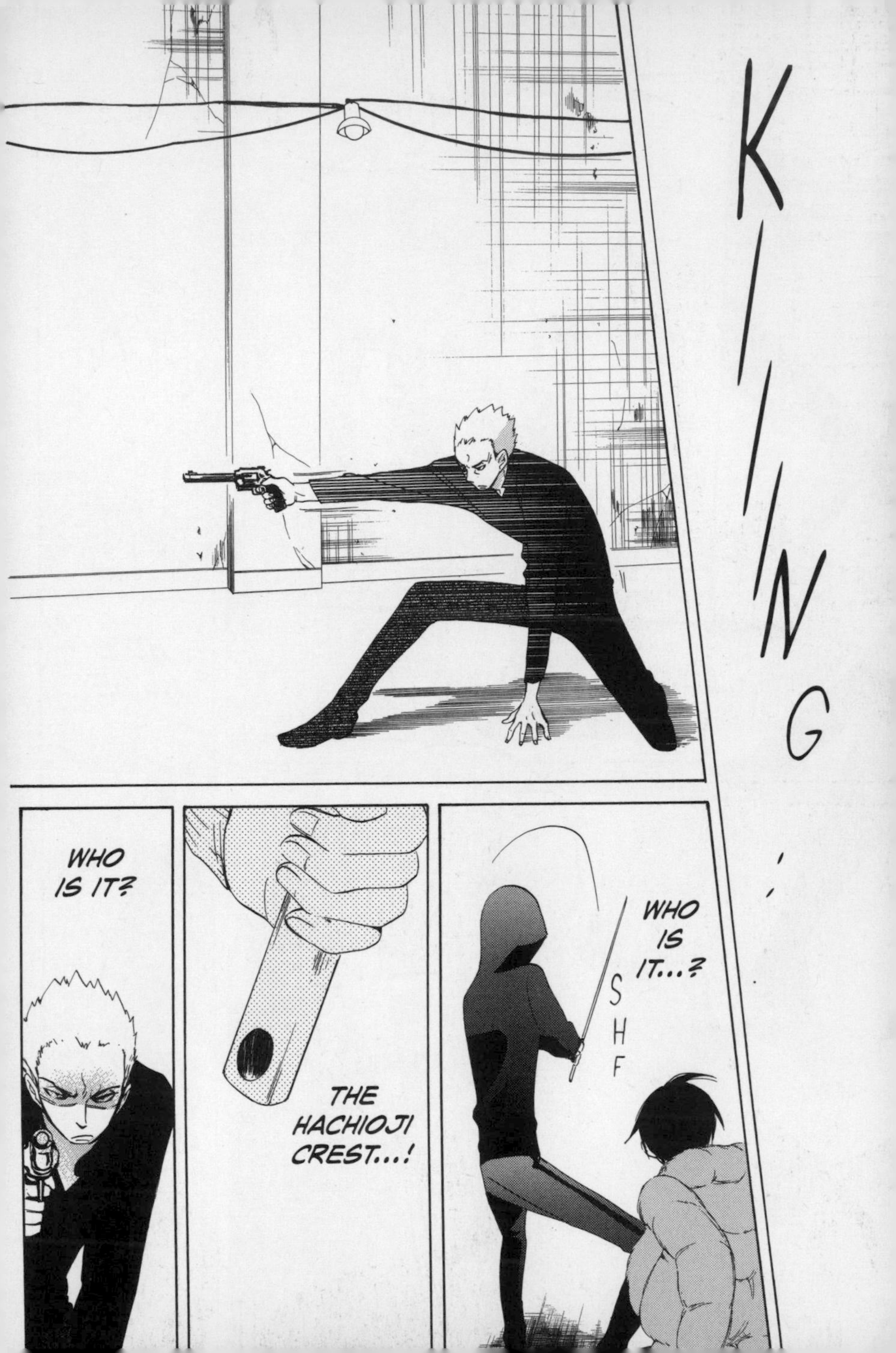
KIIIING!
WHO IS IT...?
SHF
THE HACHIOJI CREST...!
WHO IS IT?

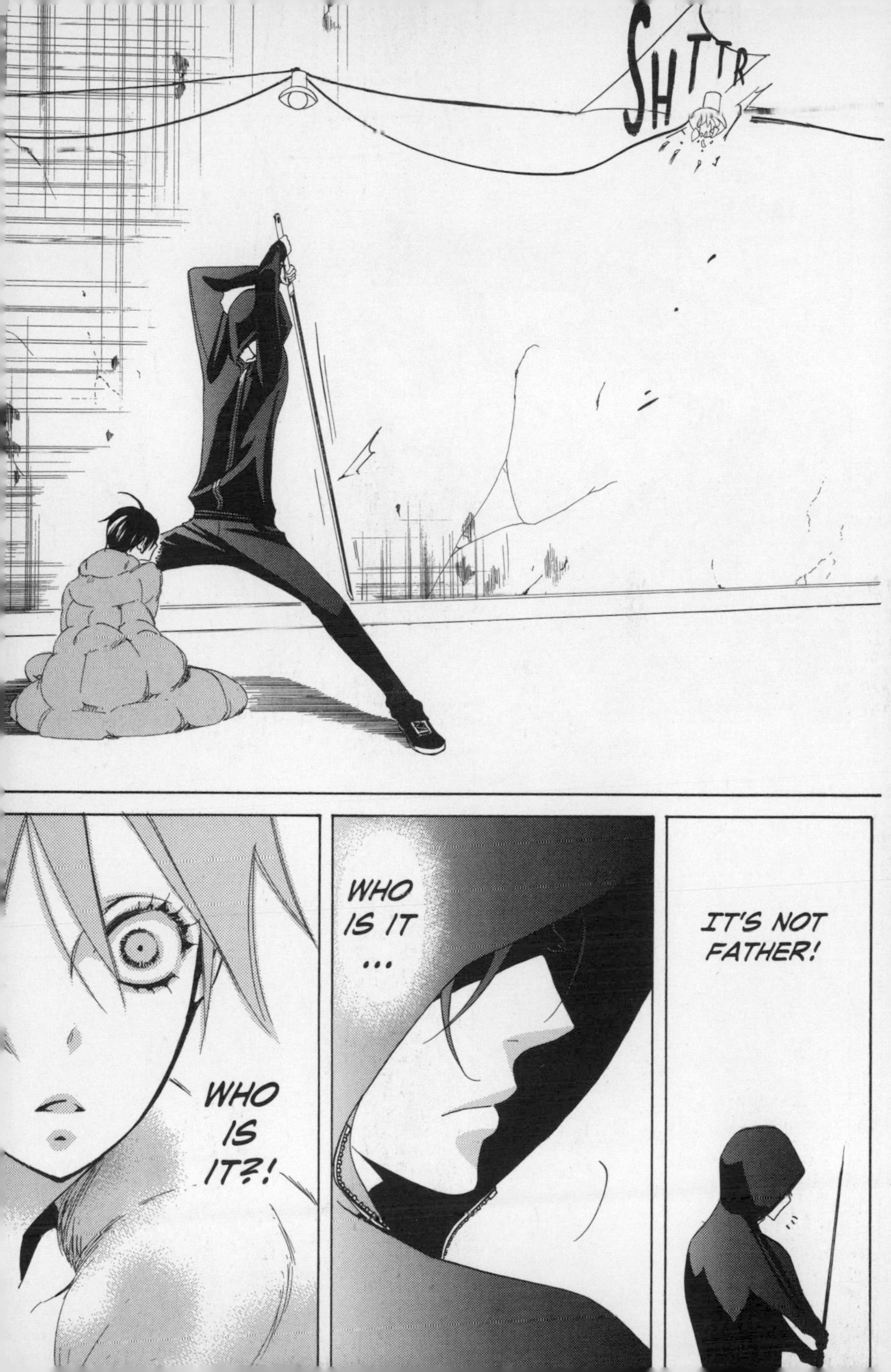
SHTTR
IT'S NOT FATHER!
WHO IS IT ...
WHO IS IT?!

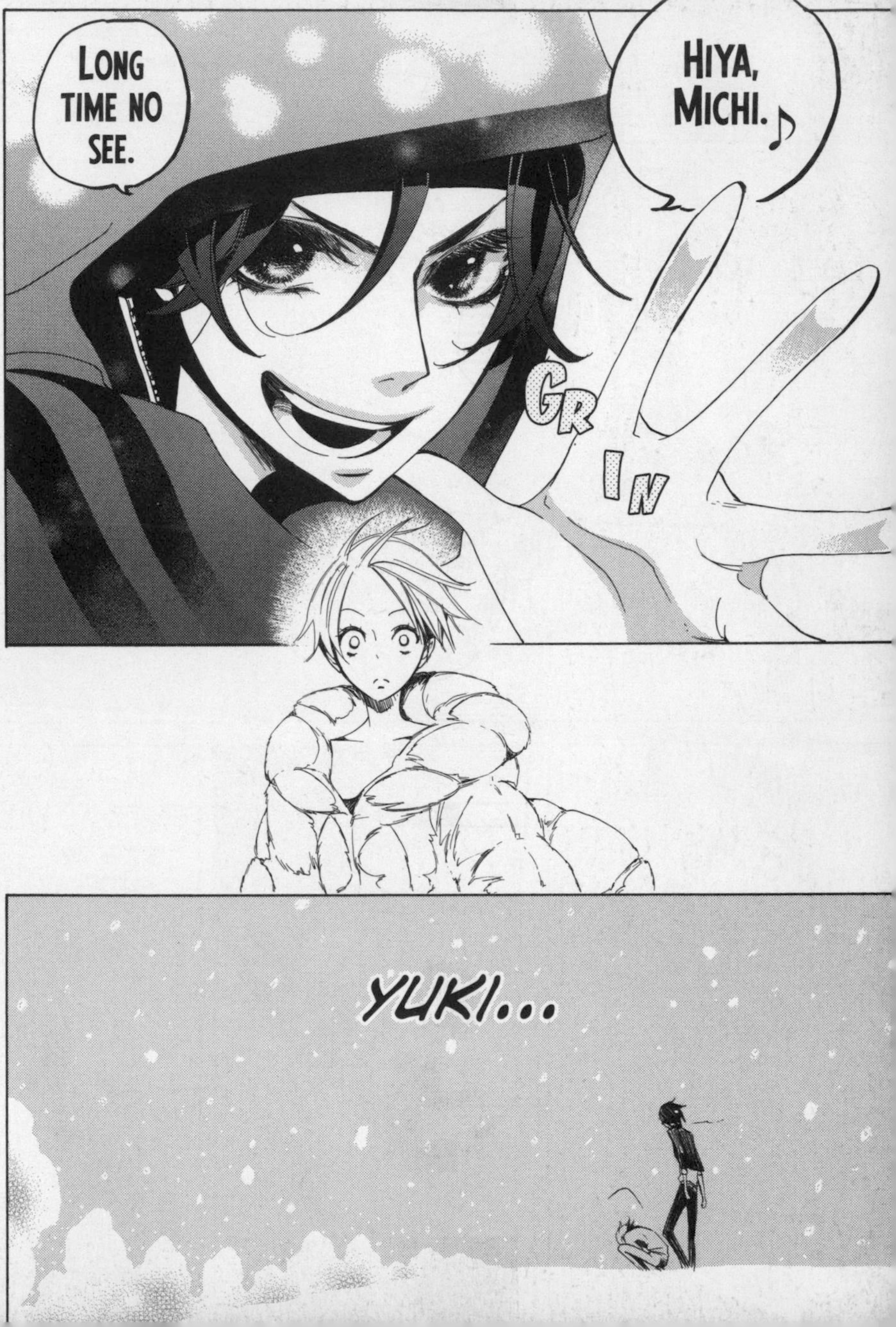

HIYA, MICHI. ♪
LONG TIME NO SEE.
GRIN
YUKI...

WALK 21: MONSTER

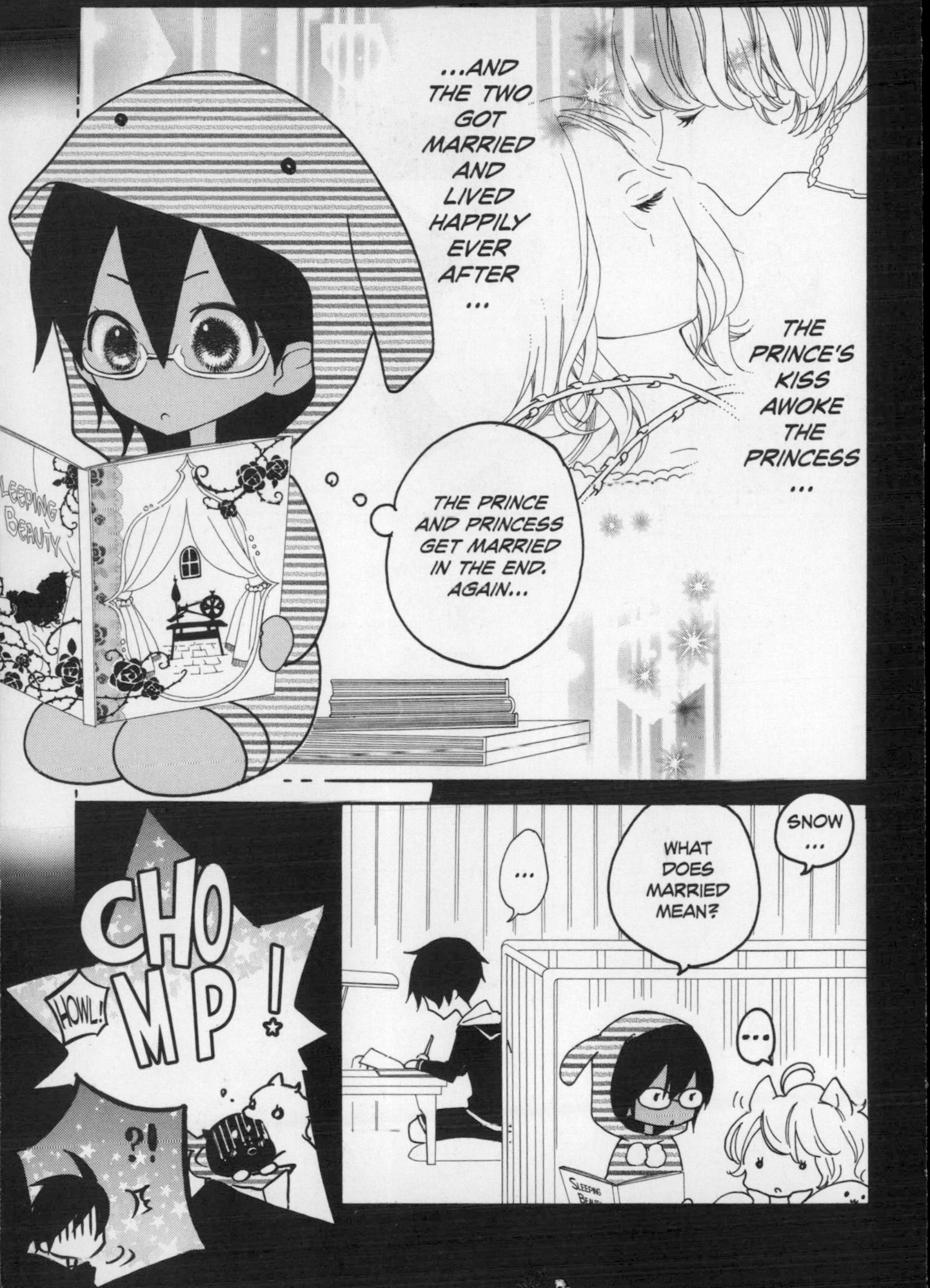
THE PRINCE'S KISS AWOKE THE PRINCESS...
...AND THE TWO GOT MARRIED AND LIVED HAPPILY EVER AFTER...
THE PRINCE AND PRINCESS GET MARRIED IN THE END. AGAIN...
SLEEPING BEAUTY
SNOW...
WHAT DOES MARRIED MEAN?
...
...
CHOMP!
HOWL!
?!

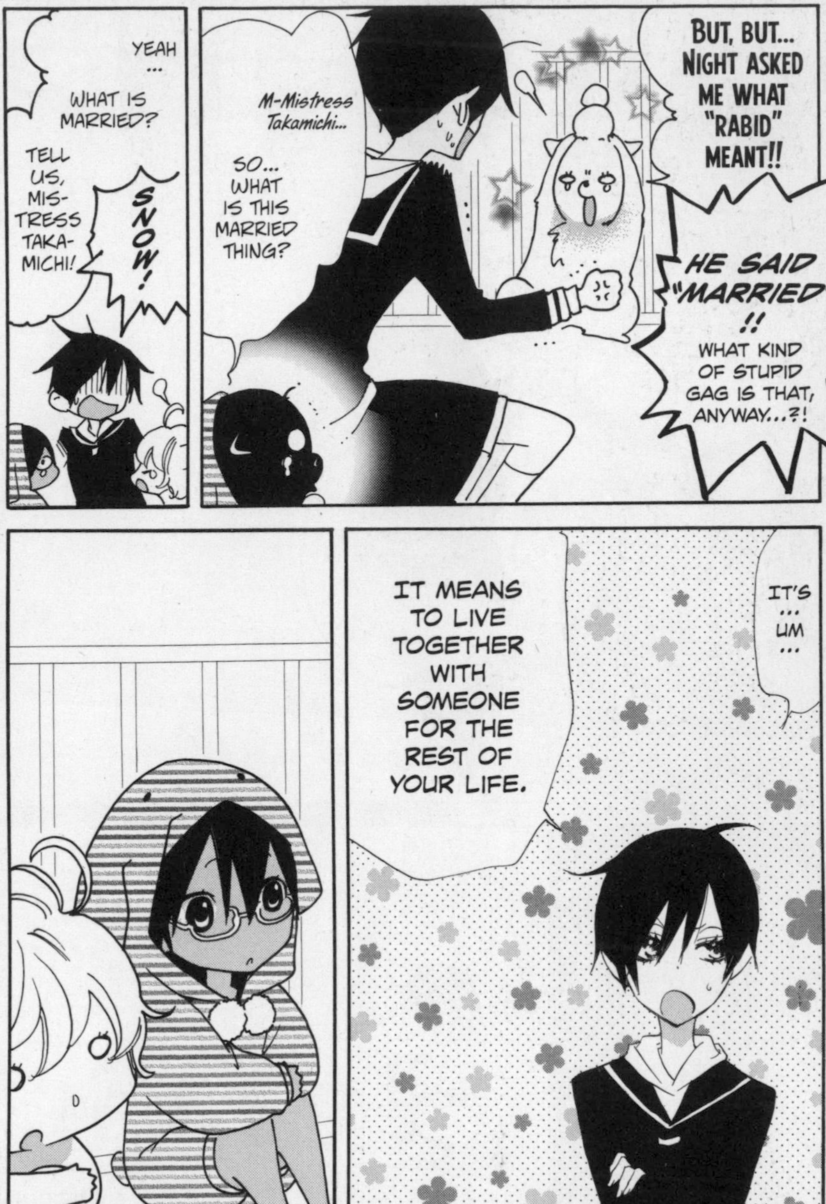
BUT, BUT... NIGHT ASKED ME WHAT "RABID" MEANT!!
HE SAID "MARRIED" !! WHAT KIND OF STUPID GAG IS THAT, ANYWAY...?!
M-Mistress Takamichi...
SO... WHAT IS THIS MARRIED THING?
YEAH ... WHAT IS MARRIED?
SNOW!
TELL US, MISTRESS TAKAMICHI!
IT'S ... UM ...
IT MEANS TO LIVE TOGETHER WITH SOMEONE FOR THE REST OF YOUR LIFE.

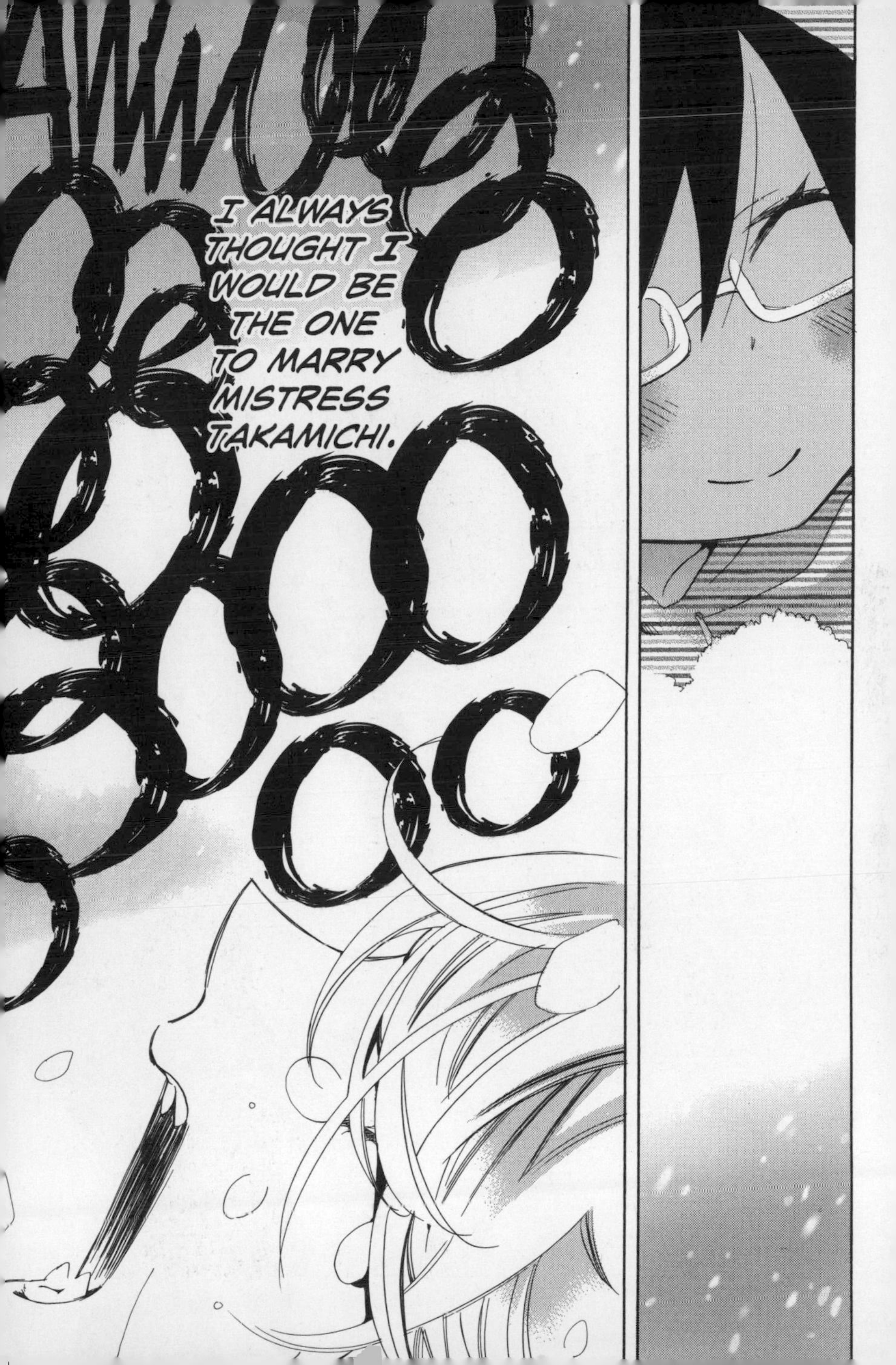
I ALWAYS THOUGHT I WOULD BE THE ONE TO MARRY MISTRESS TAKAMICHI.

WALK 21: MONSTER

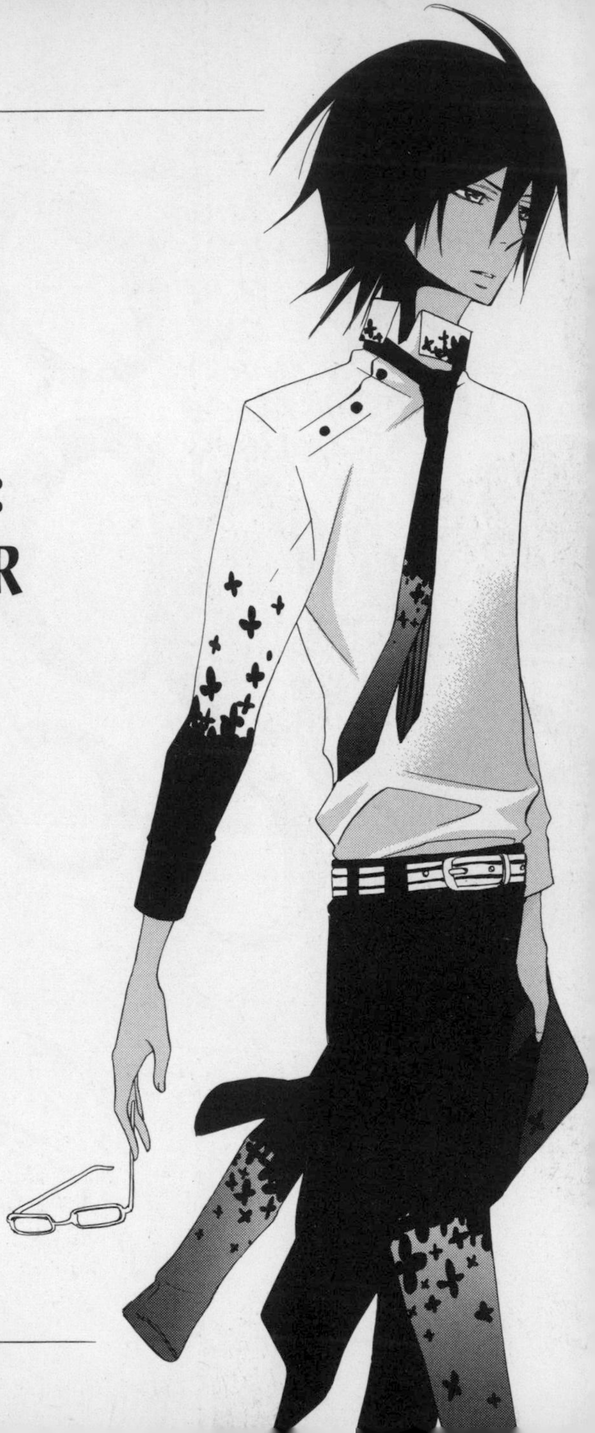

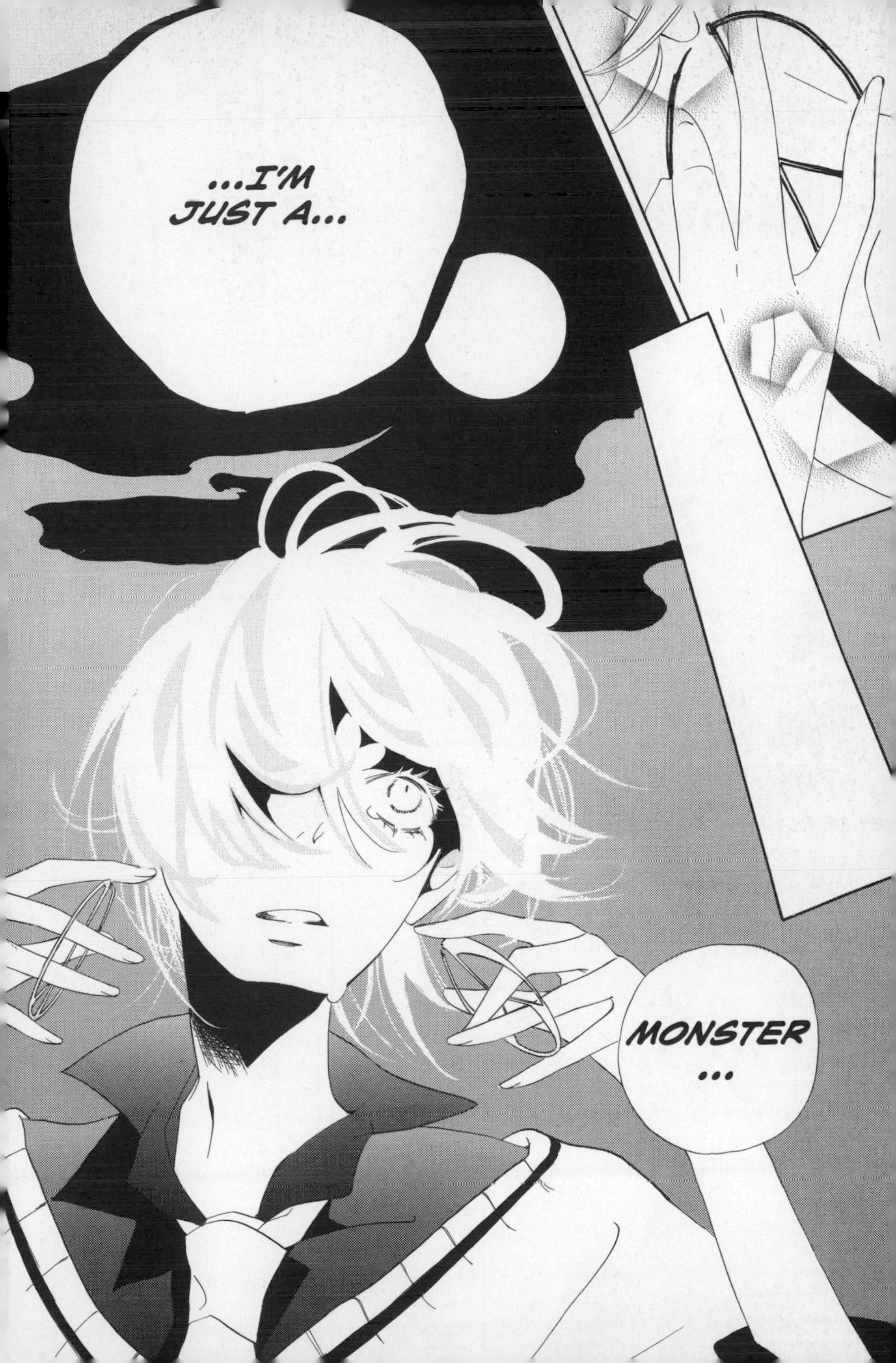
...I'M JUST A...
MONSTER ...

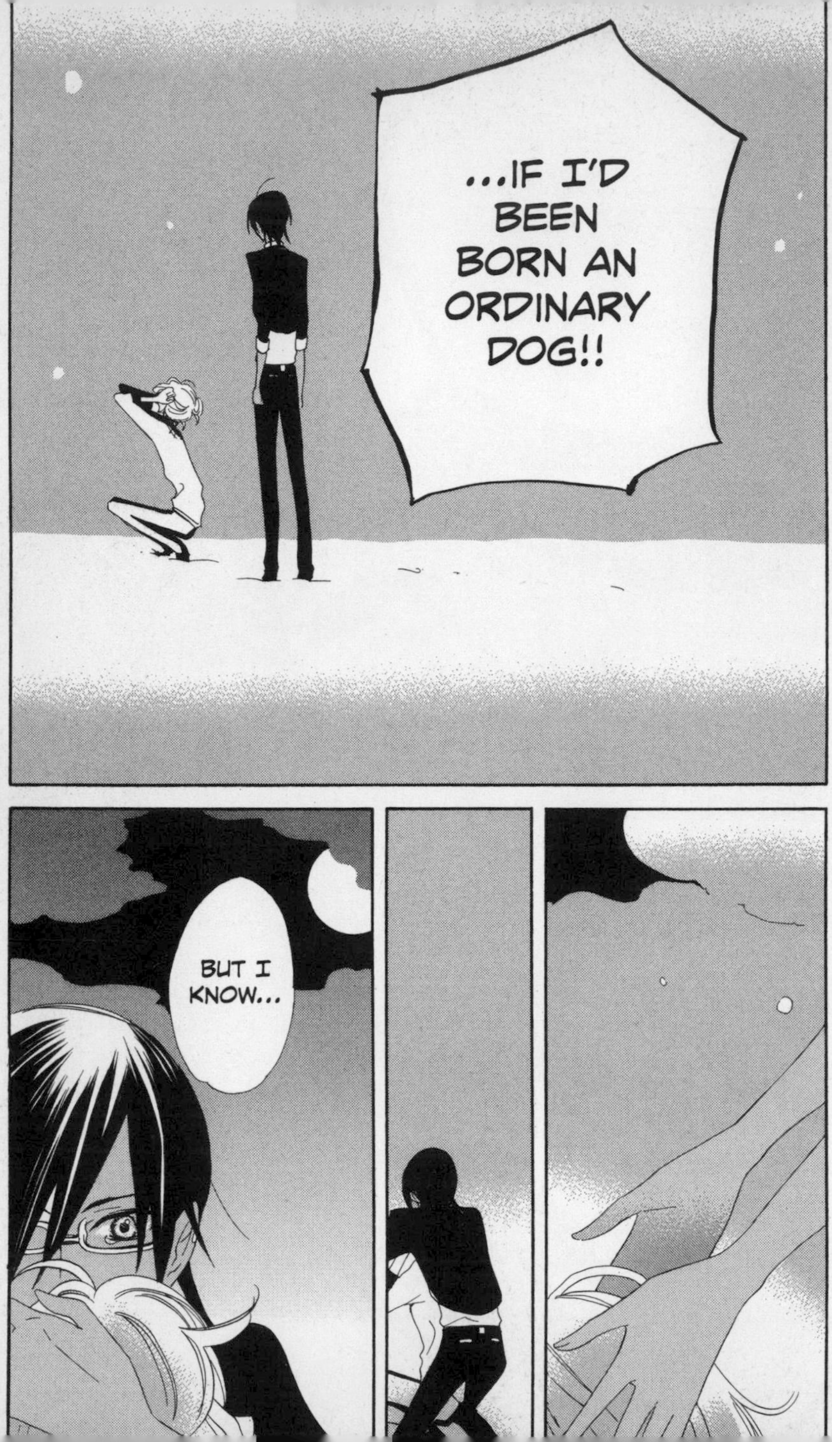
...IF I'D BEEN BORN AN ORDINARY DOG!!
BUT I KNOW...

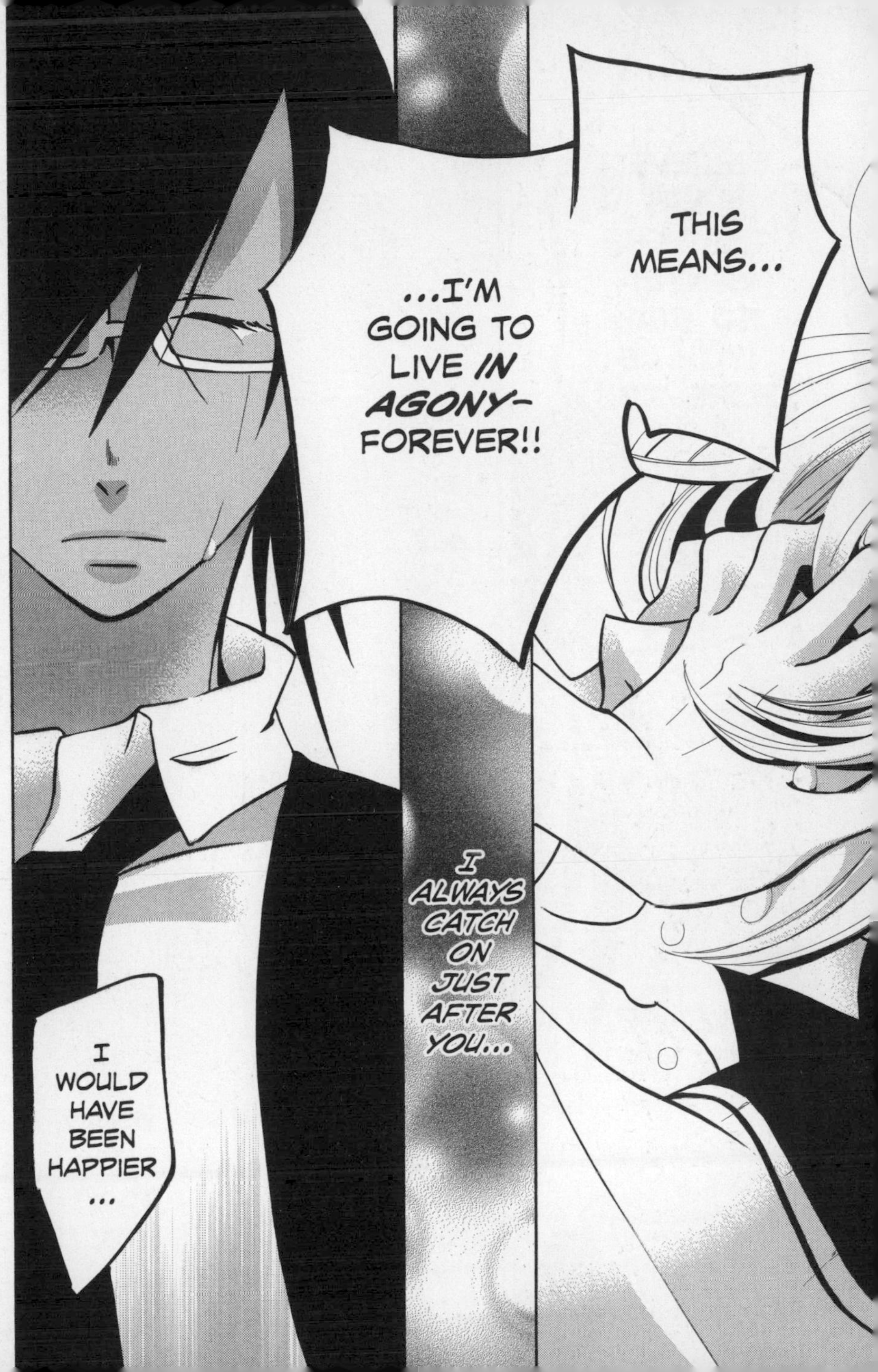
THIS MEANS...
...I'M GOING TO LIVE IN AGONY—FOREVER!!
I ALWAYS CATCH ON JUST AFTER YOU...
I WOULD HAVE BEEN HAPPIER...

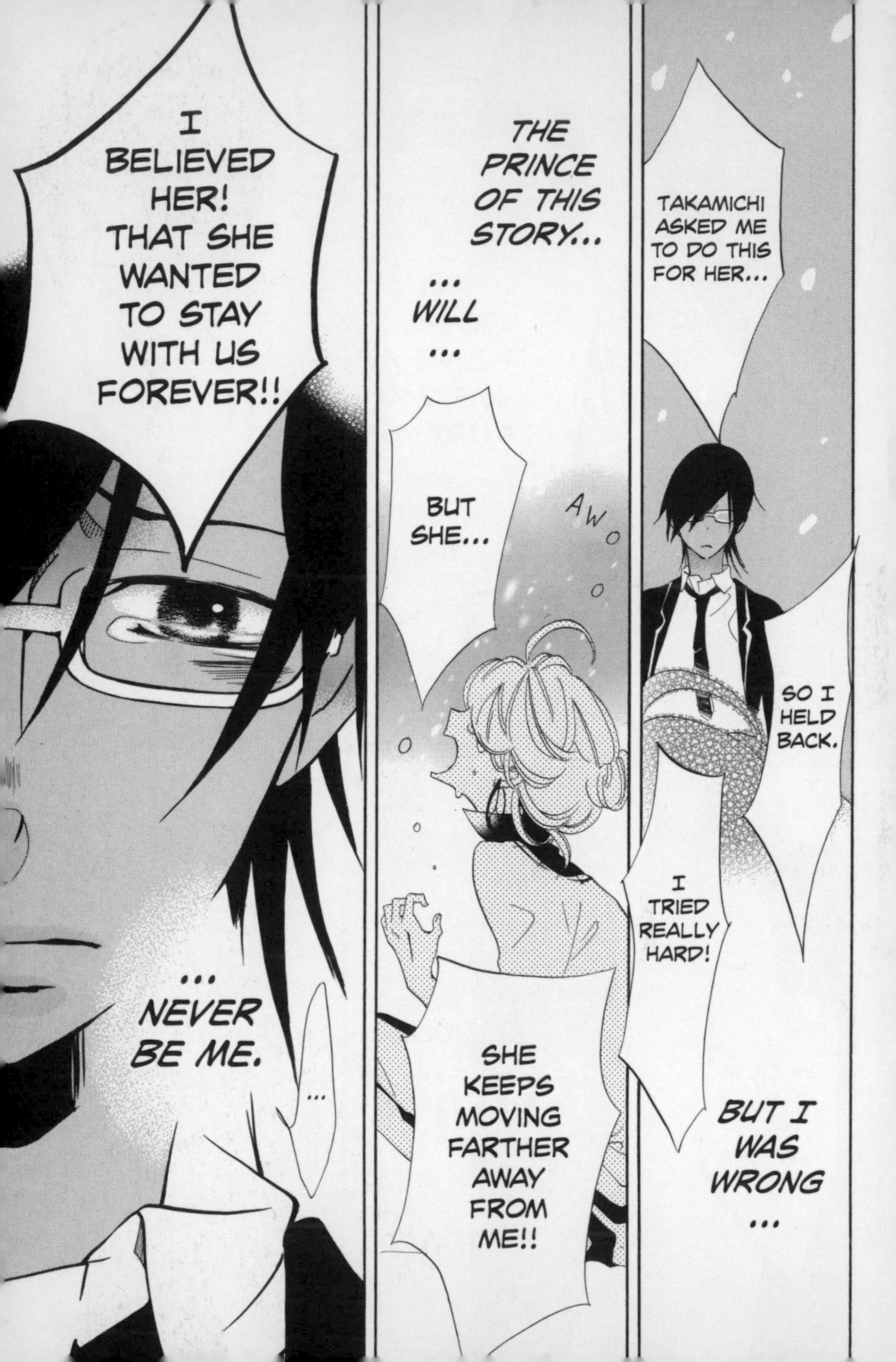
TAKAMICHI ASKED ME TO DO THIS FOR HER...
SO I HELD BACK.
I TRIED REALLY HARD!
BUT I WAS WRONG ...
THE PRINCE OF THIS STORY...
... WILL ...
BUT SHE...
AWO
SHE KEEPS MOVING FARTHER AWAY FROM ME!!
I BELIEVED HER! THAT SHE WANTED TO STAY WITH US FOREVER!!
... NEVER BE ME.
...

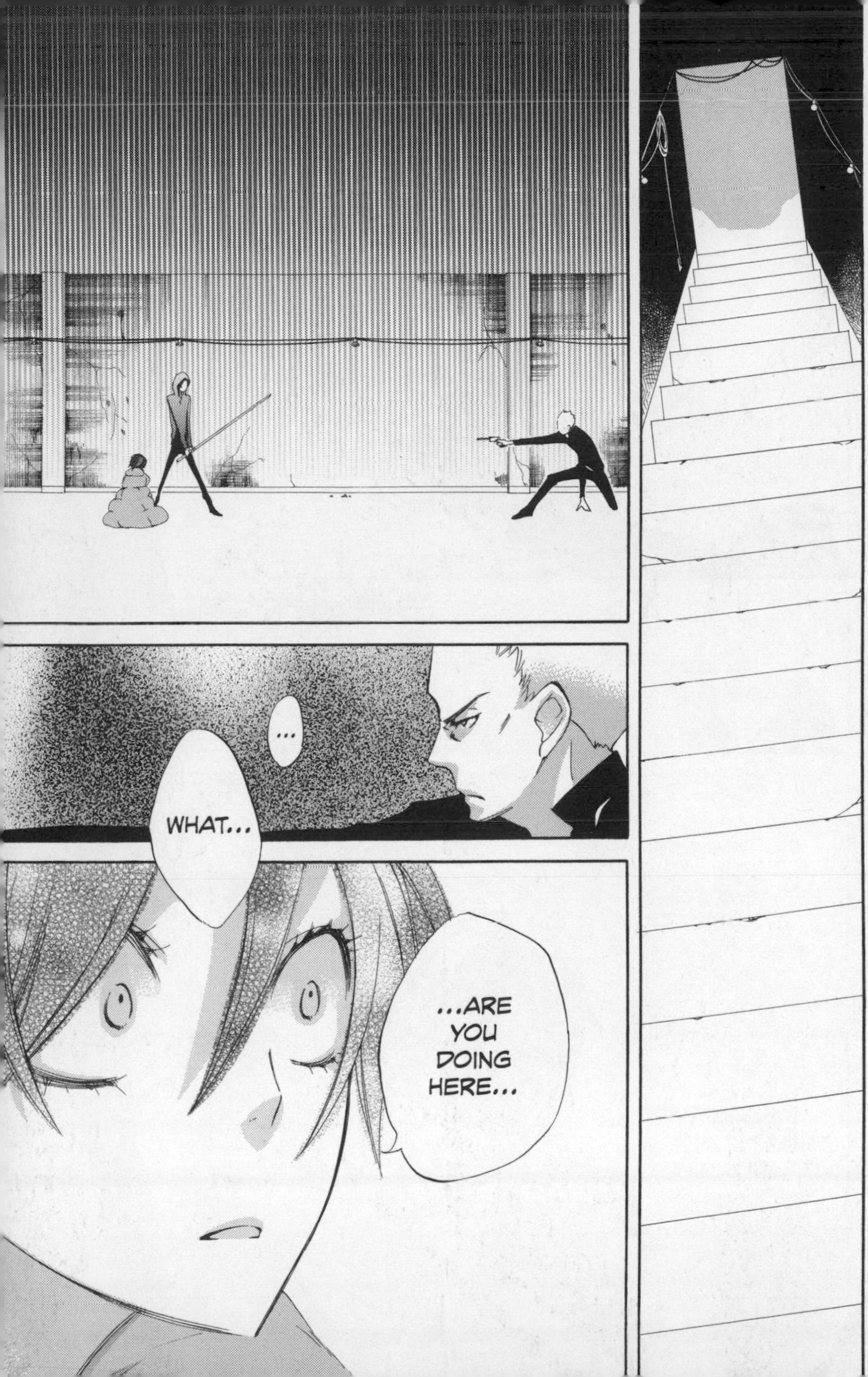
...
WHAT...
...ARE YOU DOING HERE...

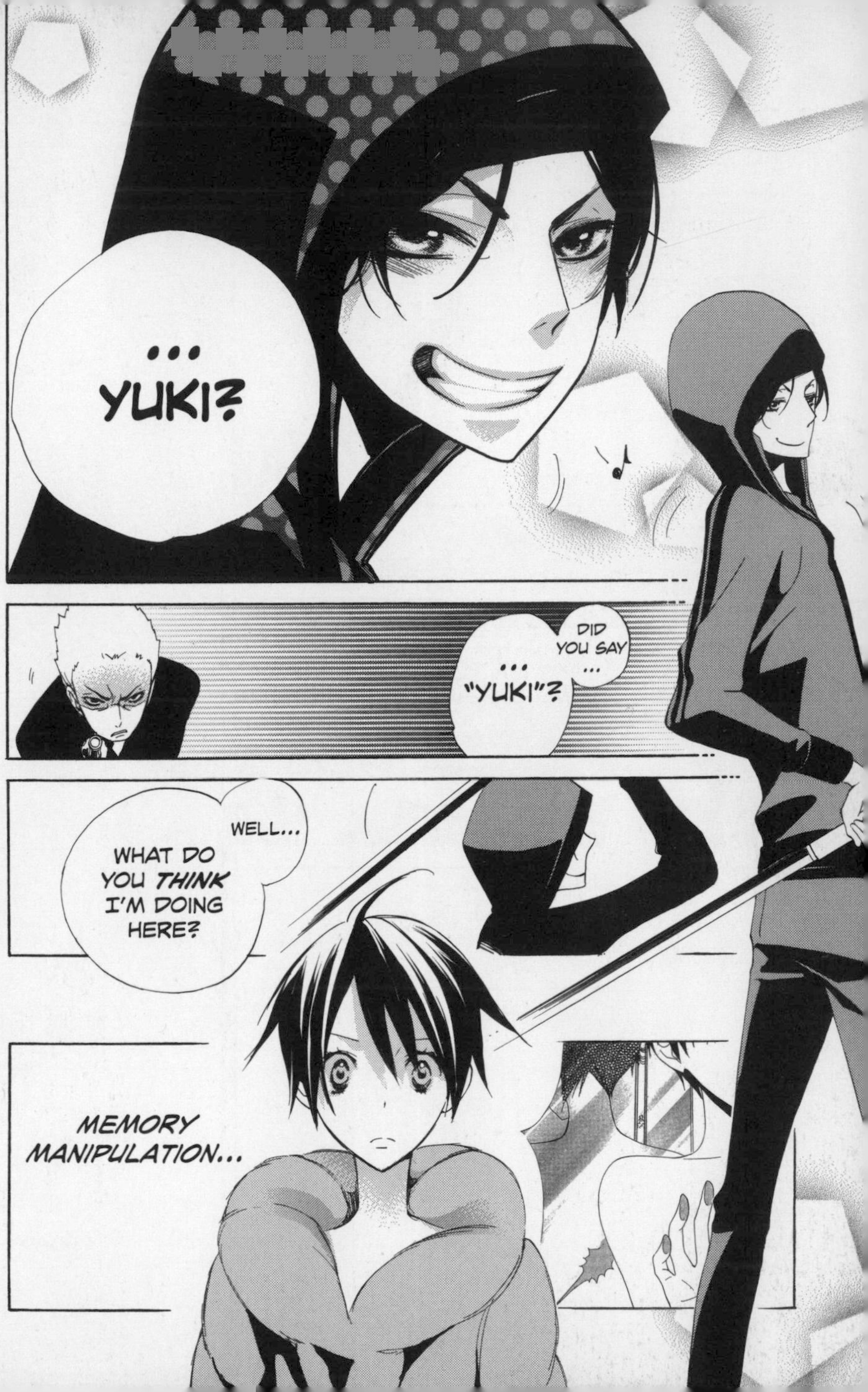
...YUKI?
DID YOU SAY ...
... "YUKI"?
WELL...
WHAT DO YOU *THINK* I'M DOING HERE?
MEMORY MANIPULATION...

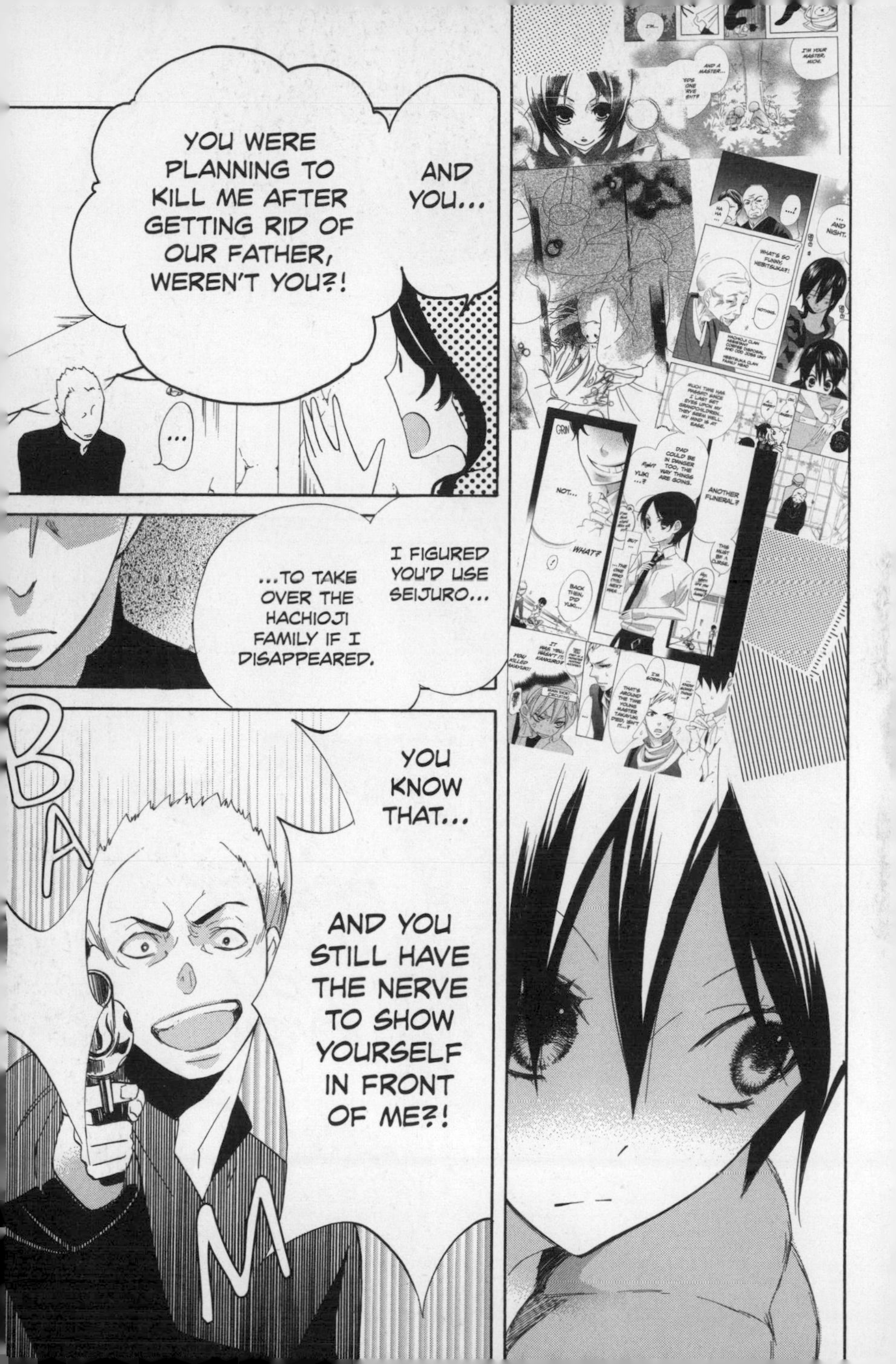
AND YOU...
YOU WERE PLANNING TO KILL ME AFTER GETTING RID OF OUR FATHER, WEREN'T YOU?!
...
I FIGURED YOU'D USE SEIJURO...
...TO TAKE OVER THE HACHIOJI FAMILY IF I DISAPPEARED.
YOU KNOW THAT...
AND YOU STILL HAVE THE NERVE TO SHOW YOURSELF IN FRONT OF ME?!
BAM

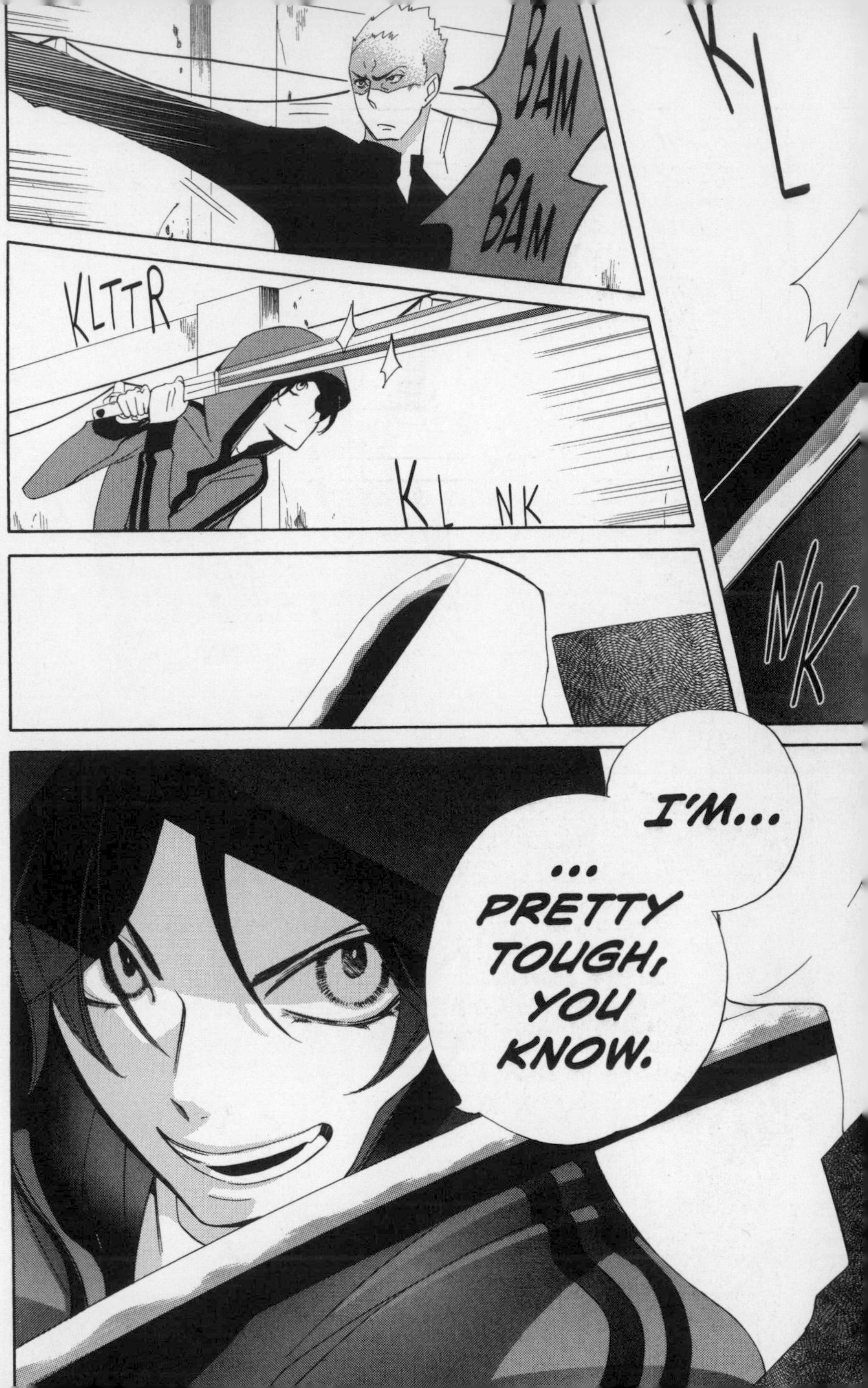
KL
NK
BAM
BAM
KLTTR
KL NK
I'M... ...PRETTY TOUGH, YOU KNOW.

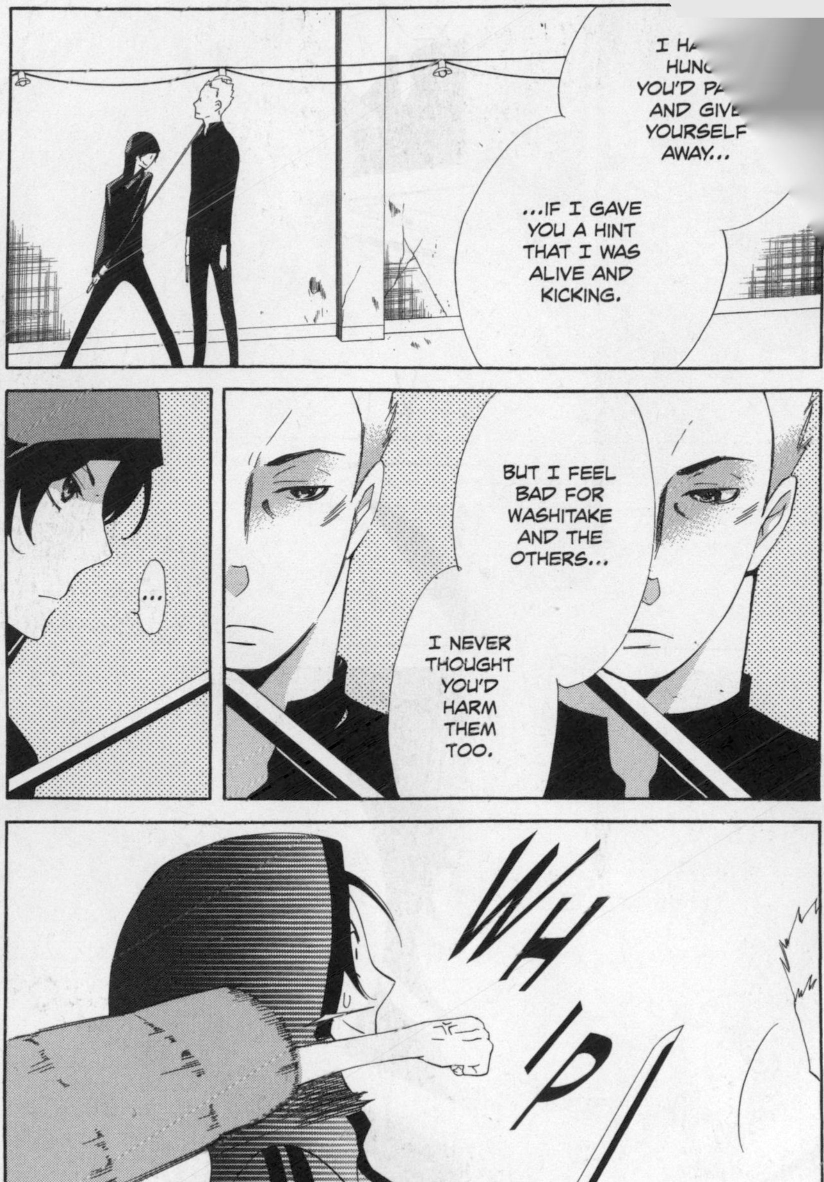
I HA HUNC YOU'D PA AND GIVE YOURSELF AWAY...
...IF I GAVE YOU A HINT THAT I WAS ALIVE AND KICKING.
BUT I FEEL BAD FOR WASHITAKE AND THE OTHERS...
I NEVER THOUGHT YOU'D HARM THEM TOO.
...
WHIP

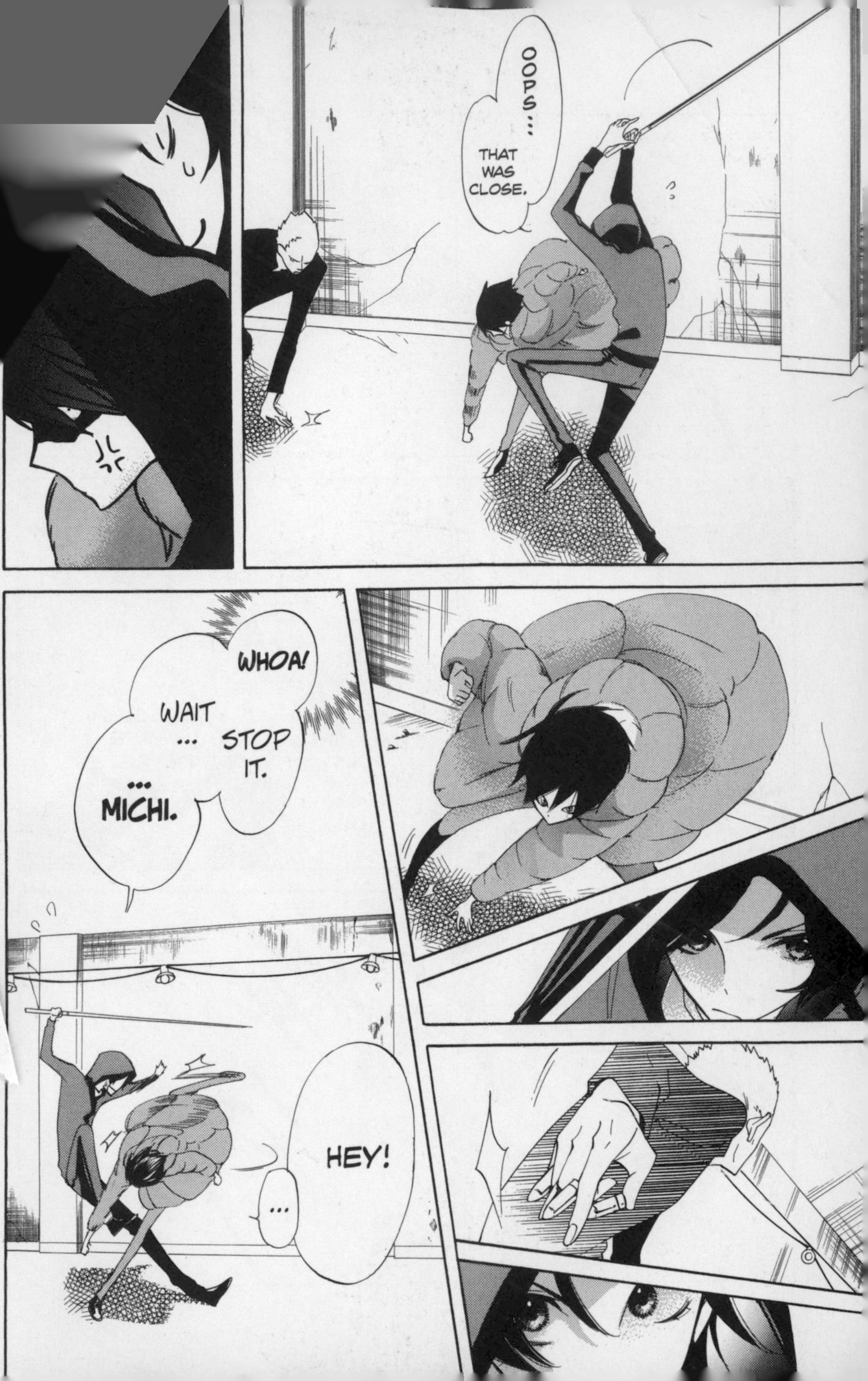
OOPS... THAT WAS CLOSE.
WHOA! WAIT... STOP IT. ...MICHI.
HEY!
...

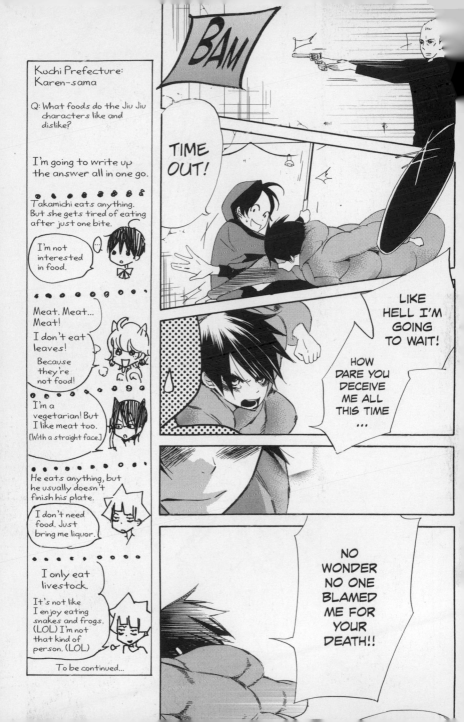

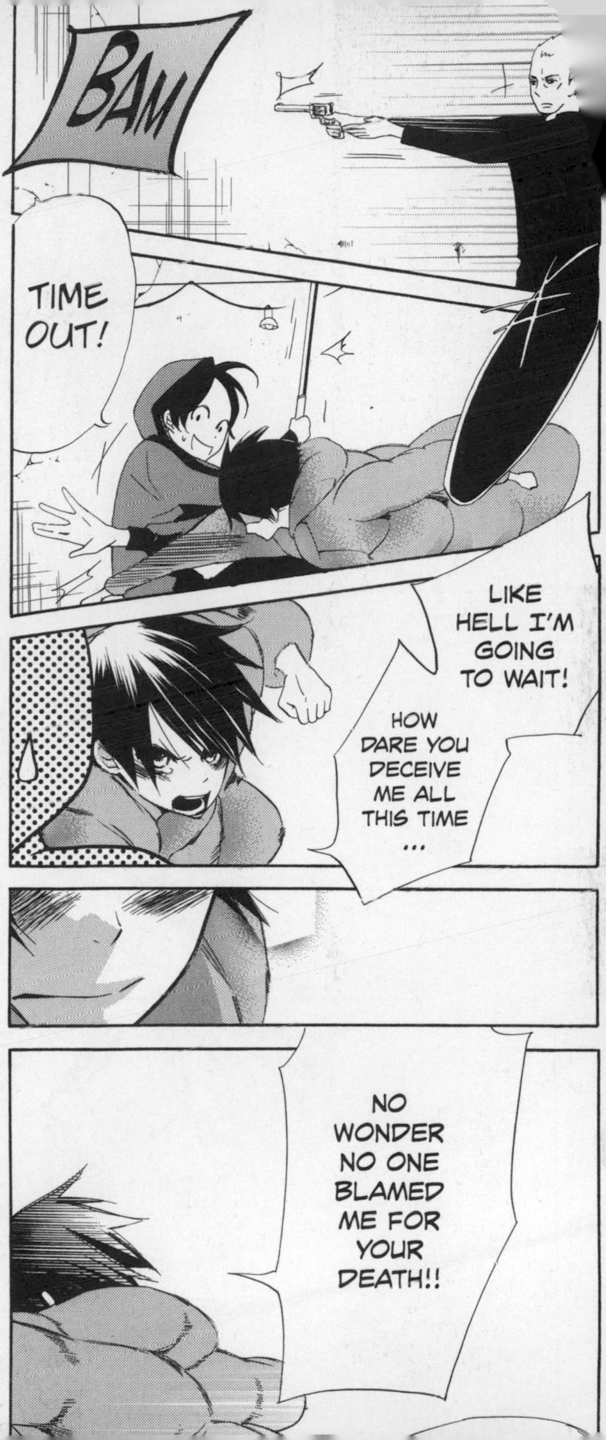
BAM
TIME OUT!
LIKE HELL I'M GOING TO WAIT!
HOW DARE YOU DECEIVE ME ALL THIS TIME ...
NO WONDER NO ONE BLAMED ME FOR YOUR DEATH!!

Kochi Prefecture:
Karen-sama

Q: What foods do the Jiu Jiu characters like and dislike?

I'm going to write up the answer all in one go.

Takamichi eats anything. But she gets tired of eating after just one bite.

I'm not interested in food.

...

Meat. Meat... Meat!

I don't eat leaves!

Because they're not food!

I'm a vegetarian! But I like meat too.

[With a straight face.]

He eats anything, but he usually doesn't finish his plate.

I don't need food. Just bring me liquor.

I only eat livestock.

It's not like I enjoy eating snakes and frogs. (LOL) I'm not that kind of person. (LOL)

To be continued...

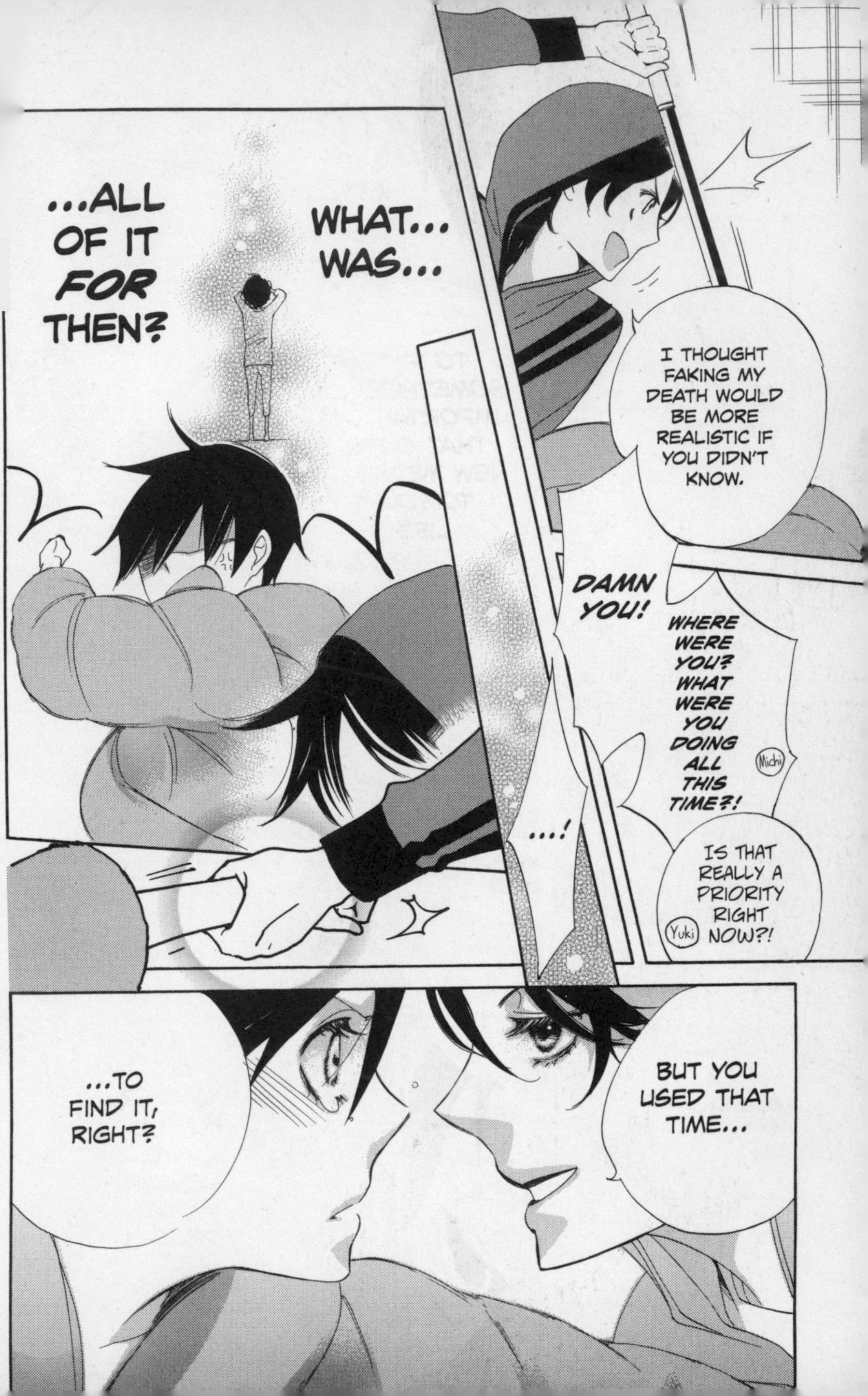
I THOUGHT FAKING MY DEATH WOULD BE MORE REALISTIC IF YOU DIDN'T KNOW.
WHAT... WAS...
...ALL OF IT *FOR* THEN?
DAMN YOU!
WHERE WERE YOU? WHAT WERE YOU DOING ALL THIS TIME?!
Michi
...!
IS THAT REALLY A PRIORITY RIGHT NOW?!
Yuki
BUT YOU USED THAT TIME...
...TO FIND IT, RIGHT?

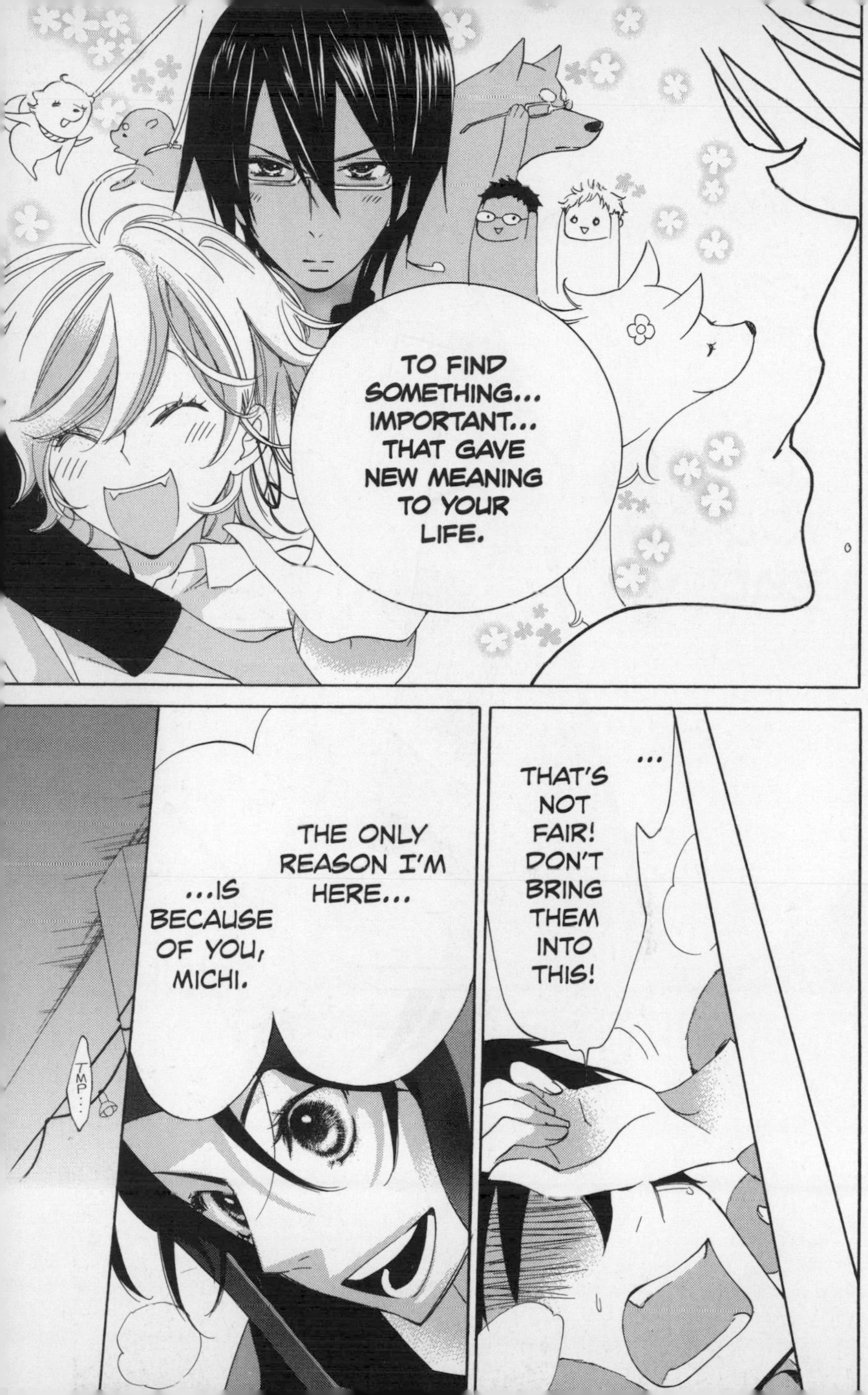
TO FIND SOMETHING... IMPORTANT... THAT GAVE NEW MEANING TO YOUR LIFE.
...
THAT'S NOT FAIR! DON'T BRING THEM INTO THIS!
THE ONLY REASON I'M HERE...
...IS BECAUSE OF YOU, MICHI.
TMP...

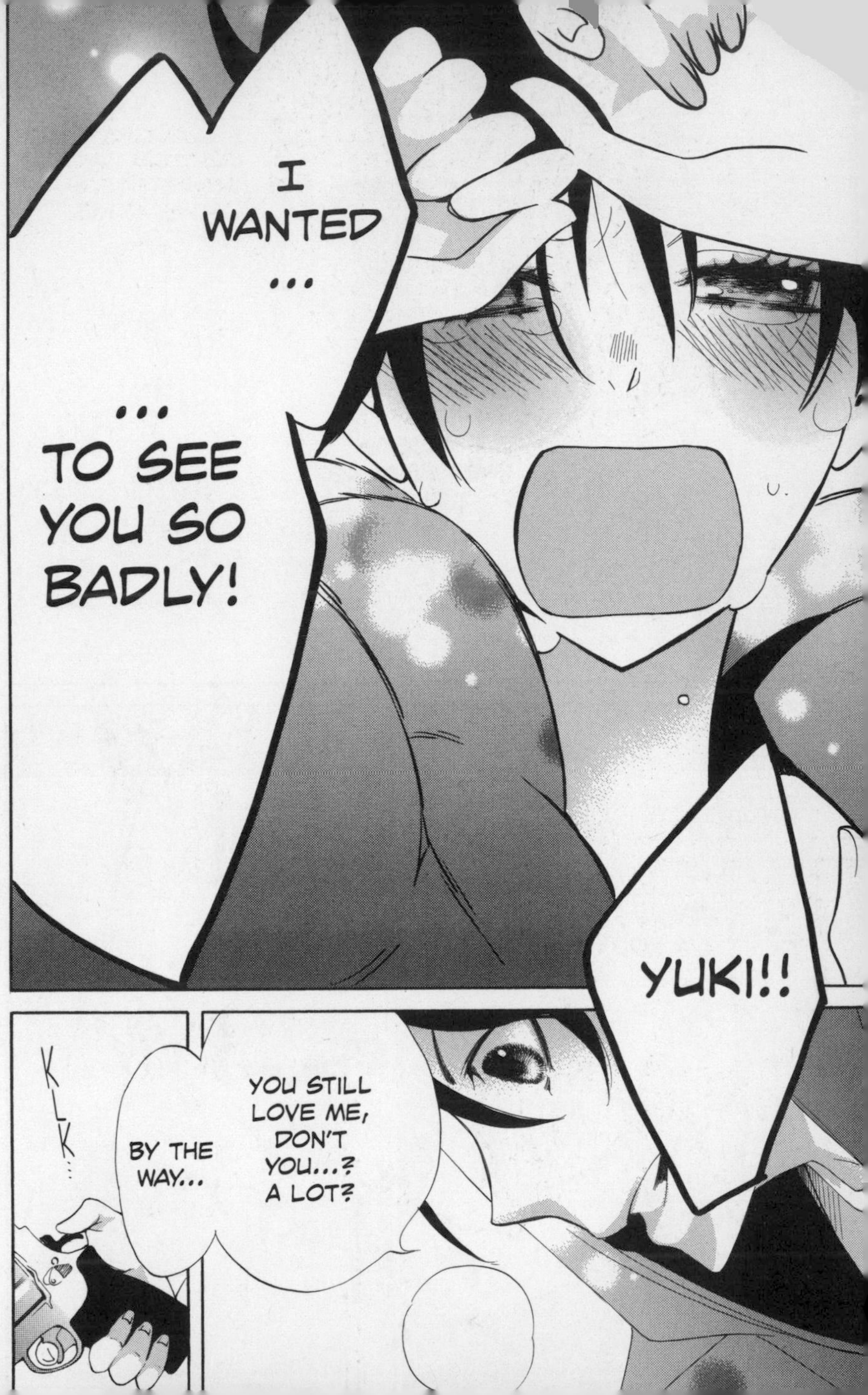
I WANTED ... ... TO SEE YOU SO BADLY!
YUKI!!
BY THE WAY... YOU STILL LOVE ME, DON'T YOU...? A LOT?
KLK...

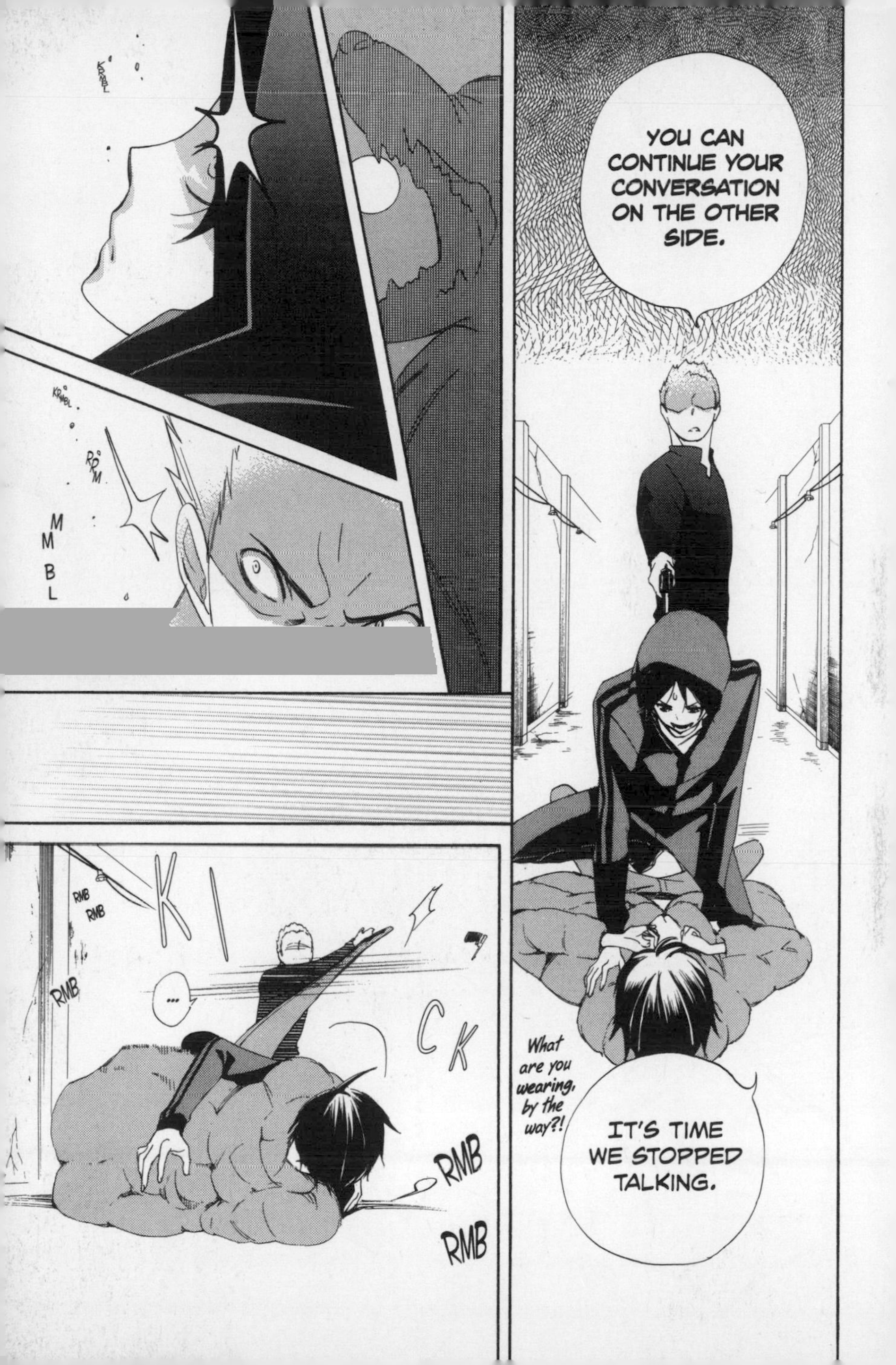
YOU CAN CONTINUE YOUR CONVERSATION ON THE OTHER SIDE.
What are you wearing, by the way?!
IT'S TIME WE STOPPED TALKING.
KRMBL
KRMBL
RRM
MMBL
KICK
RMB
RMB
RMB
...
RMB
RMB

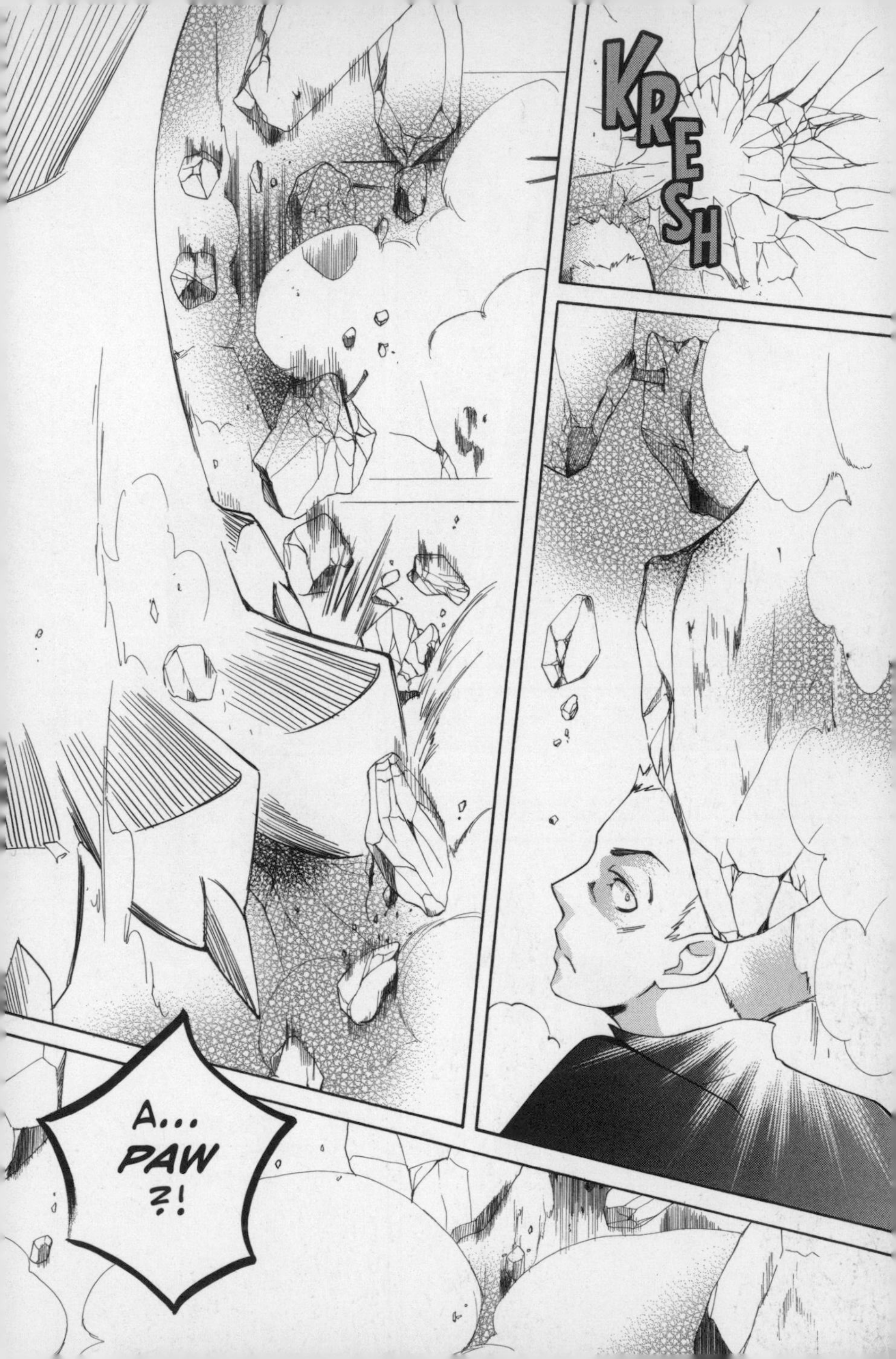
KRESH
A... PAW ?!

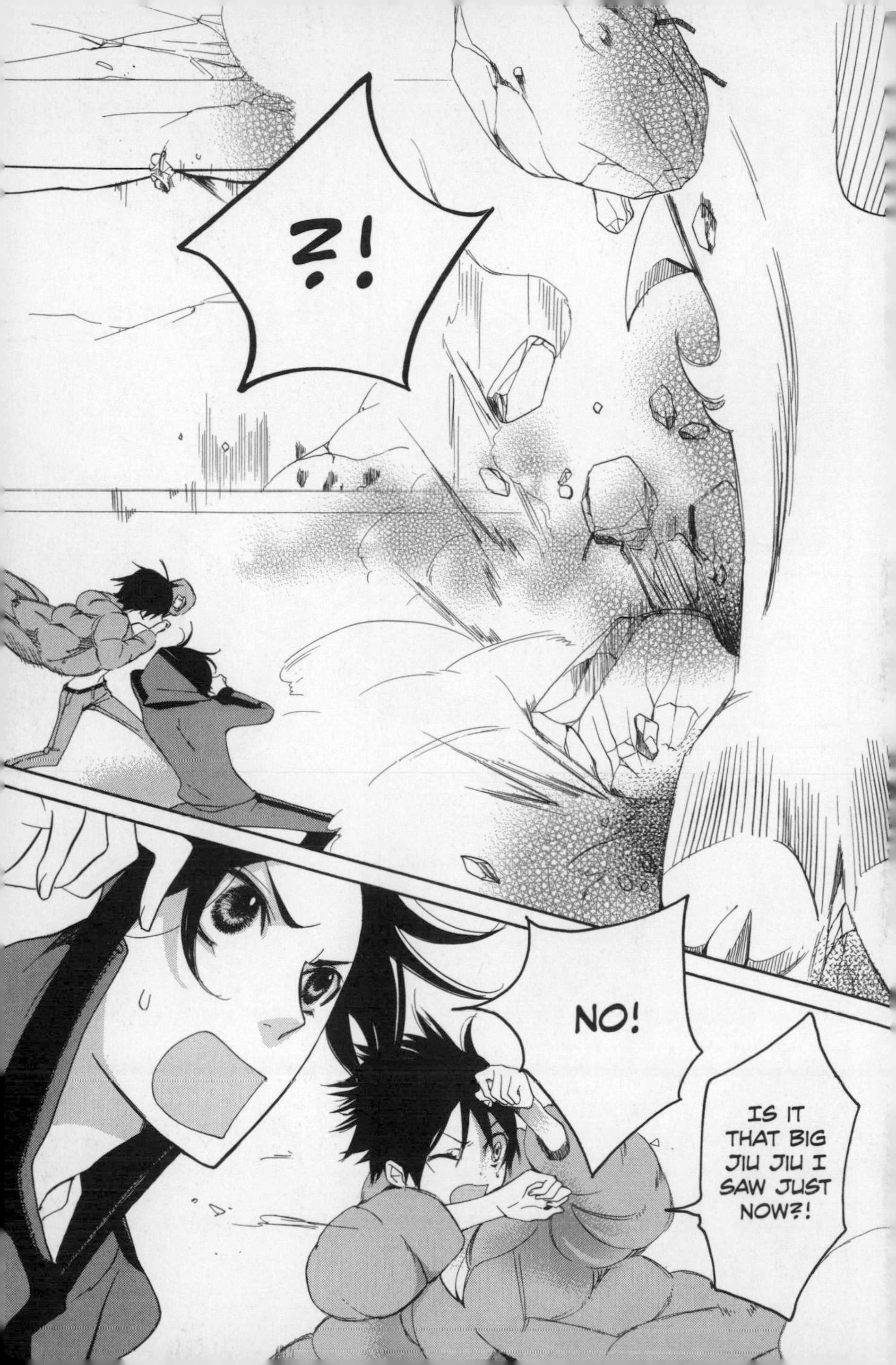
?!
NO!
IS IT THAT BIG JIU JIU I SAW JUST NOW?!

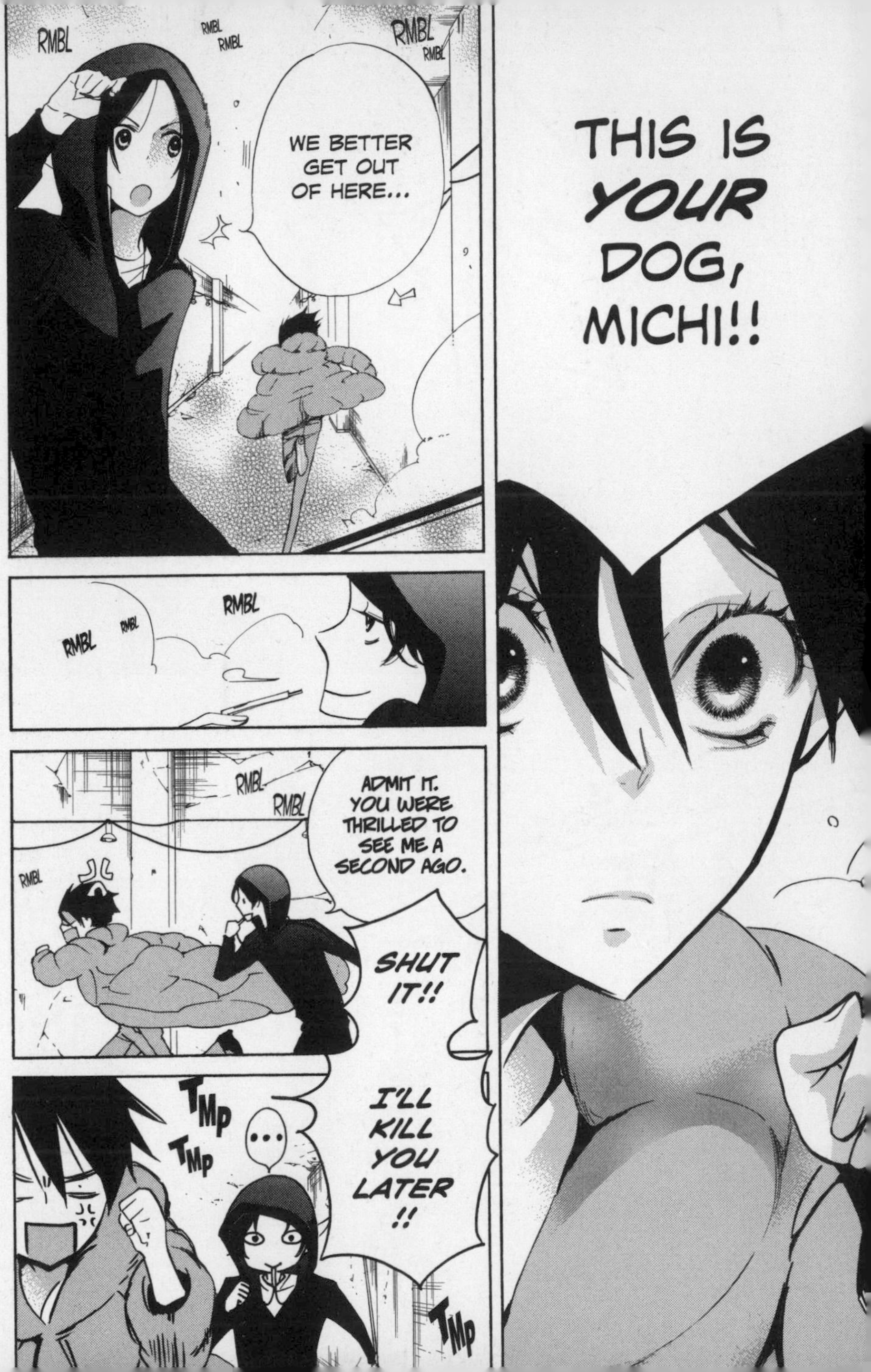

THIS IS YOUR DOG, MICHI!!
RMBL
RMBL RMBL
RMBL RMBL
WE BETTER GET OUT OF HERE...
RMBL
RMBL RMBL
RMBL
RMBL
RMBL
ADMIT IT. YOU WERE THRILLED TO SEE ME A SECOND AGO.
SHUT IT!!
I'LL KILL YOU LATER!!
TMP TMP
...
TMP

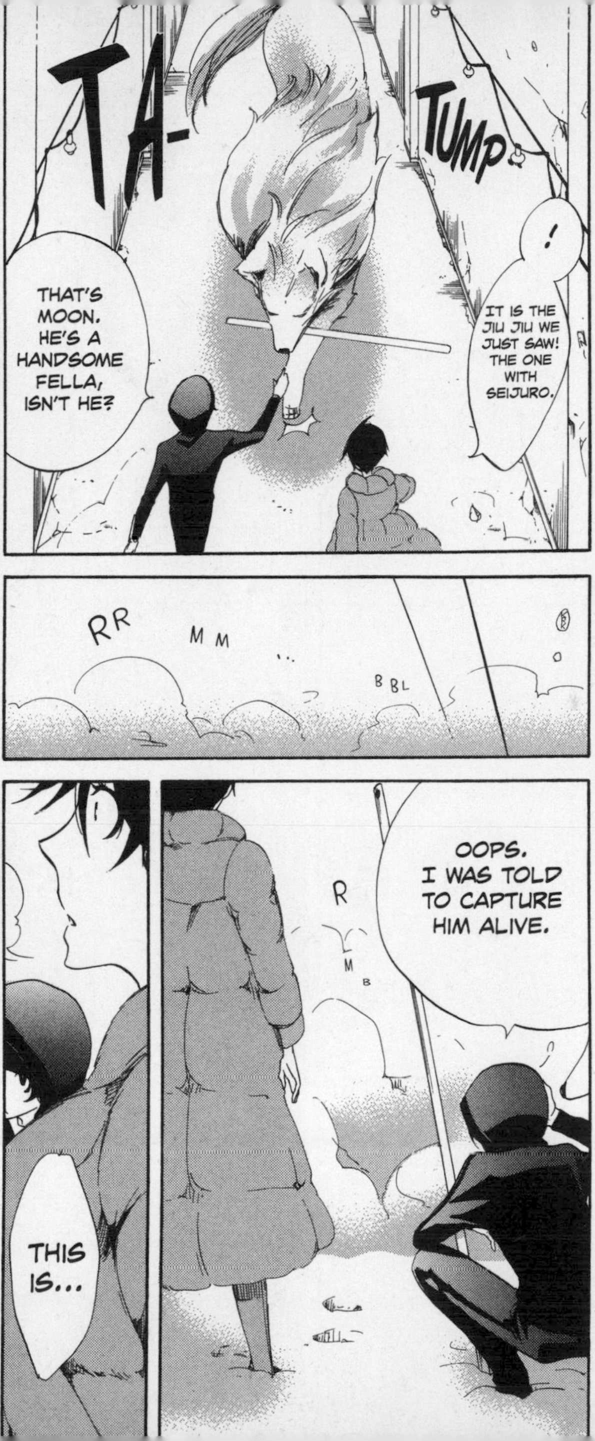
TA-
TUMP
!
IT IS THE JIU JIU WE JUST SAW! THE ONE WITH SEIJURO.
THAT'S MOON. HE'S A HANDSOME FELLA, ISN'T HE?
RR MM BBL
OOPS. I WAS TOLD TO CAPTURE HIM ALIVE.
R MB
THIS IS...

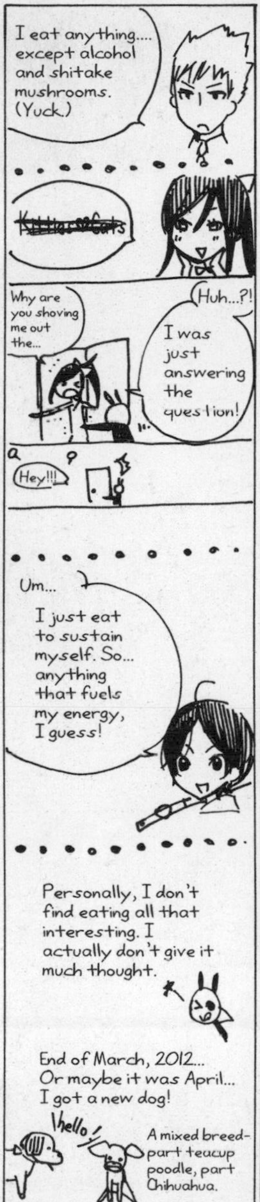
I eat anything.... except alcohol and shitake mushrooms. (Yuck.)
~~Kitties & Cats~~
Huh...?! I was just answering the question!
Why are you shoving me out the...
Hey!!!
Um... I just eat to sustain myself. So... anything that fuels my energy, I guess!
Personally, I don't find eating all that interesting. I actually don't give it much thought.
End of March, 2012... Or maybe it was April... I got a new dog!
hello!
A mixed breed-part teacup poodle, part Chihuahua.

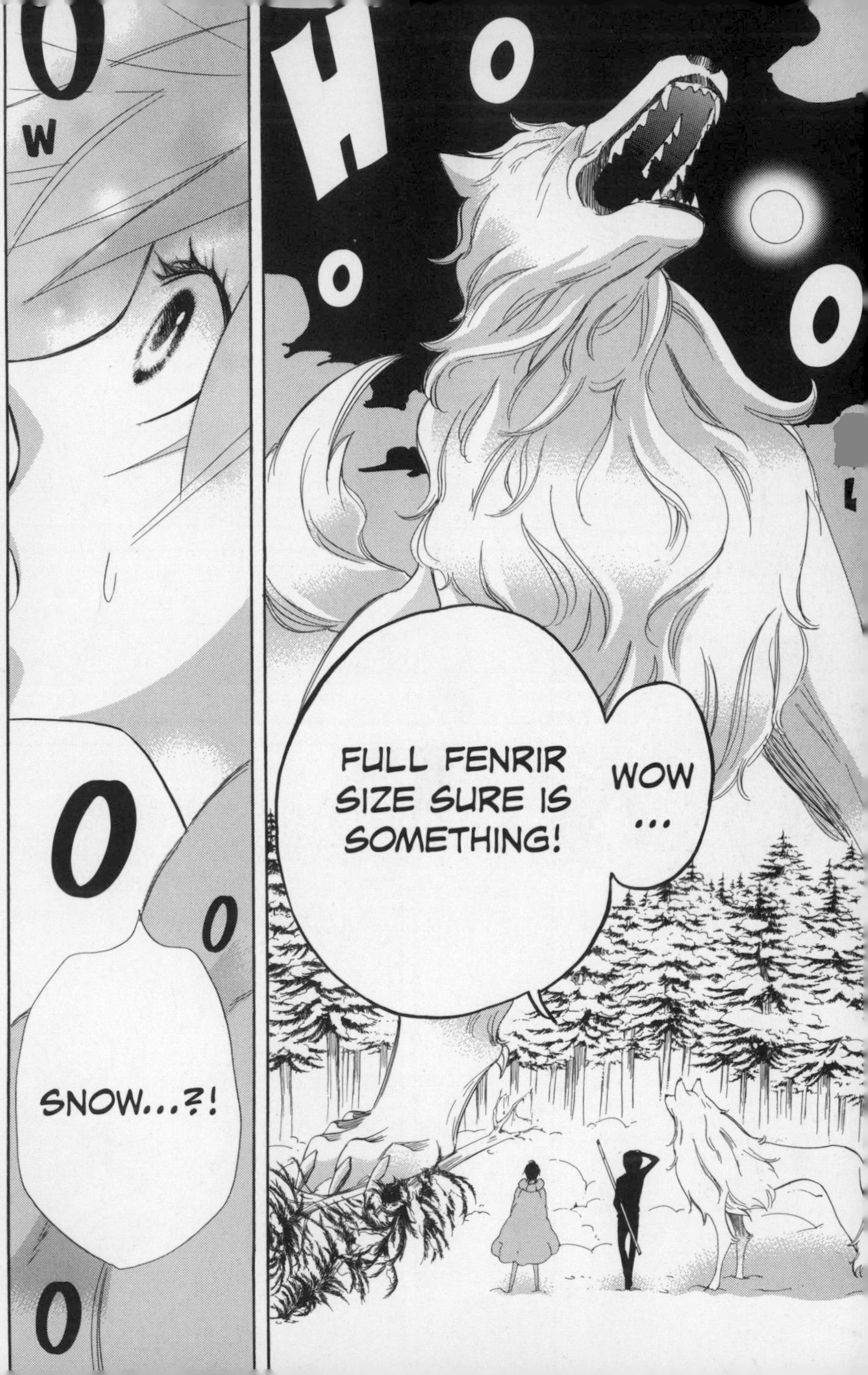
HOOOO
WOW ...
FULL FENRIR SIZE SURE IS SOMETHING!
OWOOO
SNOW...?!

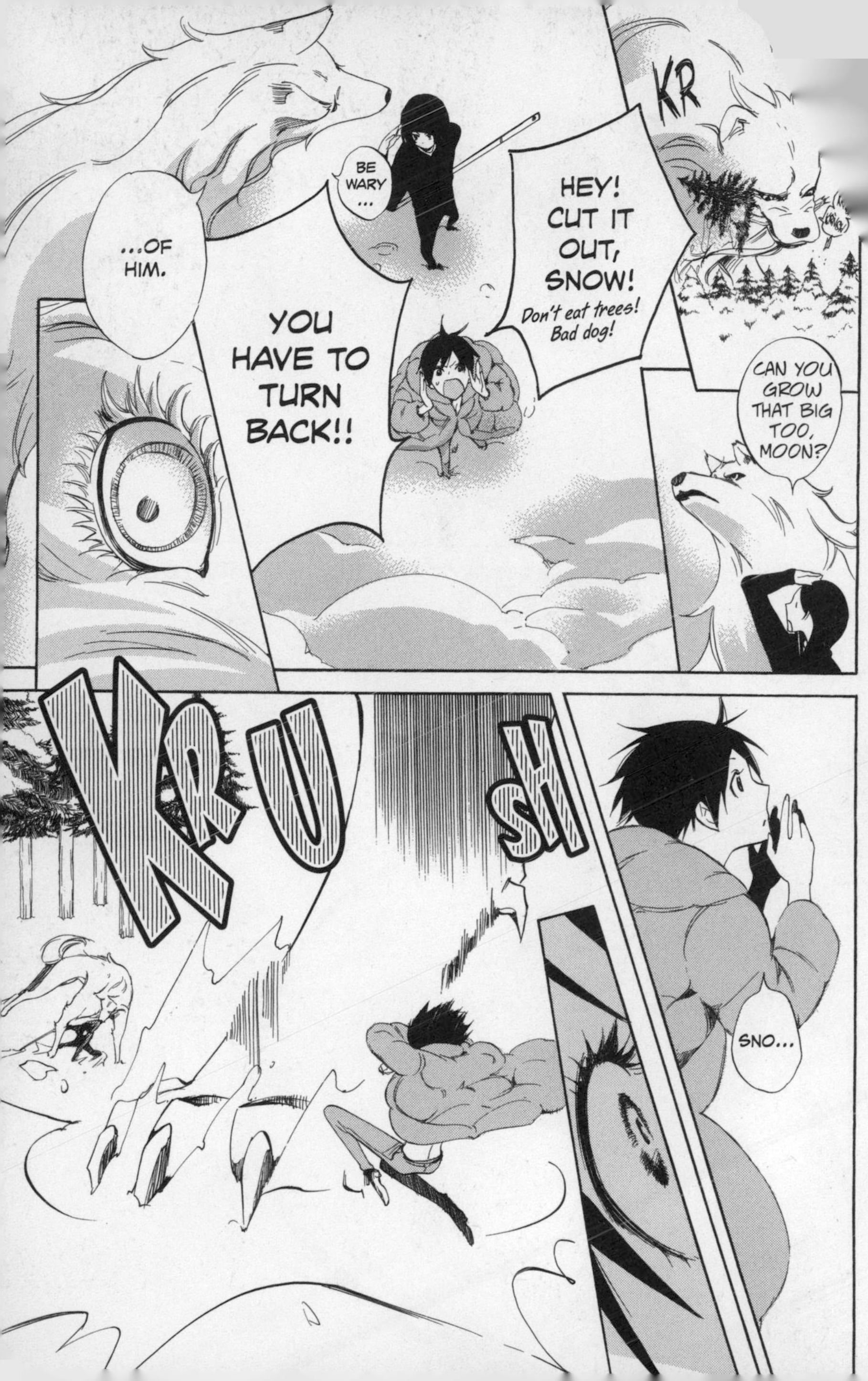
KR
CAN YOU GROW THAT BIG TOO, MOON?
HEY! CUT IT OUT, SNOW!
Don't eat trees! Bad dog!
BE WARY...
...OF HIM.
YOU HAVE TO TURN BACK!!
SNO...
KRUSH

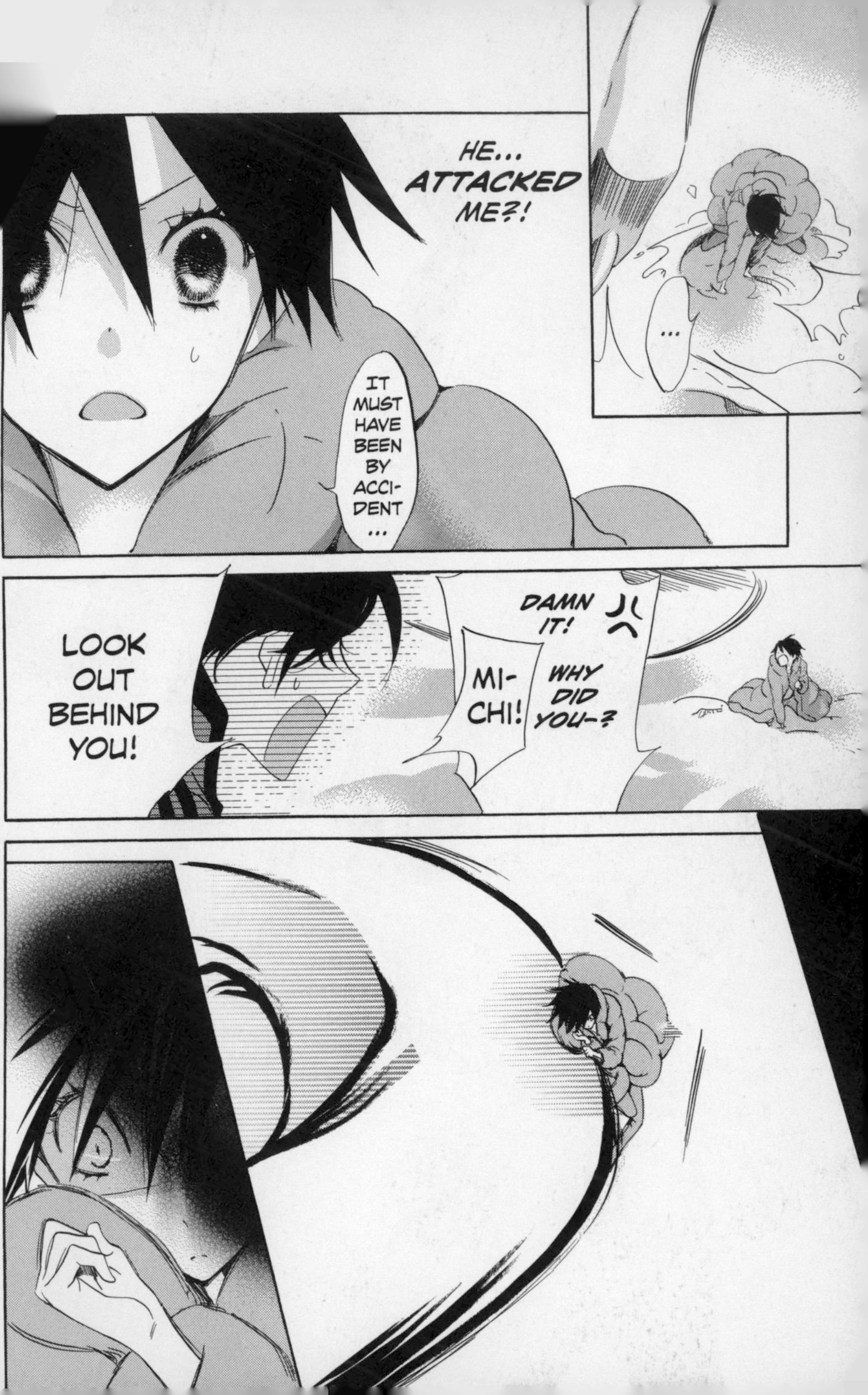
...
HE... ATTACKED ME?!
IT MUST HAVE BEEN BY ACCIDENT...
DAMN IT! WHY DID YOU-?
MI-CHI!
LOOK OUT BEHIND YOU!

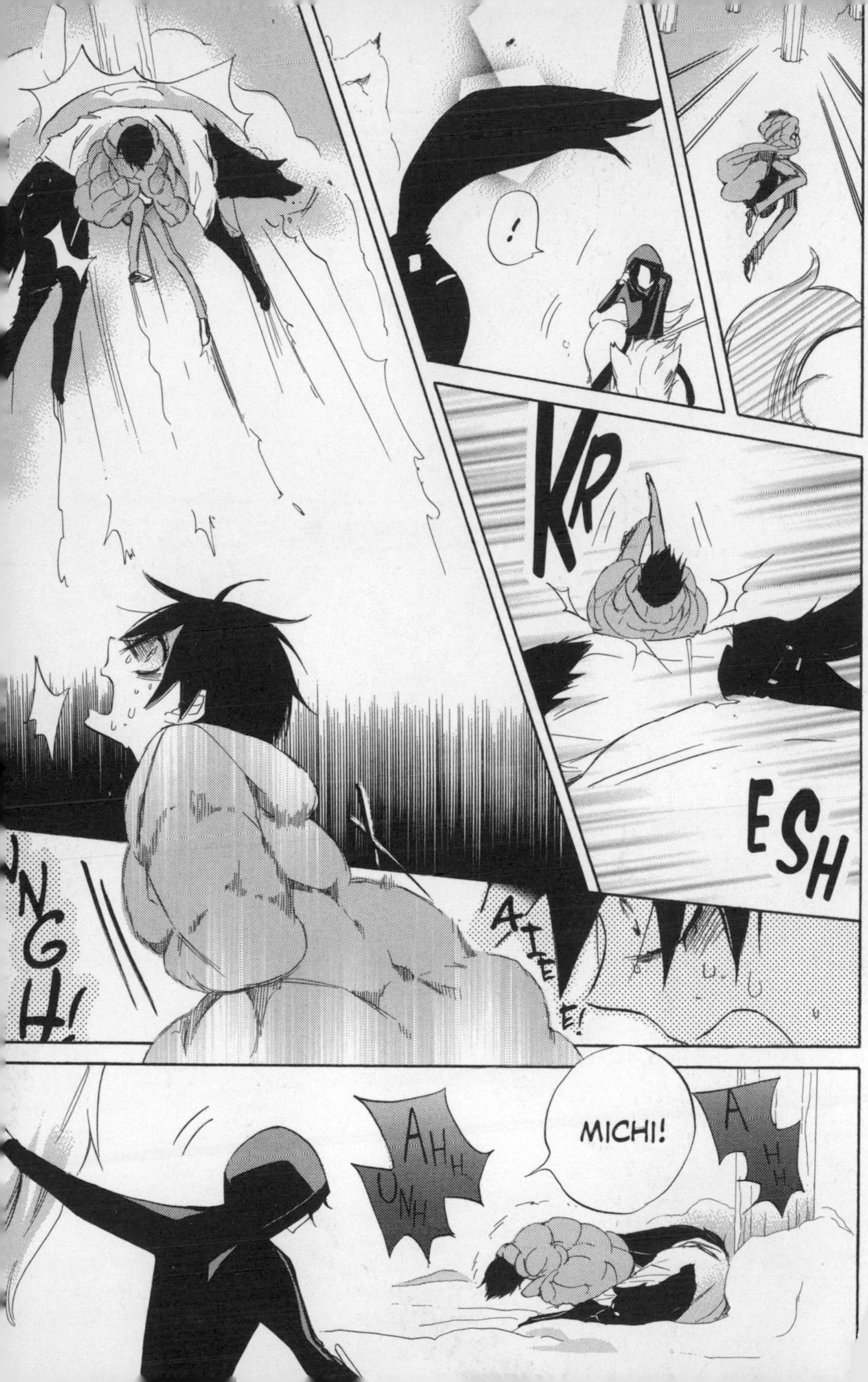
!
KR
ESH
AIEEE!
NNGH!
AHH
MICHI!
AHH
UNH

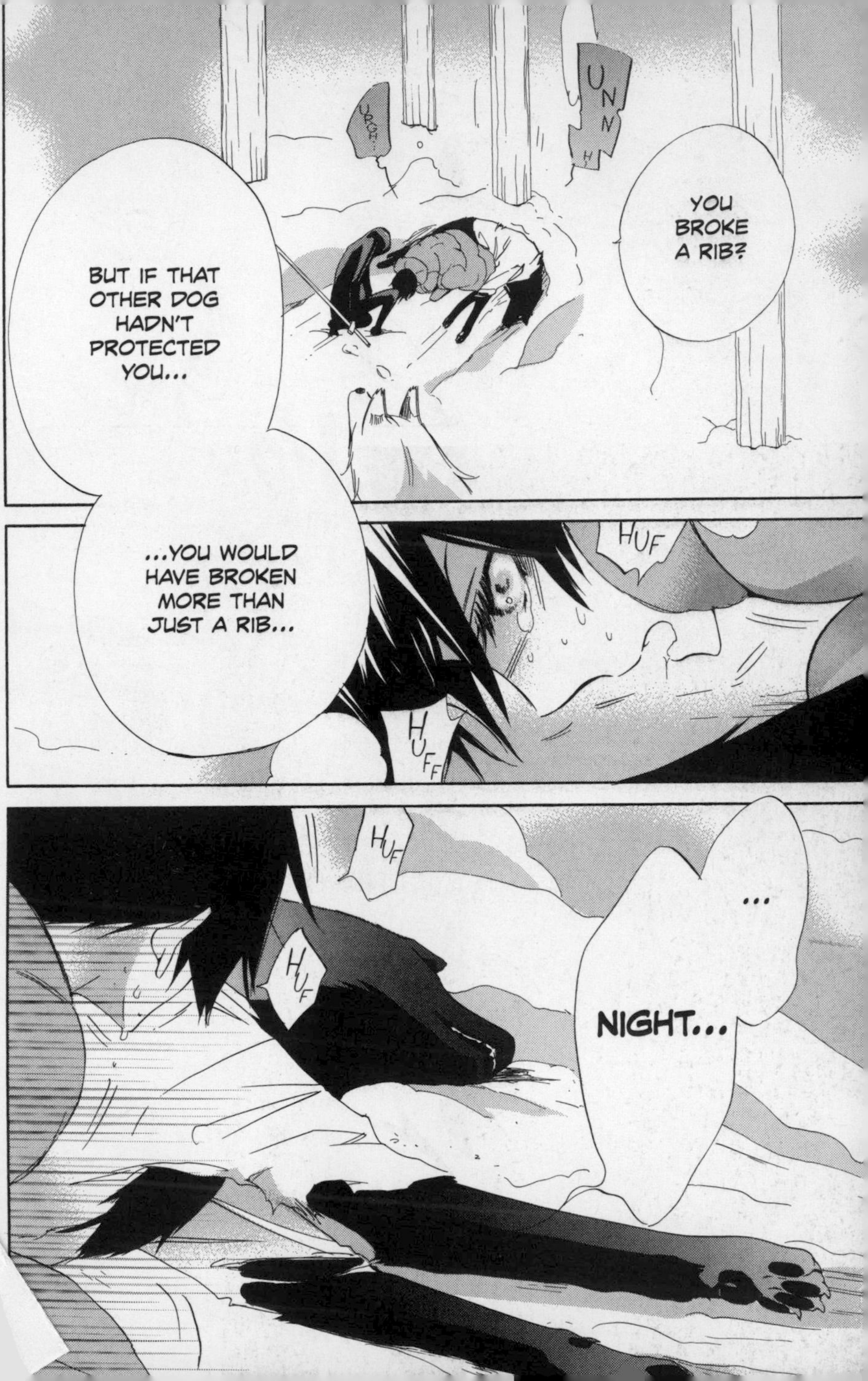
UNNH
YOU BROKE A RIB?
URGH!
BUT IF THAT OTHER DOG HADN'T PROTECTED YOU...
HUF
...YOU WOULD HAVE BROKEN MORE THAN JUST A RIB...
HUFF
...
NIGHT...
HUF
HUF

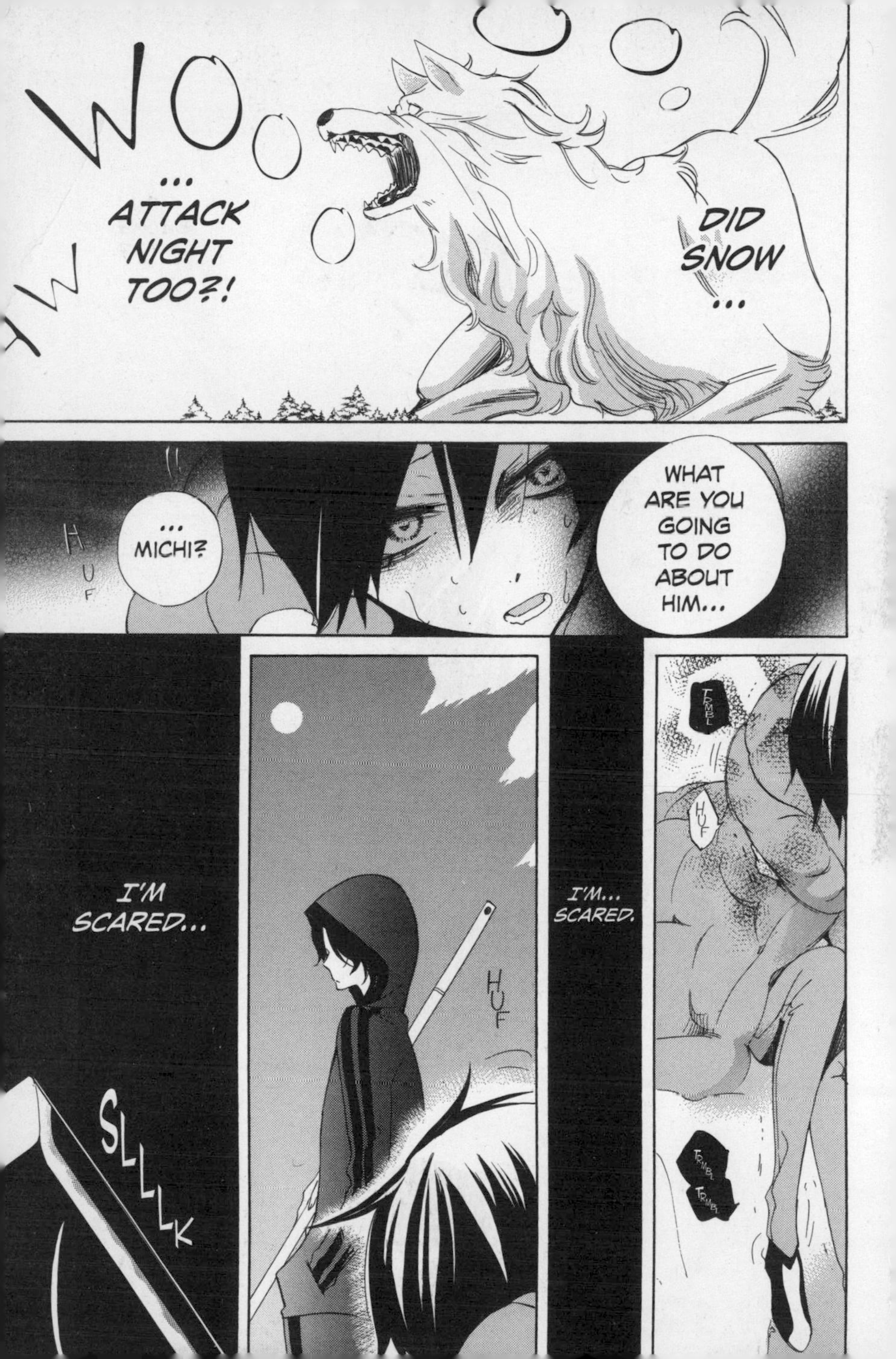
DID SNOW...
...ATTACK NIGHT TOO?!
WOOOO
WHAT ARE YOU GOING TO DO ABOUT HIM...
...MICHI?
HUF
TRMBL
HUF
TRMBL TRMBL
I'M... SCARED.
HUF
SLLLLK
I'M SCARED...

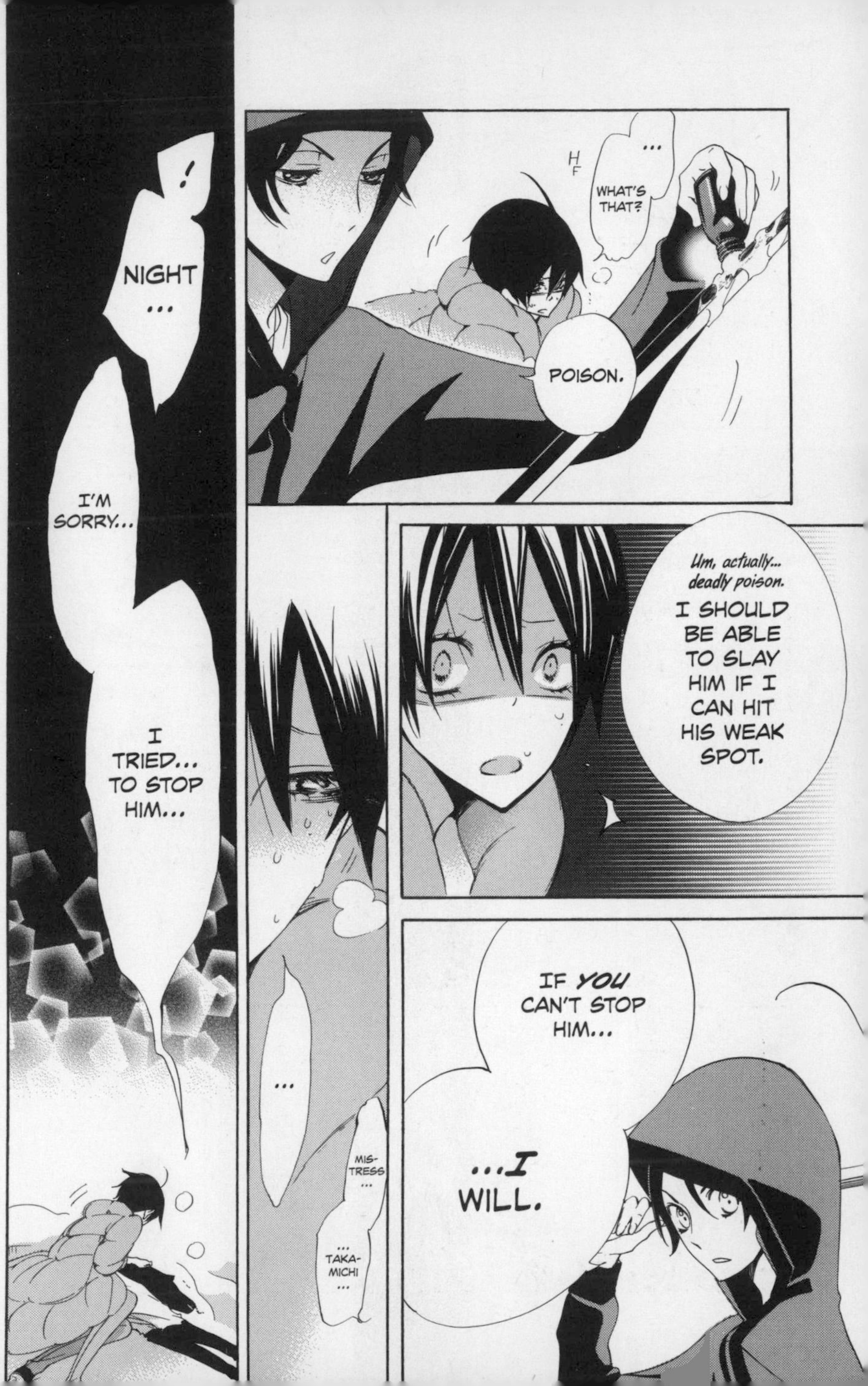

HF
... WHAT'S THAT?
POISON.
Um, actually... deadly poison. I SHOULD BE ABLE TO SLAY HIM IF I CAN HIT HIS WEAK SPOT.
IF *YOU* CAN'T STOP HIM...
...*I* WILL.
...
MIS-TRESS...
...TAKA-MICHI...
!
NIGHT...
I'M SORRY...
I TRIED... TO STOP HIM...

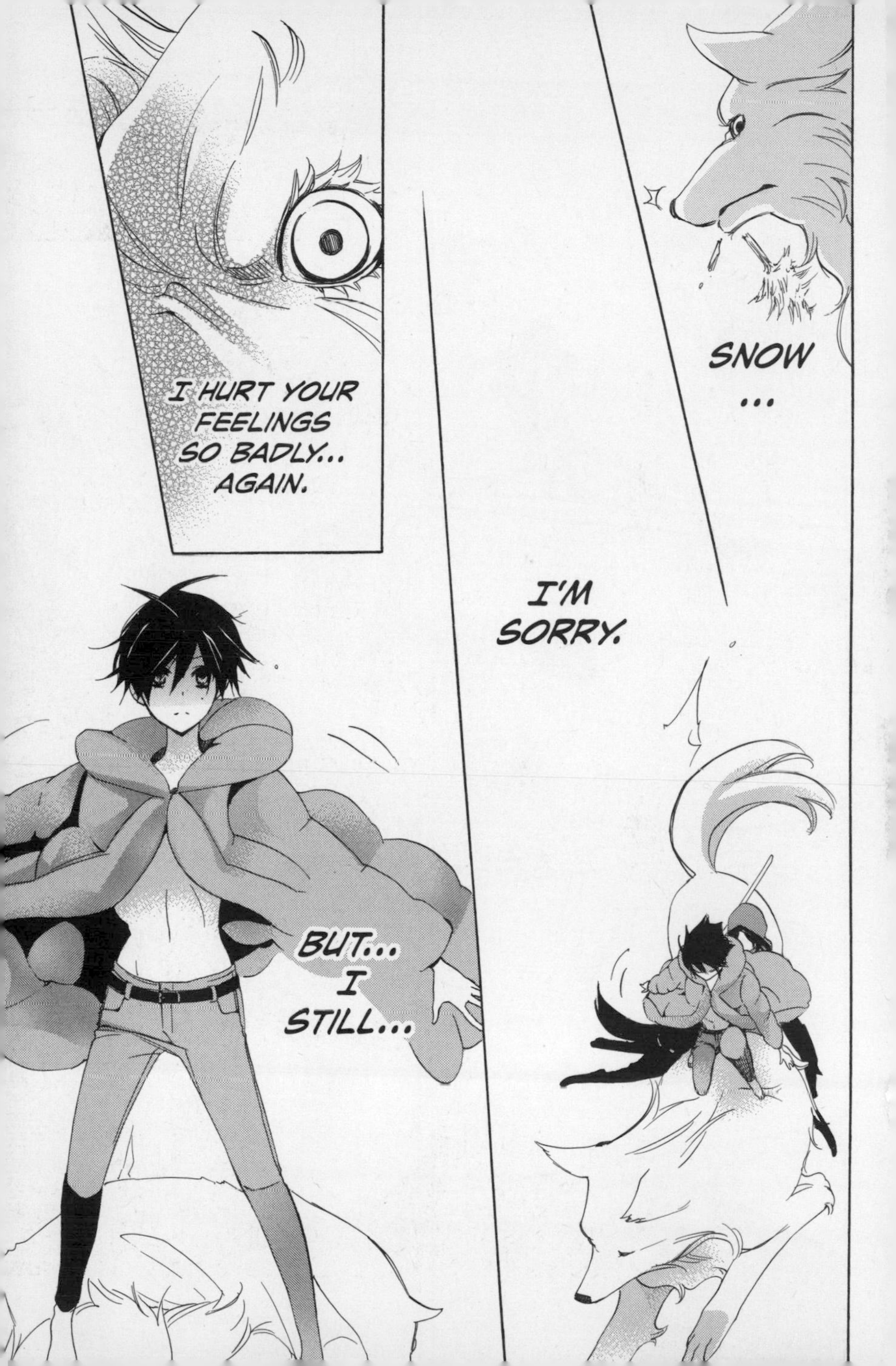
SNOW ...
I HURT YOUR FEELINGS SO BADLY... AGAIN.
I'M SORRY.
BUT... I STILL...

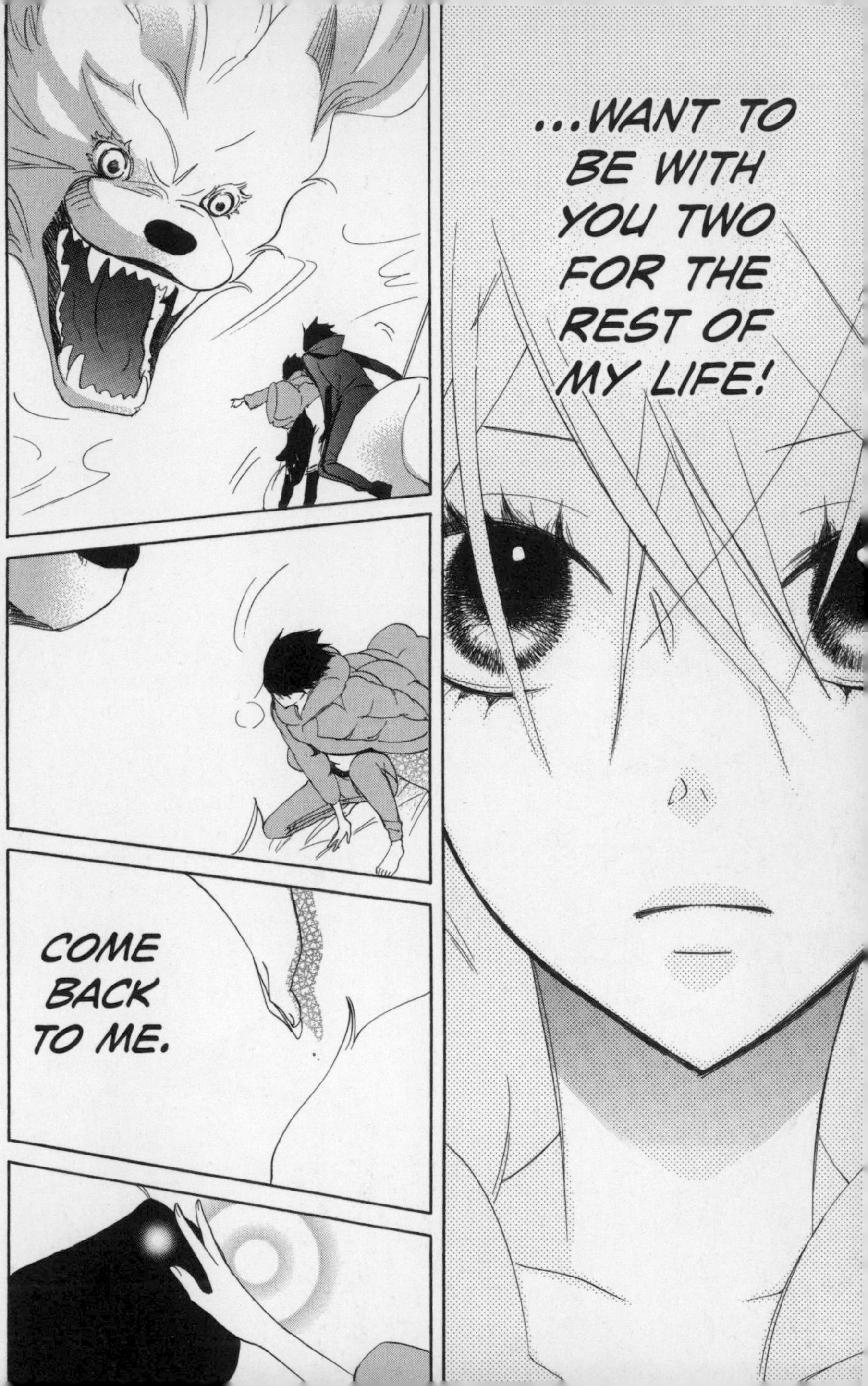
...WANT TO BE WITH YOU TWO FOR THE REST OF MY LIFE!
COME BACK TO ME.

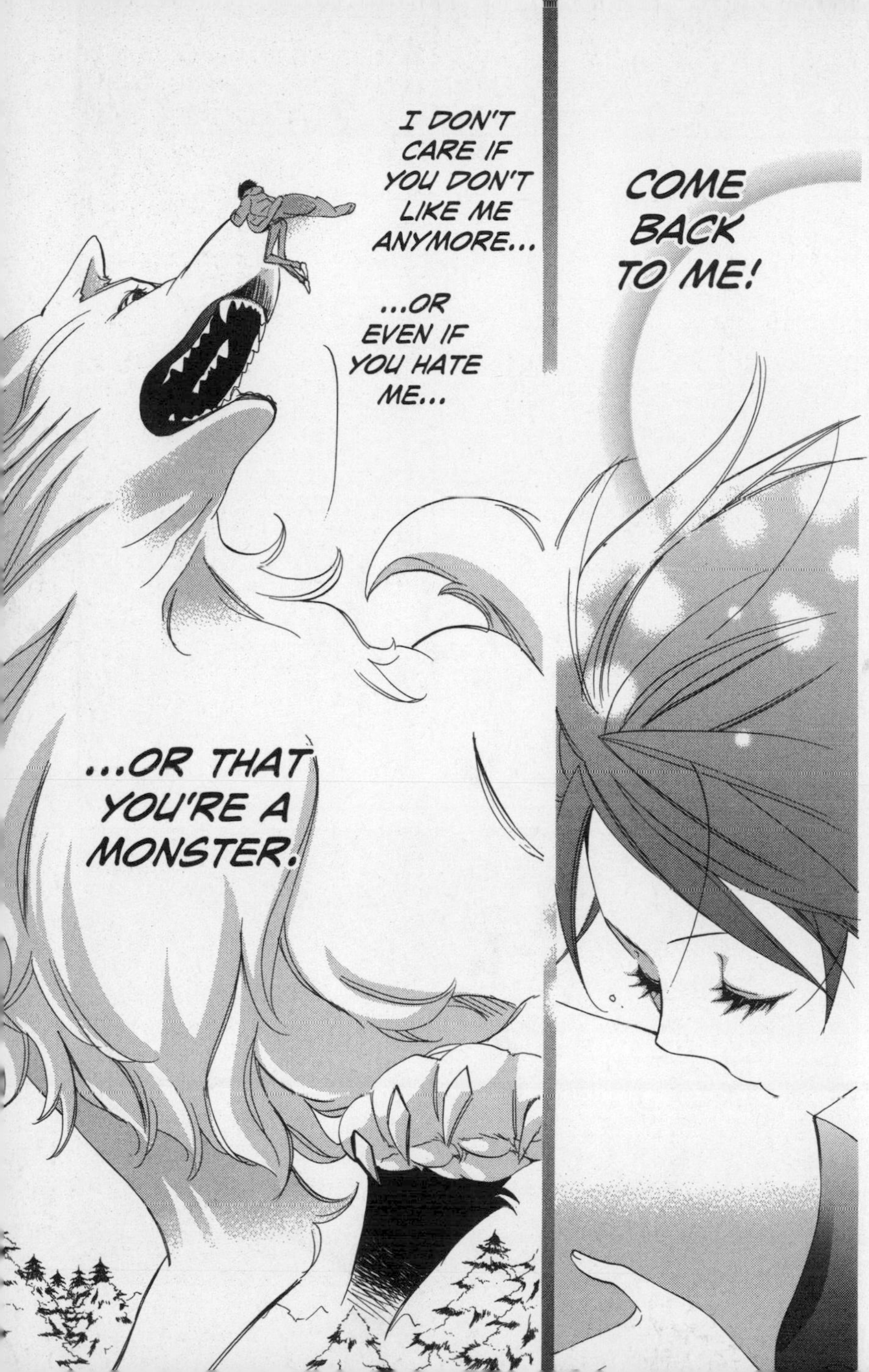
COME BACK TO ME!
I DON'T CARE IF YOU DON'T LIKE ME ANYMORE...
...OR EVEN IF YOU HATE ME...
...OR THAT YOU'RE A MONSTER.

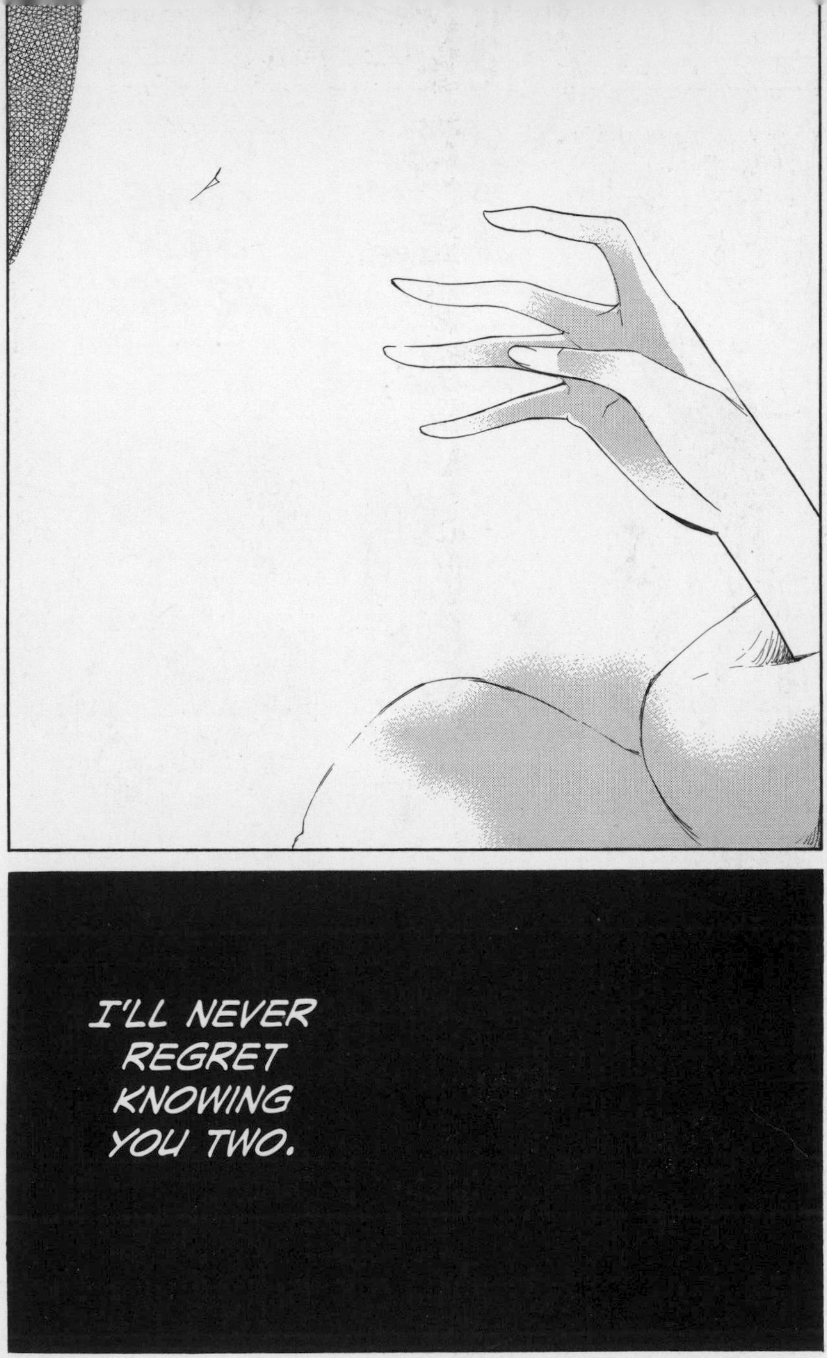
I'LL NEVER REGRET KNOWING YOU TWO.

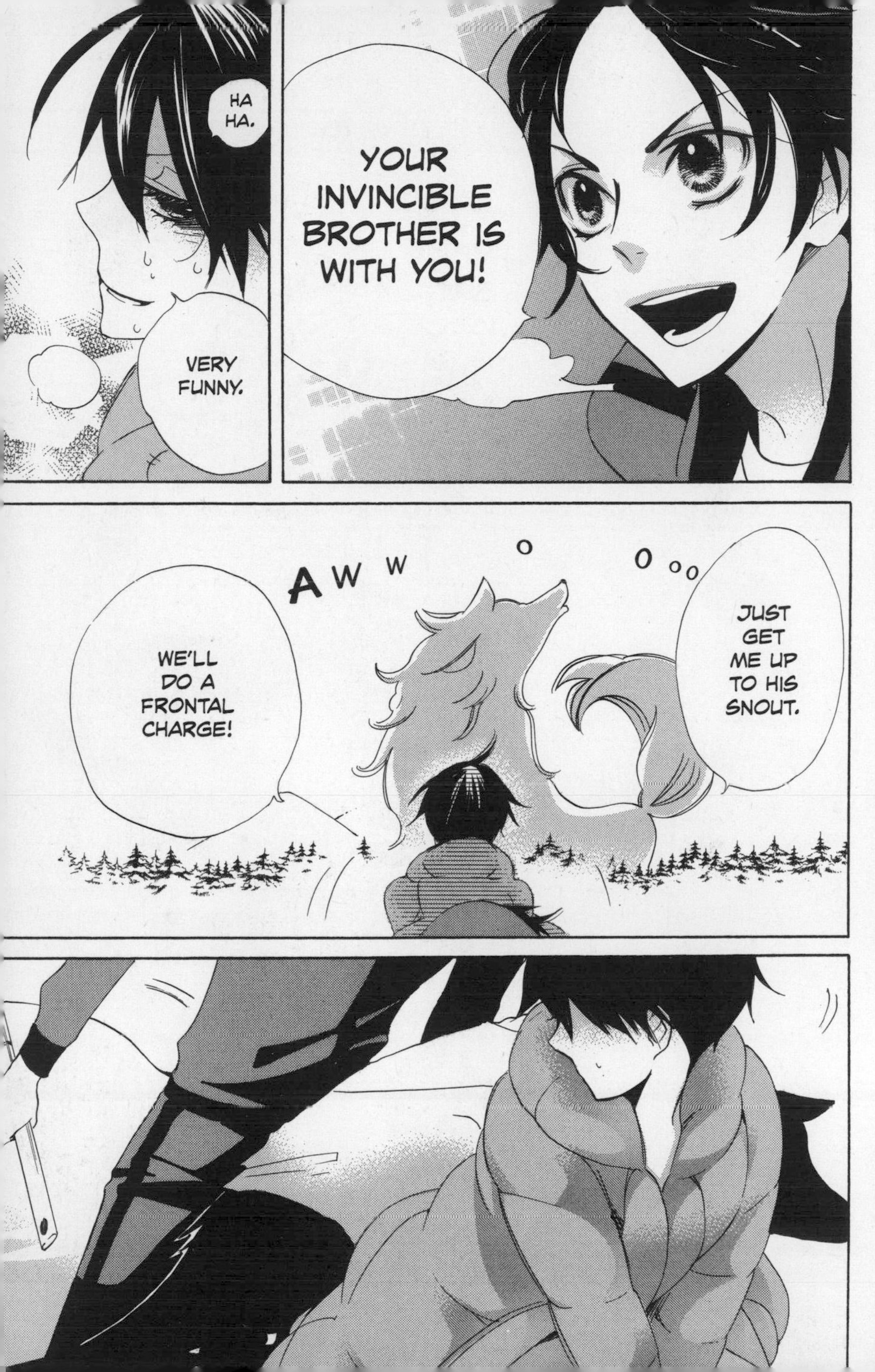
YOUR INVINCIBLE BROTHER IS WITH YOU!
HA HA.
VERY FUNNY.
AWWOOOoo
JUST GET ME UP TO HIS SNOUT.
WE'LL DO A FRONTAL CHARGE!

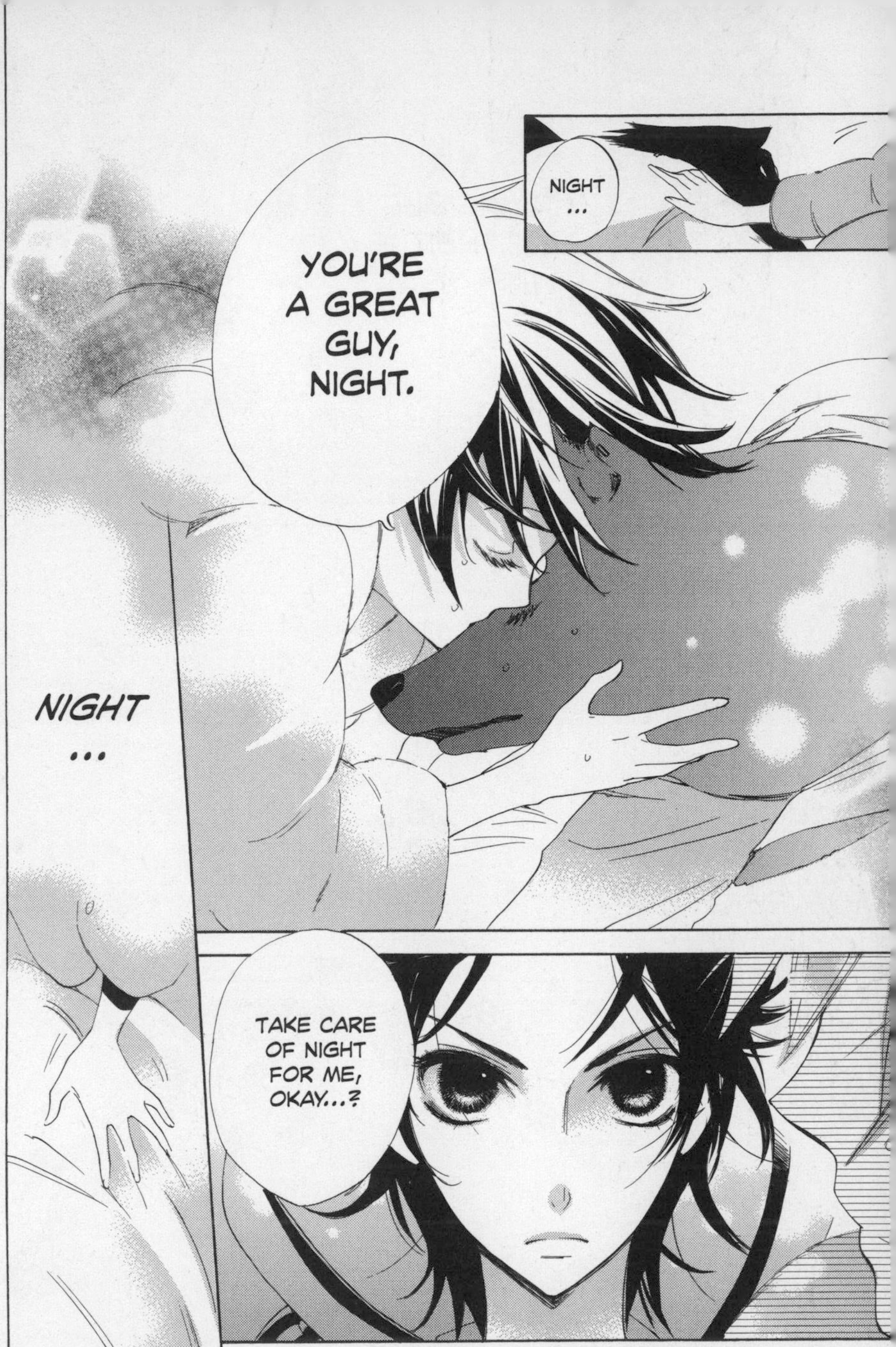
NIGHT ...
YOU'RE A GREAT GUY, NIGHT.
TAKE CARE OF NIGHT FOR ME, OKAY...?
NIGHT ...

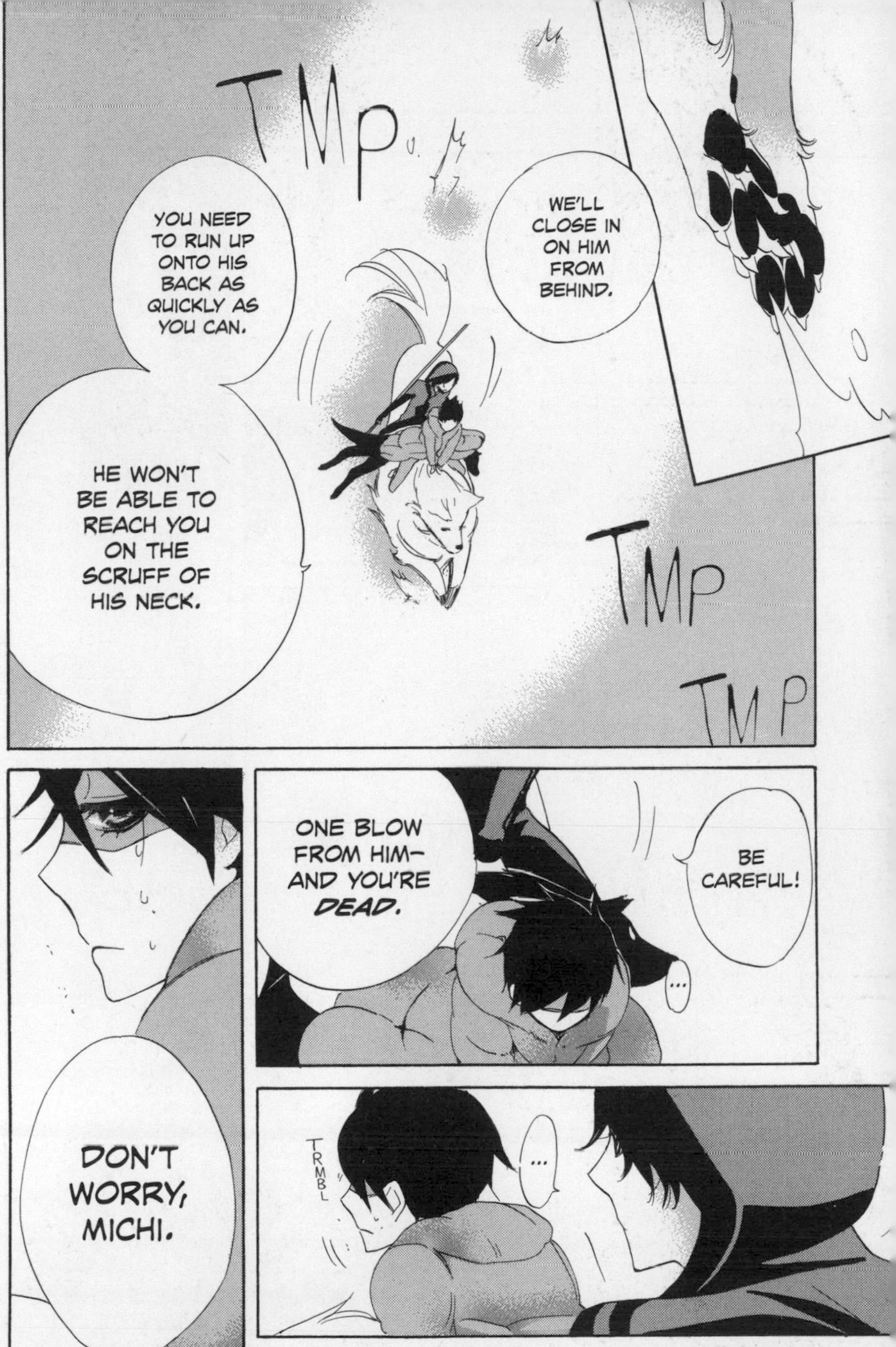
TMP
WE'LL CLOSE IN ON HIM FROM BEHIND.
YOU NEED TO RUN UP ONTO HIS BACK AS QUICKLY AS YOU CAN.
HE WON'T BE ABLE TO REACH YOU ON THE SCRUFF OF HIS NECK.
TMP
TMP
BE CAREFUL!
ONE BLOW FROM HIM—AND YOU'RE *DEAD*.
...
...
TRMBL
DON'T WORRY, MICHI.

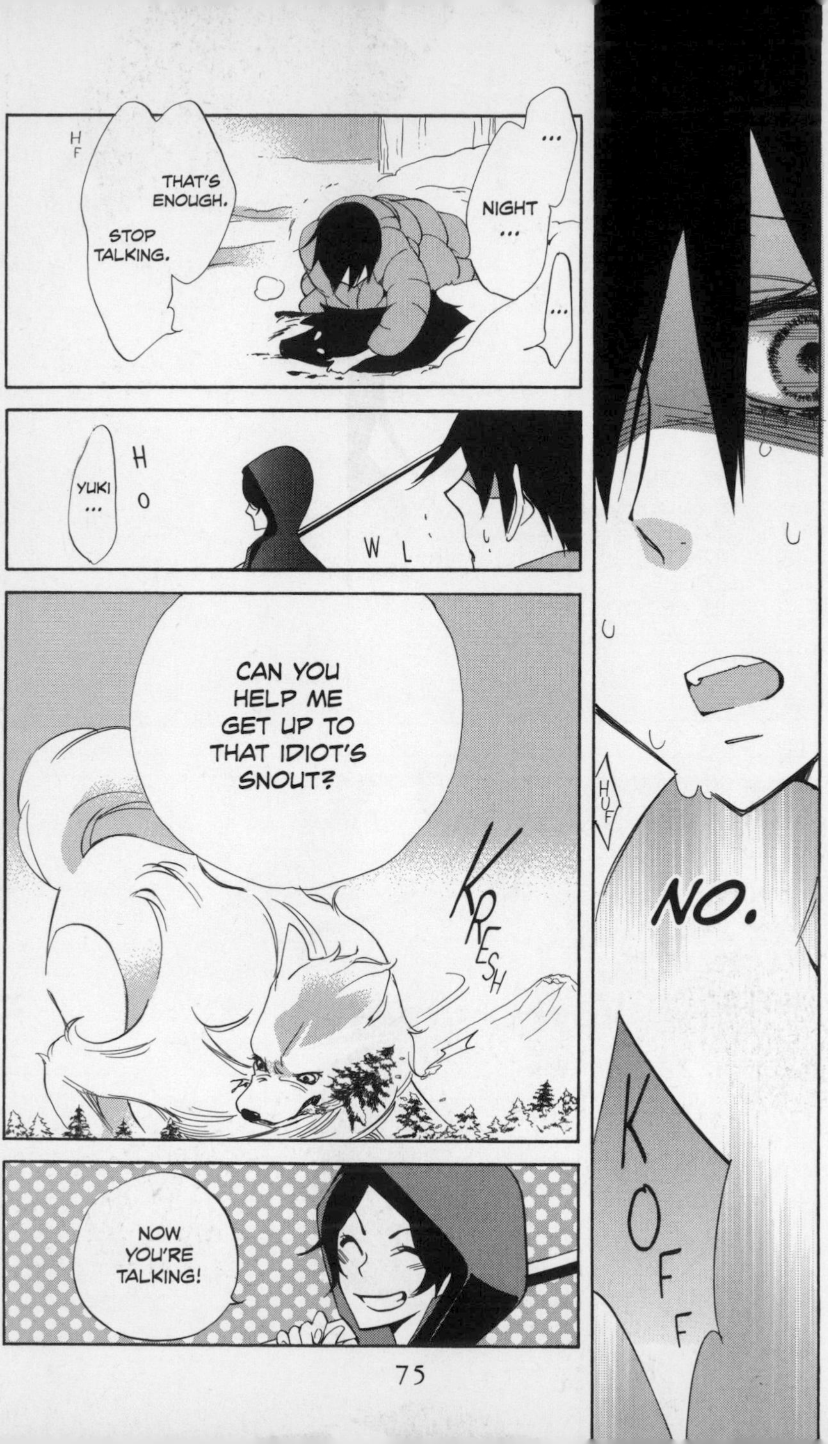
HUF
NO.
KOFF
...
NIGHT ...
...
HF
THAT'S ENOUGH.
STOP TALKING.
YUKI ...
HOWL
CAN YOU HELP ME GET UP TO THAT IDIOT'S SNOUT?
KRESH
NOW YOU'RE TALKING!

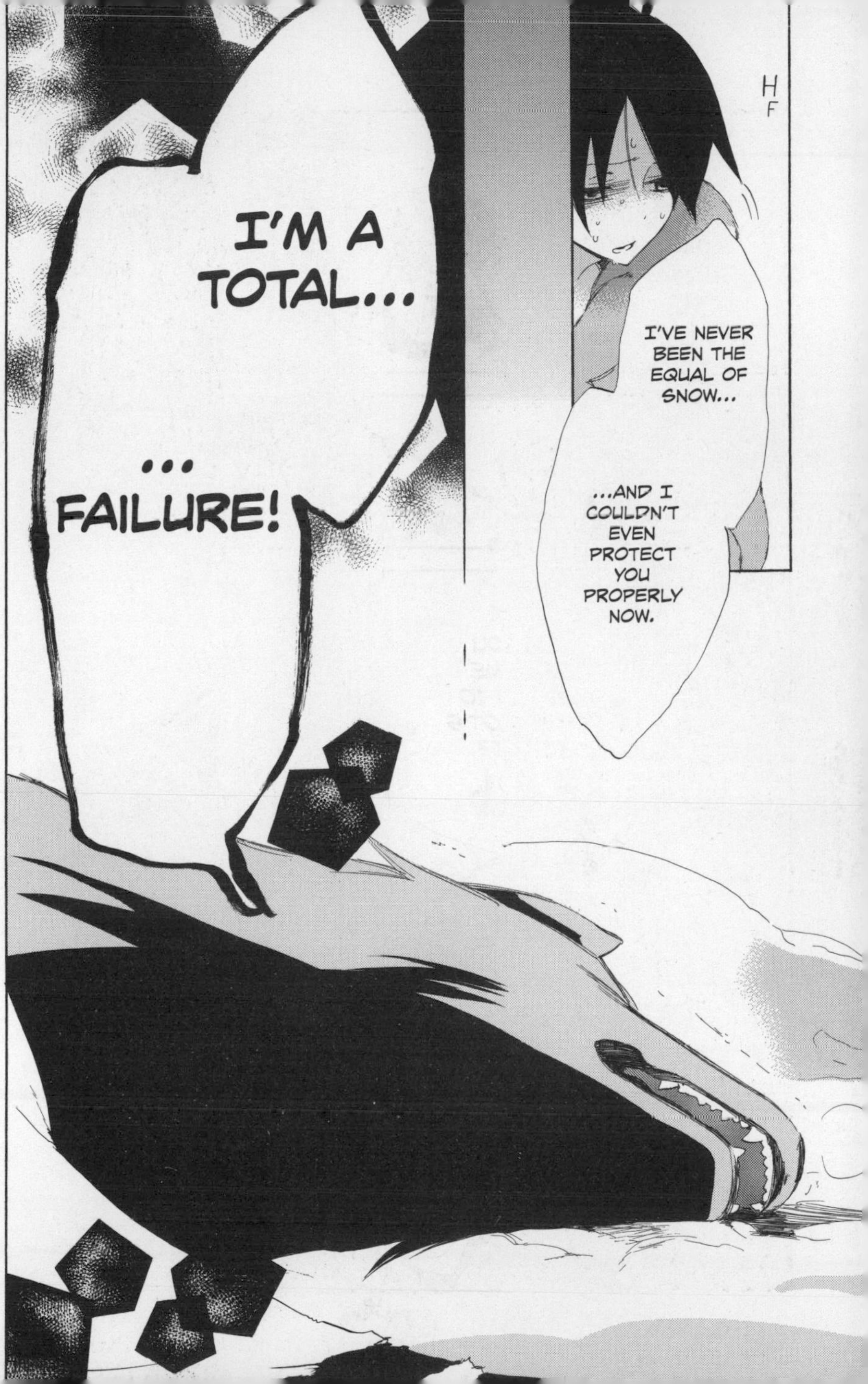
HF
I'VE NEVER BEEN THE EQUAL OF SNOW...
...AND I COULDN'T EVEN PROTECT YOU PROPERLY NOW.
I'M A TOTAL...
...FAILURE!

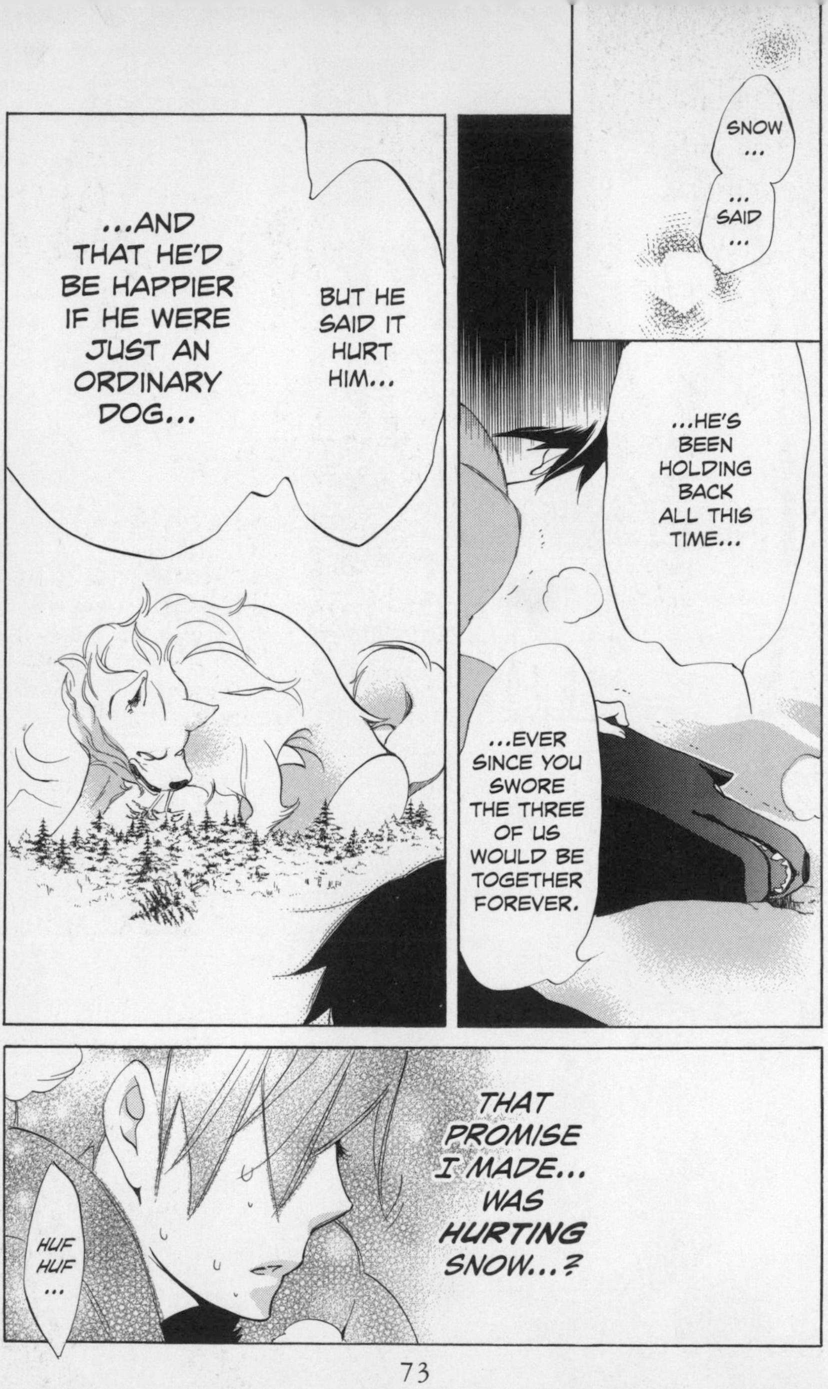
SNOW ...
... SAID ...
...HE'S BEEN HOLDING BACK ALL THIS TIME...
...EVER SINCE YOU SWORE THE THREE OF US WOULD BE TOGETHER FOREVER.
BUT HE SAID IT HURT HIM...
...AND THAT HE'D BE HAPPIER IF HE WERE JUST AN ORDINARY DOG...
THAT PROMISE I MADE... WAS HURTING SNOW...?
HUF HUF ...

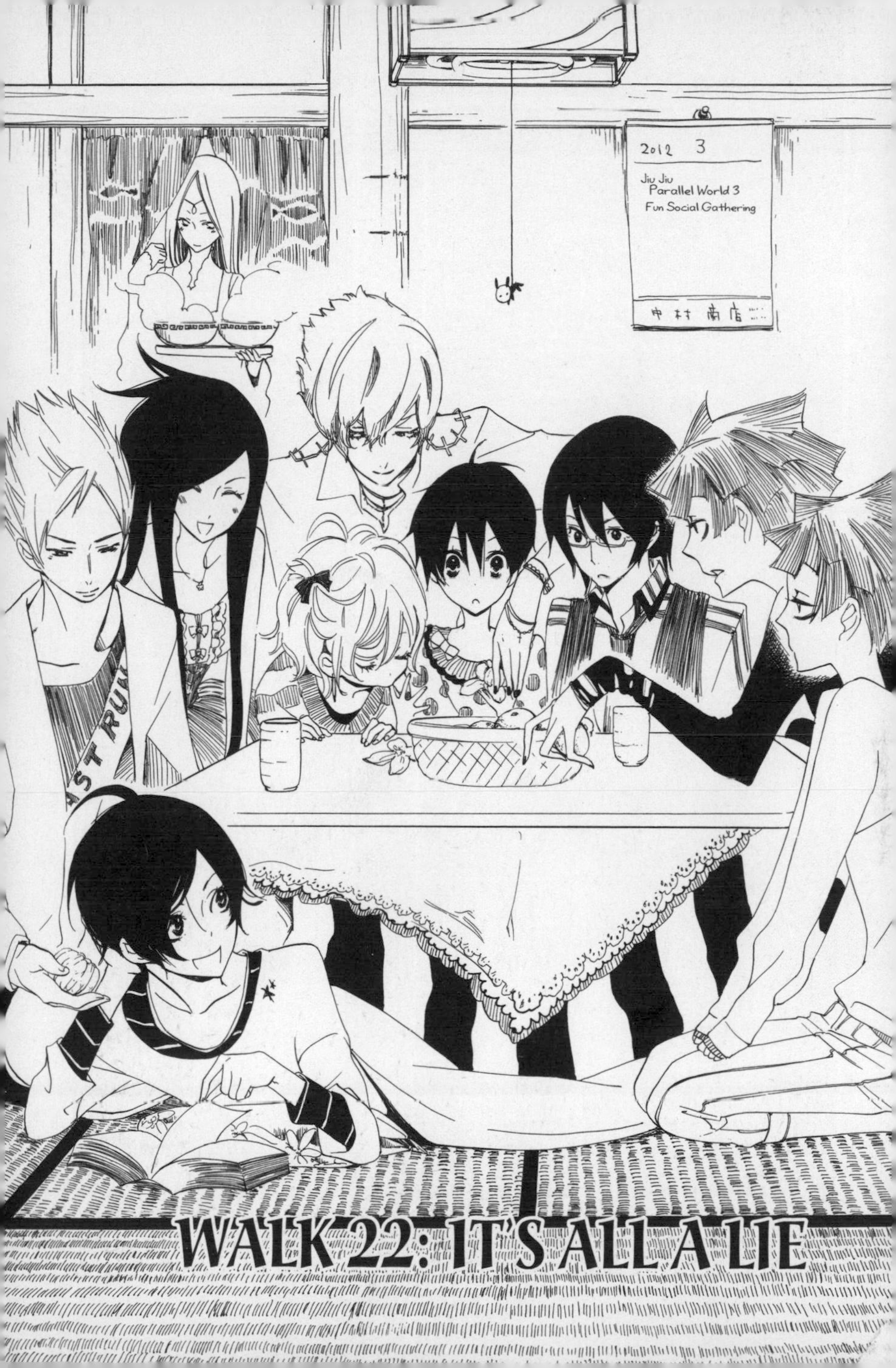
2012 3
Jiu Jiu
Parallel World 3
Fun Social Gathering
中村商店
WALK 22: IT'S ALL A LIE

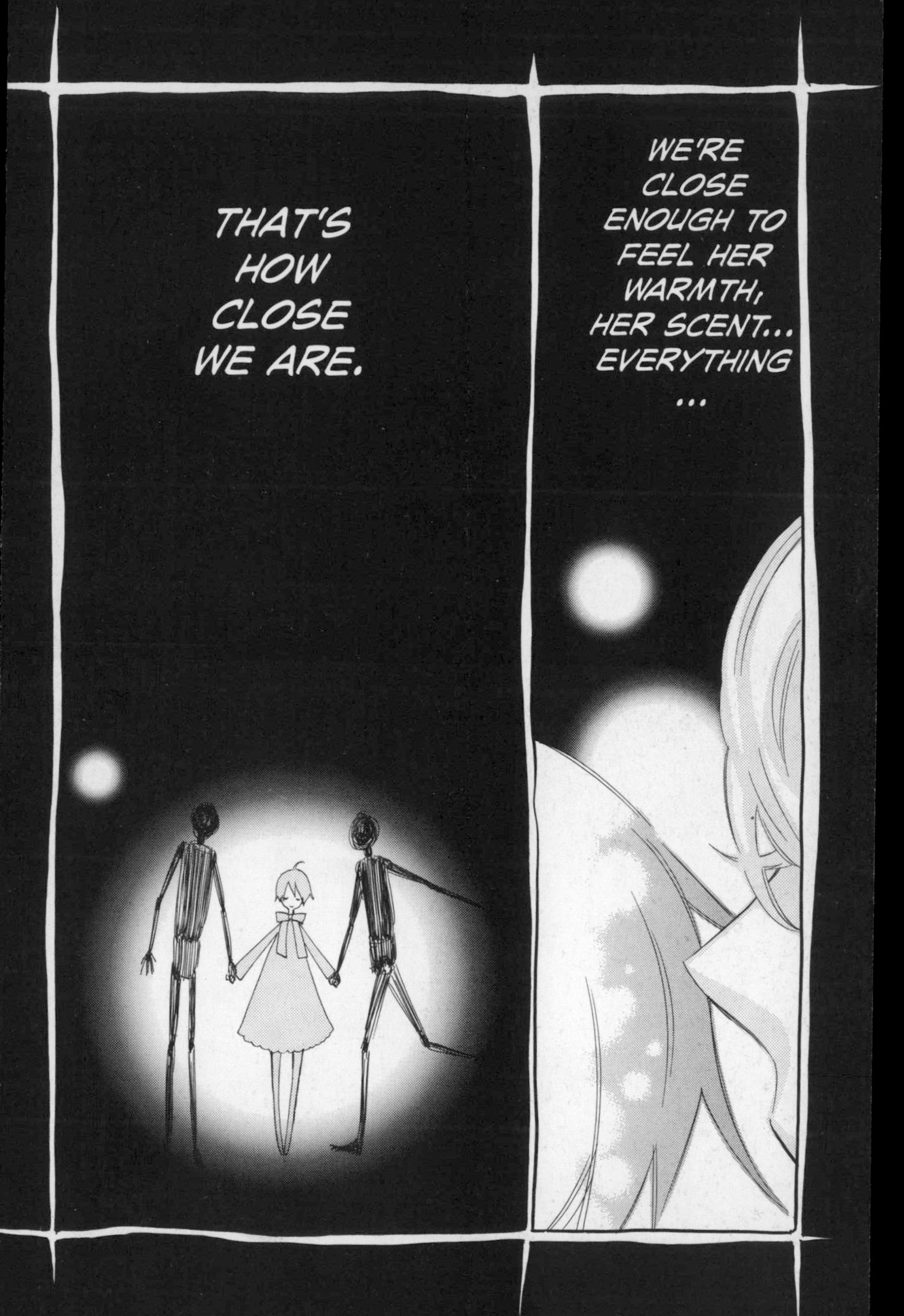
WE'RE CLOSE ENOUGH TO FEEL HER WARMTH, HER SCENT... EVERYTHING ...
THAT'S HOW CLOSE WE ARE.

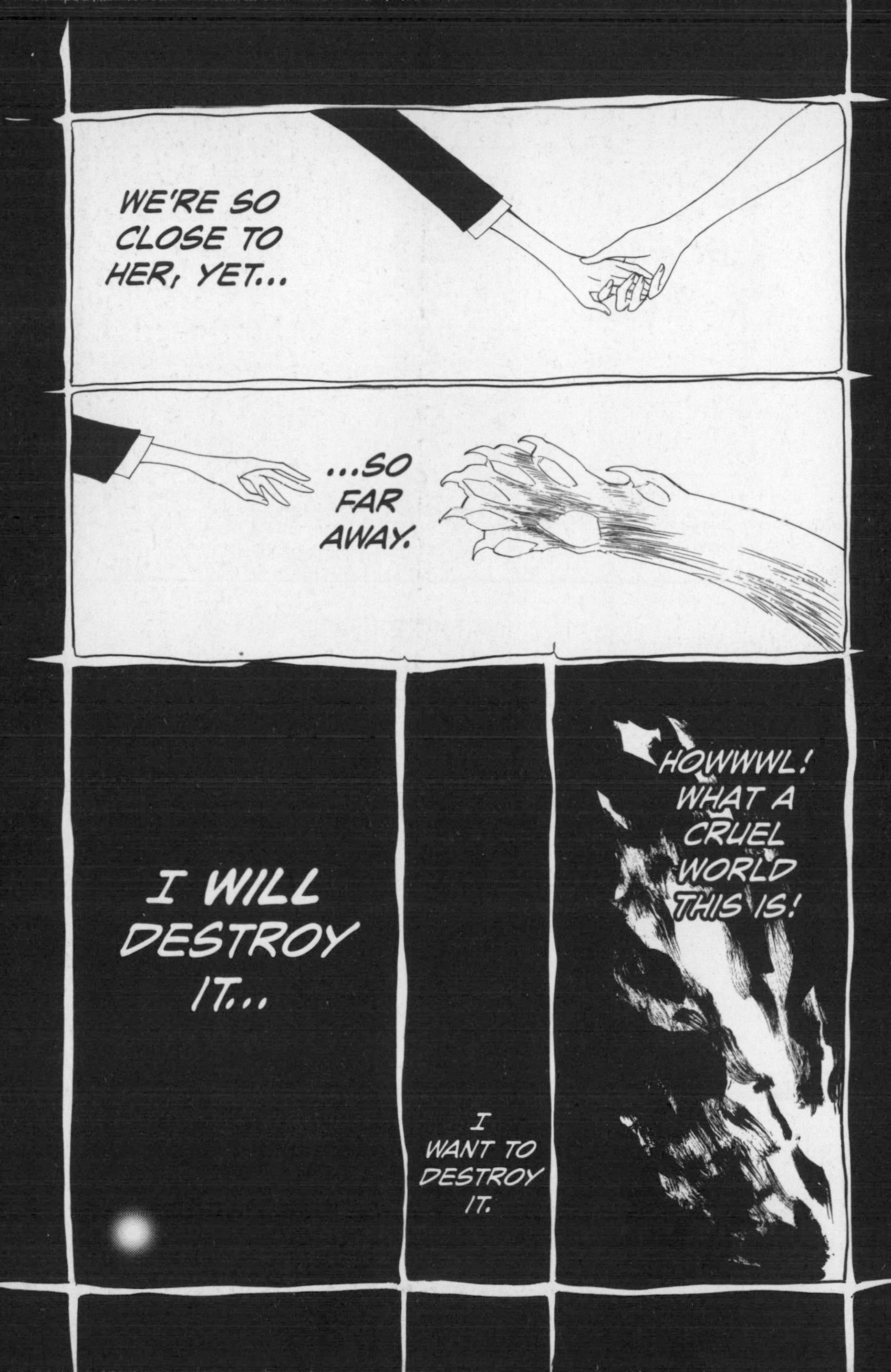
WE'RE SO CLOSE TO HER, YET...
...SO FAR AWAY.
HOWWWL! WHAT A CRUEL WORLD THIS IS!
I WANT TO DESTROY IT.
I WILL DESTROY IT...

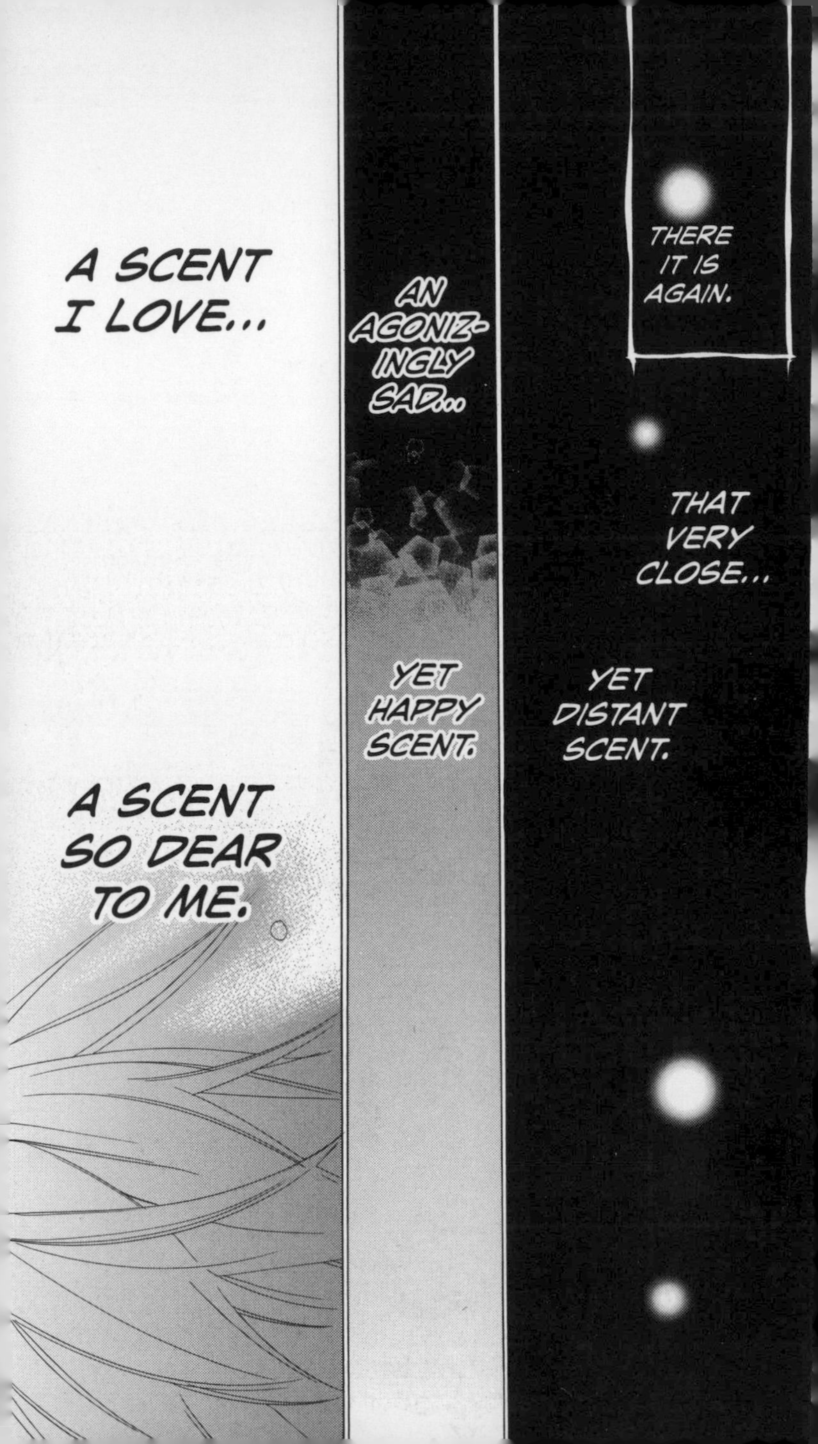
THERE IT IS AGAIN.
THAT VERY CLOSE...
YET DISTANT SCENT.
AN AGONIZINGLY SAD...
YET HAPPY SCENT.
A SCENT I LOVE...
A SCENT SO DEAR TO ME.

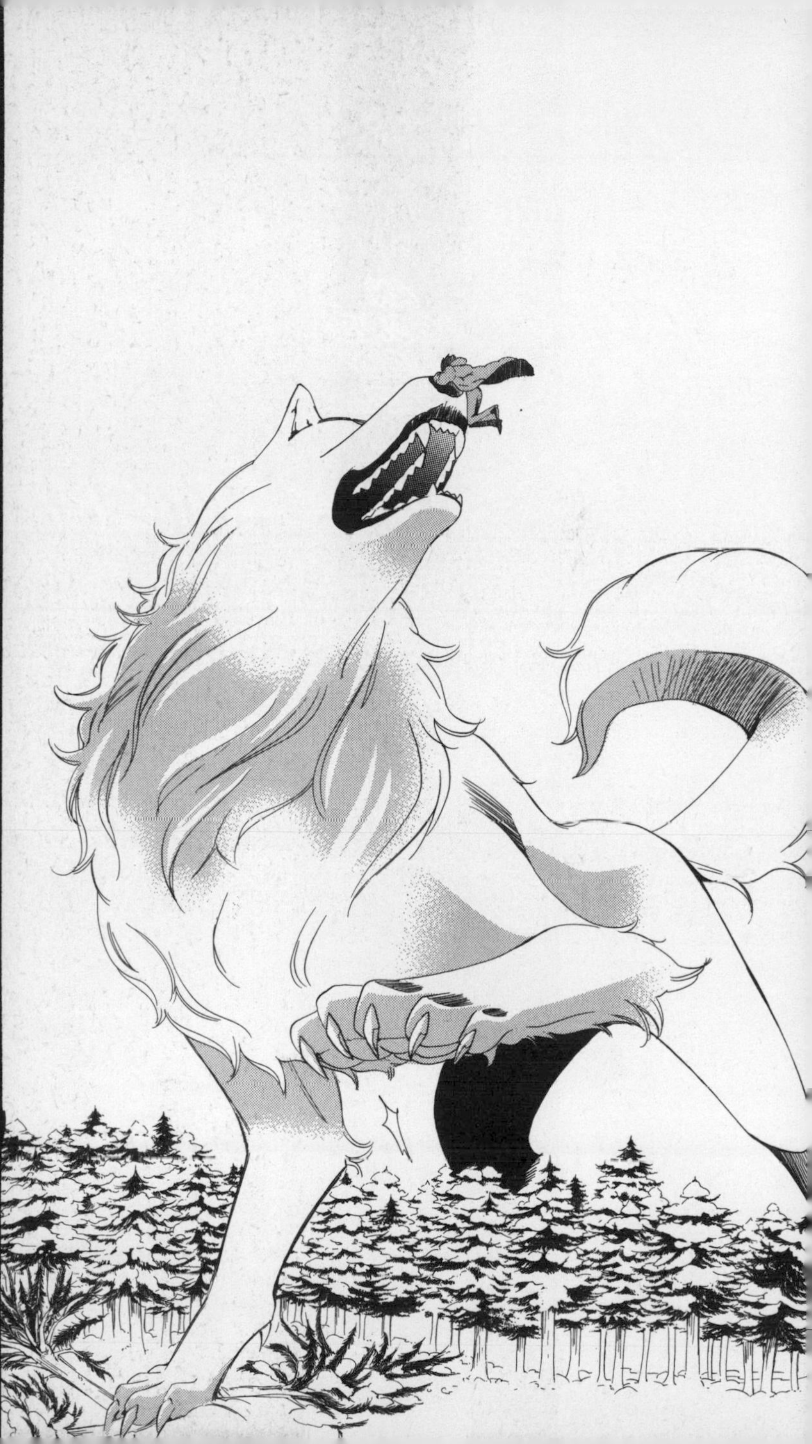

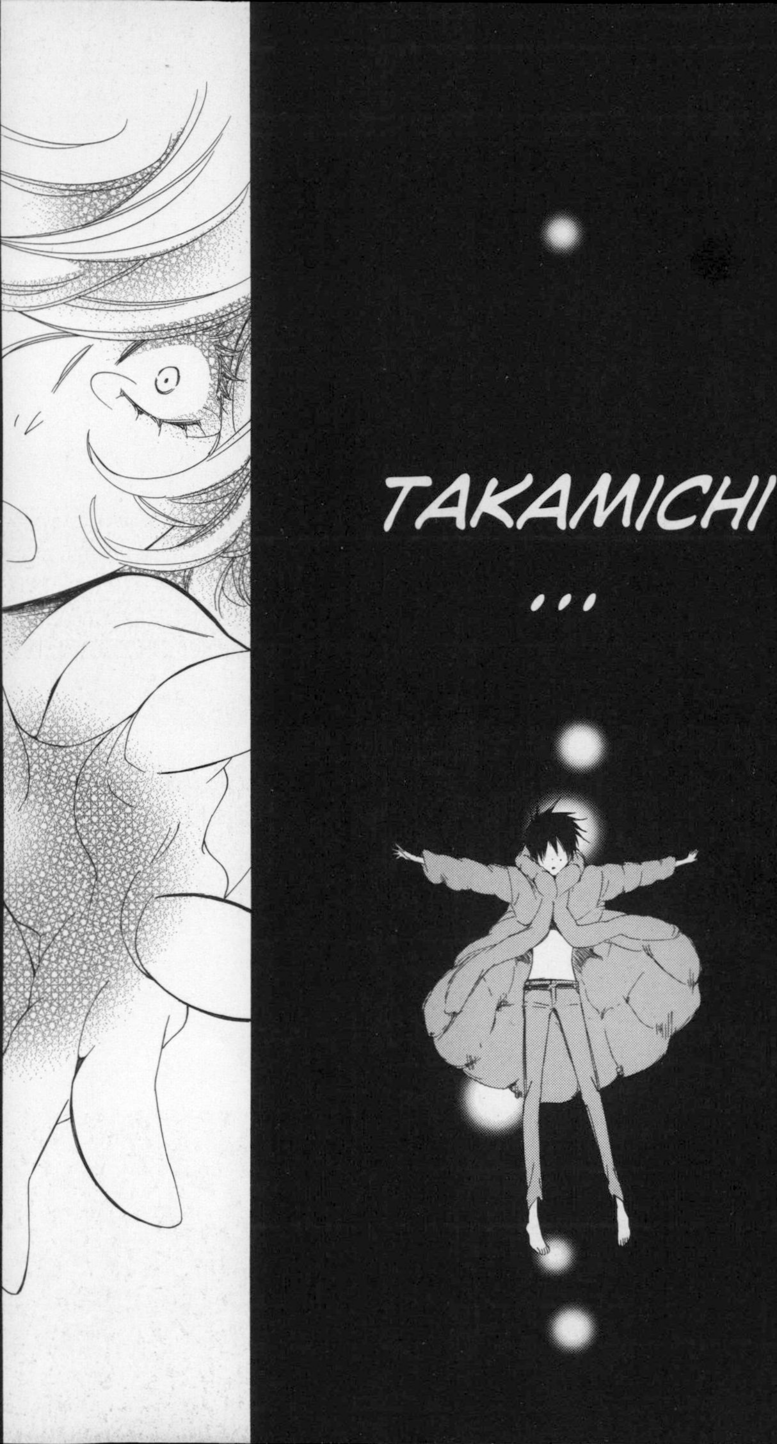
TAKAMICHI
...

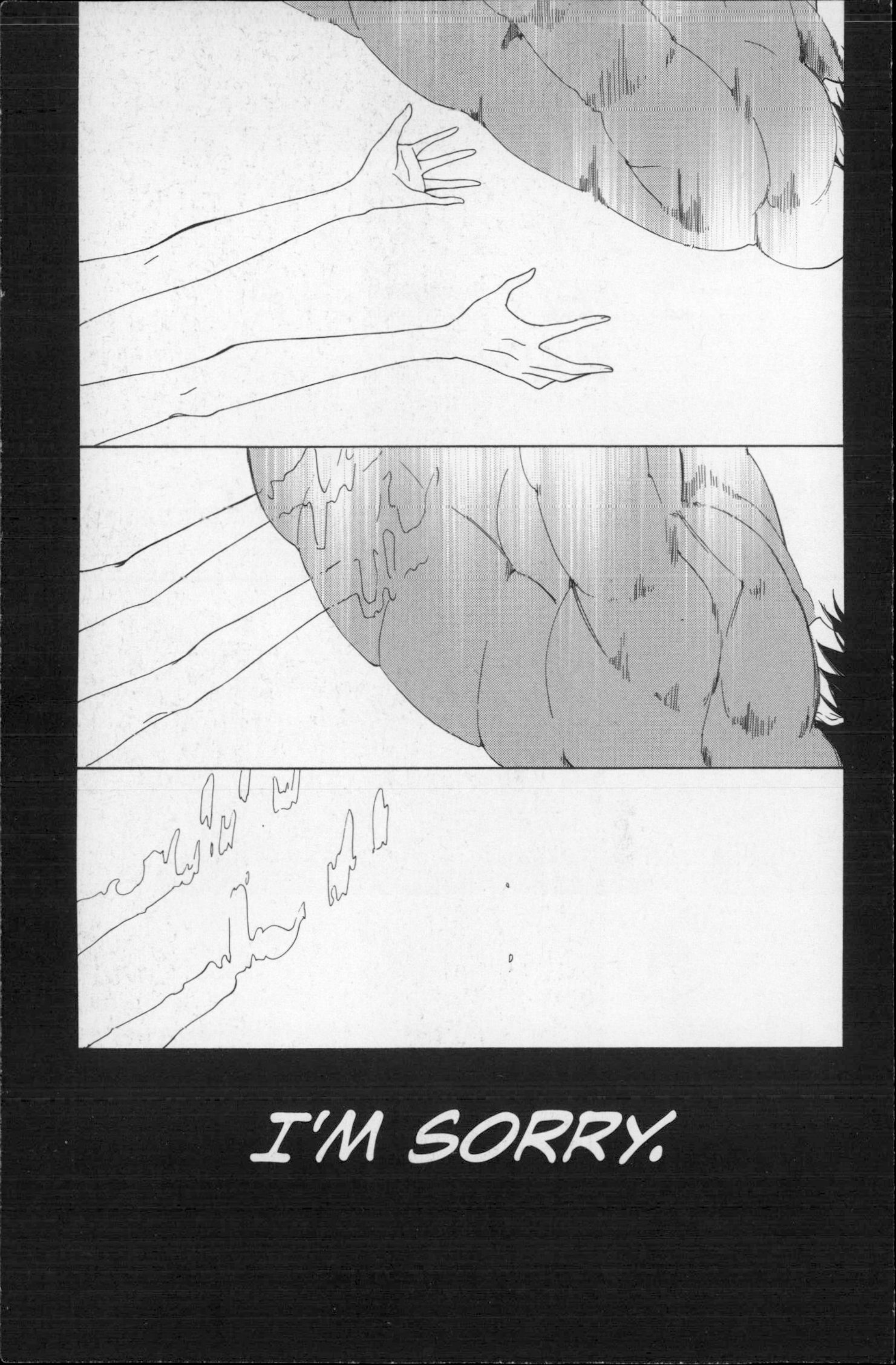

I'M SORRY.

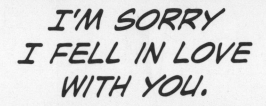

I'M SORRY
I FELL IN LOVE
WITH YOU.

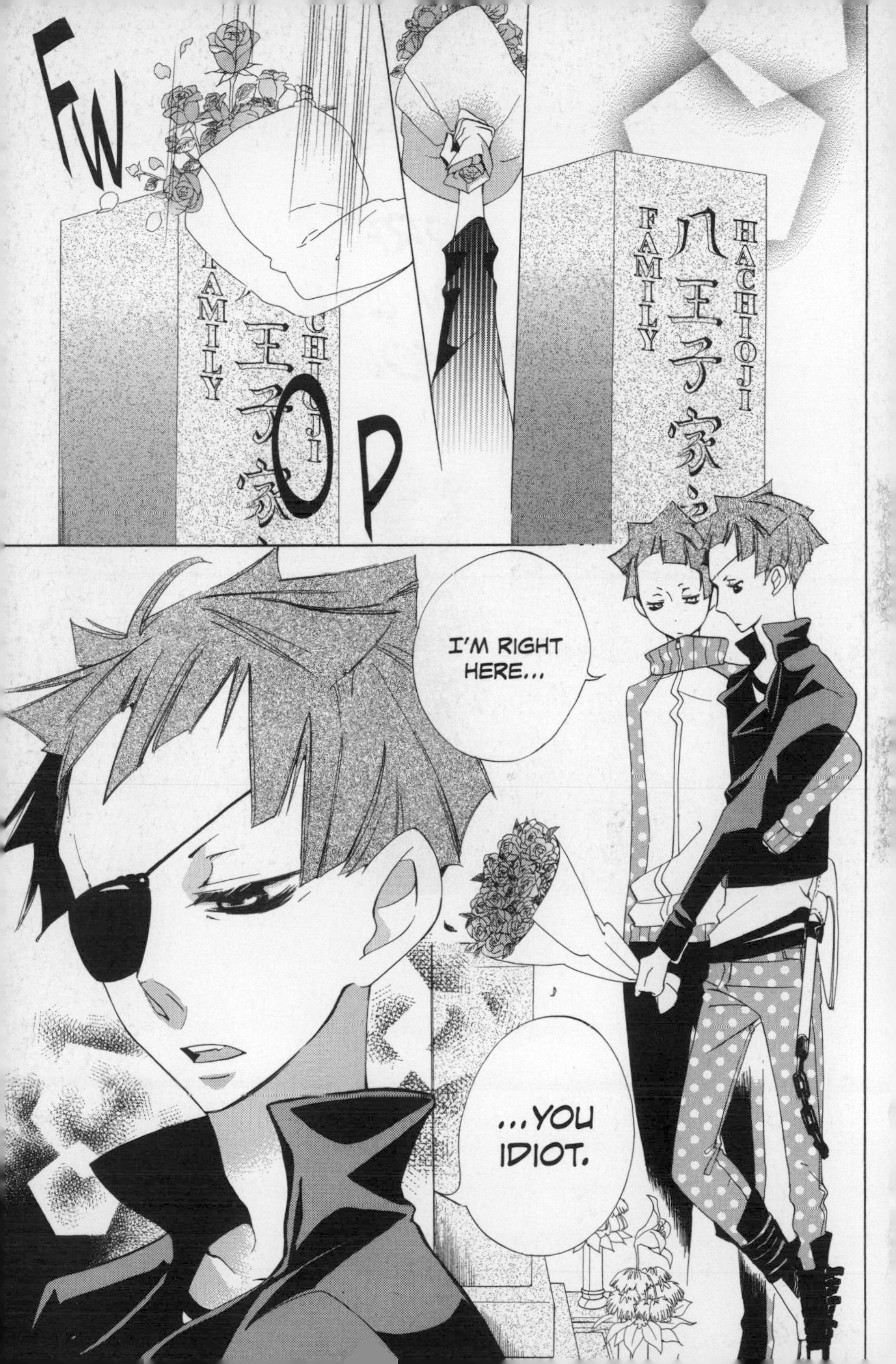
HACHIOJI
八王子家
FAMILY
FWOOP
I'M RIGHT HERE...
...YOU IDIOT.

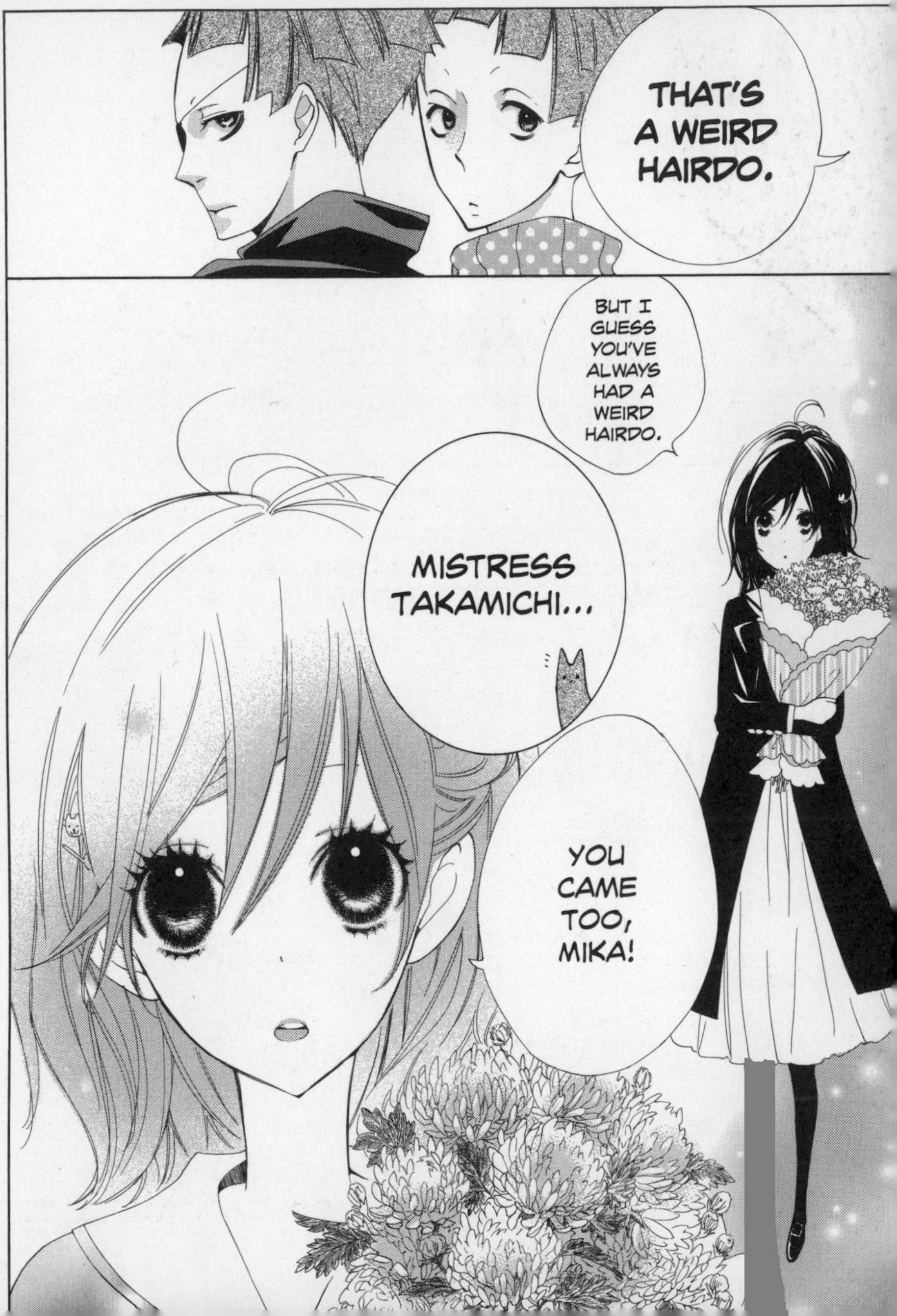
THAT'S A WEIRD HAIRDO.
BUT I GUESS YOU'VE ALWAYS HAD A WEIRD HAIRDO.
MISTRESS TAKAMICHI...
YOU CAME TOO, MIKA!

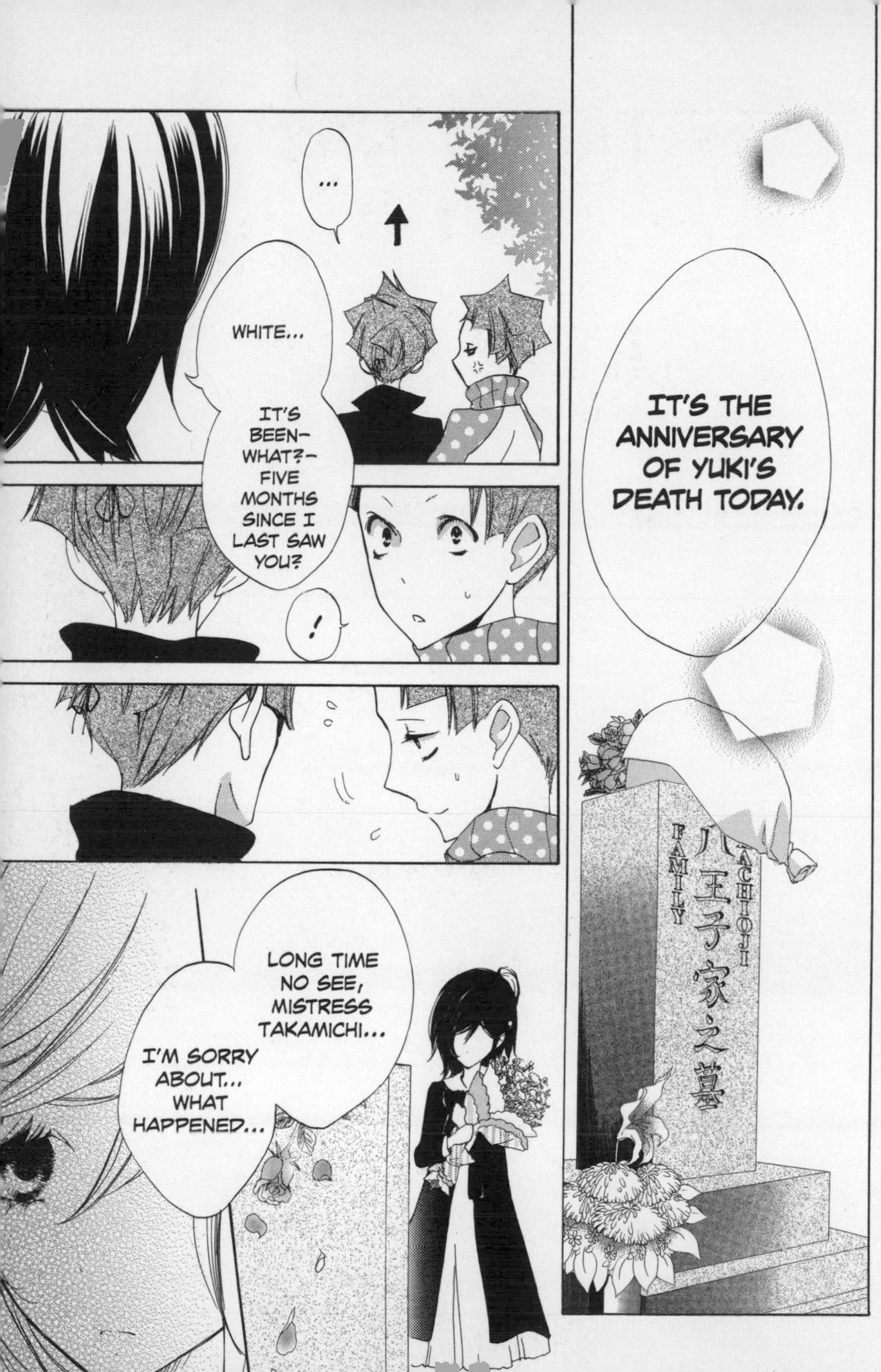
IT'S THE ANNIVERSARY OF YUKI'S DEATH TODAY.
ACHIOJI
八王子家之墓
FAMILY
...
WHITE...
IT'S BEEN—WHAT?—FIVE MONTHS SINCE I LAST SAW YOU?
!
LONG TIME NO SEE, MISTRESS TAKAMICHI...
I'M SORRY ABOUT... WHAT HAPPENED...

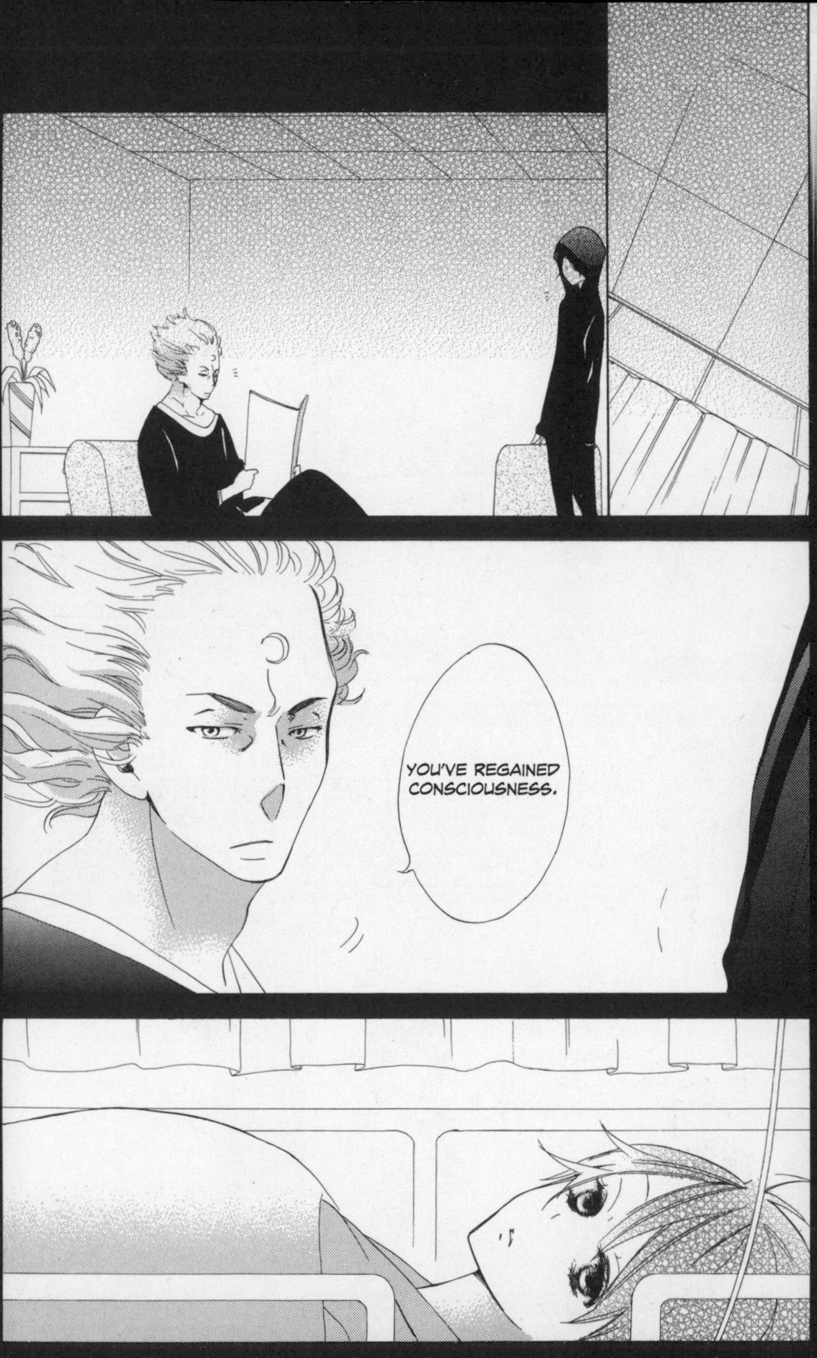
YOU'VE REGAINED CONSCIOUSNESS.

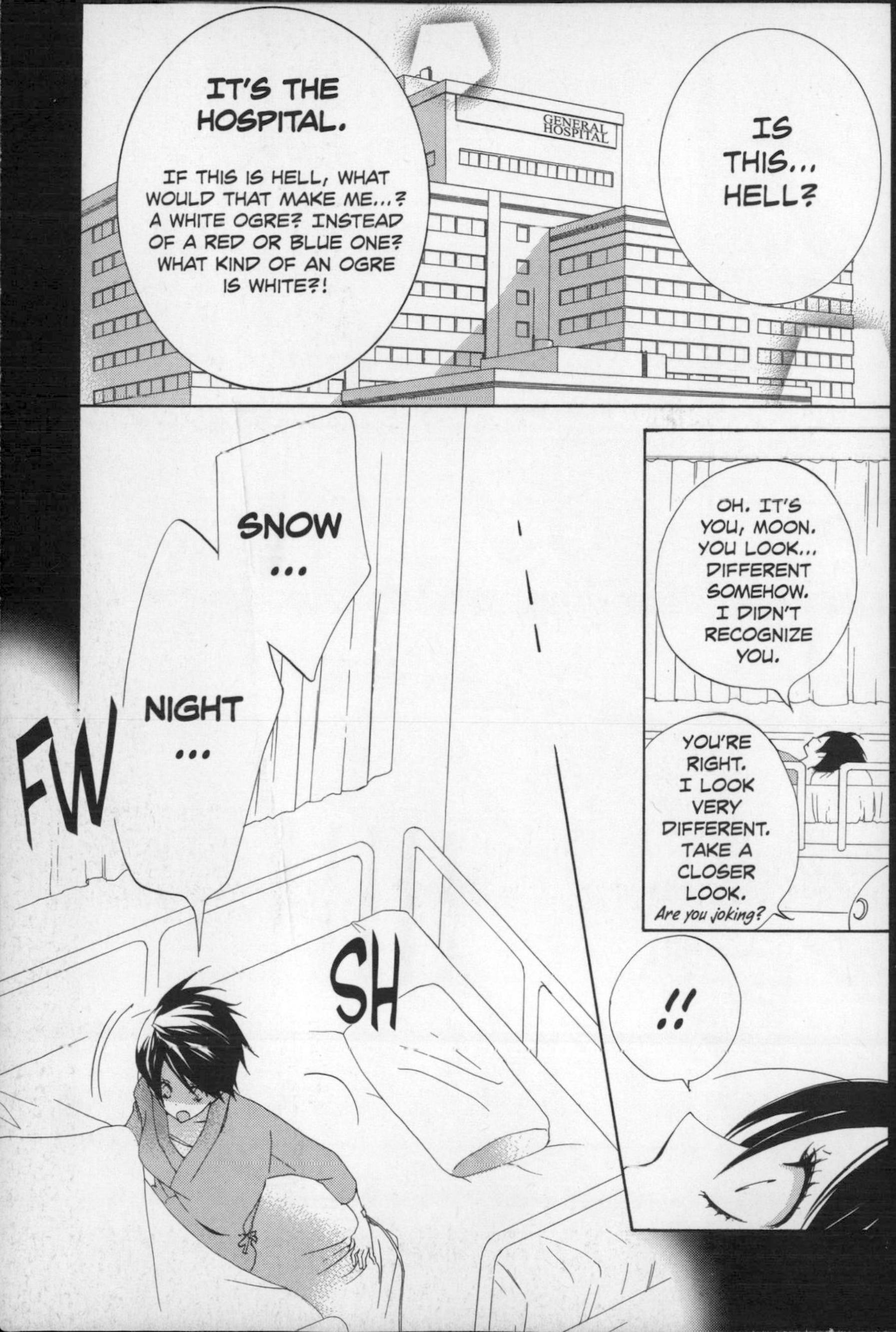
IS THIS... HELL?
GENERAL HOSPITAL
IT'S THE HOSPITAL.
IF THIS IS HELL, WHAT WOULD THAT MAKE ME...? A WHITE OGRE? INSTEAD OF A RED OR BLUE ONE? WHAT KIND OF AN OGRE IS WHITE?!
OH. IT'S YOU, MOON. YOU LOOK... DIFFERENT SOMEHOW. I DIDN'T RECOGNIZE YOU.
YOU'RE RIGHT. I LOOK VERY DIFFERENT. TAKE A CLOSER LOOK.
Are you joking?
!!
SNOW ...
NIGHT ...
FW
SH

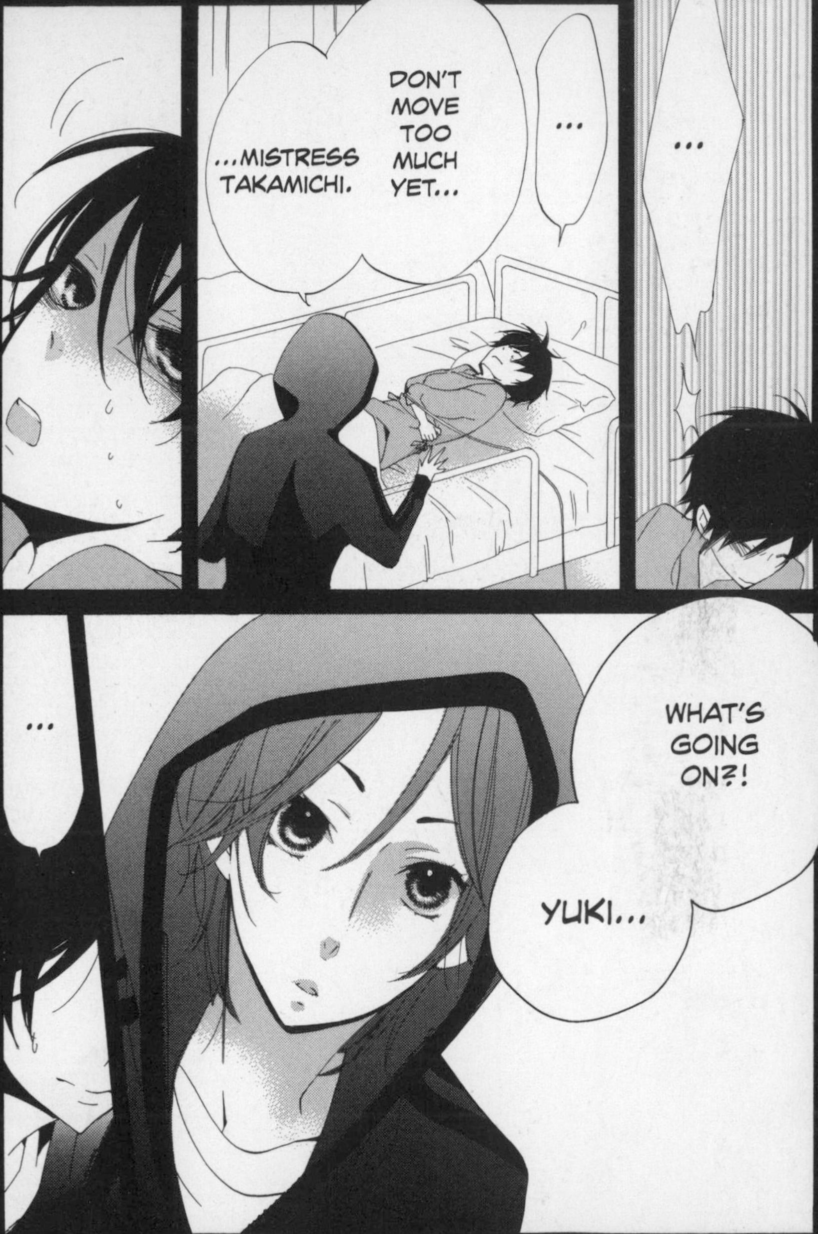
...
...
DON'T MOVE TOO MUCH YET...
...MISTRESS TAKAMICHI.
WHAT'S GOING ON?!
YUKI...
...

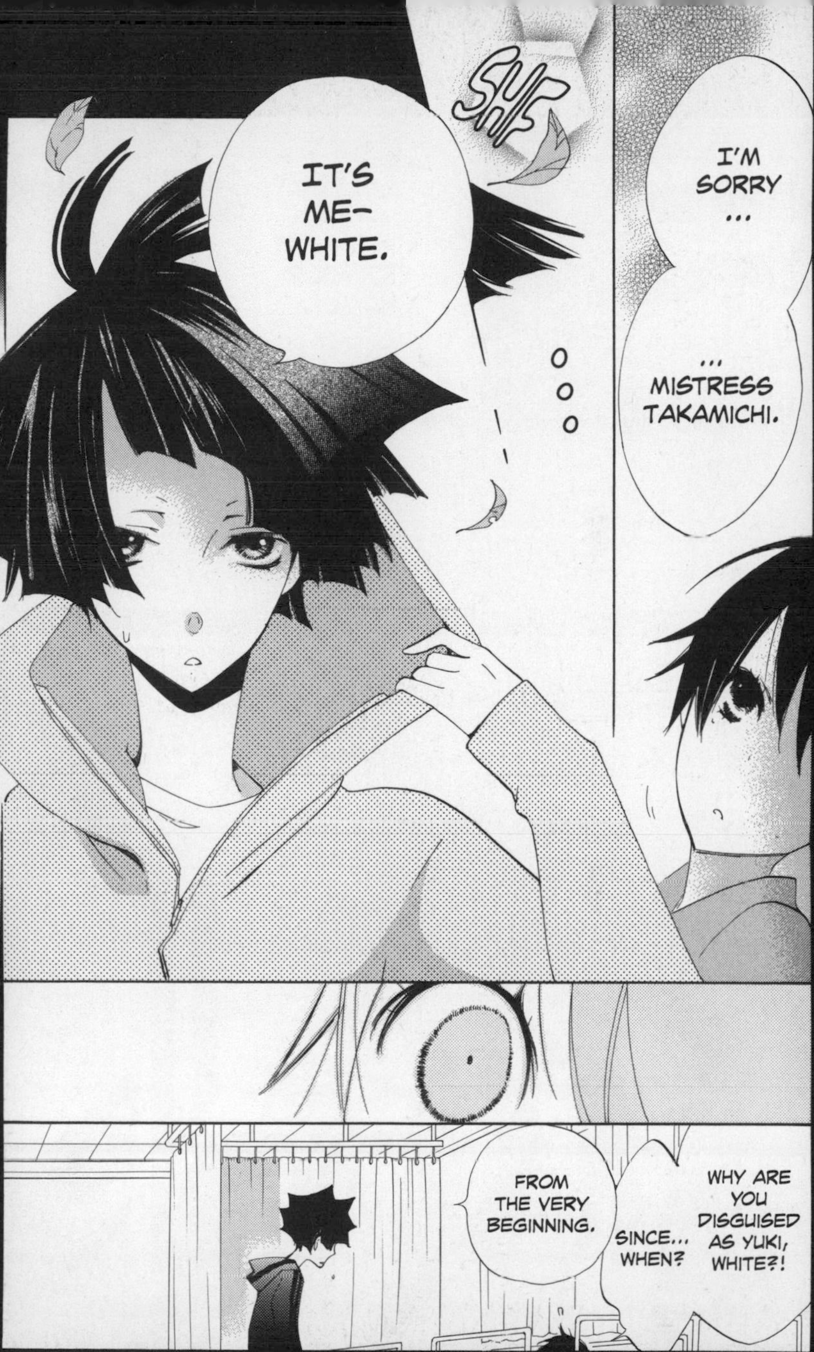
I'M SORRY ...
... MISTRESS TAKAMICHI.
SHF
IT'S ME-WHITE.
WHY ARE YOU DISGUISED AS YUKI, WHITE?!
SINCE... WHEN?
FROM THE VERY BEGINNING.

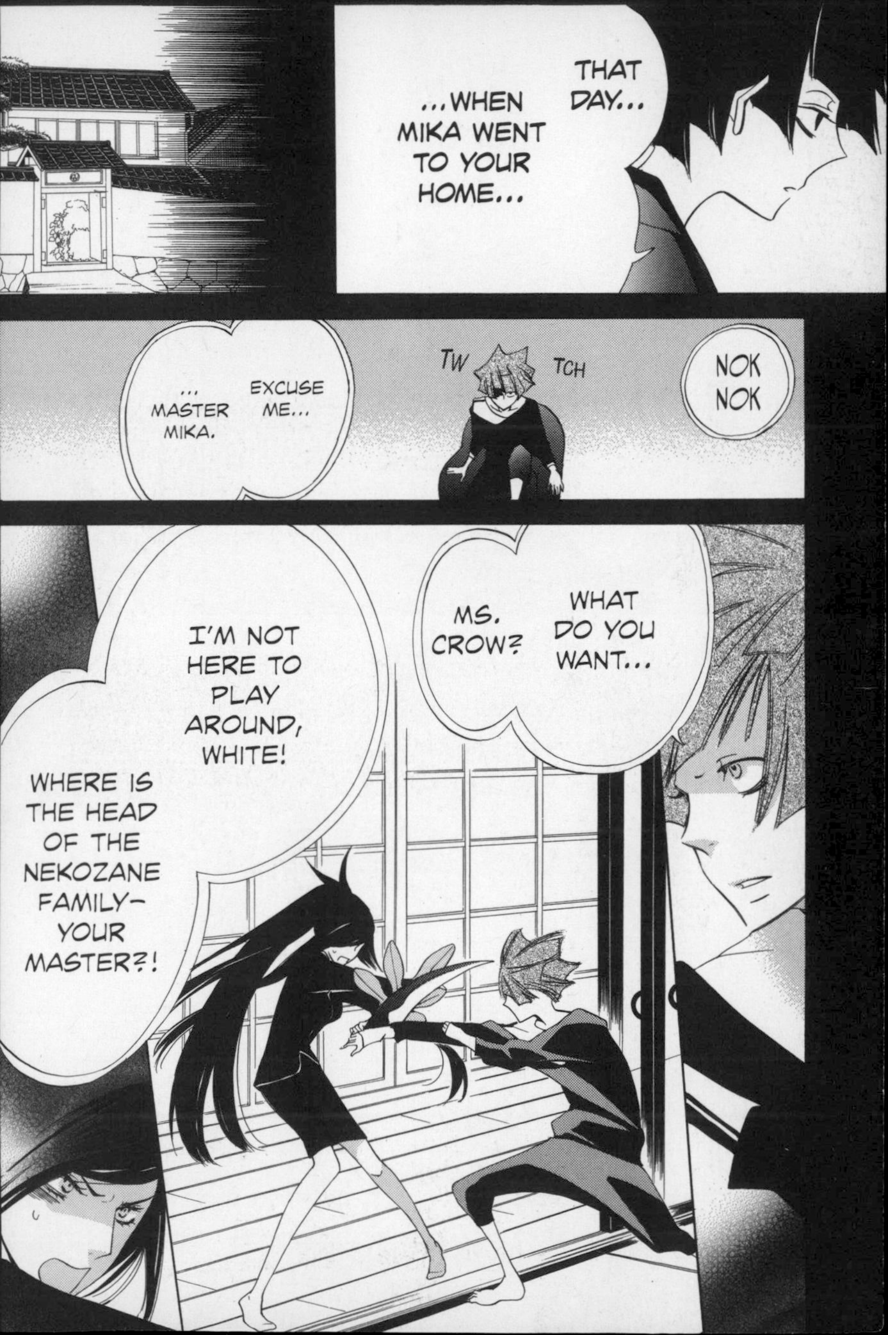
THAT DAY...
...WHEN MIKA WENT TO YOUR HOME...
NOK NOK
TW TCH
EXCUSE ME...
... MASTER MIKA.
WHAT DO YOU WANT...
MS. CROW?
I'M NOT HERE TO PLAY AROUND, WHITE!
WHERE IS THE HEAD OF THE NEKOZANE FAMILY—YOUR MASTER?!

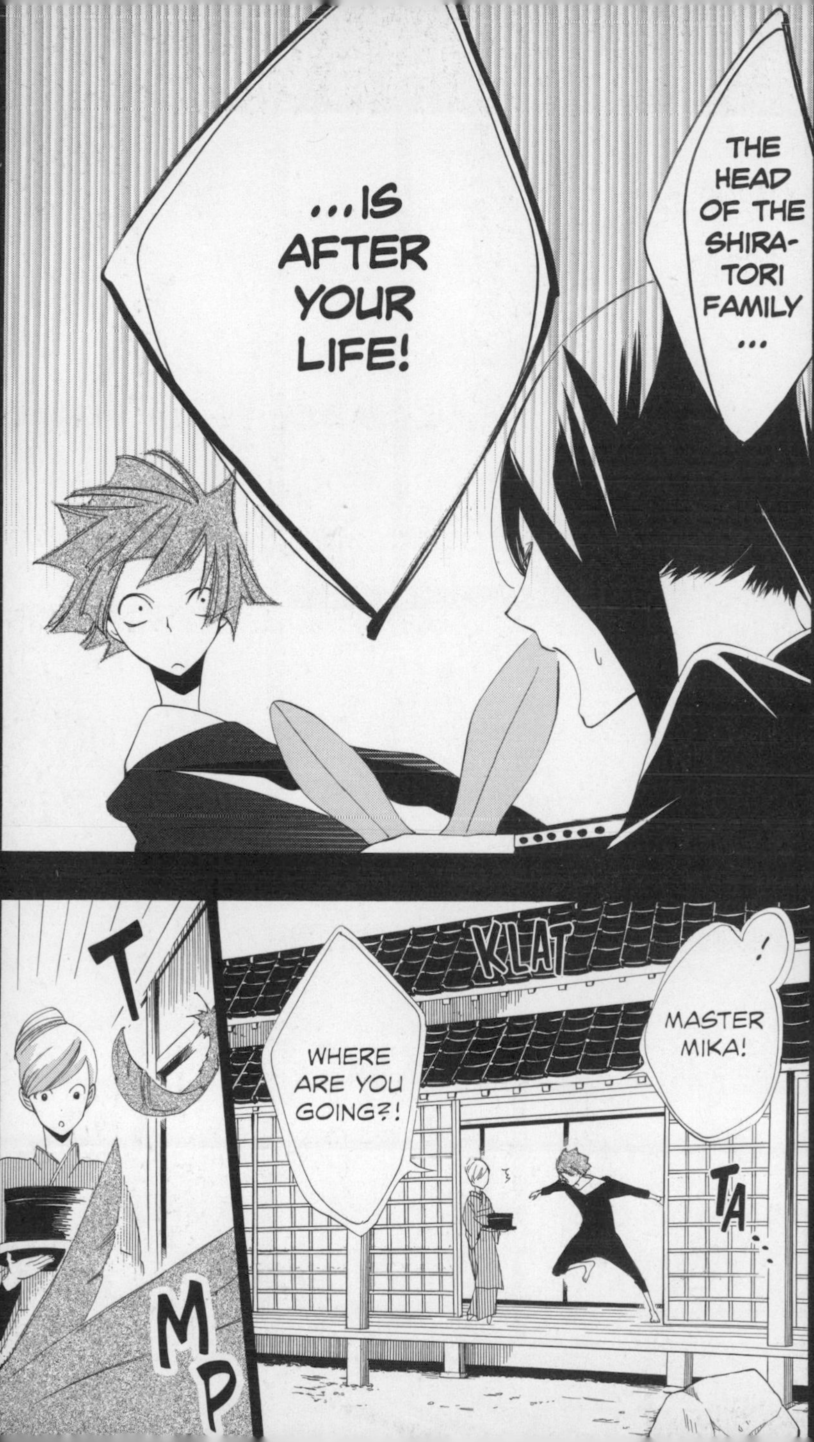
THE HEAD OF THE SHIRA-TORI FAMILY...
...IS AFTER YOUR LIFE!
!
MASTER MIKA!
KLAT
WHERE ARE YOU GOING?!
TA
T
MP

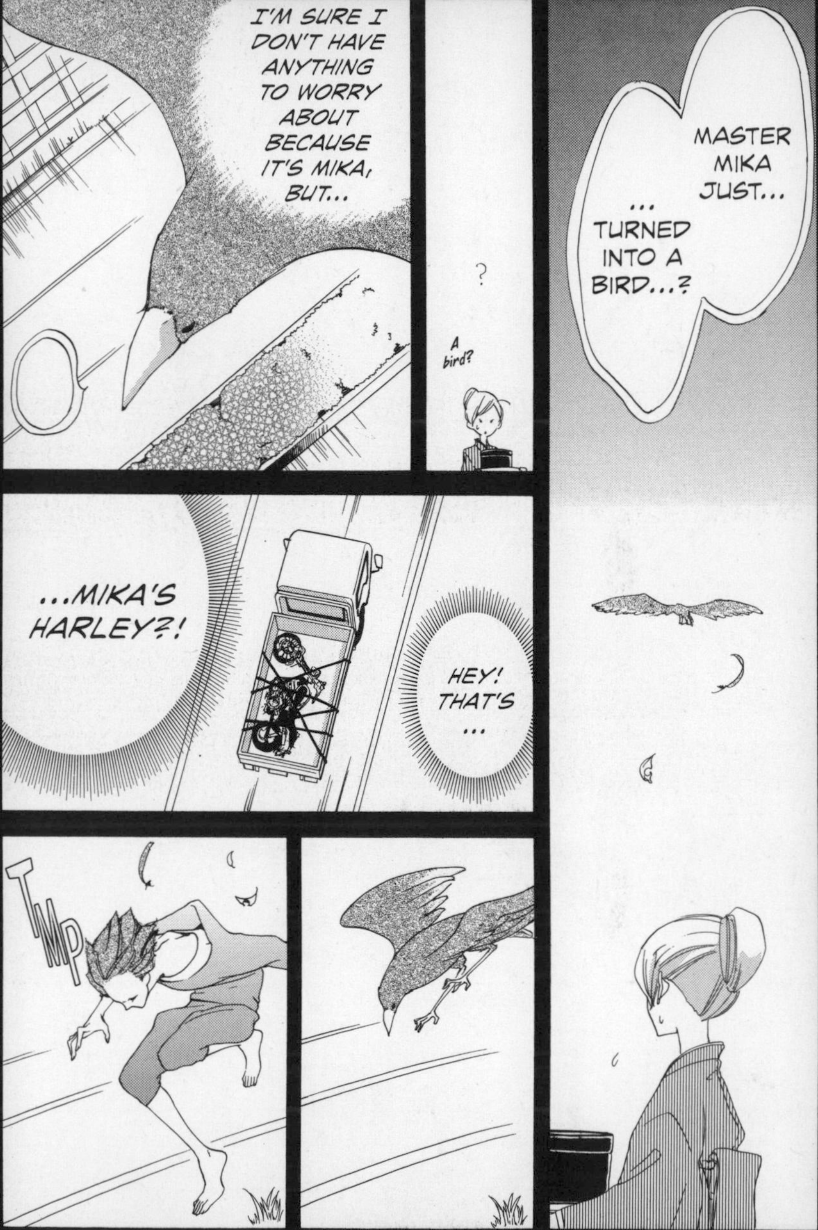
MASTER MIKA JUST...
...TURNED INTO A BIRD...?
?
A bird?
I'M SURE I DON'T HAVE ANYTHING TO WORRY ABOUT BECAUSE IT'S MIKA, BUT...
HEY! THAT'S...
...MIKA'S HARLEY?!
TMP

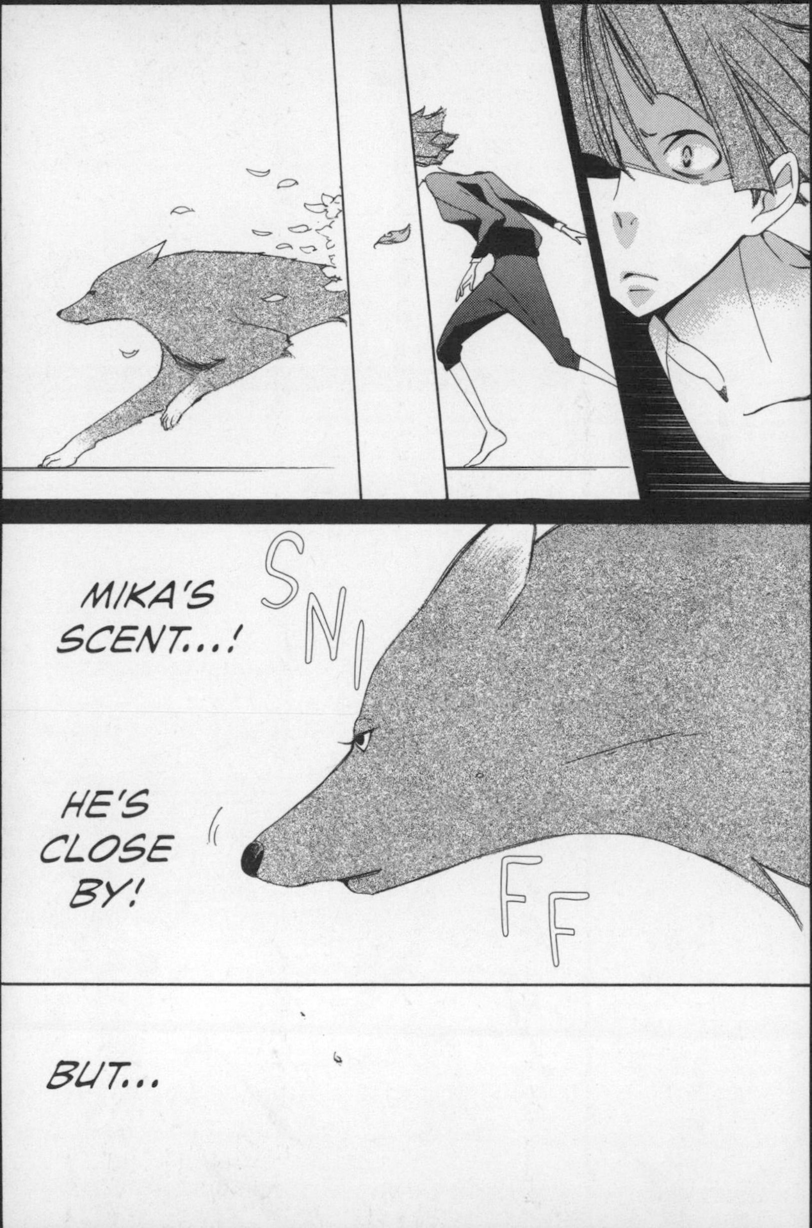
MIKA'S SCENT...!
SNIFF
HE'S CLOSE BY!
BUT...

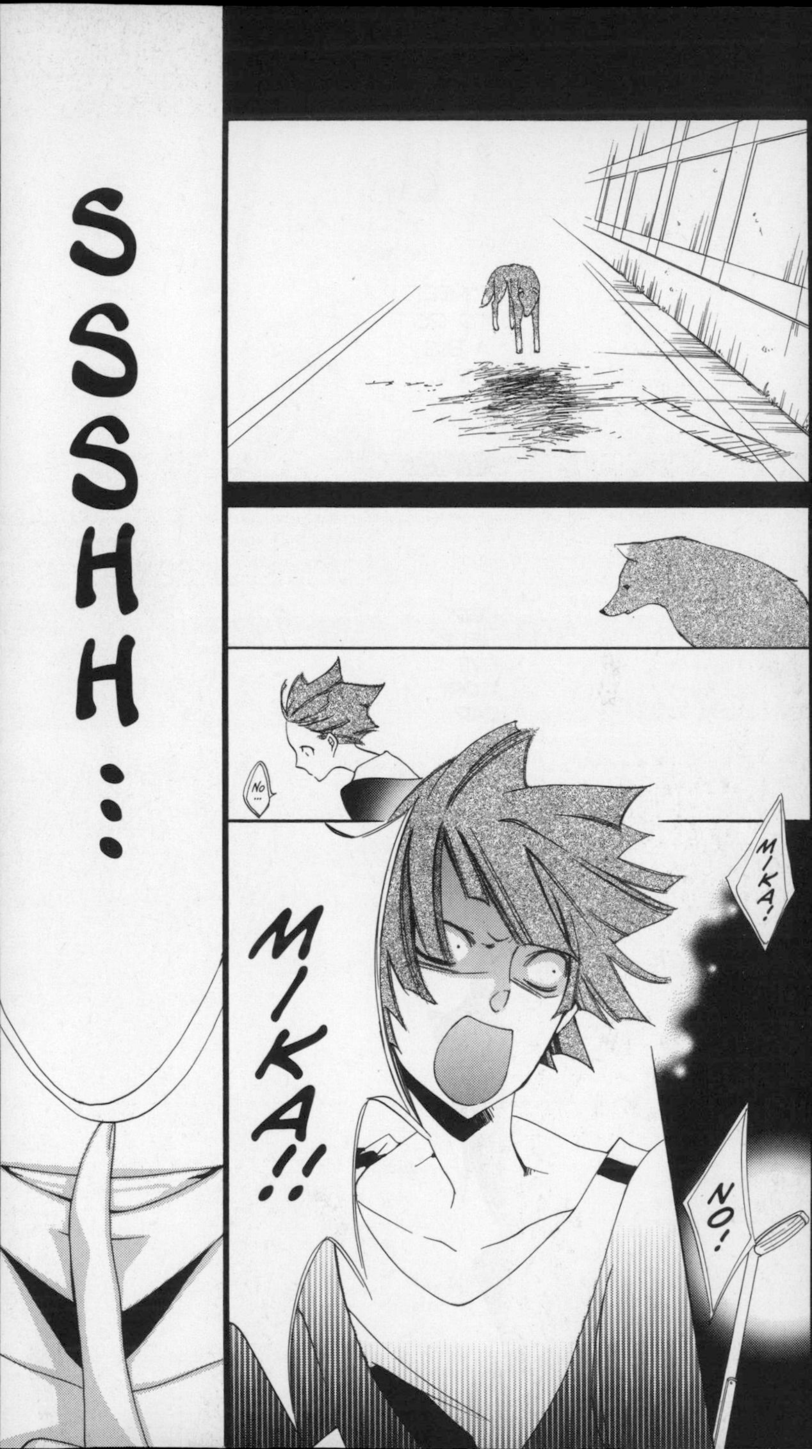
NO...
MIKA!
NO!
MIKA!!
SSSHH...

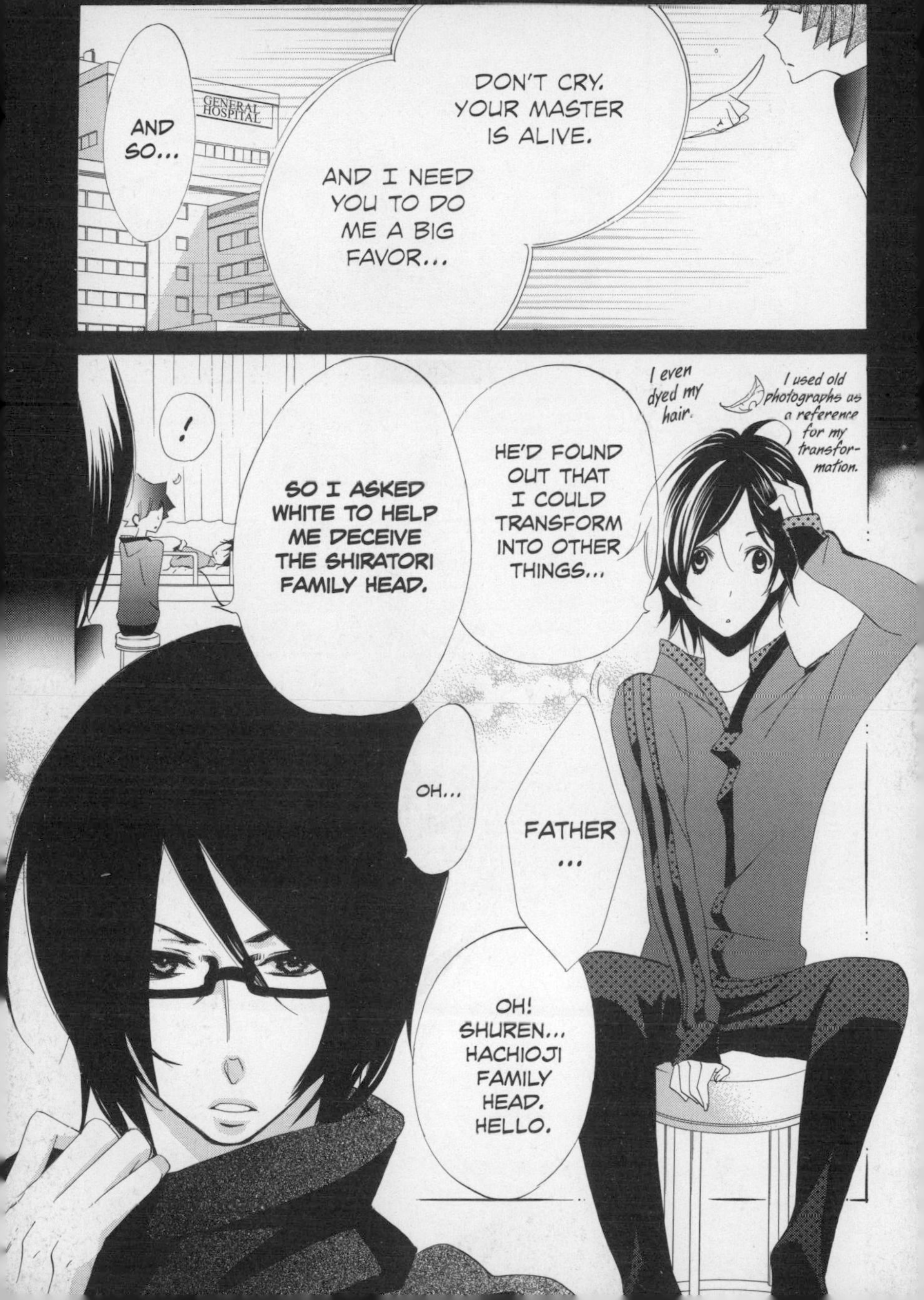
DON'T CRY. YOUR MASTER IS ALIVE.
AND I NEED YOU TO DO ME A BIG FAVOR...
GENERAL HOSPITAL
AND SO...
I used old photographs as a reference for my transformation.
I even dyed my hair.
HE'D FOUND OUT THAT I COULD TRANSFORM INTO OTHER THINGS...
SO I ASKED WHITE TO HELP ME DECEIVE THE SHIRATORI FAMILY HEAD.
!
FATHER...
OH...
OH! SHUREN... HACHIOJI FAMILY HEAD. HELLO.

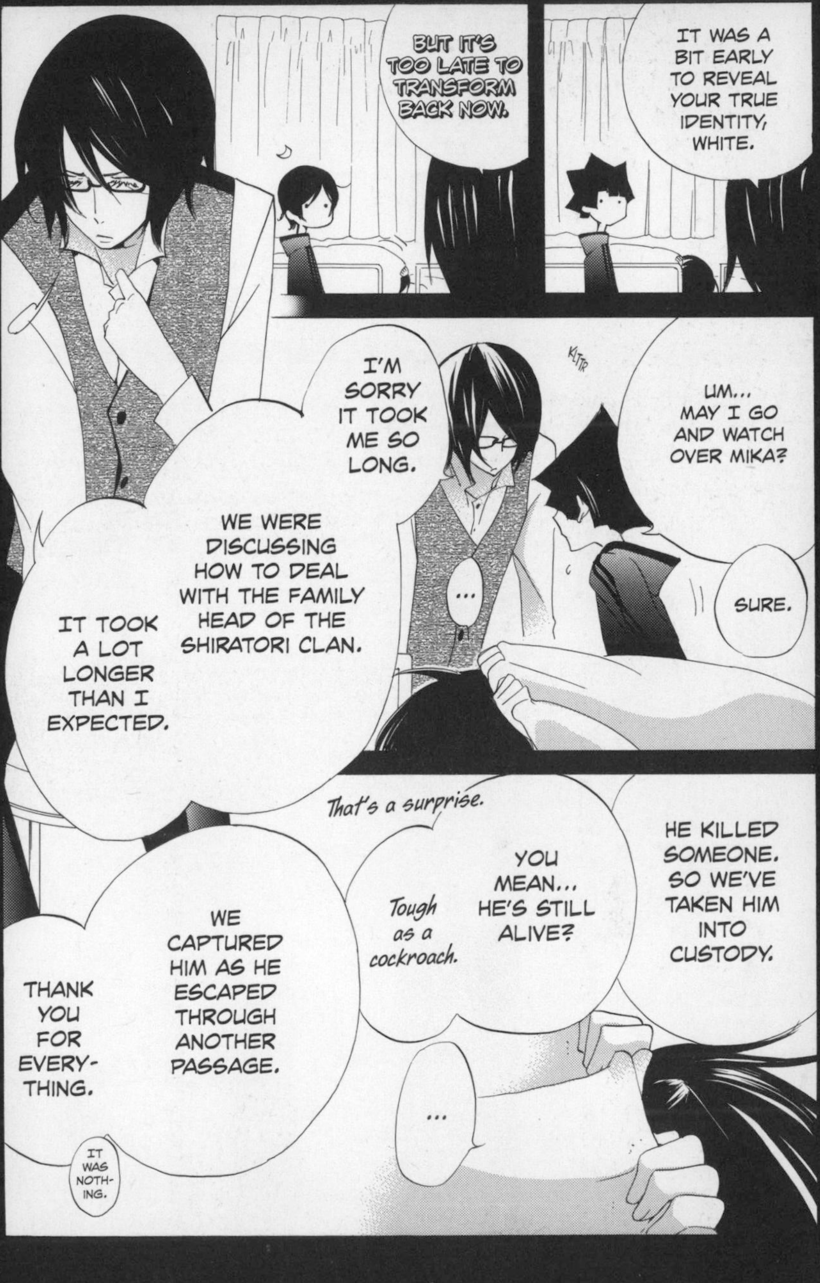
IT WAS A BIT EARLY TO REVEAL YOUR TRUE IDENTITY, WHITE.
BUT IT'S TOO LATE TO TRANSFORM BACK NOW.
KLTTR
UM... MAY I GO AND WATCH OVER MIKA?
SURE.
...
I'M SORRY IT TOOK ME SO LONG.
WE WERE DISCUSSING HOW TO DEAL WITH THE FAMILY HEAD OF THE SHIRATORI CLAN.
IT TOOK A LOT LONGER THAN I EXPECTED.
HE KILLED SOMEONE. SO WE'VE TAKEN HIM INTO CUSTODY.
YOU MEAN... HE'S STILL ALIVE?
That's a surprise.
Tough as a cockroach.
WE CAPTURED HIM AS HE ESCAPED THROUGH ANOTHER PASSAGE.
...
THANK YOU FOR EVERYTHING.
IT WAS NOTHING.

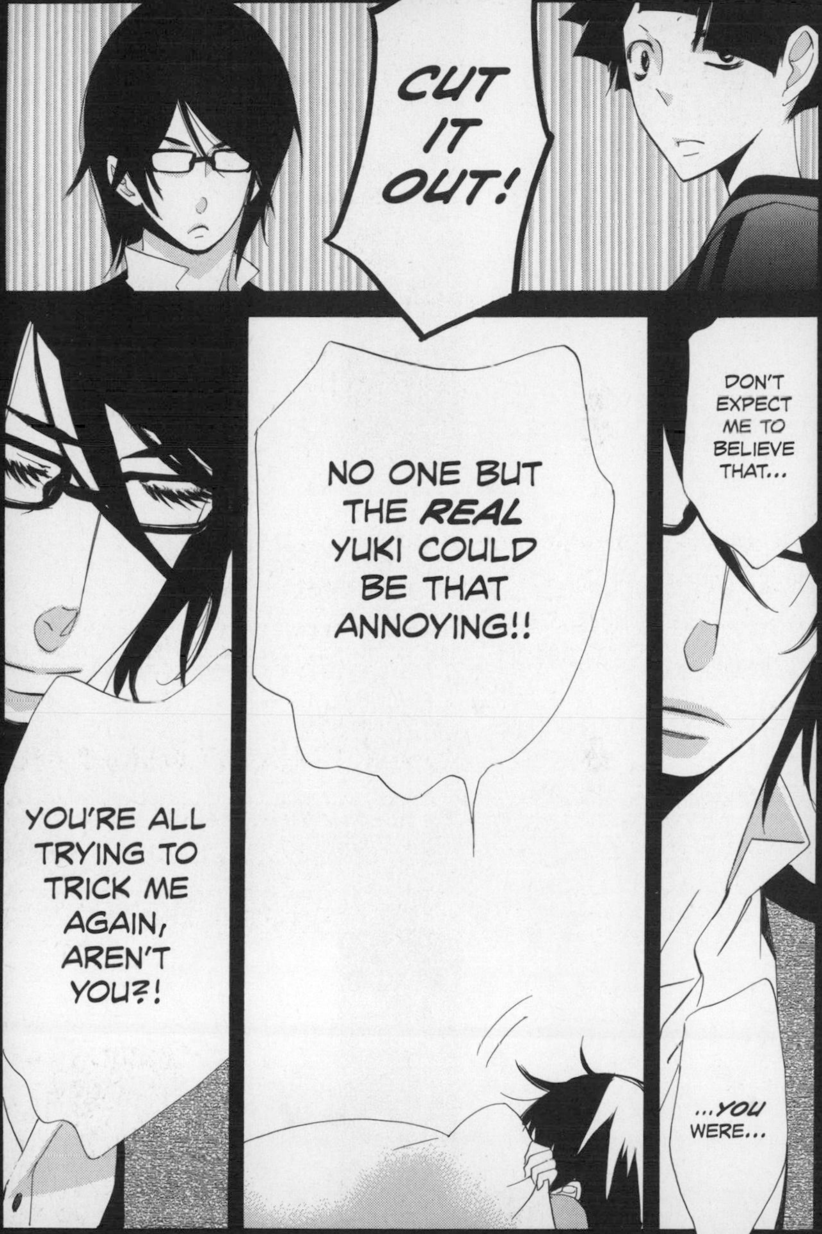
CUT IT OUT!
DON'T EXPECT ME TO BELIEVE THAT...
...*YOU* WERE...
NO ONE BUT THE *REAL* YUKI COULD BE THAT ANNOYING!!
YOU'RE ALL TRYING TO TRICK ME AGAIN, AREN'T YOU?!

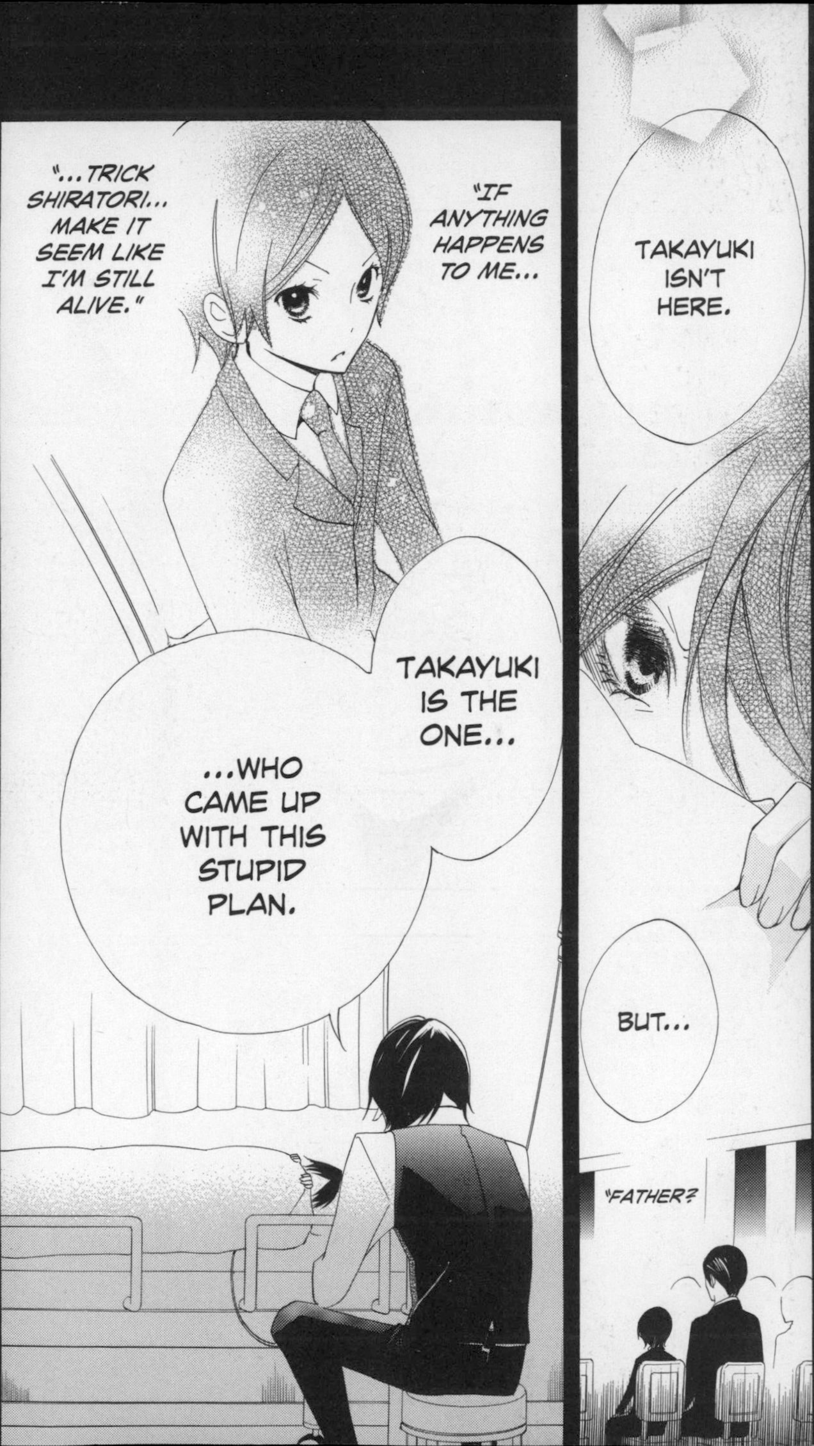
TAKAYUKI ISN'T HERE.
BUT...
"FATHER?
"IF ANYTHING HAPPENS TO ME...
"...TRICK SHIRATORI... MAKE IT SEEM LIKE I'M STILL ALIVE."
TAKAYUKI IS THE ONE...
...WHO CAME UP WITH THIS STUPID PLAN.

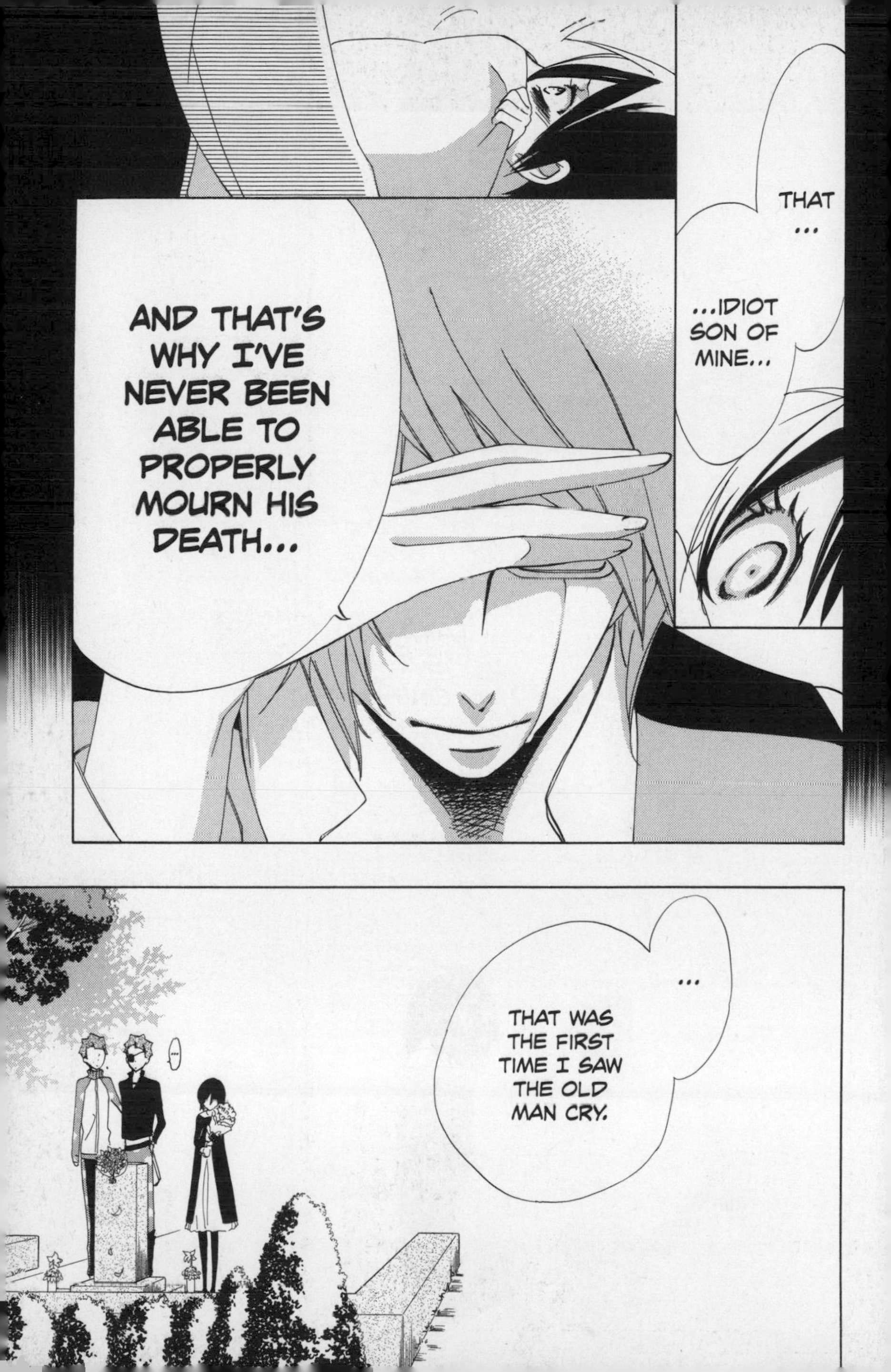
THAT ...
...IDIOT SON OF MINE...
AND THAT'S WHY I'VE NEVER BEEN ABLE TO PROPERLY MOURN HIS DEATH...
...
THAT WAS THE FIRST TIME I SAW THE OLD MAN CRY.

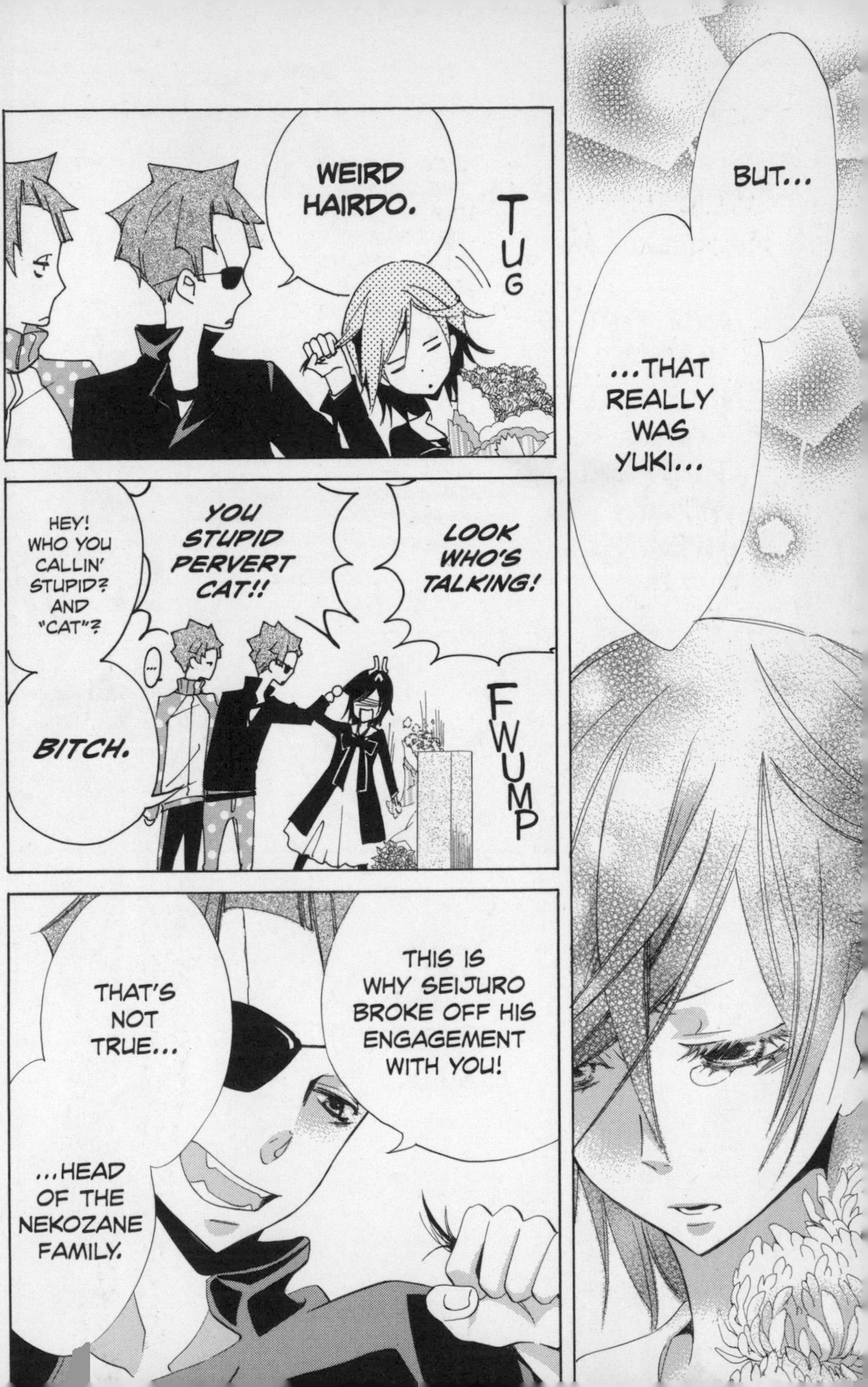
BUT...
...THAT REALLY WAS YUKI...
TUG
WEIRD HAIRDO.
LOOK WHO'S TALKING!
FWUMP
YOU STUPID PERVERT CAT!!
HEY! WHO YOU CALLIN' STUPID? AND "CAT"?
...
BITCH.
THIS IS WHY SEIJURO BROKE OFF HIS ENGAGEMENT WITH YOU!
THAT'S NOT TRUE...
...HEAD OF THE NEKOZANE FAMILY.

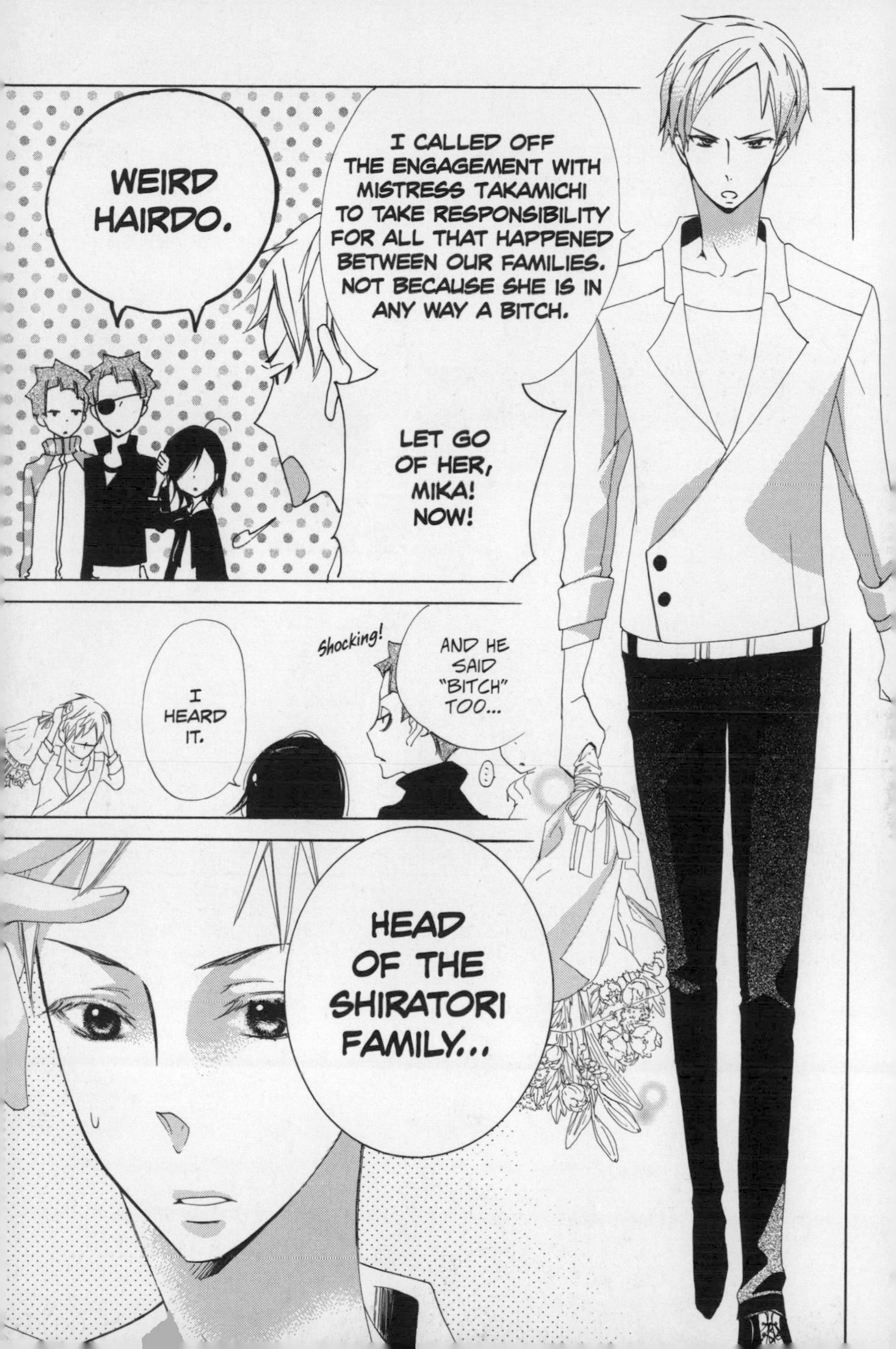
I CALLED OFF THE ENGAGEMENT WITH MISTRESS TAKAMICHI TO TAKE RESPONSIBILITY FOR ALL THAT HAPPENED BETWEEN OUR FAMILIES. NOT BECAUSE SHE IS IN ANY WAY A BITCH.
LET GO OF HER, MIKA! NOW!
WEIRD HAIRDO.
AND HE SAID "BITCH" TOO...
Shocking!
I HEARD IT.
HEAD OF THE SHIRATORI FAMILY...

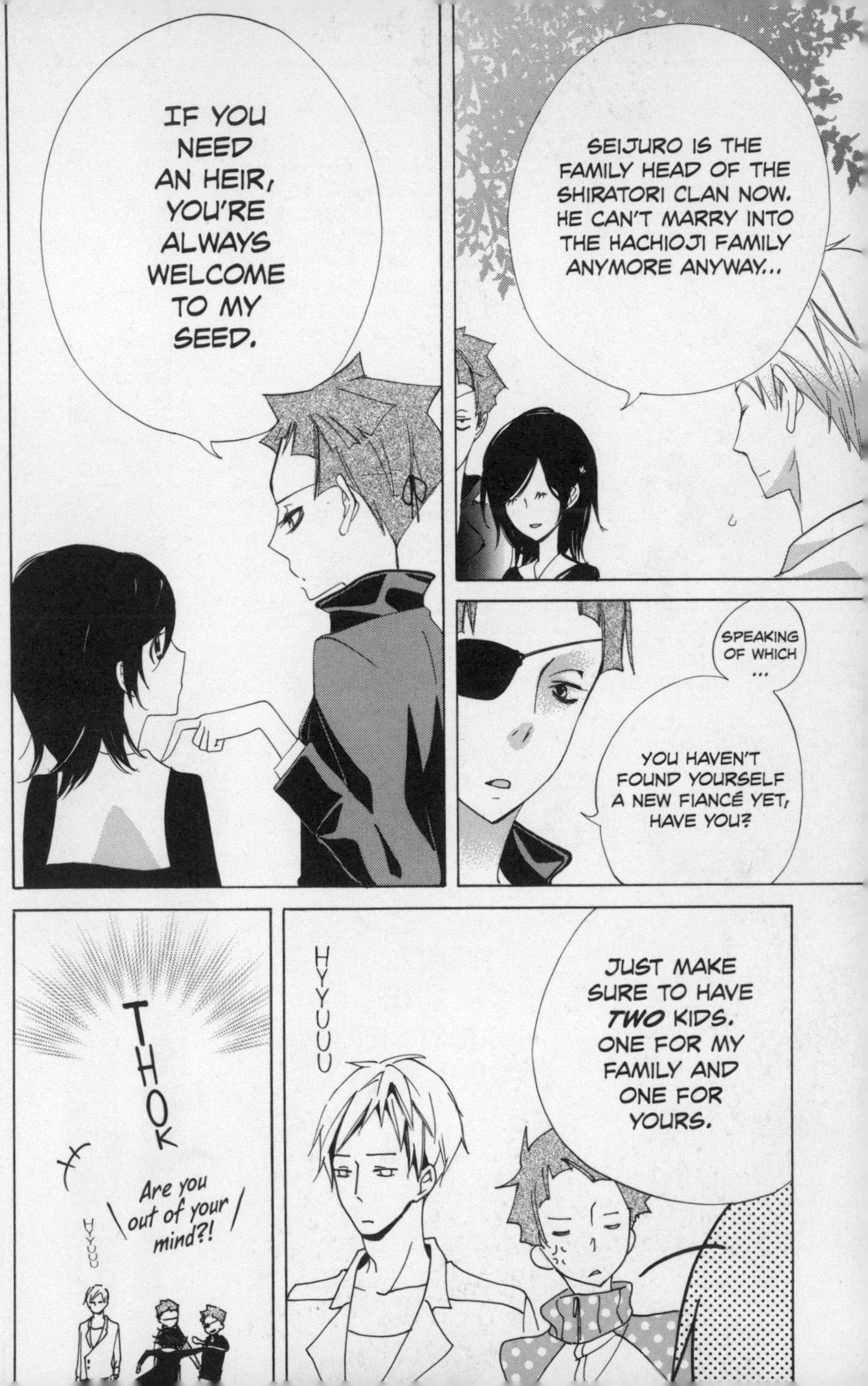
SEIJURO IS THE FAMILY HEAD OF THE SHIRATORI CLAN NOW. HE CAN'T MARRY INTO THE HACHIOJI FAMILY ANYMORE ANYWAY...
SPEAKING OF WHICH ...
YOU HAVEN'T FOUND YOURSELF A NEW FIANCÉ YET, HAVE YOU?
IF YOU NEED AN HEIR, YOU'RE ALWAYS WELCOME TO MY SEED.
JUST MAKE SURE TO HAVE *TWO* KIDS. ONE FOR MY FAMILY AND ONE FOR YOURS.
HYYUUU
THOK
Are you out of your mind?!
HYYUUU

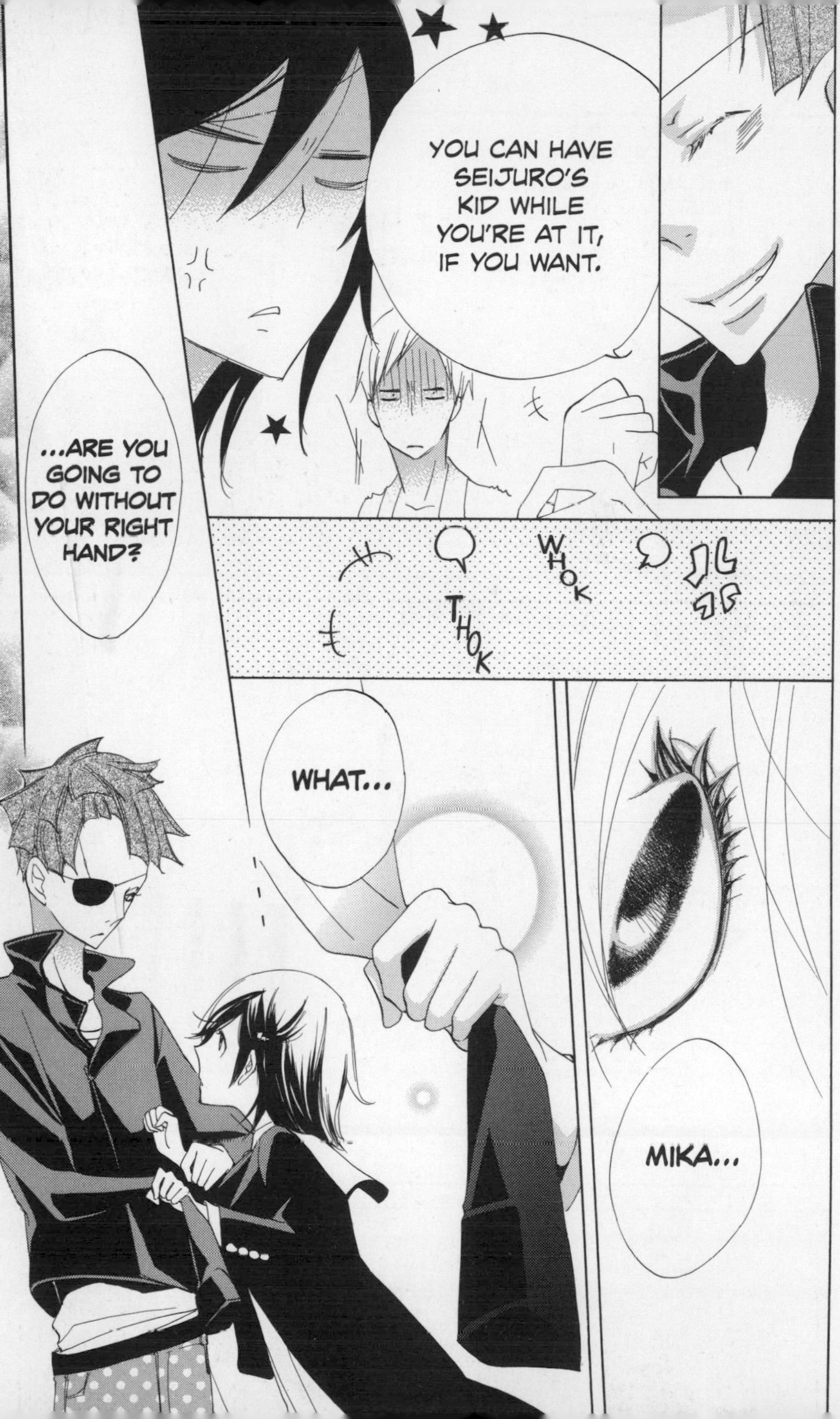
YOU CAN HAVE SEIJURO'S KID WHILE YOU'RE AT IT, IF YOU WANT.
...ARE YOU GOING TO DO WITHOUT YOUR RIGHT HAND?
WHOK
THOK
MIKA...
WHAT...

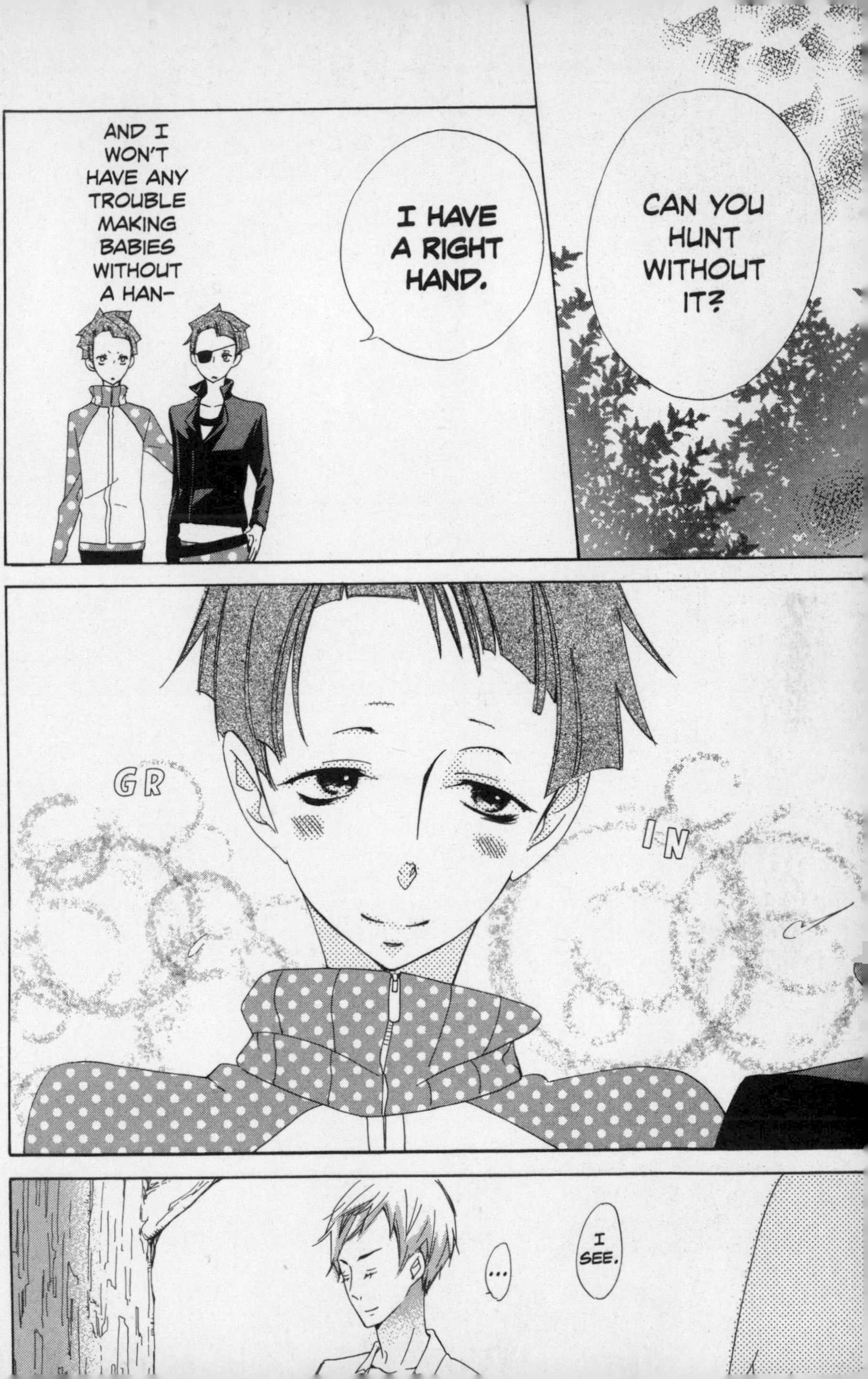
CAN YOU HUNT WITHOUT IT?
I HAVE A RIGHT HAND.
AND I WON'T HAVE ANY TROUBLE MAKING BABIES WITHOUT A HAN-
GR
IN
I SEE.
...

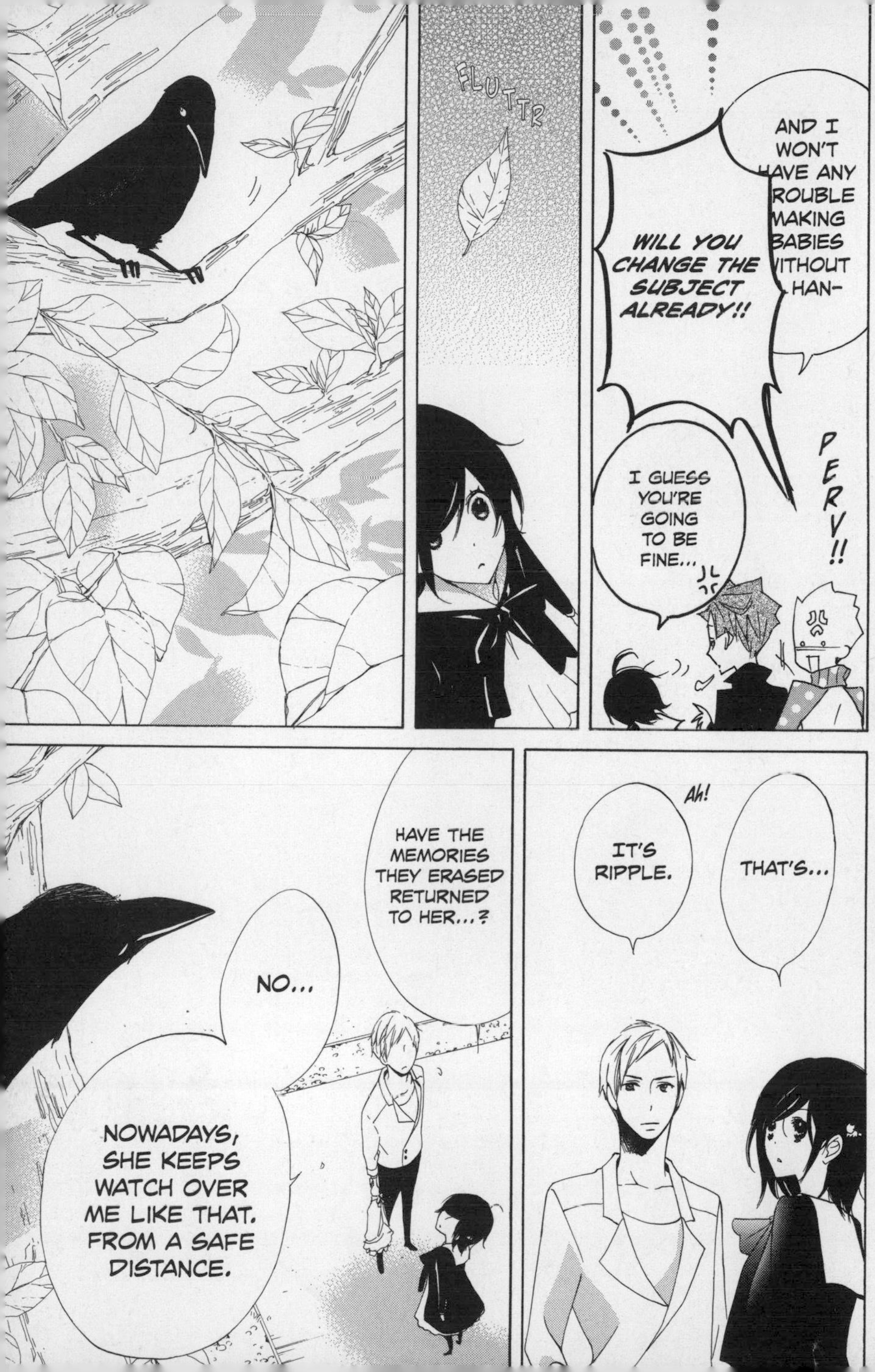
AND I WON'T HAVE ANY TROUBLE MAKING BABIES WITHOUT HAN-
WILL YOU CHANGE THE SUBJECT ALREADY!!
PERV!!
I GUESS YOU'RE GOING TO BE FINE...
FLUTTR
THAT'S...
Ah!
IT'S RIPPLE.
HAVE THE MEMORIES THEY ERASED RETURNED TO HER...?
NO...
NOWADAYS, SHE KEEPS WATCH OVER ME LIKE THAT. FROM A SAFE DISTANCE.

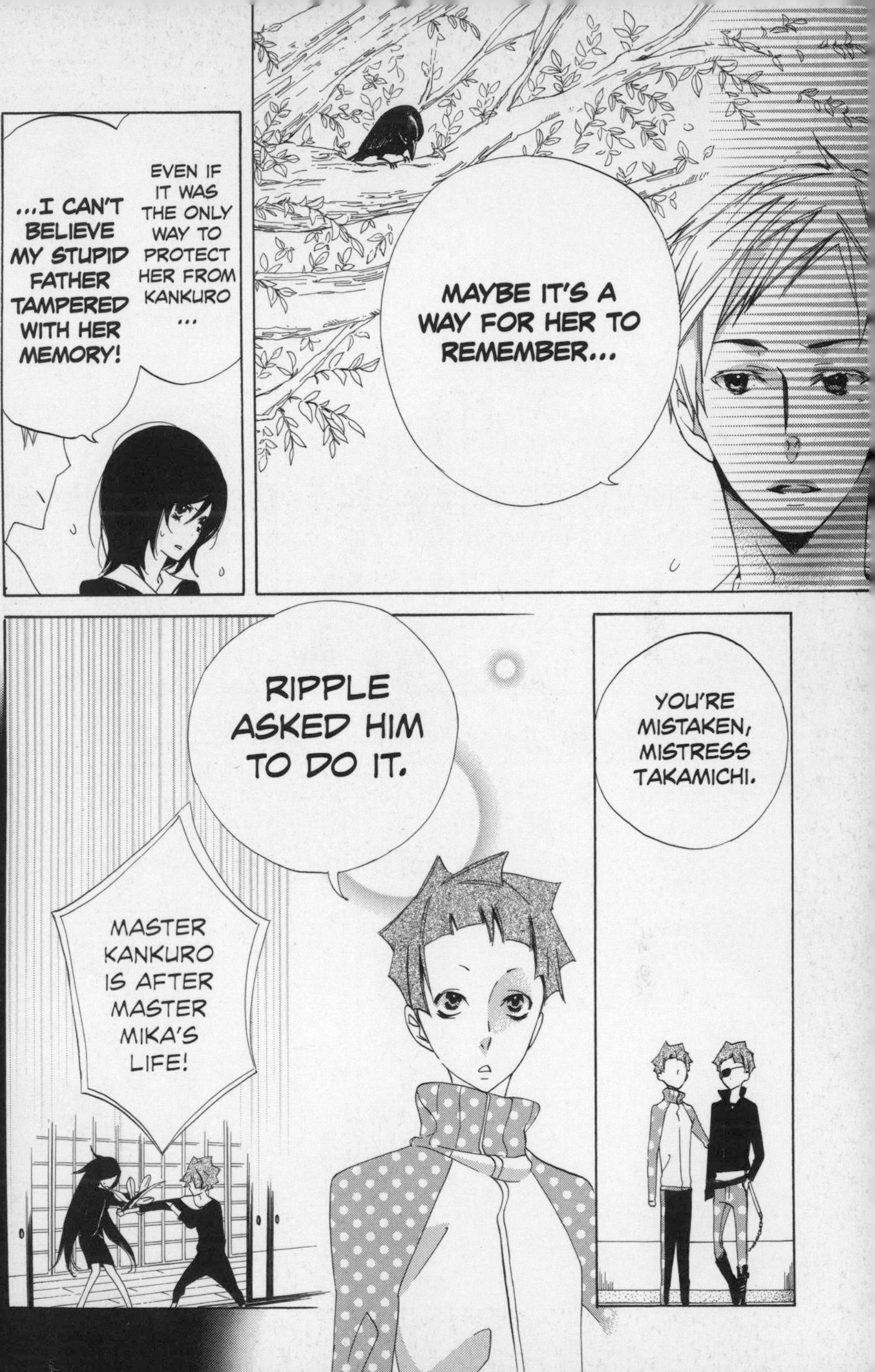
MAYBE IT'S A WAY FOR HER TO REMEMBER...
EVEN IF IT WAS THE ONLY WAY TO PROTECT HER FROM KANKURO ...
...I CAN'T BELIEVE MY STUPID FATHER TAMPERED WITH HER MEMORY!
YOU'RE MISTAKEN, MISTRESS TAKAMICHI.
RIPPLE ASKED HIM TO DO IT.
MASTER KANKURO IS AFTER MASTER MIKA'S LIFE!

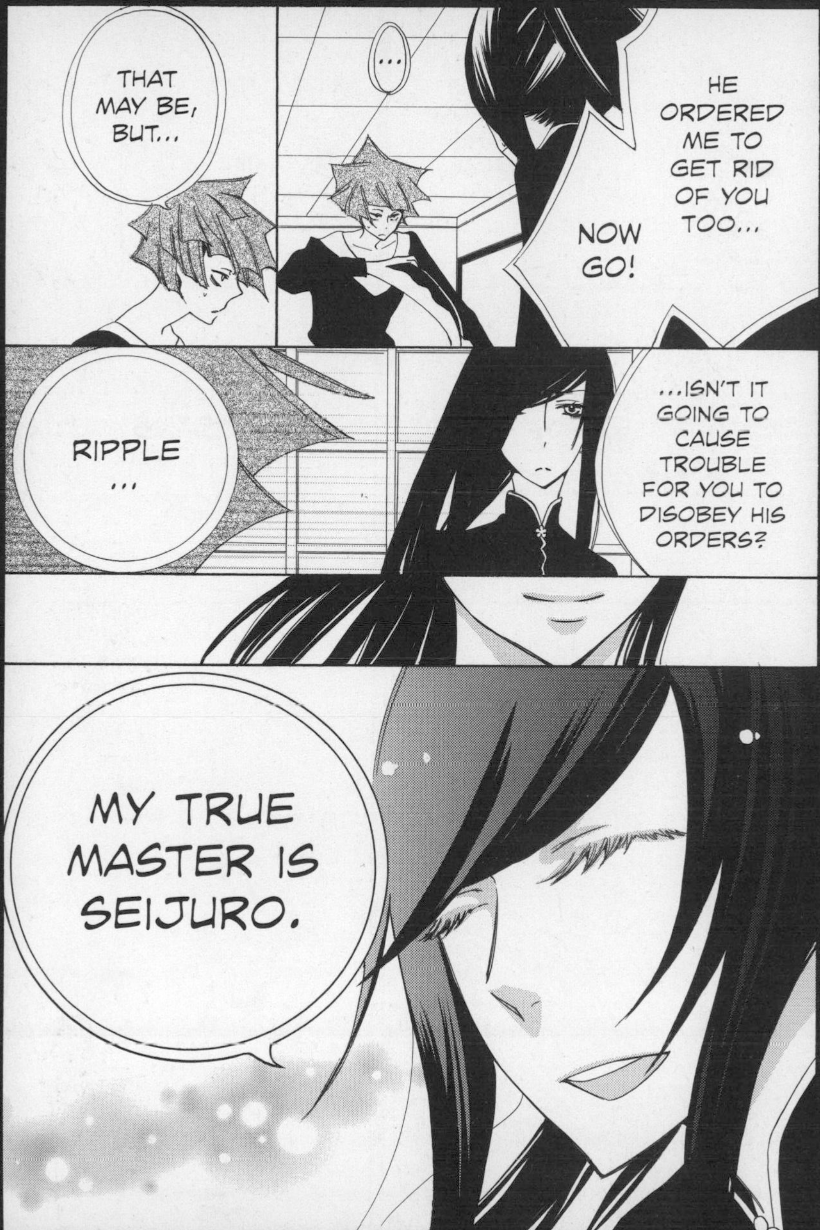
HE ORDERED ME TO GET RID OF YOU TOO...
NOW GO!
...
THAT MAY BE, BUT...
...ISN'T IT GOING TO CAUSE TROUBLE FOR YOU TO DISOBEY HIS ORDERS?
RIPPLE ...
MY TRUE MASTER IS SEIJURO.

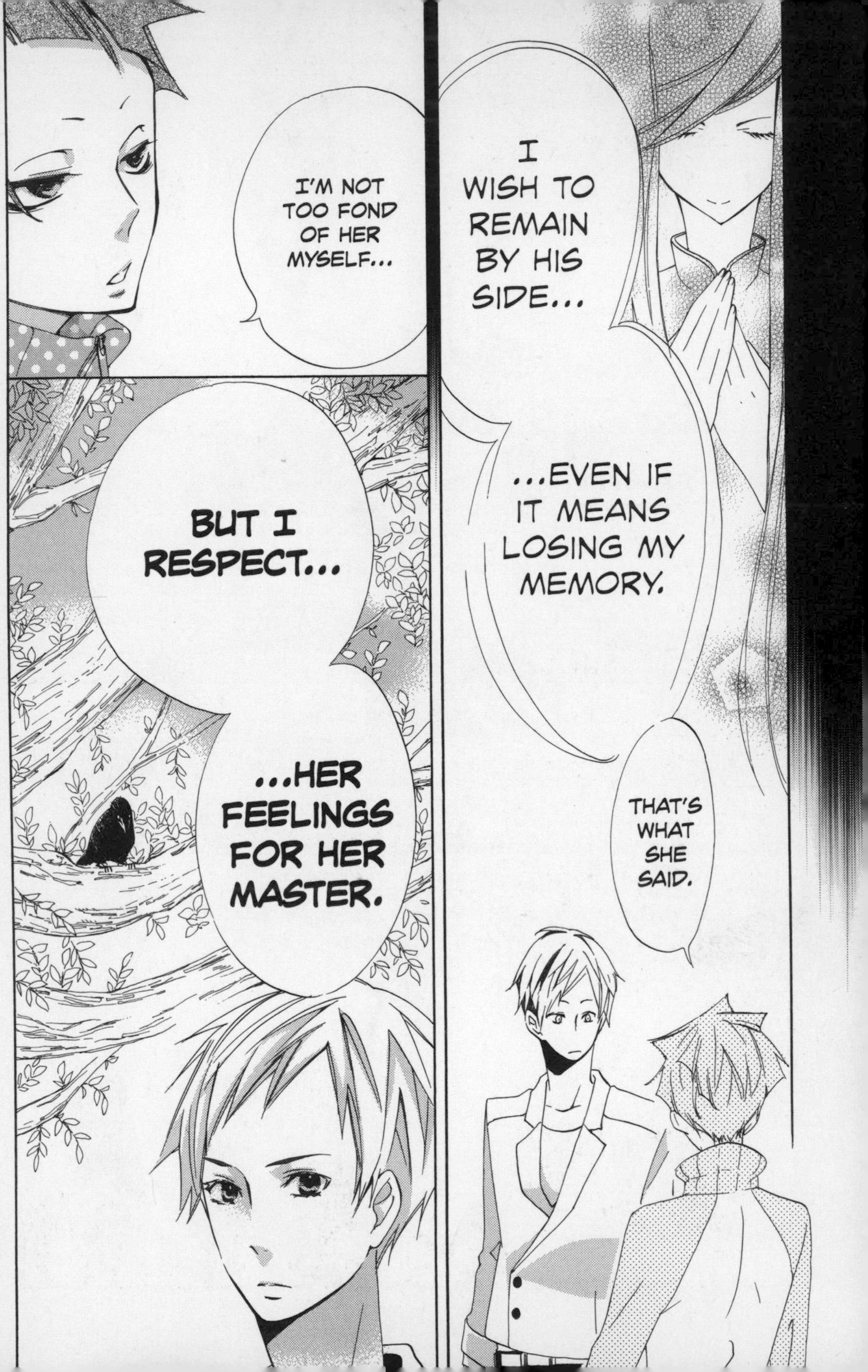
I WISH TO REMAIN BY HIS SIDE...
...EVEN IF IT MEANS LOSING MY MEMORY.
THAT'S WHAT SHE SAID.
I'M NOT TOO FOND OF HER MYSELF...
BUT I RESPECT...
...HER FEELINGS FOR HER MASTER.

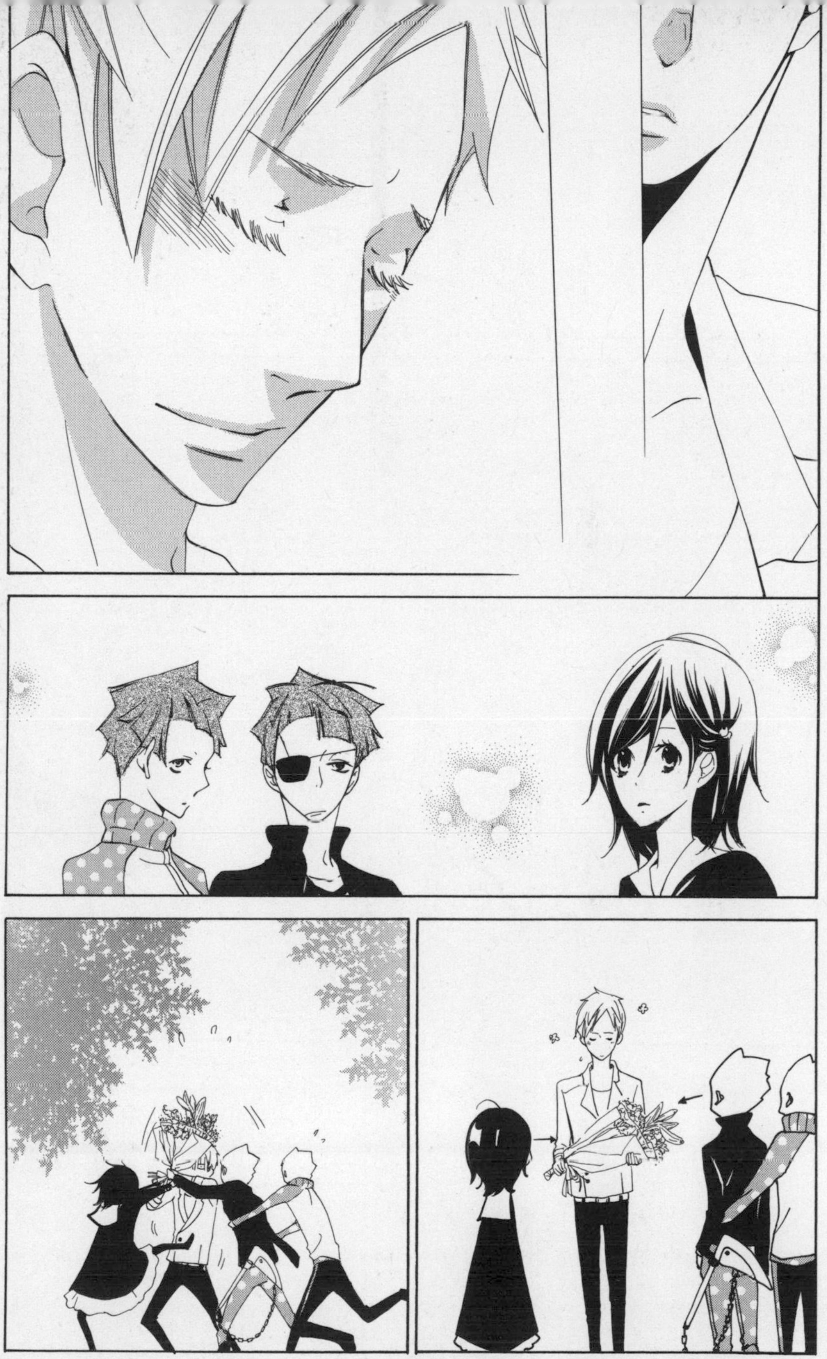

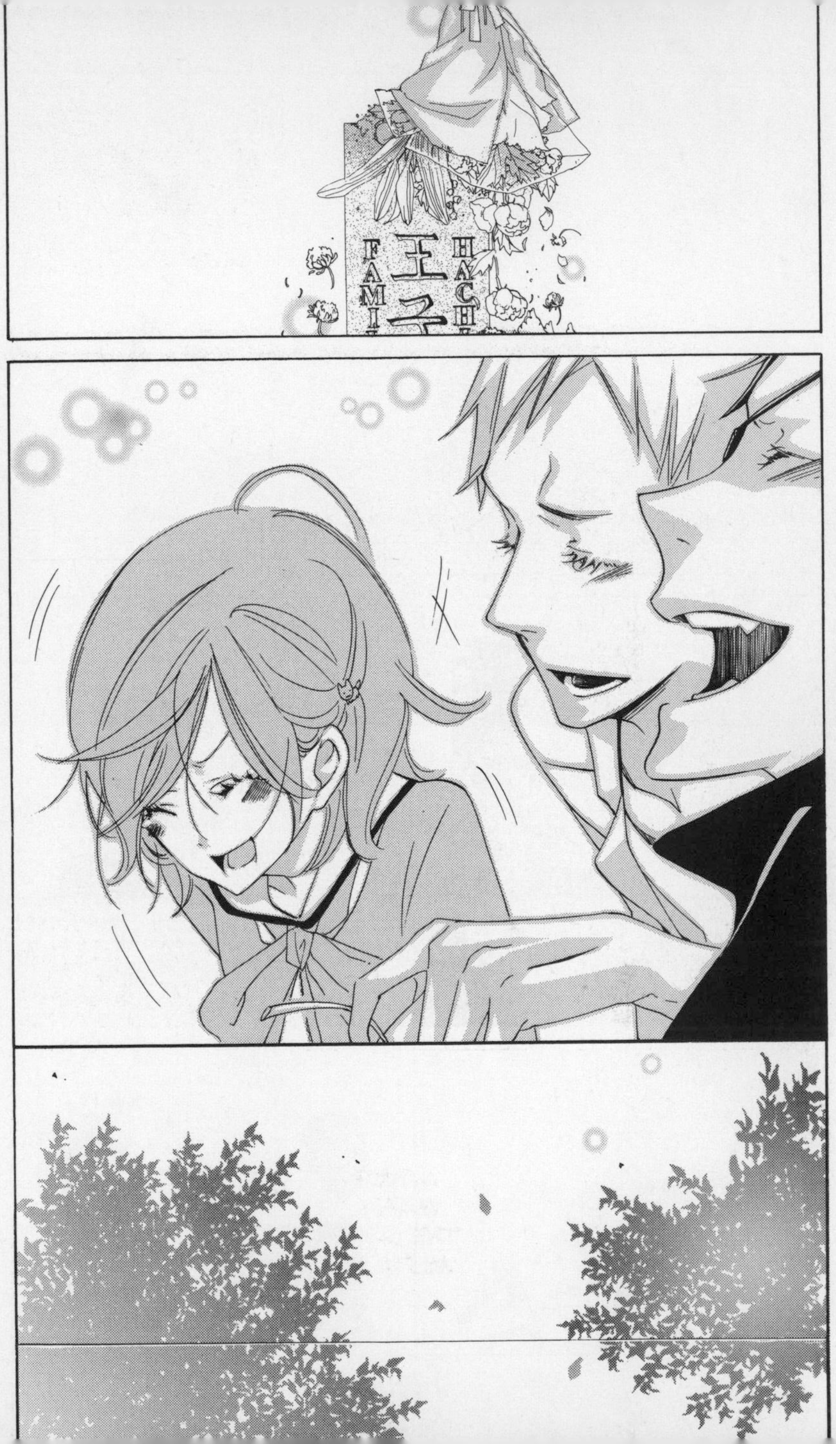

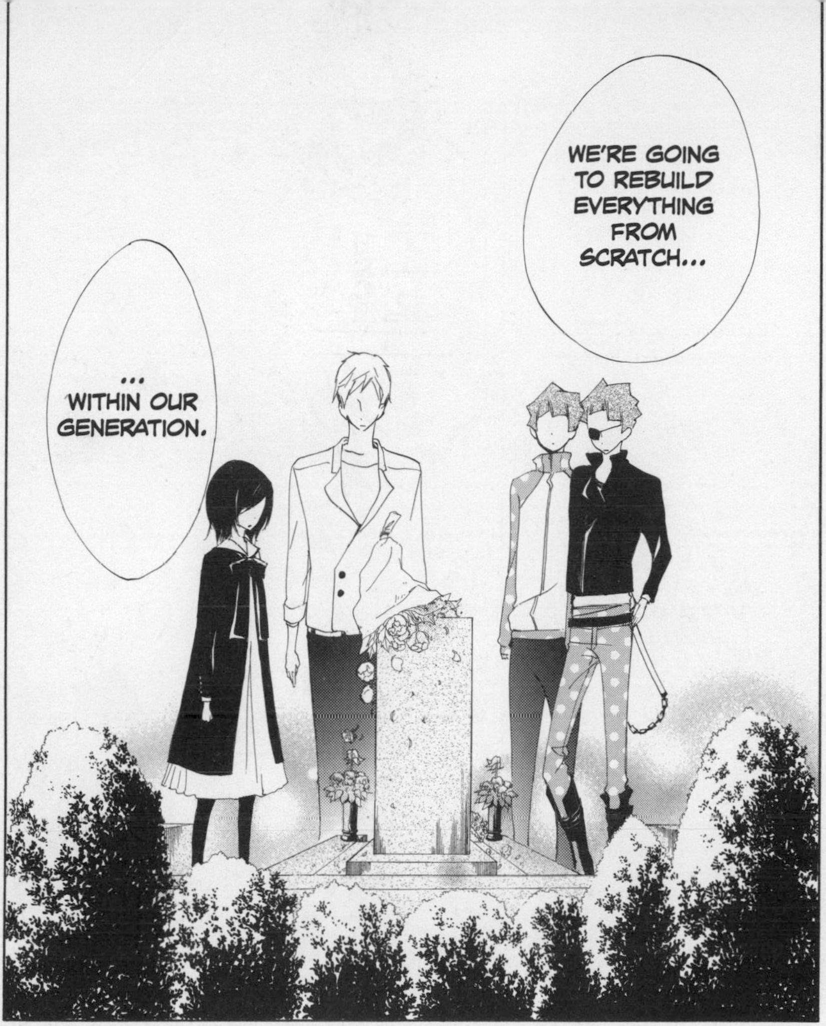
WE'RE GOING TO REBUILD EVERYTHING FROM SCRATCH...
... WITHIN OUR GENERATION.

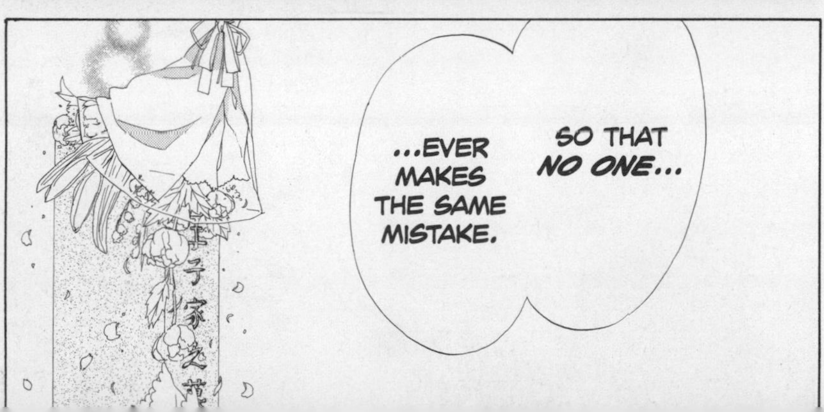
SO THAT *NO ONE*...
...EVER MAKES THE SAME MISTAKE.

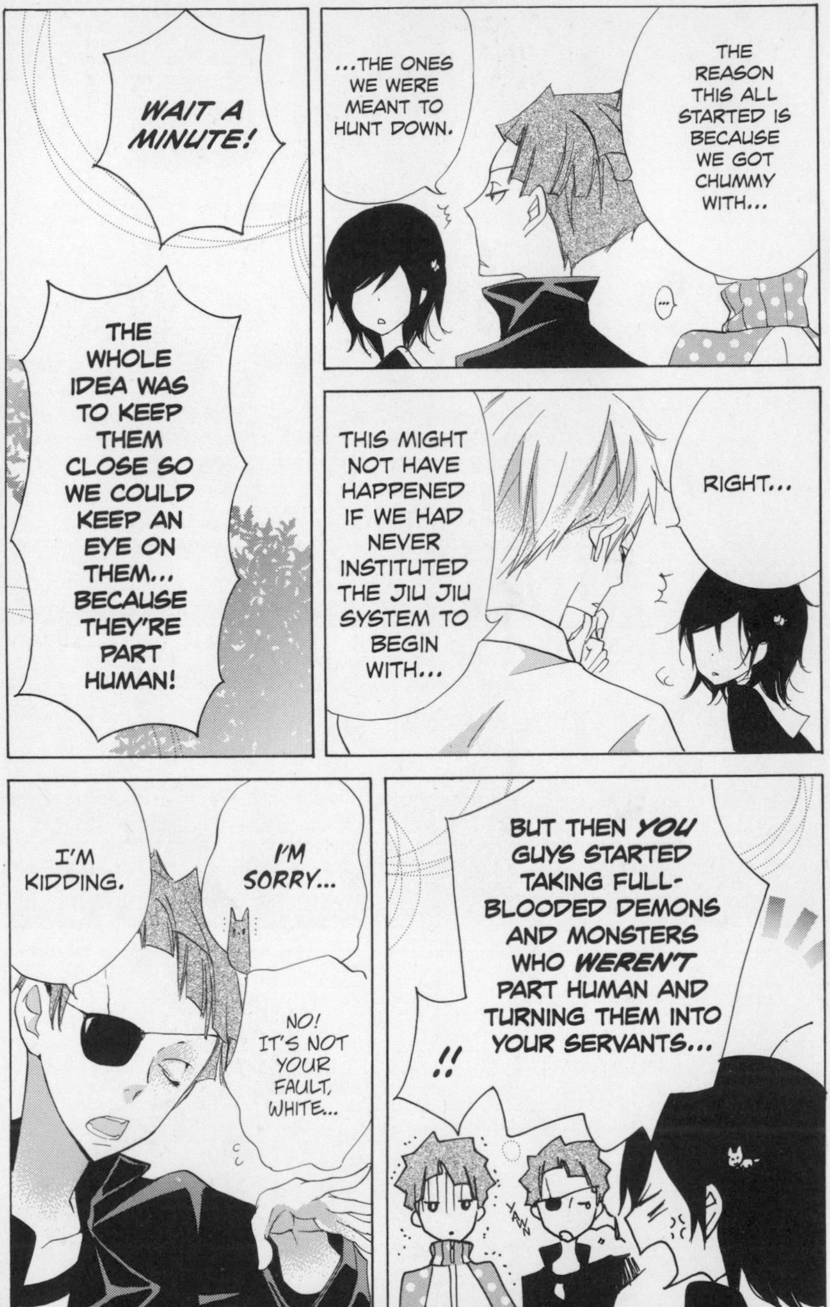
THE REASON THIS ALL STARTED IS BECAUSE WE GOT CHUMMY WITH...
...THE ONES WE WERE MEANT TO HUNT DOWN.
...
RIGHT...
THIS MIGHT NOT HAVE HAPPENED IF WE HAD NEVER INSTITUTED THE JIU JIU SYSTEM TO BEGIN WITH...
WAIT A MINUTE!
THE WHOLE IDEA WAS TO KEEP THEM CLOSE SO WE COULD KEEP AN EYE ON THEM... BECAUSE THEY'RE PART HUMAN!
BUT THEN YOU GUYS STARTED TAKING FULL-BLOODED DEMONS AND MONSTERS WHO WEREN'T PART HUMAN AND TURNING THEM INTO YOUR SERVANTS...
!!
YAWN
I'M SORRY...
I'M KIDDING.
NO! IT'S NOT YOUR FAULT, WHITE...

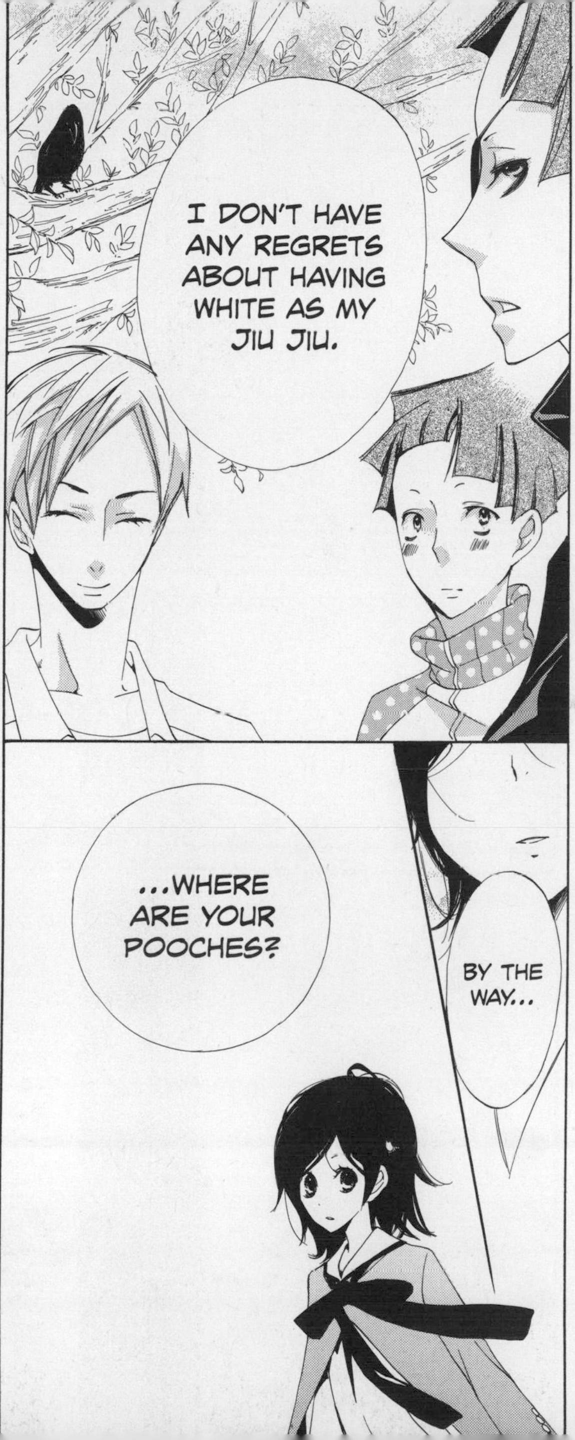
I DON'T HAVE ANY REGRETS ABOUT HAVING WHITE AS MY JIU JIU.
BY THE WAY...
...WHERE ARE YOUR POOCHES?

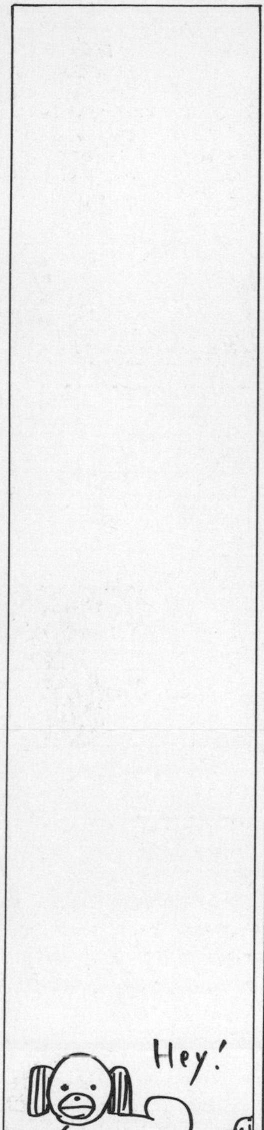
Hey!

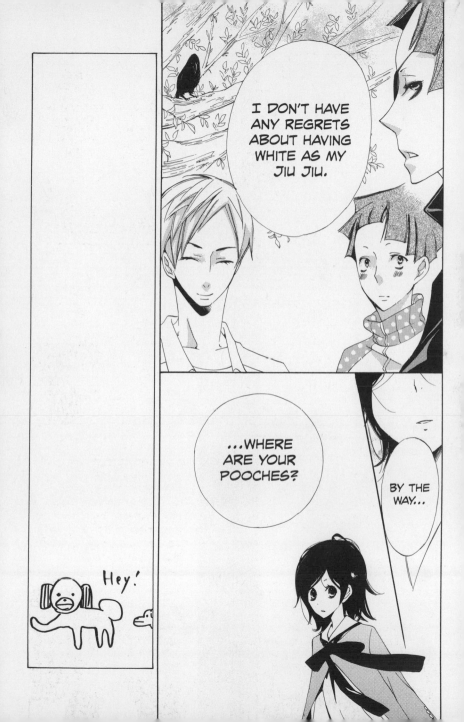

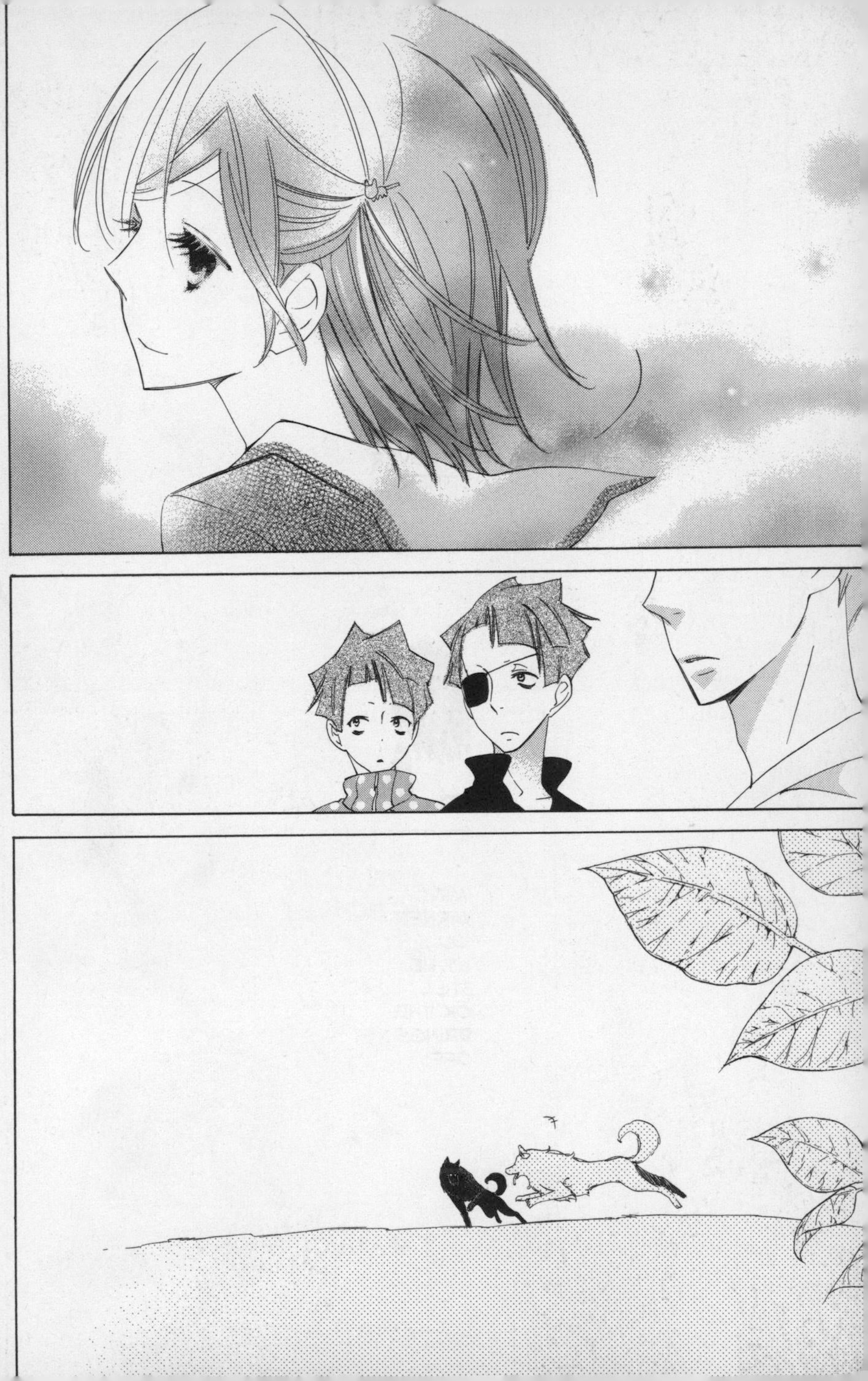
チ

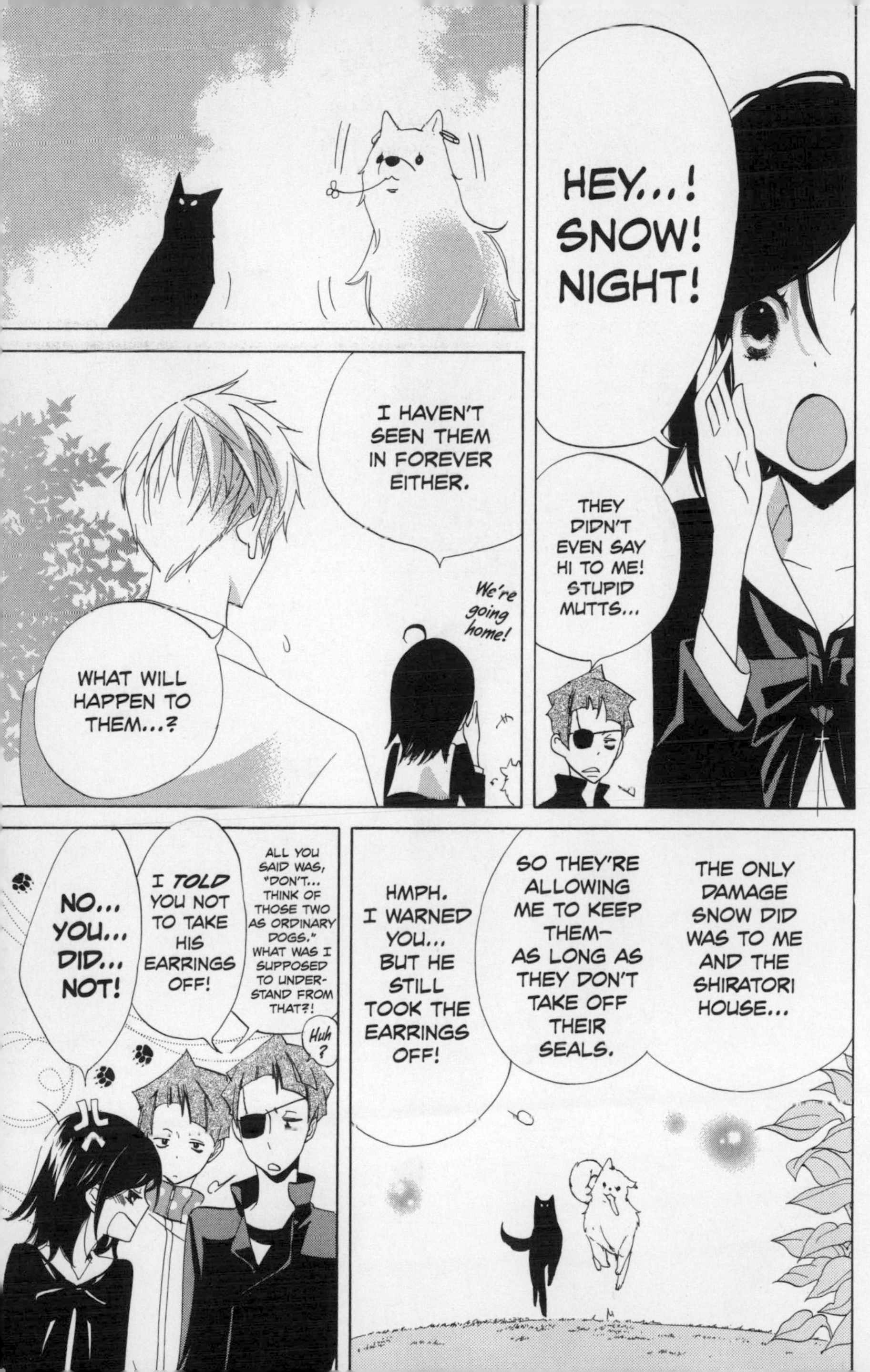
HEY...! SNOW! NIGHT!
THEY DIDN'T EVEN SAY HI TO ME! STUPID MUTTS...
I HAVEN'T SEEN THEM IN FOREVER EITHER.
We're going home!
WHAT WILL HAPPEN TO THEM...?
THE ONLY DAMAGE SNOW DID WAS TO ME AND THE SHIRATORI HOUSE...
SO THEY'RE ALLOWING ME TO KEEP THEM— AS LONG AS THEY DON'T TAKE OFF THEIR SEALS.
HMPH. I WARNED YOU... BUT HE STILL TOOK THE EARRINGS OFF!
ALL YOU SAID WAS, "DON'T... THINK OF THOSE TWO AS ORDINARY DOGS." WHAT WAS I SUPPOSED TO UNDER-STAND FROM THAT?!
Huh?
I *TOLD* YOU NOT TO TAKE HIS EARRINGS OFF!
NO... YOU... DID... NOT!

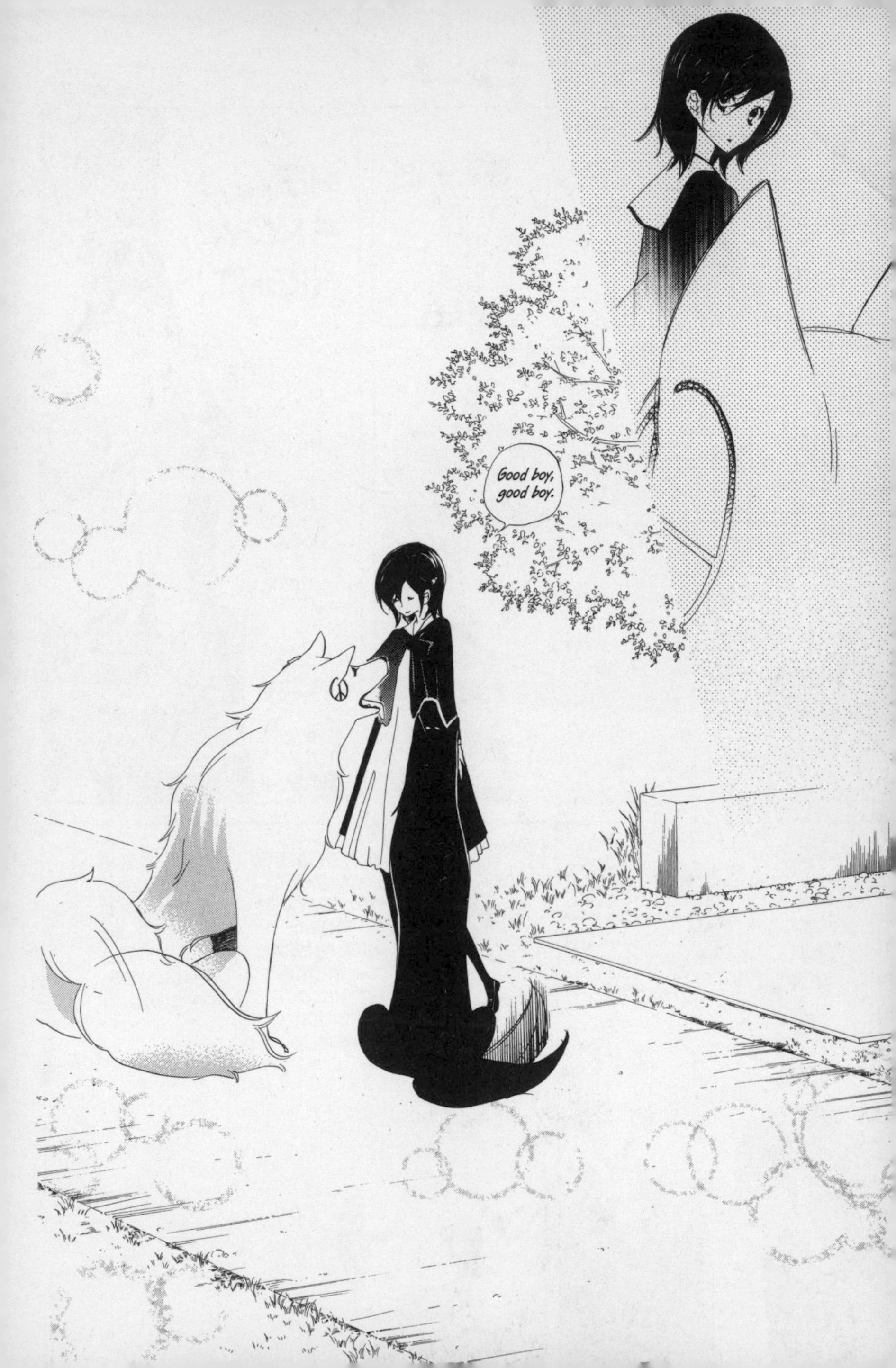
Good boy, good boy.

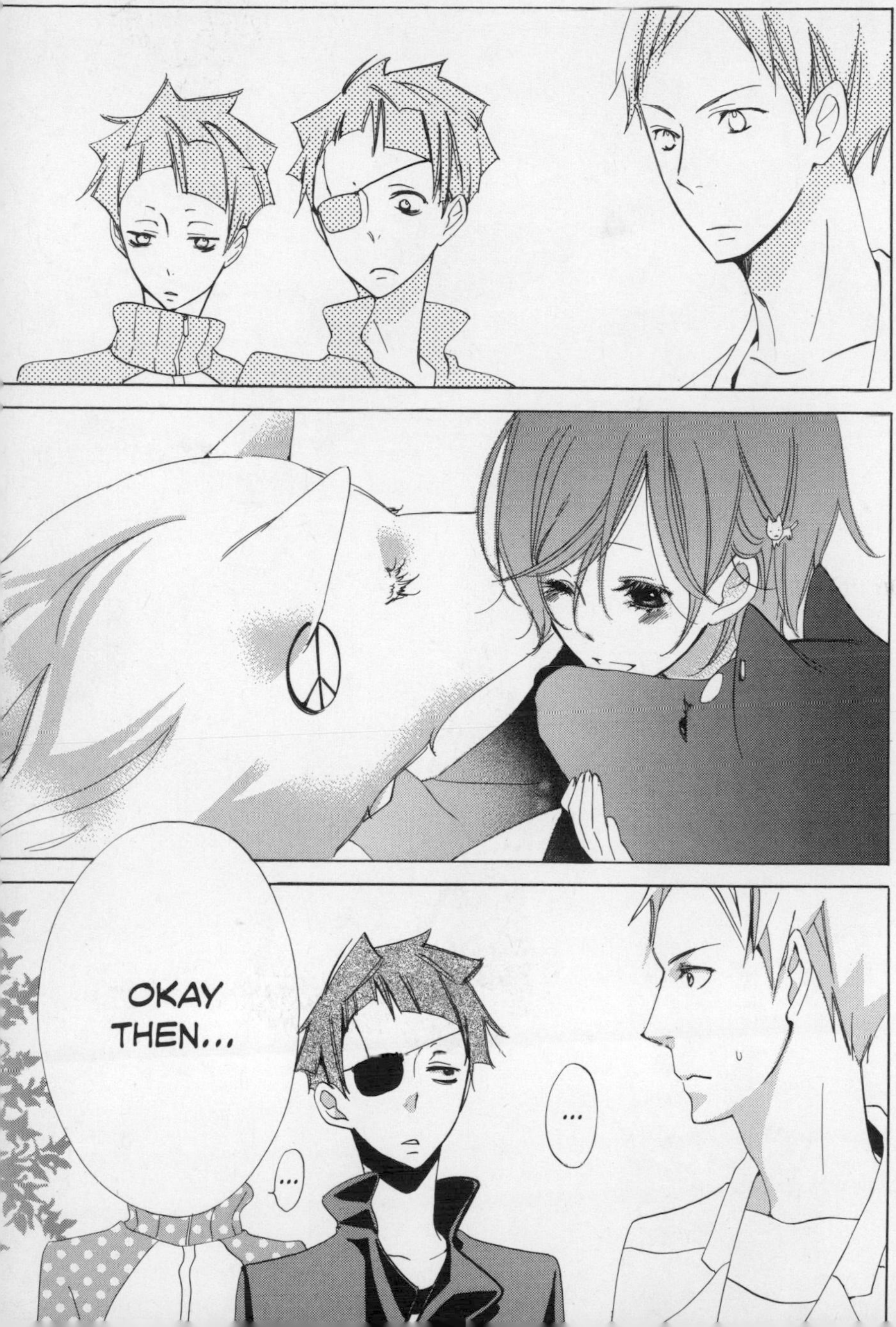
OKAY THEN...
...
...

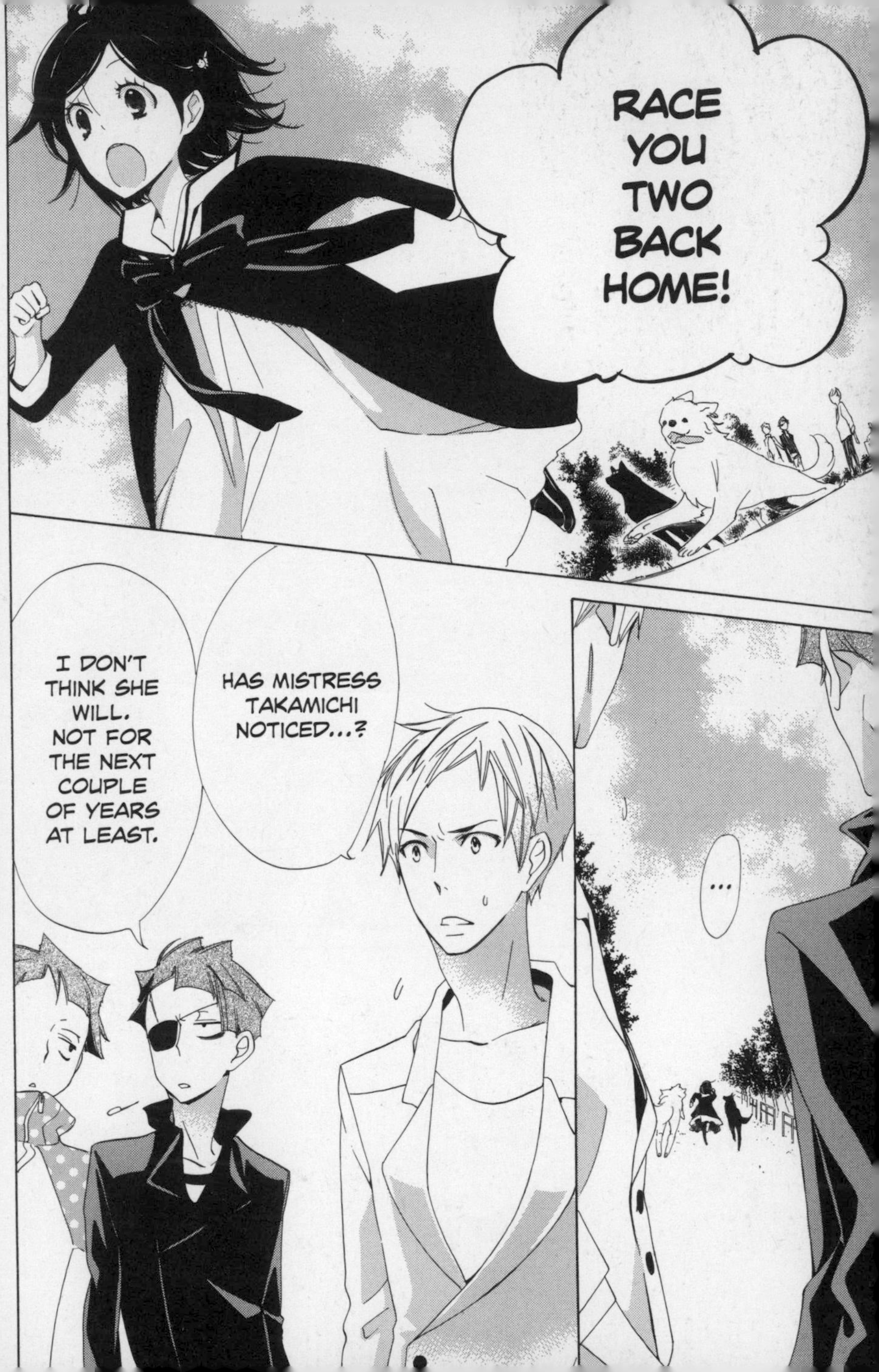
RACE YOU TWO BACK HOME!
...
HAS MISTRESS TAKAMICHI NOTICED...?
I DON'T THINK SHE WILL. NOT FOR THE NEXT COUPLE OF YEARS AT LEAST.

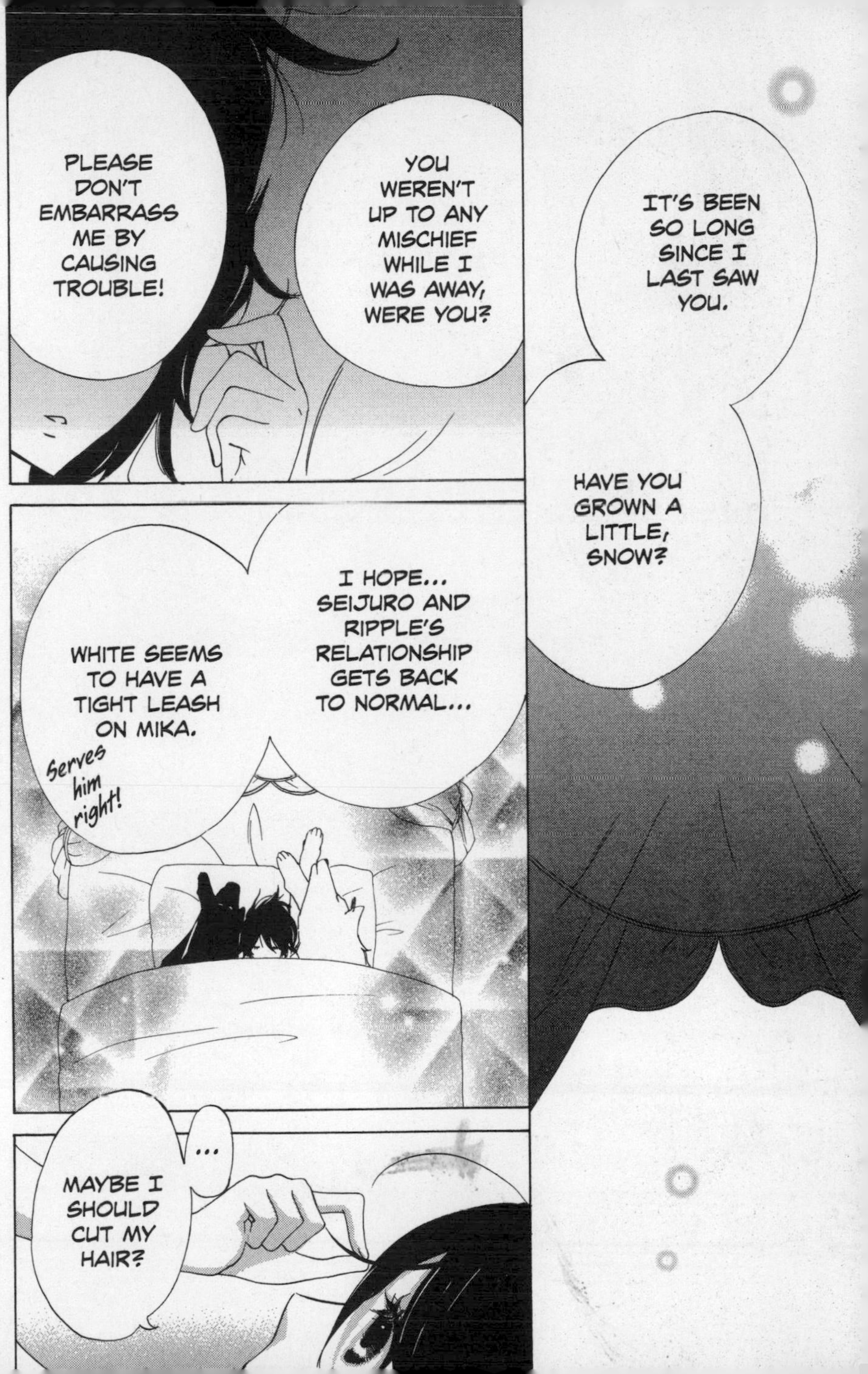
IT'S BEEN SO LONG SINCE I LAST SAW YOU.
HAVE YOU GROWN A LITTLE, SNOW?
YOU WEREN'T UP TO ANY MISCHIEF WHILE I WAS AWAY, WERE YOU?
PLEASE DON'T EMBARRASS ME BY CAUSING TROUBLE!
I HOPE... SEIJURO AND RIPPLE'S RELATIONSHIP GETS BACK TO NORMAL...
WHITE SEEMS TO HAVE A TIGHT LEASH ON MIKA.
Serves him right!
...
MAYBE I SHOULD CUT MY HAIR?

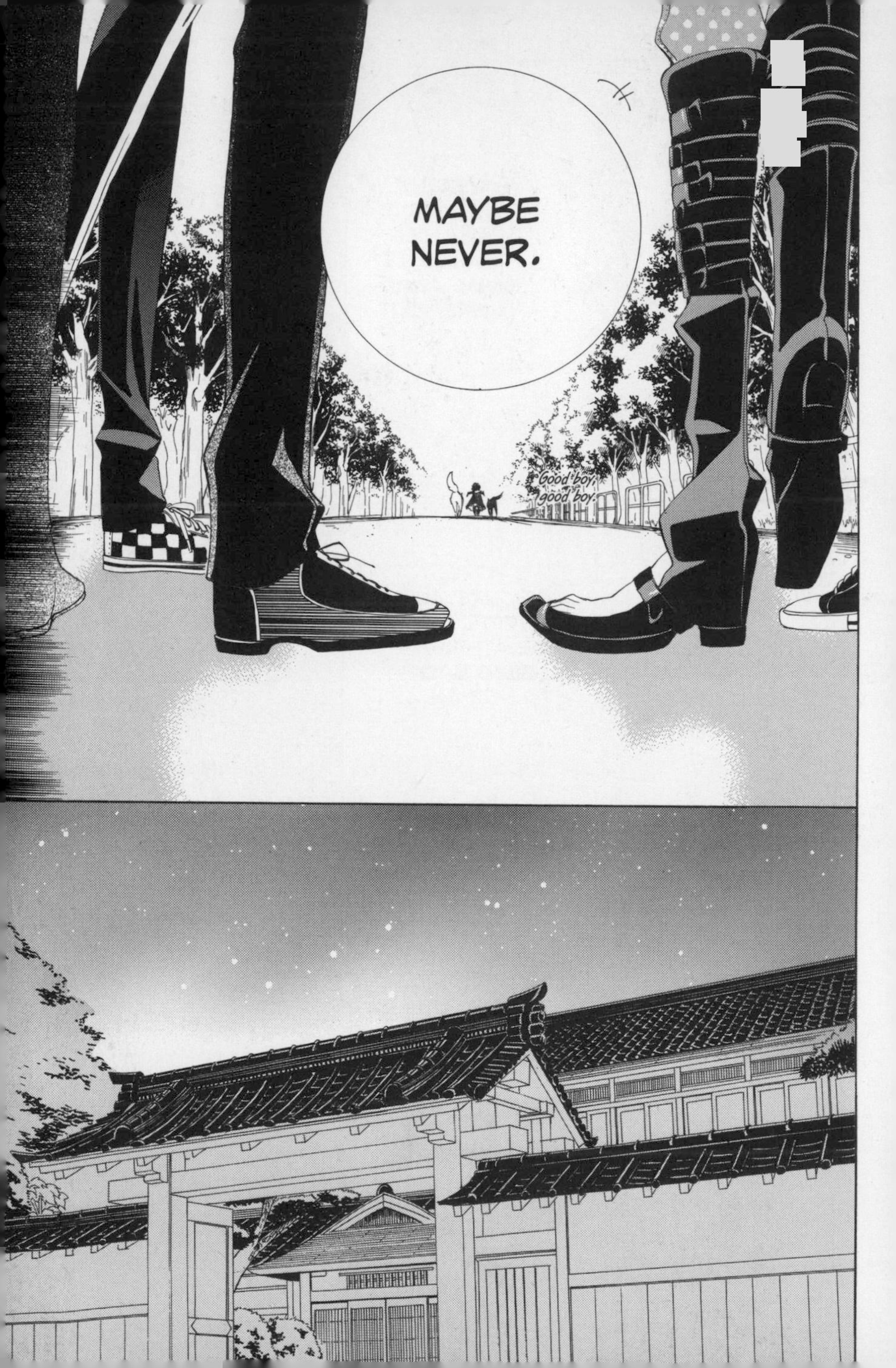
MAYBE NEVER.
Good boy, good boy.

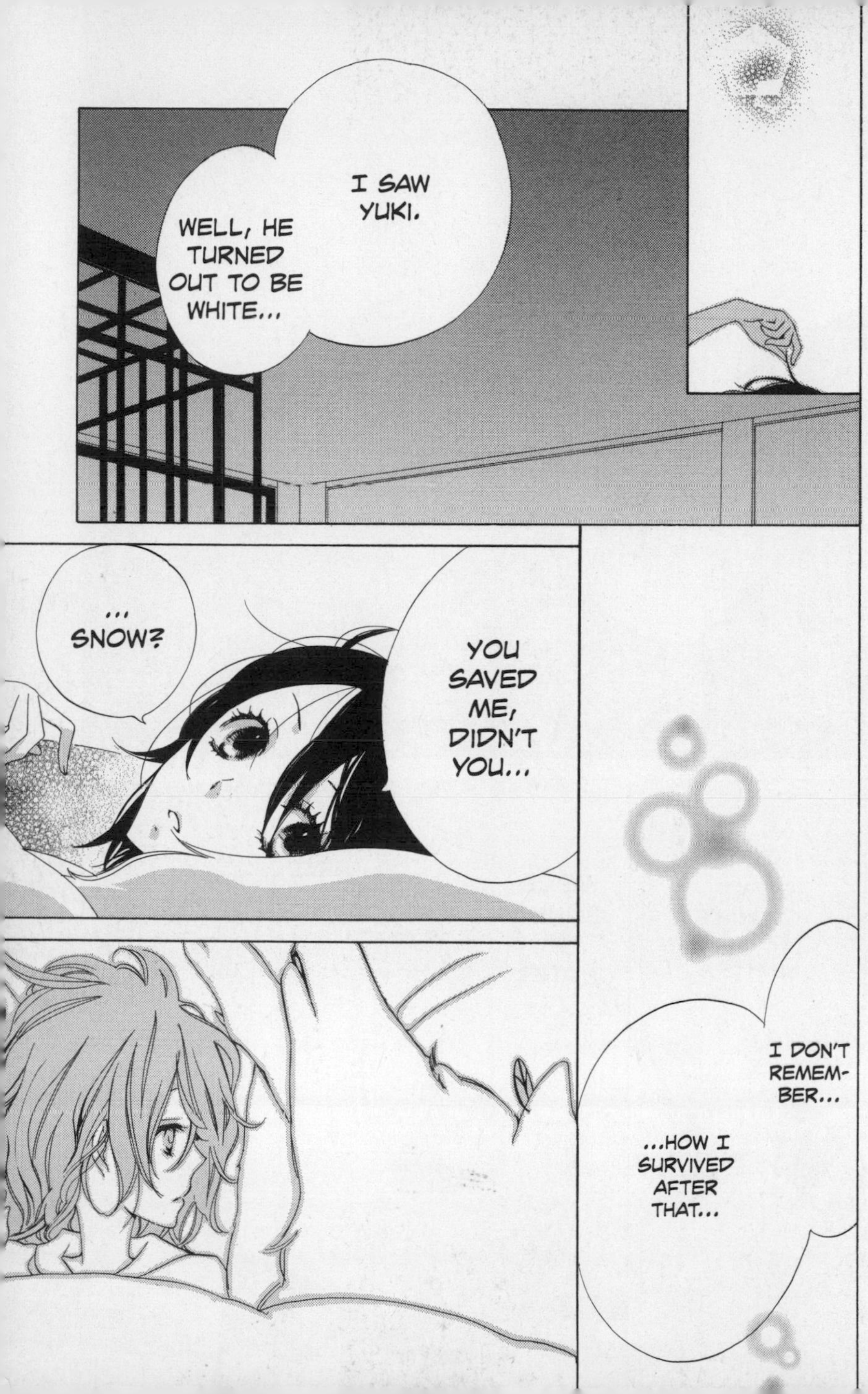
I SAW YUKI.
WELL, HE TURNED OUT TO BE WHITE...
I DON'T REMEMBER...
...HOW I SURVIVED AFTER THAT...
YOU SAVED ME, DIDN'T YOU...
... SNOW?

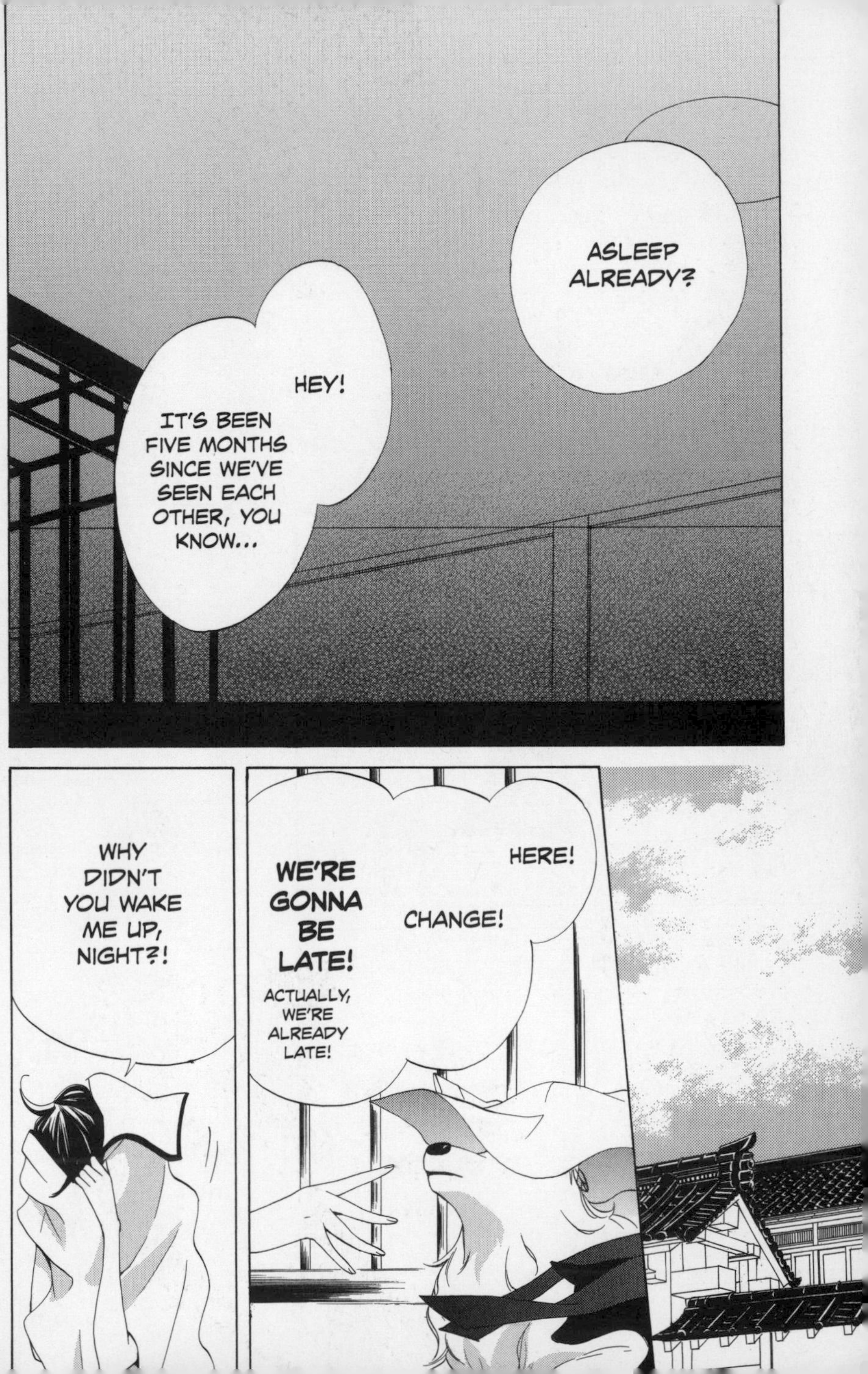
ASLEEP ALREADY?
HEY! IT'S BEEN FIVE MONTHS SINCE WE'VE SEEN EACH OTHER, YOU KNOW...
HERE!
CHANGE!
WE'RE GONNA BE LATE!
ACTUALLY, WE'RE ALREADY LATE!
WHY DIDN'T YOU WAKE ME UP, NIGHT?!

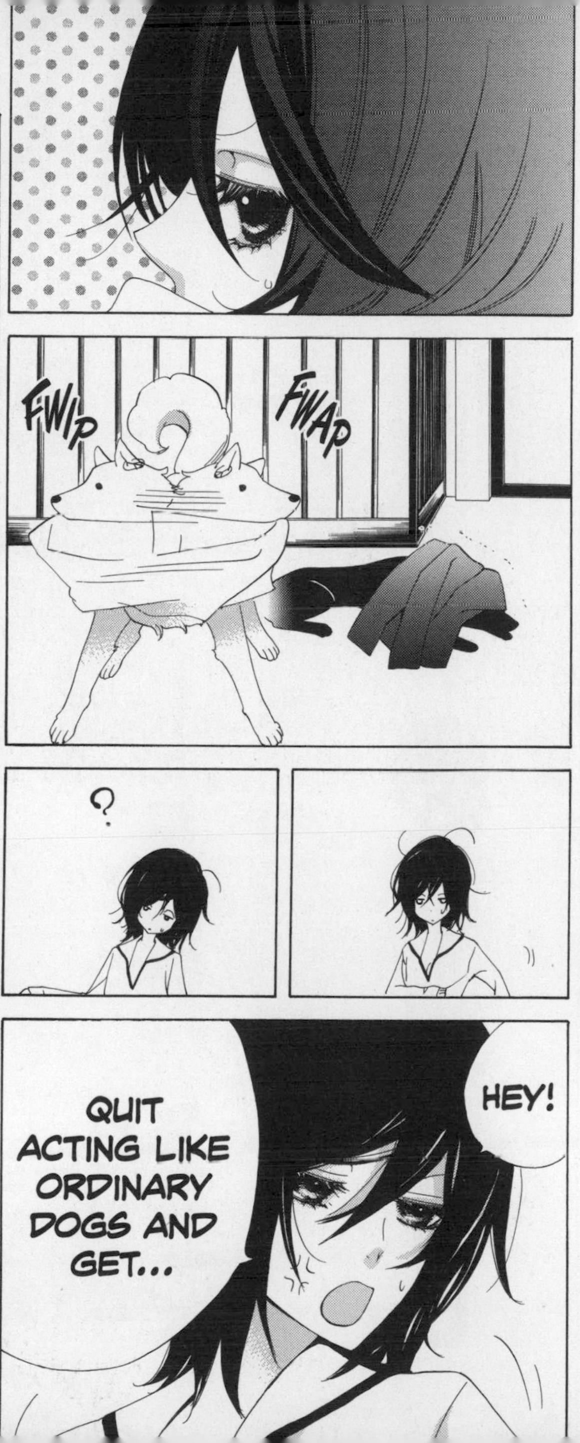
FWAP
FWIP
?
HEY!
QUIT ACTING LIKE ORDINARY DOGS AND GET...

Phew...
This is the final volume of *Jiu Jiu*! It took a while for volume 5 to come out, but thank you so much for waiting and supporting me all this time! It's not like I was taking a break from my work, you know!

December, 2008.
Hana-to-Yume Magazine, Issue 2
Chapter 1 One-Shot.

March...and so on, 2009.
Hana-to-Yume Magazine Issues 8-11
Chapters 2-5 continuously.

May...and so on, 2009.
Hana-to-Yume Magazine Issues V15-17, 19-21
Chapters 6-11 continuously.

December, 2009.
Series moved to *The-Hana-to-Yume*. (A bimonthly magazine).
February 1st to December 1st Issues
Chapters 12-17.

Series moved to *The-Hana-to-Yume Seasonal Magazine*. (It comes out once every three months)
May 1st, 2011-August 1st, 2012
Chapters 18-23.

...so, I was working on the series at designated times!

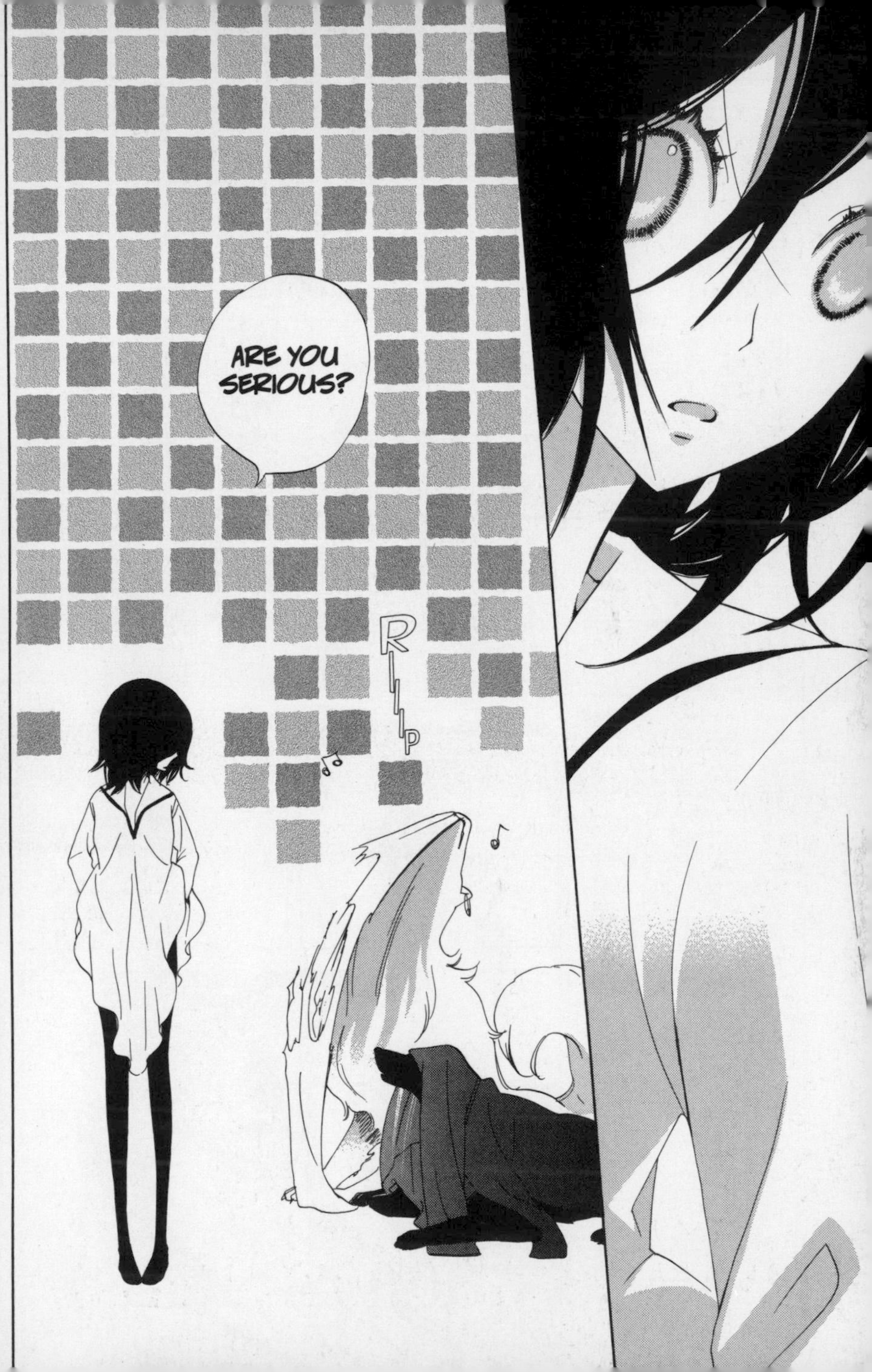
ARE YOU SERIOUS?
RIIIP

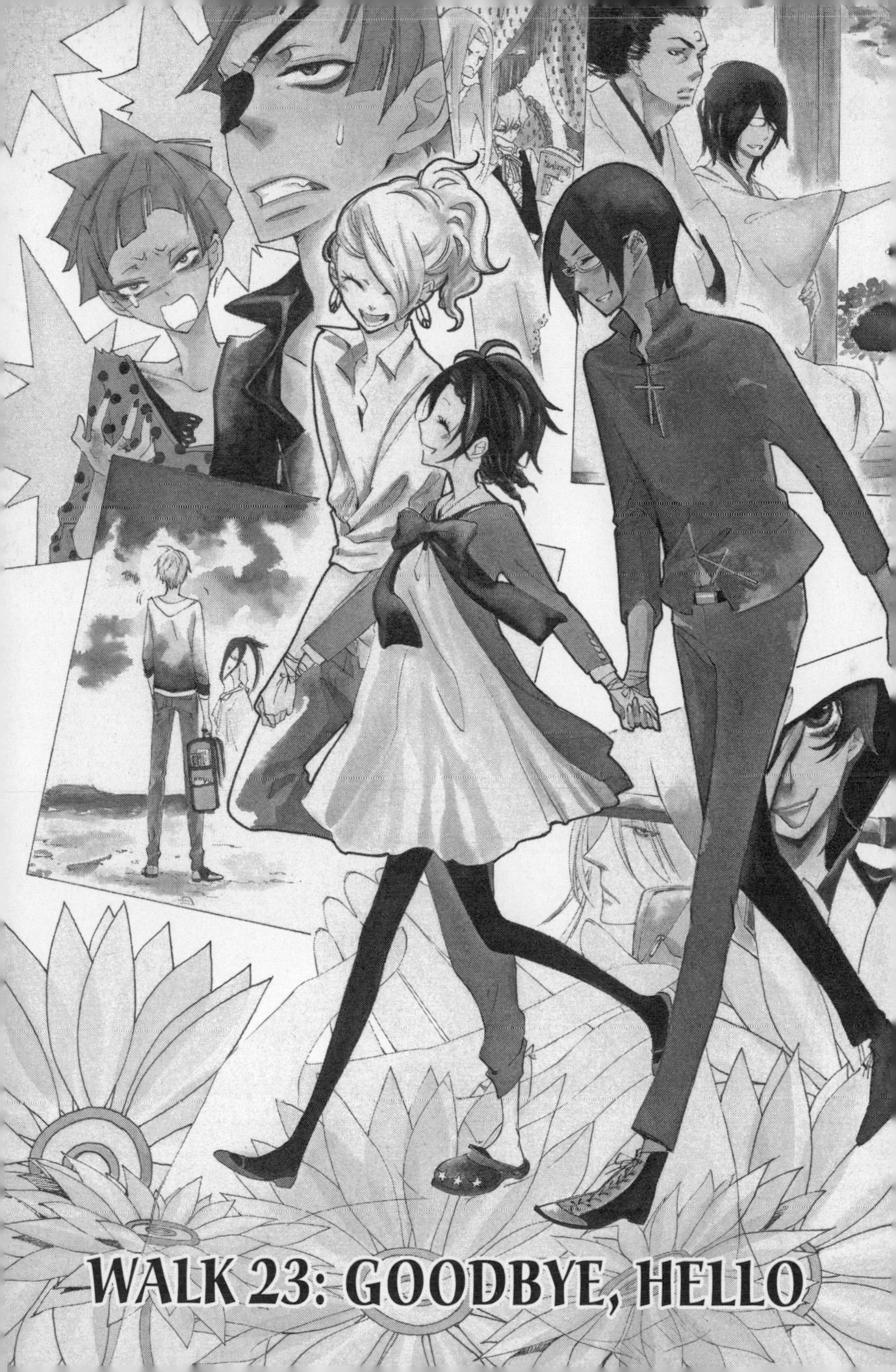

WALK 23: GOODBYE, HELLO

HEY,
TAKAMICHI...

THE REASON
MY FRONT
PAWS TURNED
INTO ARMS...

...IS SO THAT
I COULD
HOLD YOU.

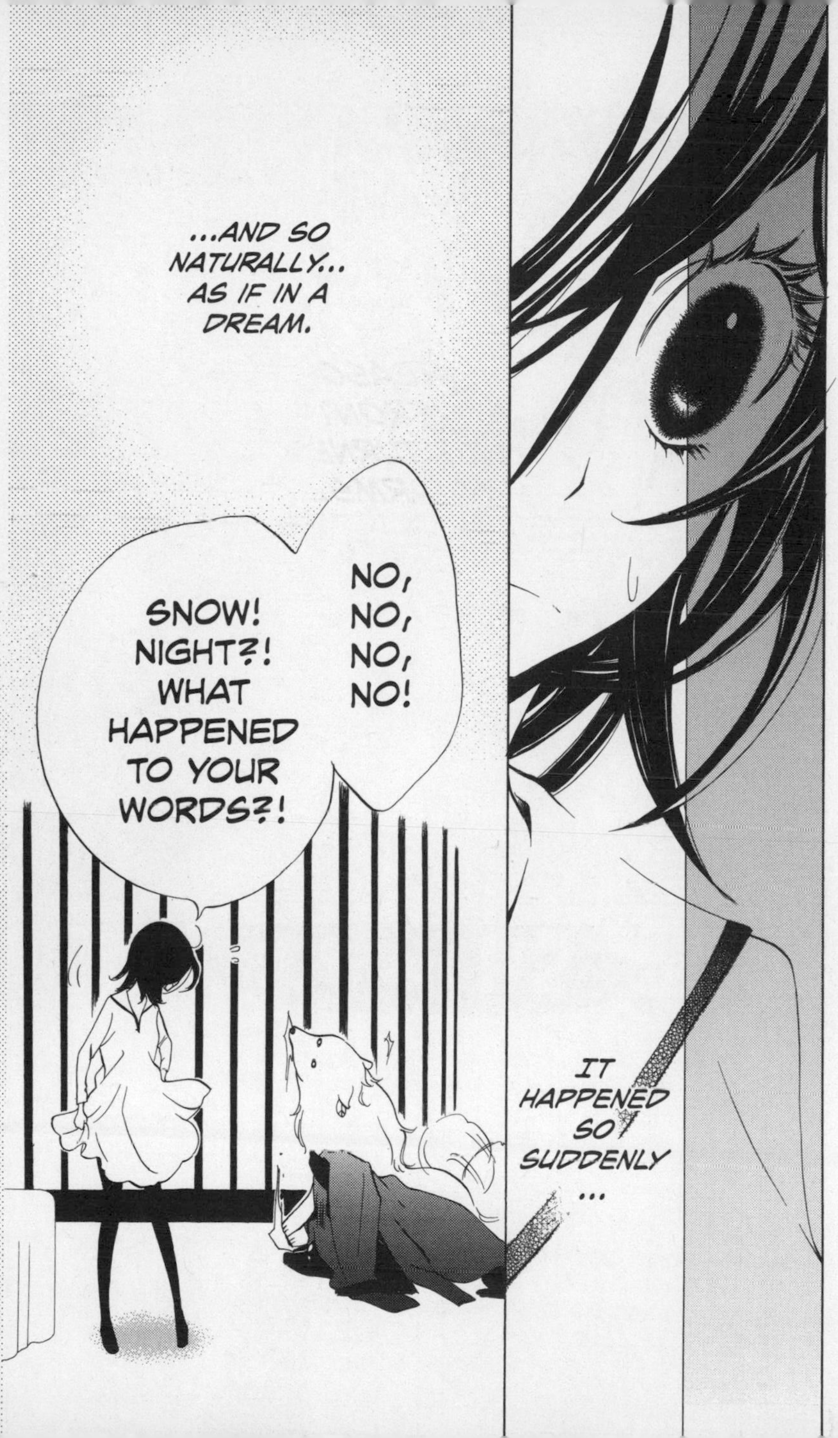
IT HAPPENED SO SUDDENLY ...
...AND SO NATURALLY... AS IF IN A DREAM.
NO, NO, NO, NO! SNOW! NIGHT?! WHAT HAPPENED TO YOUR WORDS?!

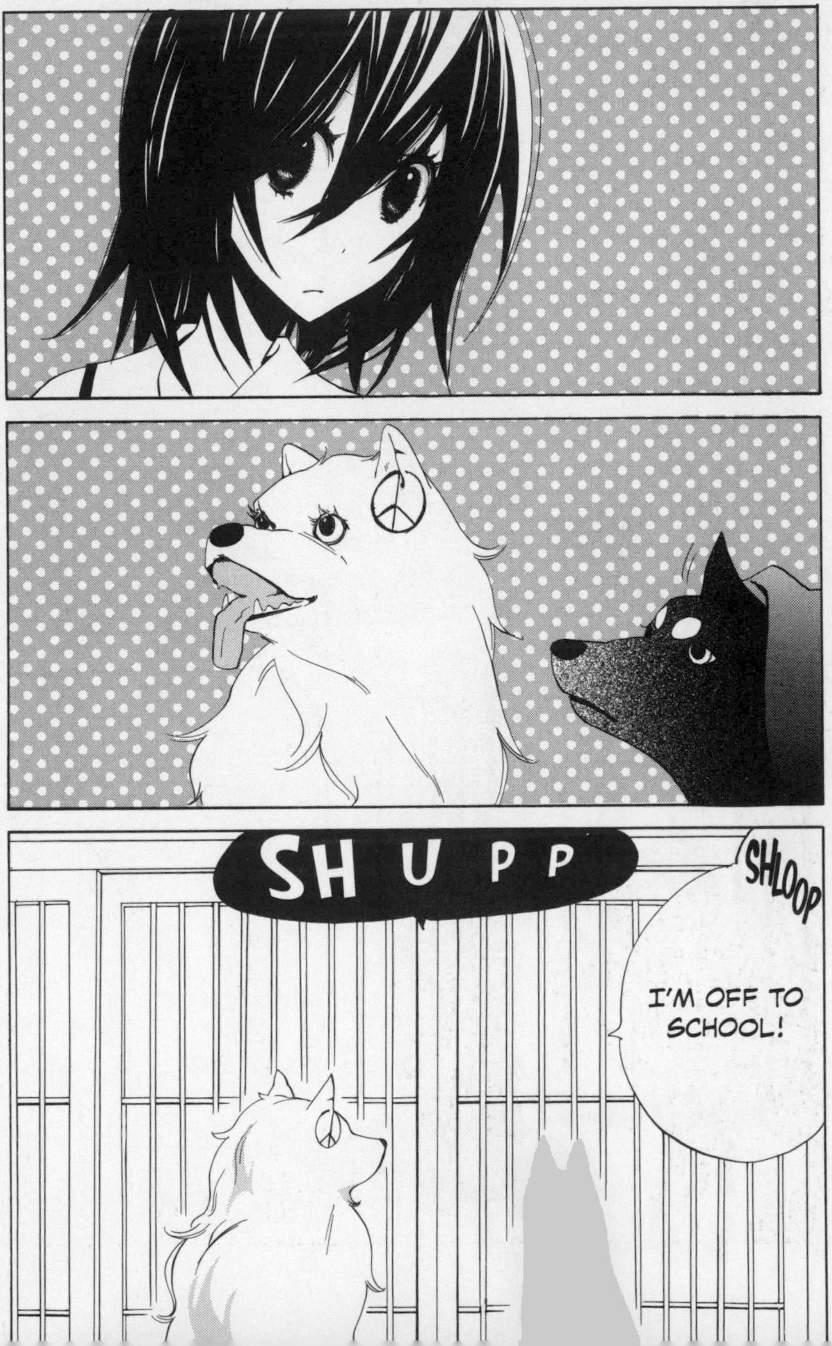
SHLOOP
I'M OFF TO SCHOOL!
SHUPP

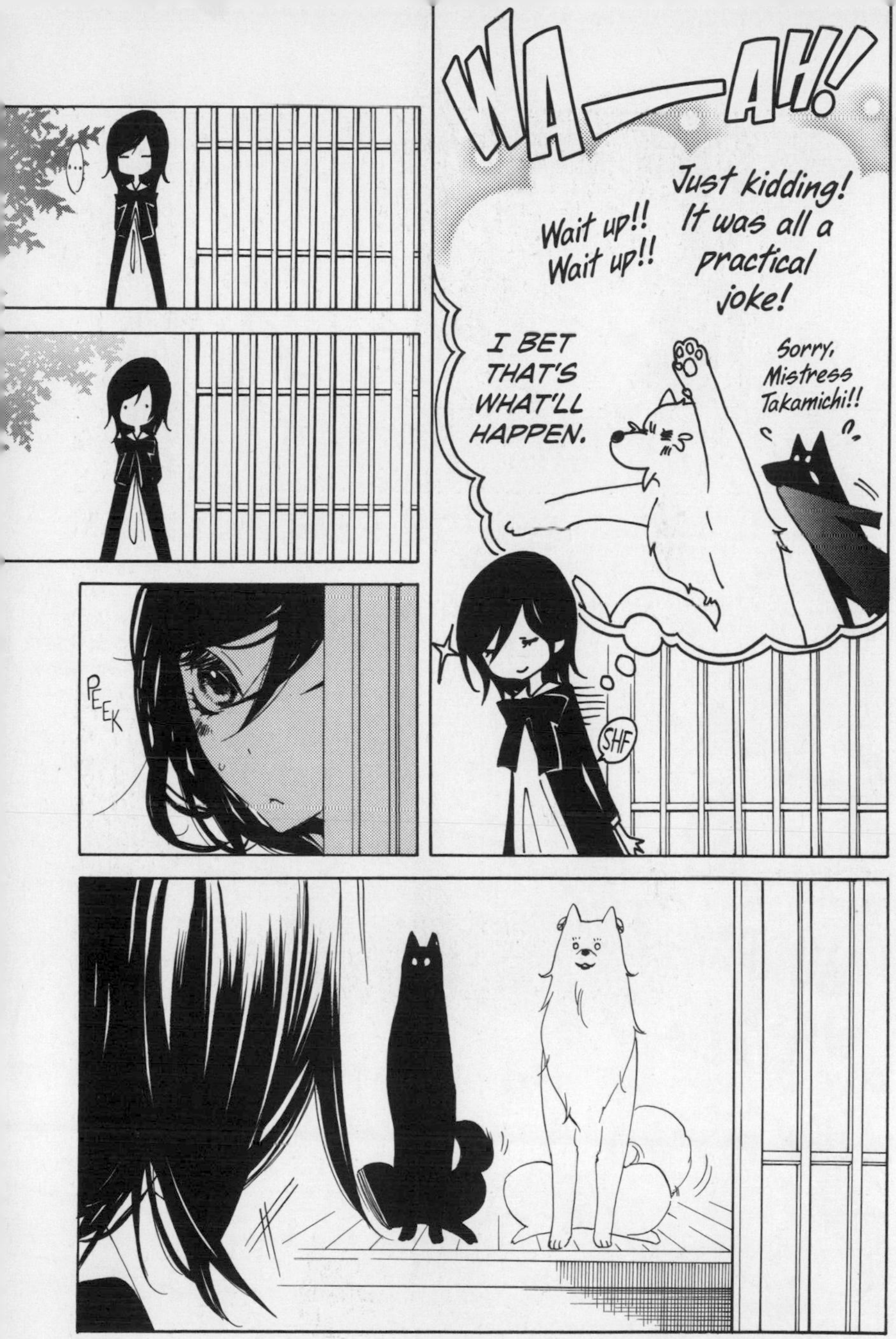
WA—AH!
Just kidding! It was all a practical joke!
Wait up!! Wait up!!
Sorry, Mistress Takamichi!!
I BET THAT'S WHAT'LL HAPPEN.
SHF
...
PEEK

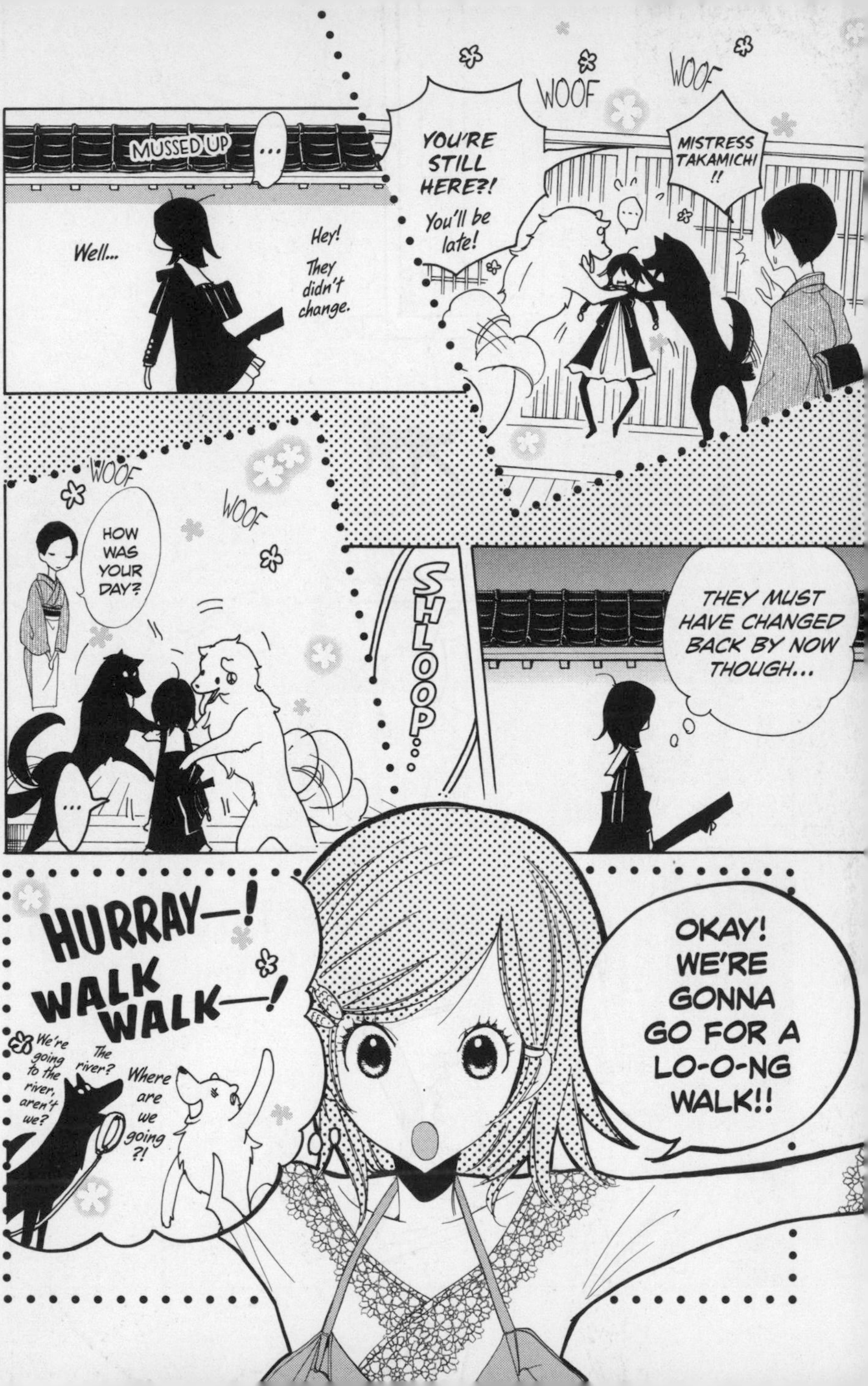
WOOF
WOOF
MISTRESS TAKAMICHI!!
YOU'RE STILL HERE?!
You'll be late!
...
...
MUSSED UP
Hey!
They didn't change.
Well...
THEY MUST HAVE CHANGED BACK BY NOW THOUGH...
SHLOOP...
WOOF
WOOF
HOW WAS YOUR DAY?
...
OKAY! WE'RE GONNA GO FOR A LO-O-NG WALK!!
HURRAY—!
WALK WALK—!
Where are we going?!
The river?
We're going to the river, aren't we?

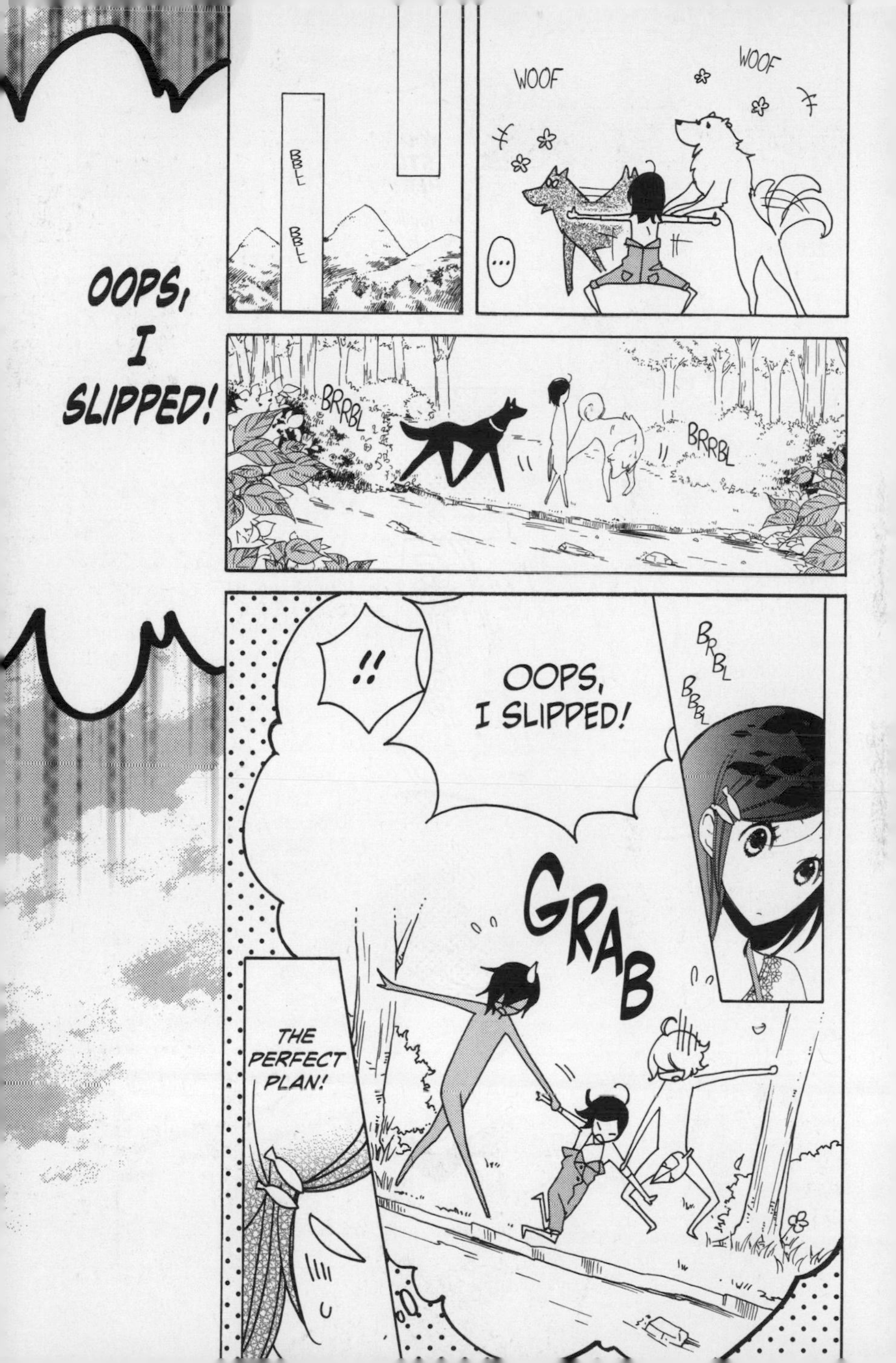

WOOF
WOOF
...
BBLL BBLL
BRRBL
BRRBL
BRBL
BBBL
!!
OOPS, I SLIPPED!
GRAB
THE PERFECT PLAN!
OOPS, I SLIPPED!

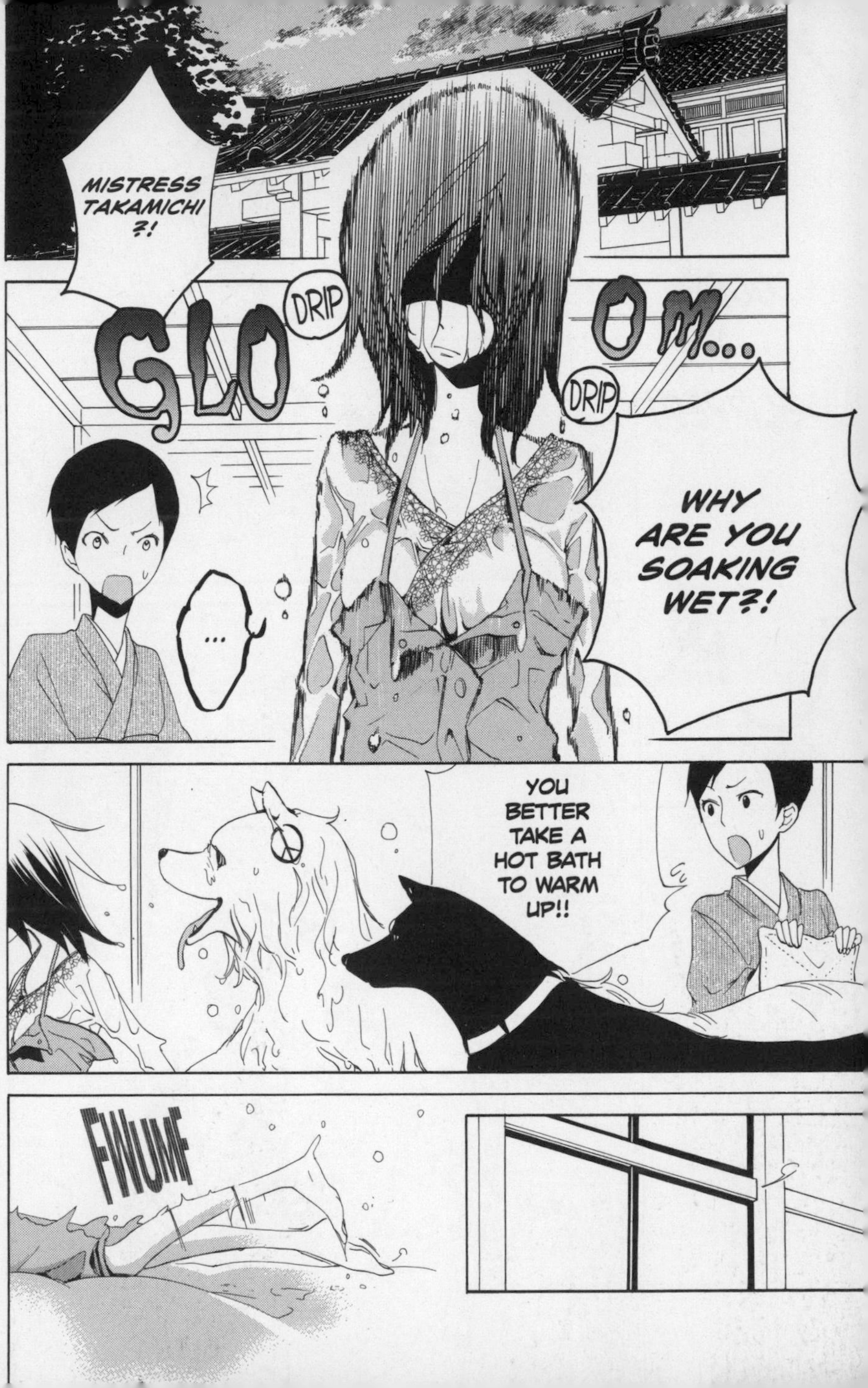
MISTRESS TAKAMICHI ?!
GLO
DRIP
OM...
DRIP
WHY ARE YOU SOAKING WET?!
...
YOU BETTER TAKE A HOT BATH TO WARM UP!!
FWUMF

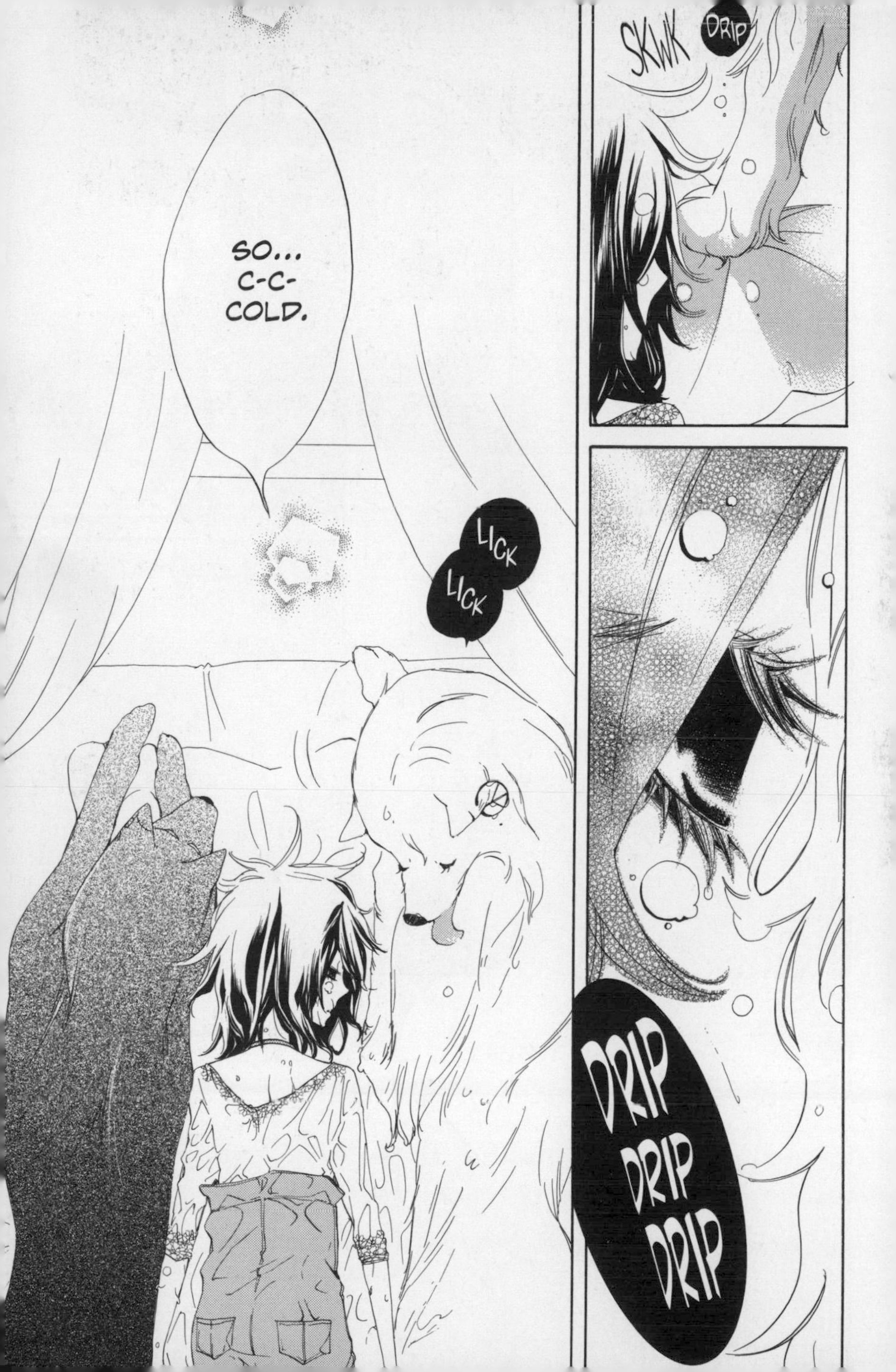
SKWK
DRIP
DRIP
DRIP
DRIP
SO... C-C- COLD.
LICK
LICK

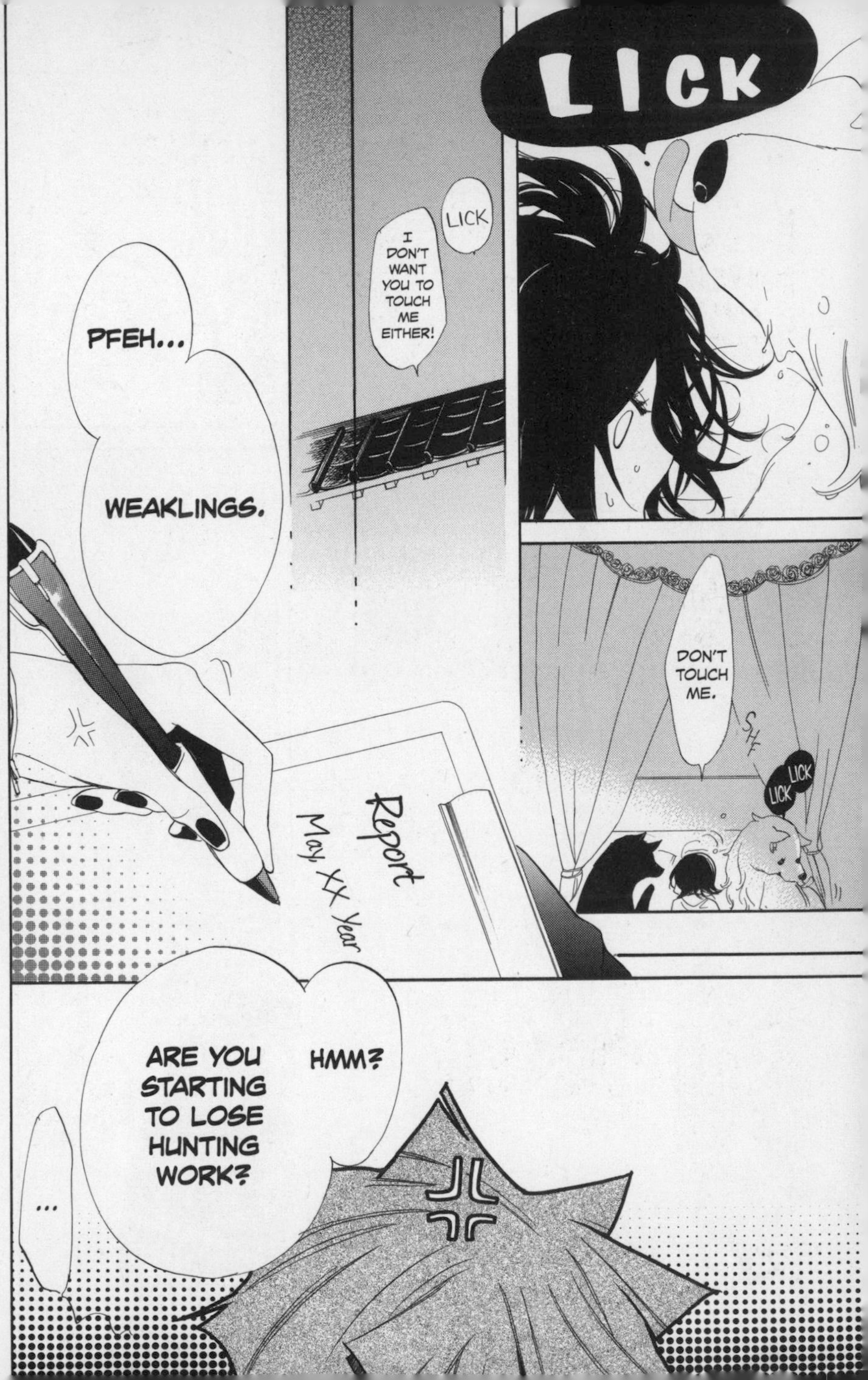
LICK
DON'T TOUCH ME.
SHF
LICK
LICK
LICK
I DON'T WANT YOU TO TOUCH ME EITHER!
PFEH...
WEAKLINGS.
Report
May, XX Year
HMM?
ARE YOU STARTING TO LOSE HUNTING WORK?
...

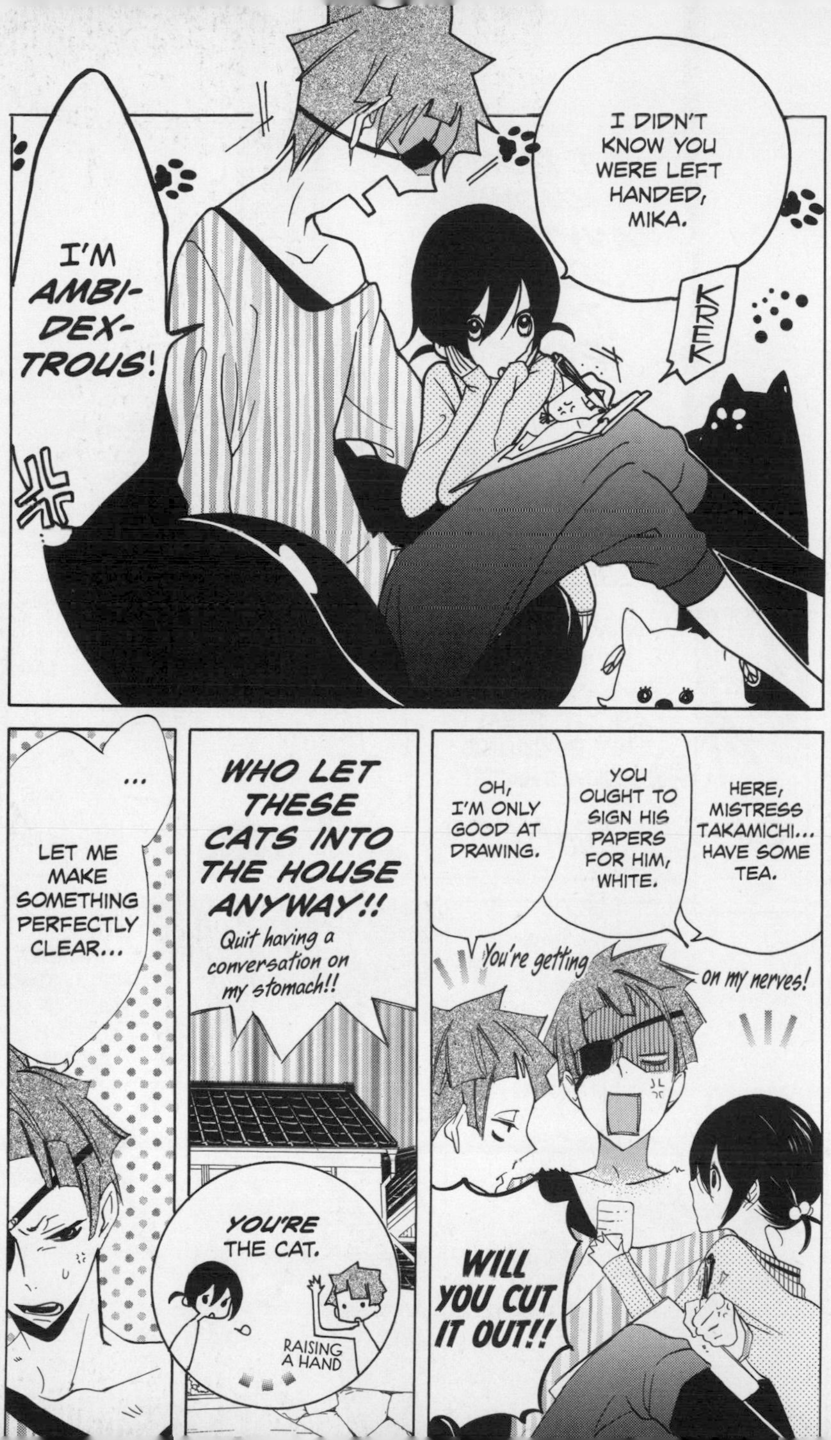
I DIDN'T KNOW YOU WERE LEFT HANDED, MIKA.
KREK
I'M AMBI-DEX-TROUS!
HERE, MISTRESS TAKAMICHI... HAVE SOME TEA.
YOU OUGHT TO SIGN HIS PAPERS FOR HIM, WHITE.
OH, I'M ONLY GOOD AT DRAWING.
You're getting on my nerves!
WILL YOU CUT IT OUT!!
WHO LET THESE CATS INTO THE HOUSE ANYWAY!!
Quit having a conversation on my stomach!!
YOU'RE THE CAT.
RAISING A HAND
...
LET ME MAKE SOMETHING PERFECTLY CLEAR...

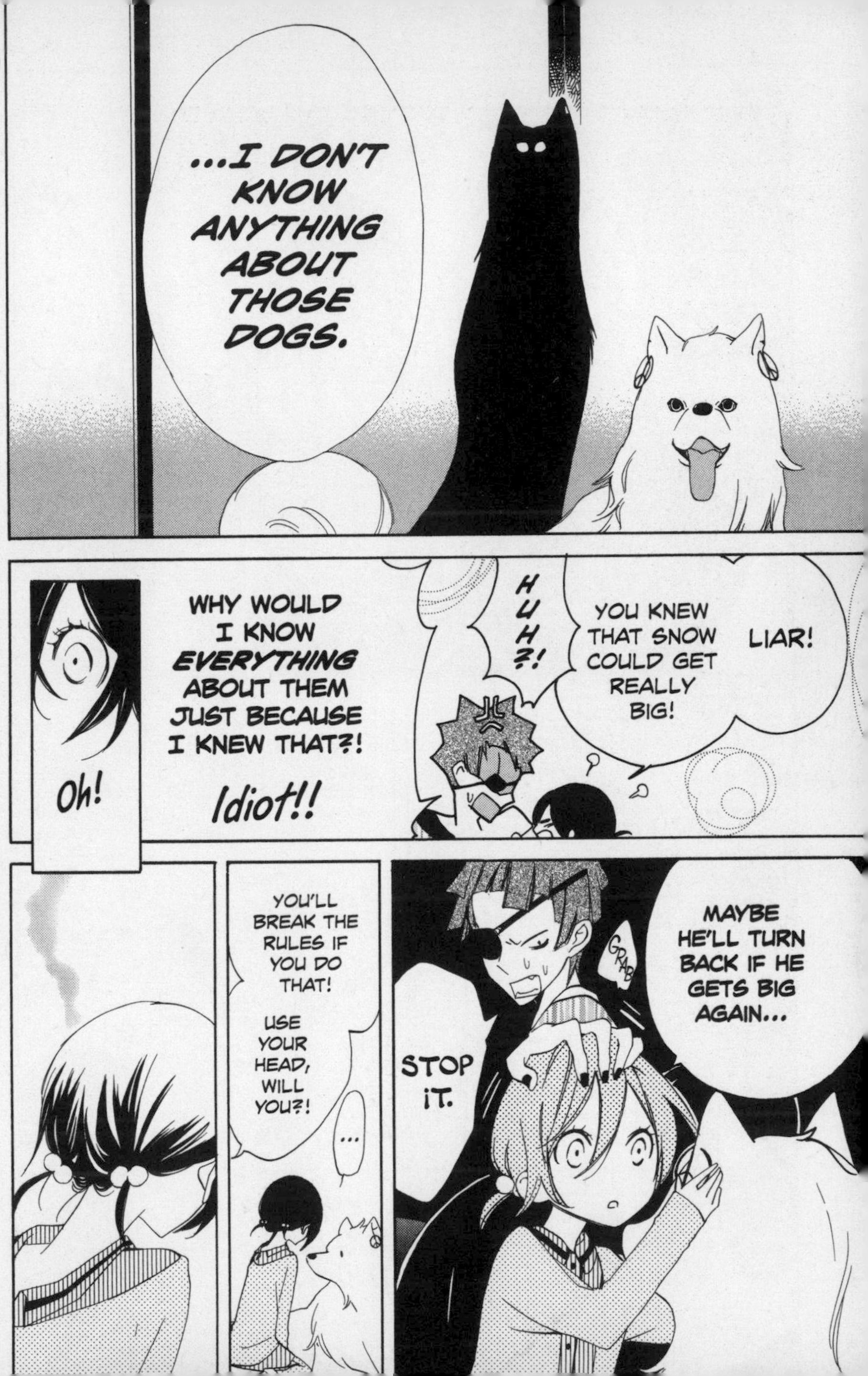
...I DON'T KNOW ANYTHING ABOUT THOSE DOGS.
LIAR!
YOU KNEW THAT SNOW COULD GET REALLY BIG!
HUH?!
WHY WOULD I KNOW EVERYTHING ABOUT THEM JUST BECAUSE I KNEW THAT?!
Idiot!!
Oh!
MAYBE HE'LL TURN BACK IF HE GETS BIG AGAIN...
GRAB
STOP IT.
YOU'LL BREAK THE RULES IF YOU DO THAT!
USE YOUR HEAD, WILL YOU?!
...

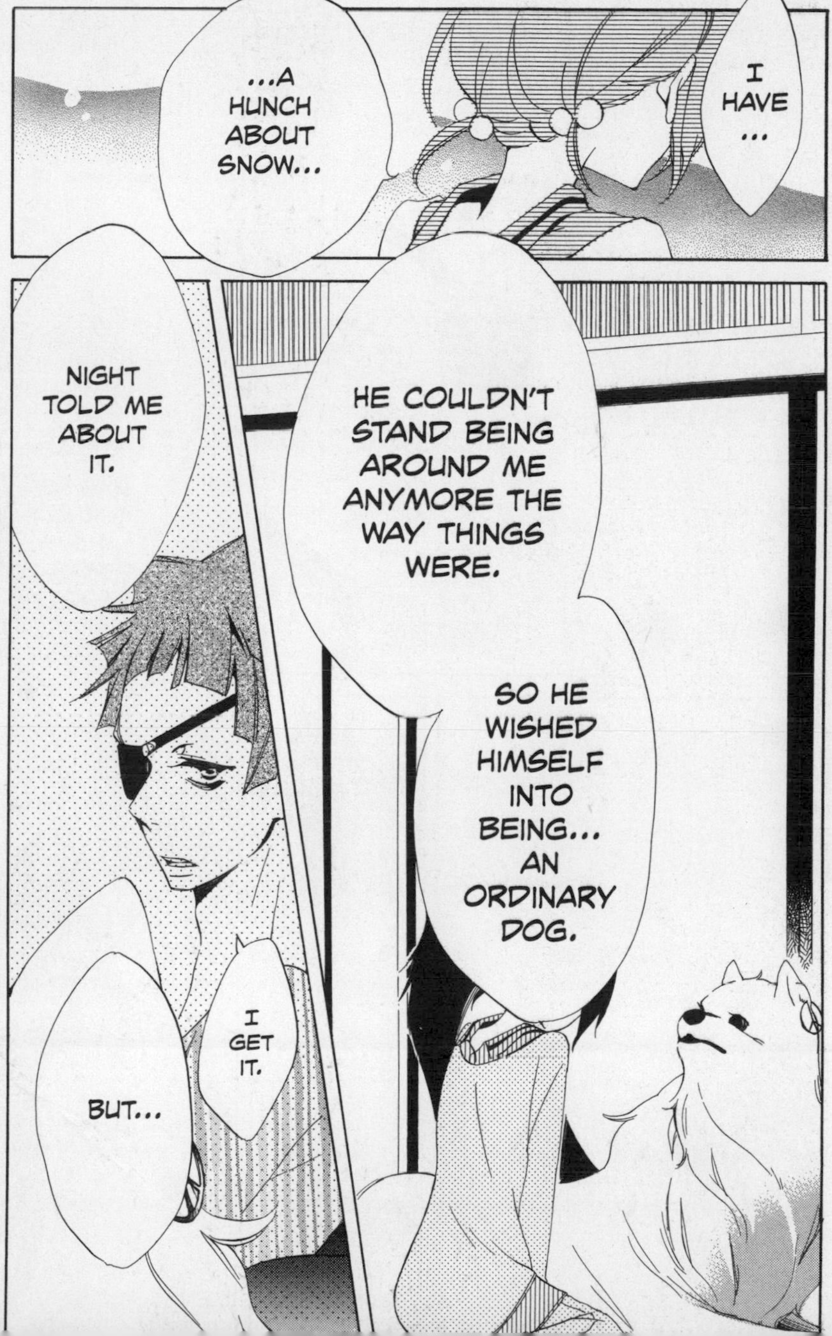
I HAVE...
...A HUNCH ABOUT SNOW...
HE COULDN'T STAND BEING AROUND ME ANYMORE THE WAY THINGS WERE.
SO HE WISHED HIMSELF INTO BEING... AN ORDINARY DOG.
NIGHT TOLD ME ABOUT IT.
I GET IT.
BUT...

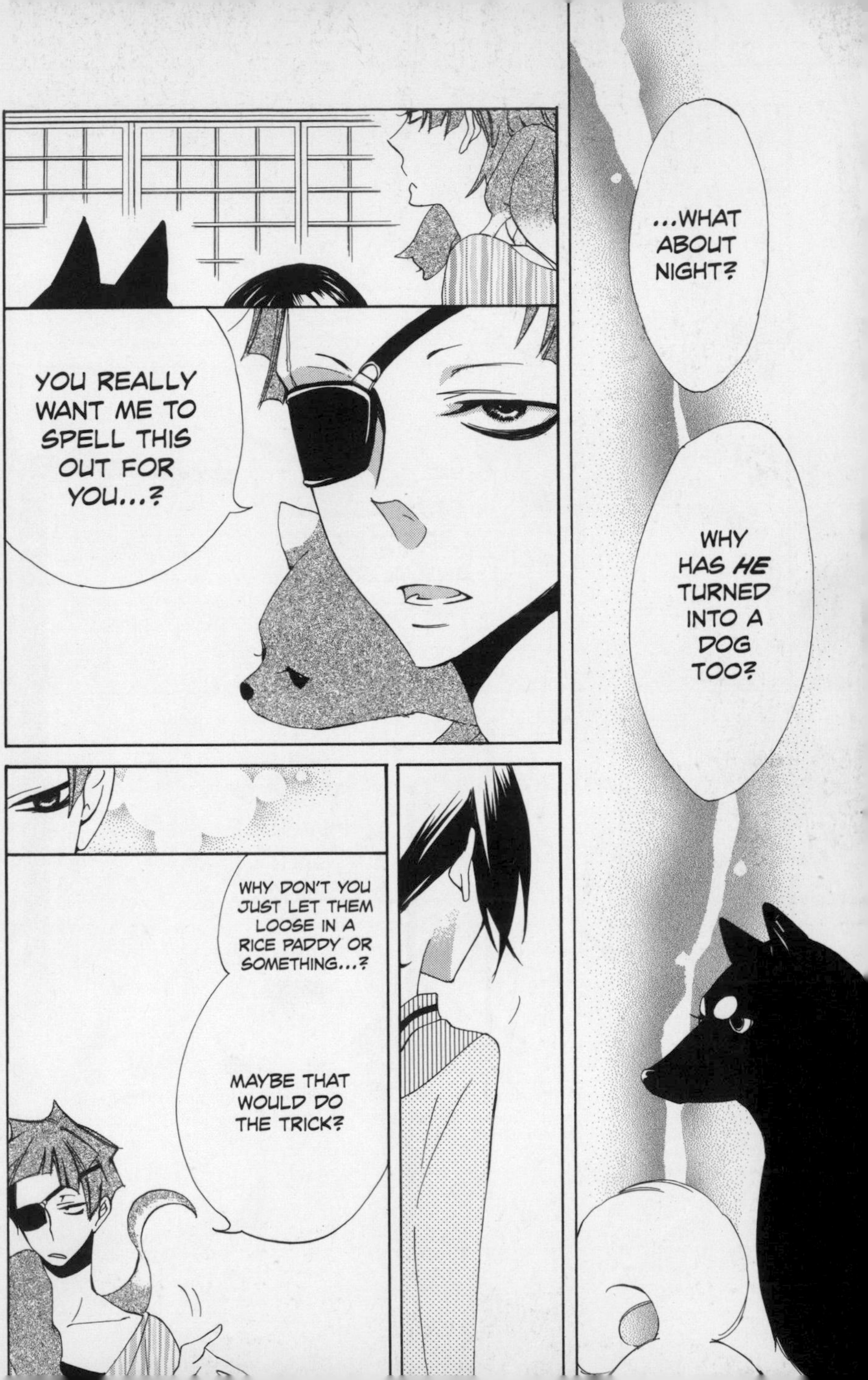
...WHAT ABOUT NIGHT?
WHY HAS *HE* TURNED INTO A DOG TOO?
YOU REALLY WANT ME TO SPELL THIS OUT FOR YOU...?
WHY DON'T YOU JUST LET THEM LOOSE IN A RICE PADDY OR SOMETHING...?
MAYBE THAT WOULD DO THE TRICK?

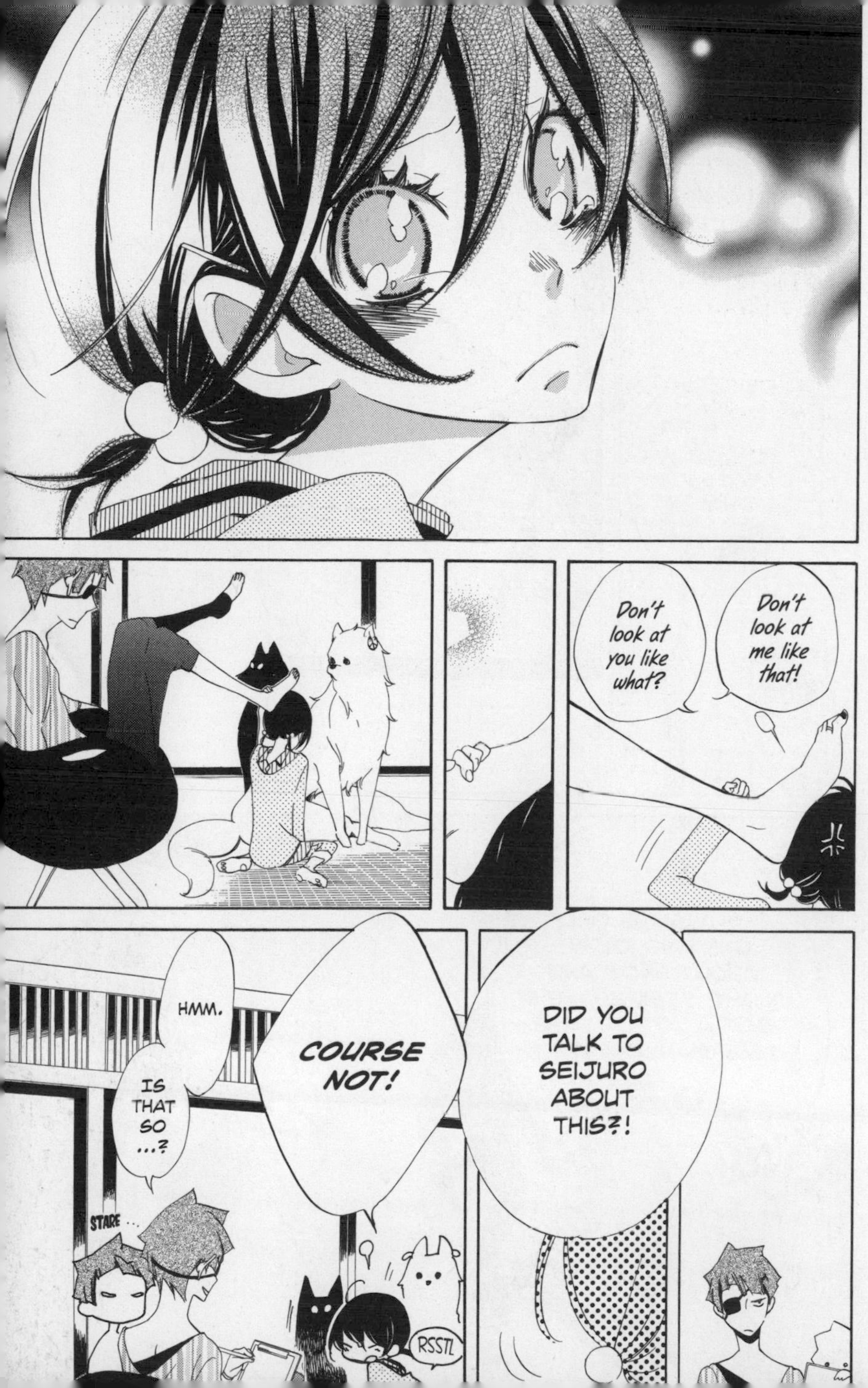

Don't look at me like that!
Don't look at you like what?
DID YOU TALK TO SEIJURO ABOUT THIS?!
COURSE NOT!
HMM.
IS THAT SO ...?
STARE ...
RSSTL

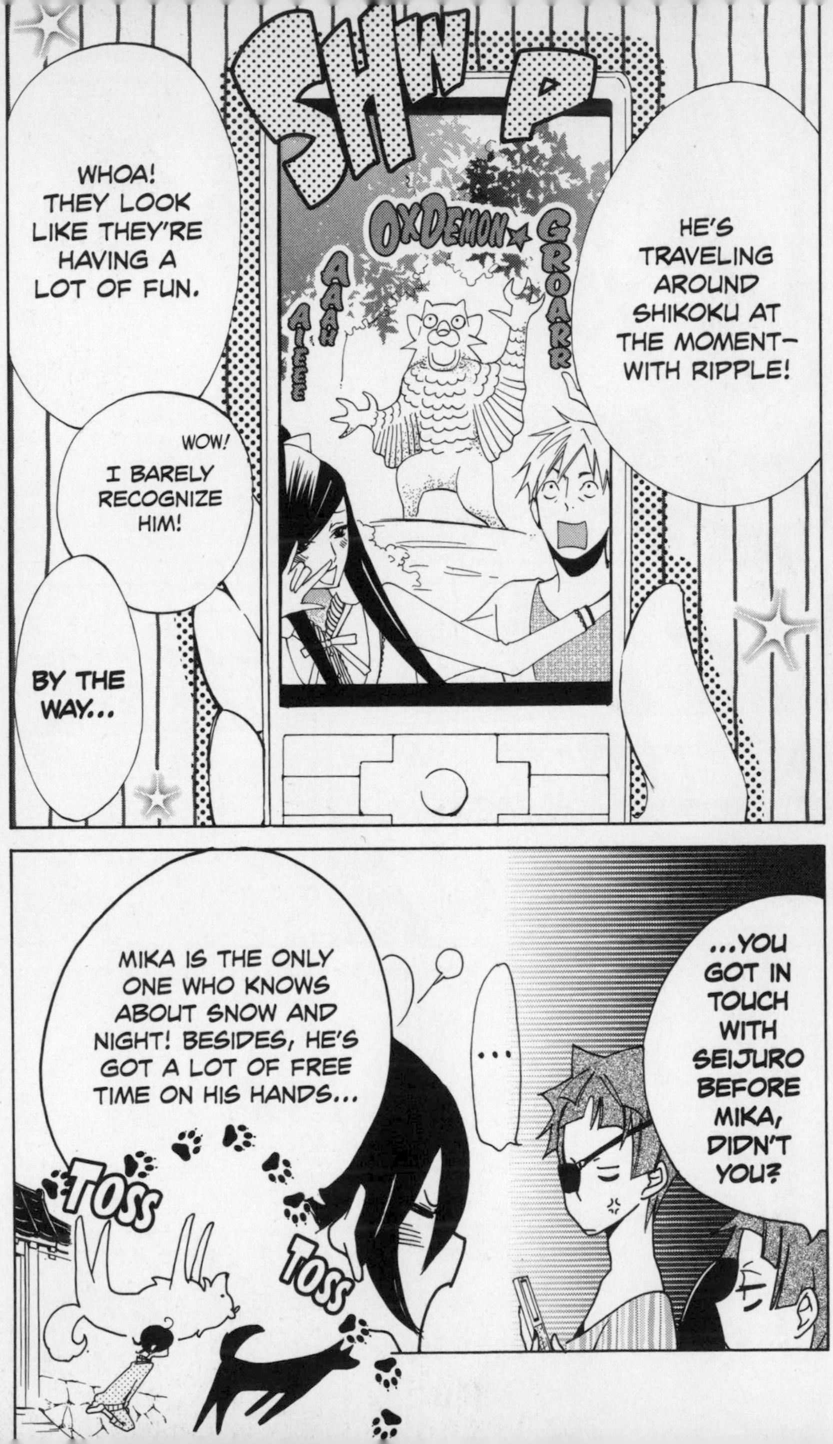
SHWP
HE'S TRAVELING AROUND SHIKOKU AT THE MOMENT—WITH RIPPLE!
OXDEMON★
GROARR
AAAH
AIEEE
WHOA! THEY LOOK LIKE THEY'RE HAVING A LOT OF FUN.
WOW! I BARELY RECOGNIZE HIM!
BY THE WAY...
...YOU GOT IN TOUCH WITH SEIJURO BEFORE MIKA, DIDN'T YOU?
...
MIKA IS THE ONLY ONE WHO KNOWS ABOUT SNOW AND NIGHT! BESIDES, HE'S GOT A LOT OF FREE TIME ON HIS HANDS...
TOSS
TOSS

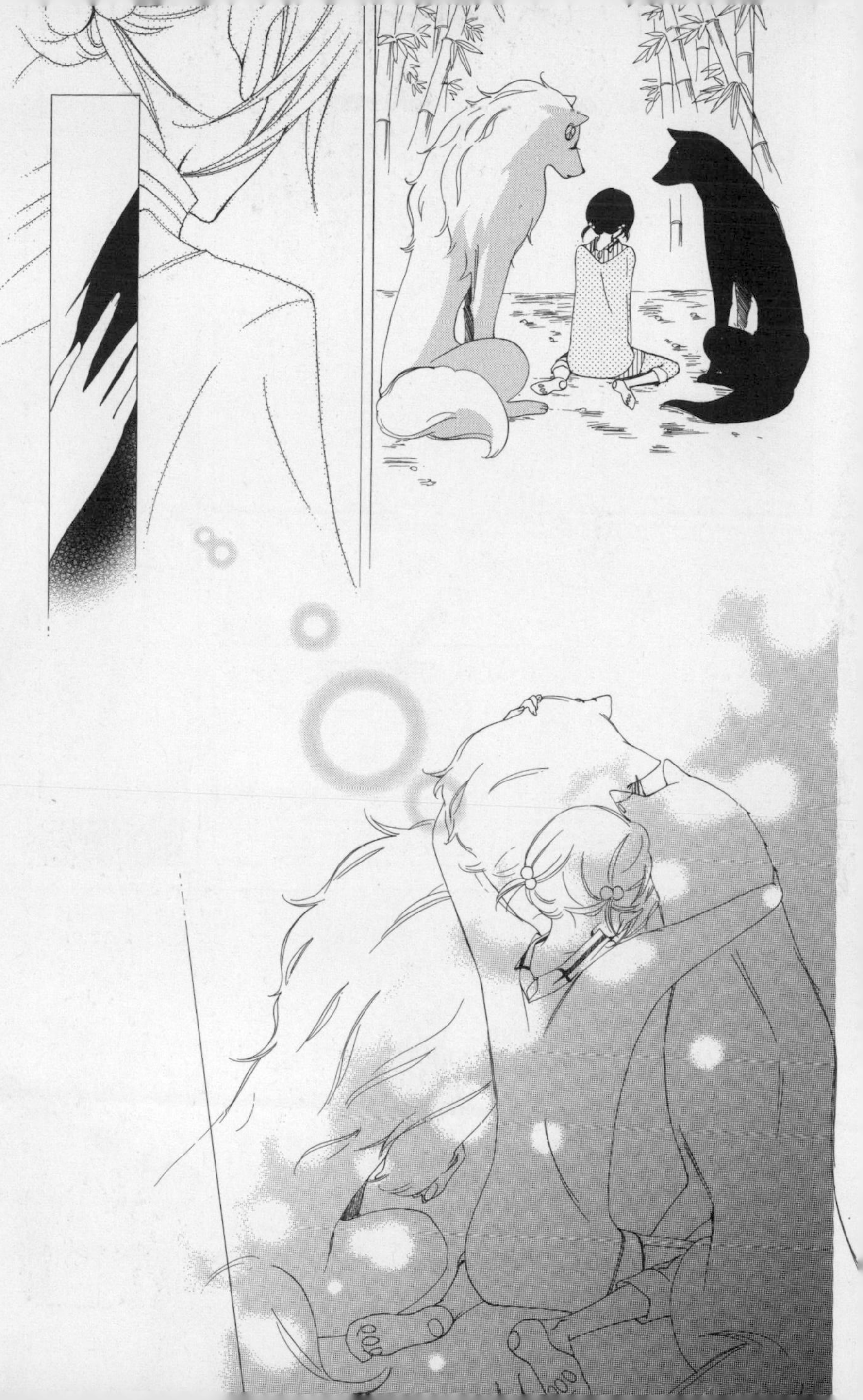

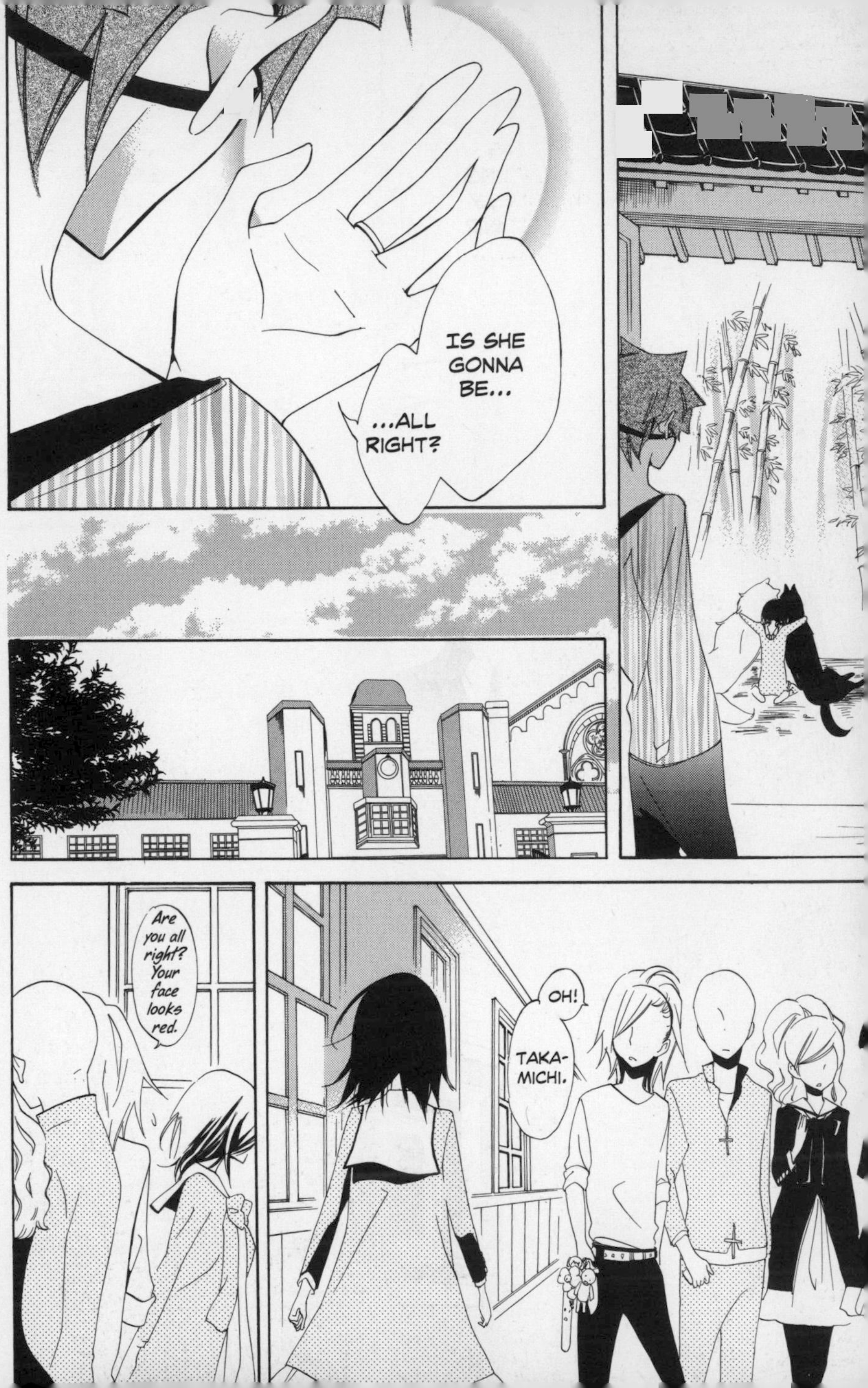
IS SHE GONNA BE...
...ALL RIGHT?
OH!
TAKA-MICHI.
Are you all right? Your face looks red.

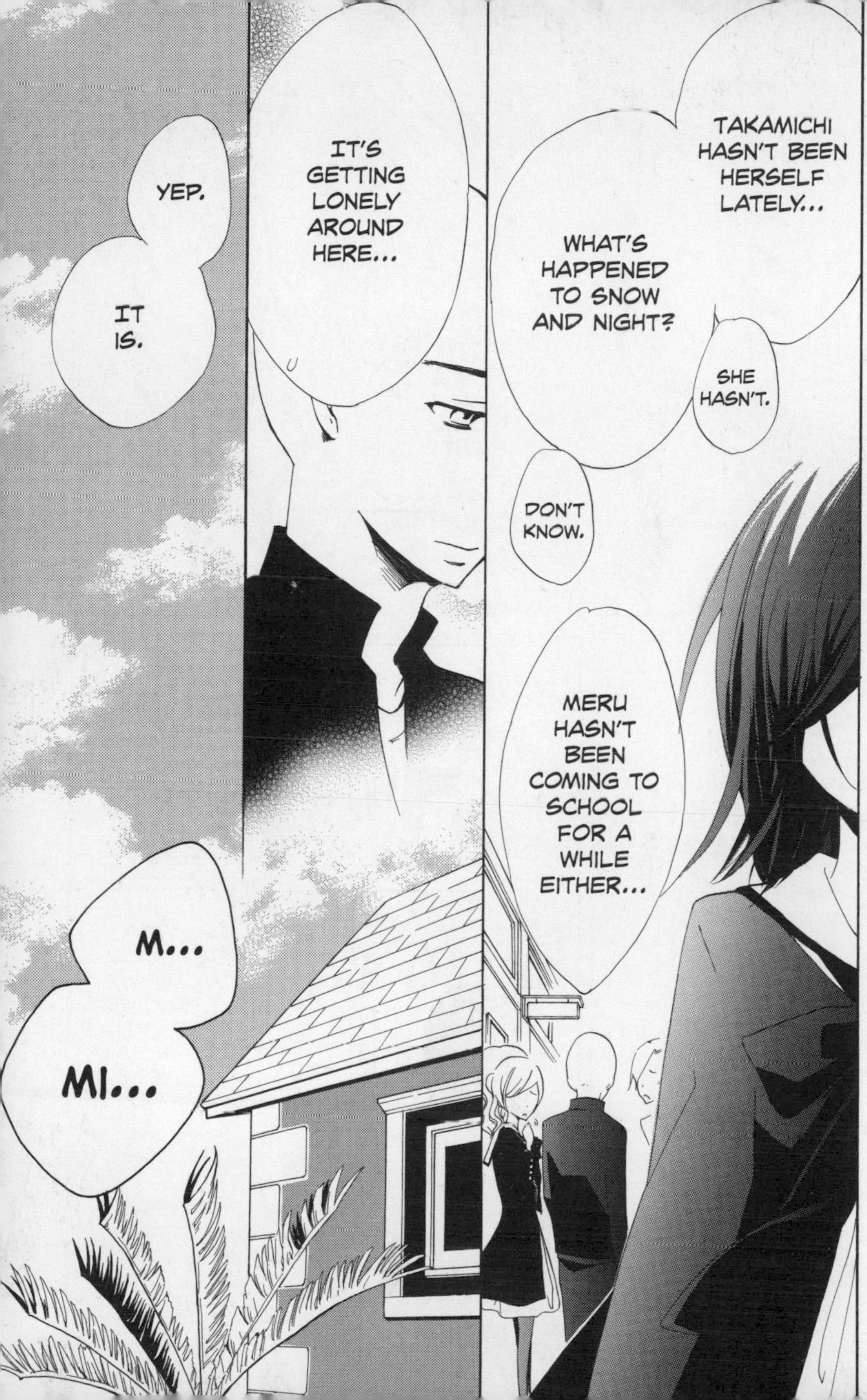
TAKAMICHI HASN'T BEEN HERSELF LATELY...
WHAT'S HAPPENED TO SNOW AND NIGHT?
SHE HASN'T.
DON'T KNOW.
MERU HASN'T BEEN COMING TO SCHOOL FOR A WHILE EITHER...
IT'S GETTING LONELY AROUND HERE...
YEP.
IT IS.
M...
MI...

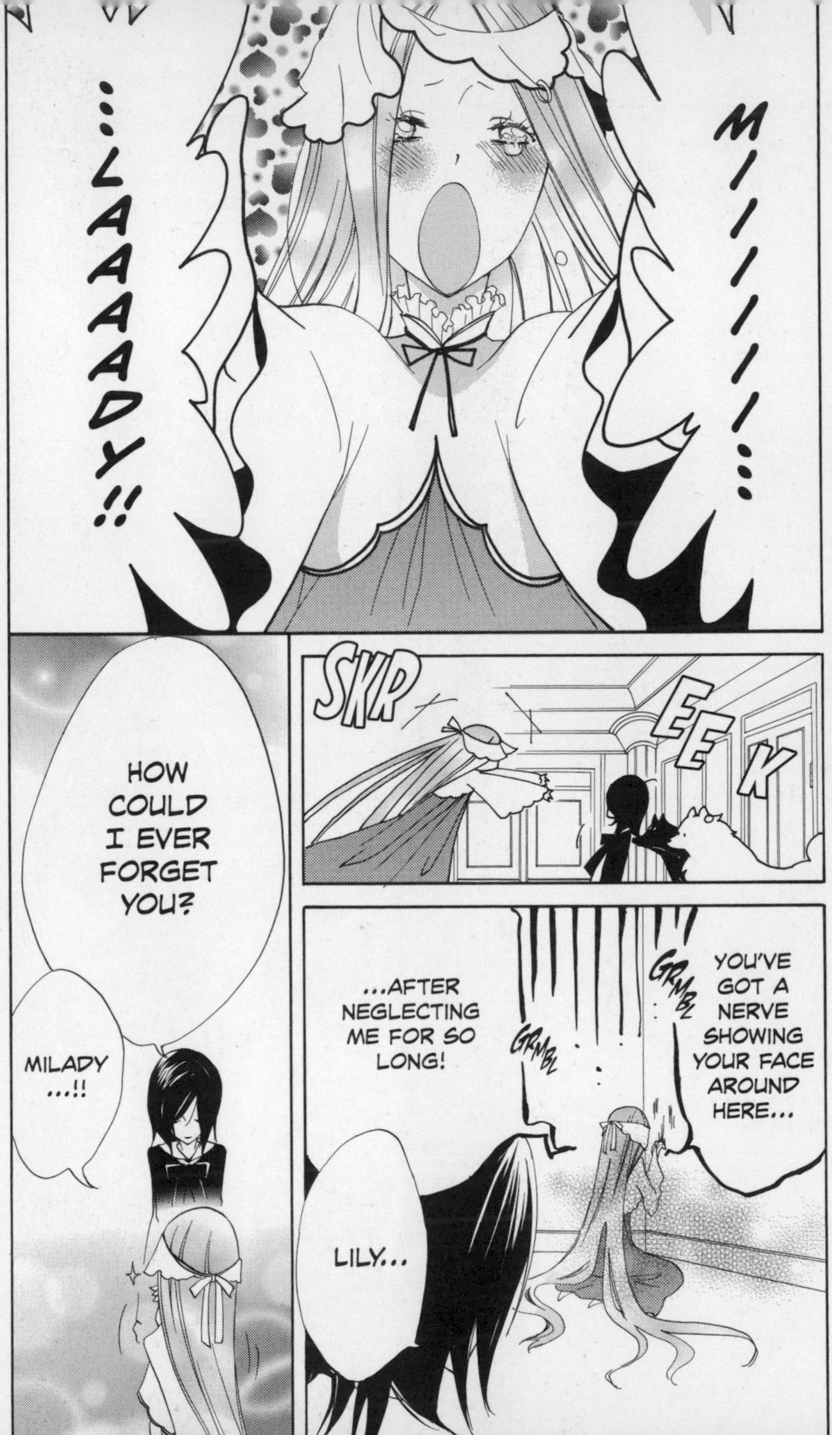
MI—————…
…LAAAAADY!!
SKR
EEEK
YOU'VE GOT A NERVE SHOWING YOUR FACE AROUND HERE…
GRMBL
GRMBL
…AFTER NEGLECTING ME FOR SO LONG!
LILY…
HOW COULD I EVER FORGET YOU?
MILADY …!!

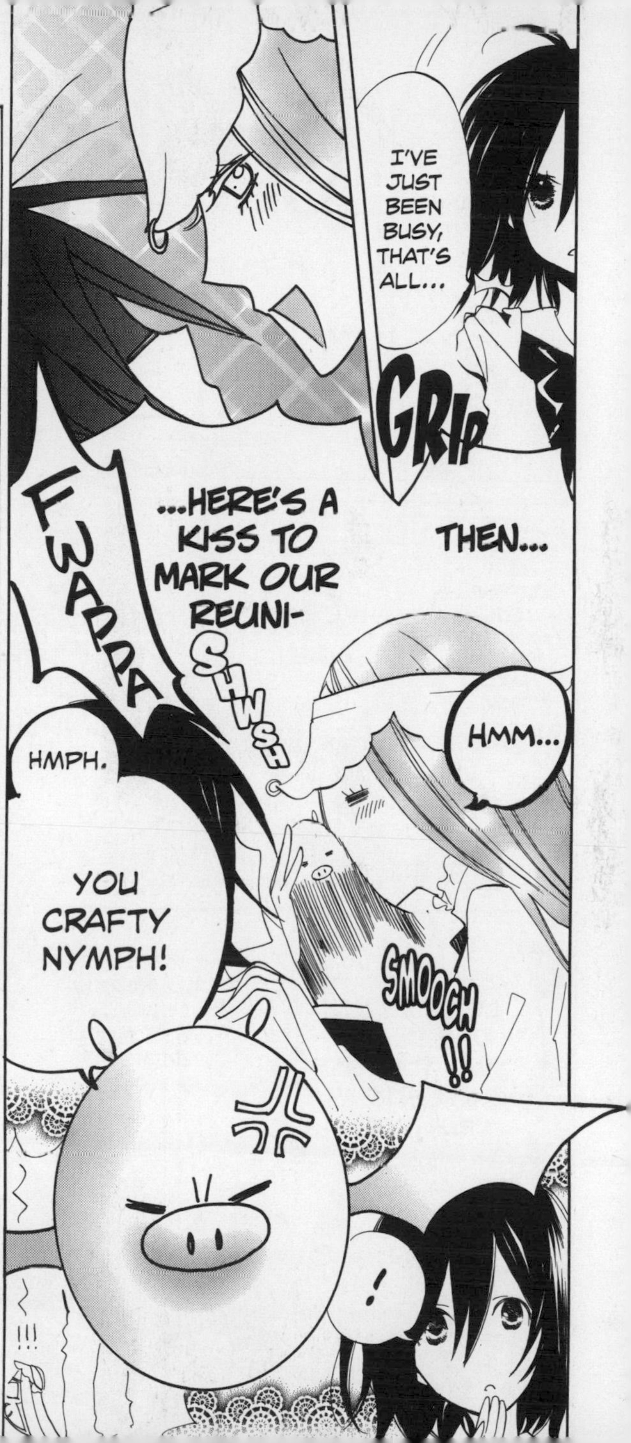
I'VE JUST BEEN BUSY, THAT'S ALL...
GRIP
THEN...
...HERE'S A KISS TO MARK OUR REUNI-
SHWSH
FWAPPA
HMM...
SMOOCH!!
HMPH.
YOU CRAFTY NYMPH!
!
!!!

In the beginning,
I was working on this series alongside my series *Sarashi-Asobi*.

During vol. 5, I was working on this series alongside *Roppan!!*.

I complained a lot, but I had so much fun thanks to the support of all my readers! I'm actually working on this at the same time as *Roppan!!*.

I'm worried you'll be unsatisfied with a lot of parts because I just couldn't spend enough time on vol. 5....
But please, give me a smile and forgive me!

Well then...
Thank you very, very much for following *Jiu Jiu* all the way to the end!

I know it sounds selfish, but I'd be overjoyed if you could continue to support me by reading *Roppan!!*.

With lots of love...

Touya Tobina

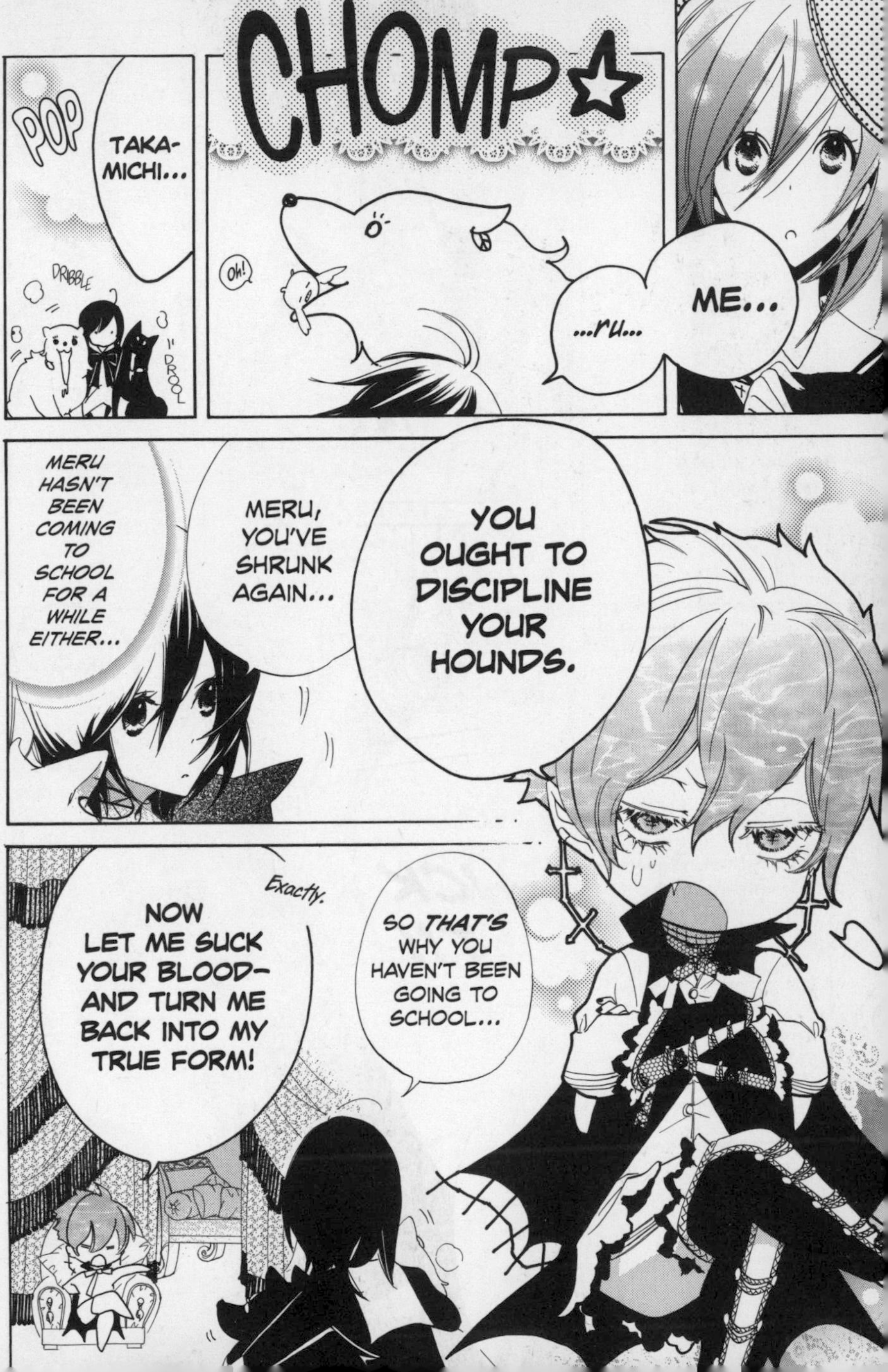
ME...
...ru...
CHOMP☆
Oh!
POP
TAKA-MICHI...
DRIBBLE
DROOL
YOU OUGHT TO DISCIPLINE YOUR HOUNDS.
MERU, YOU'VE SHRUNK AGAIN...
MERU HASN'T BEEN COMING TO SCHOOL FOR A WHILE EITHER...
SO *THAT'S* WHY YOU HAVEN'T BEEN GOING TO SCHOOL...
Exactly.
NOW LET ME SUCK YOUR BLOOD—AND TURN ME BACK INTO MY TRUE FORM!

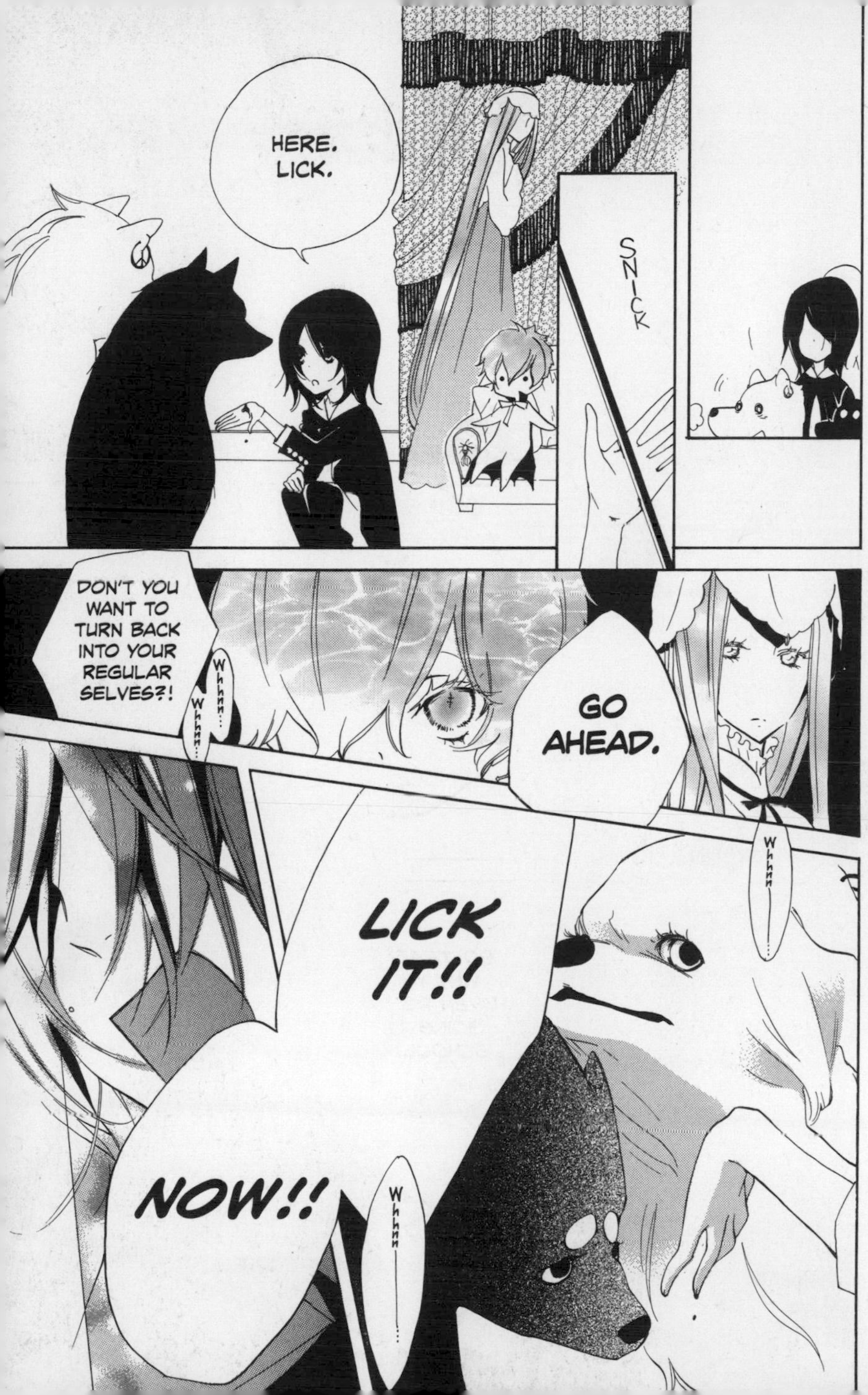
SNICK
HERE. LICK.
GO AHEAD.
DON'T YOU WANT TO TURN BACK INTO YOUR REGULAR SELVES?!
Whhn...
Whhn...
Whhn...
LICK IT!!
NOW!!
Whhn...

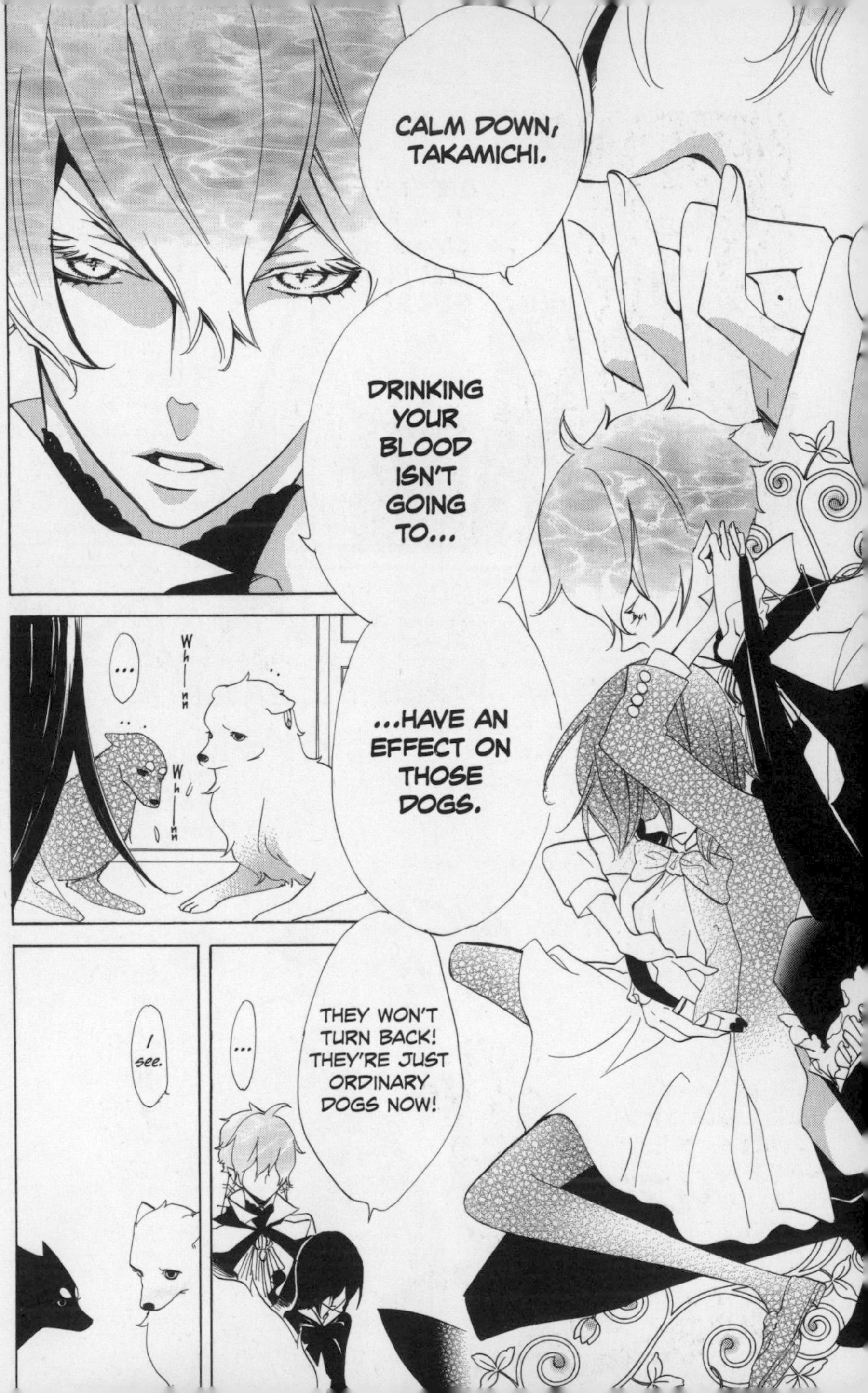
CALM DOWN, TAKAMICHI.
DRINKING YOUR BLOOD ISN'T GOING TO...
...HAVE AN EFFECT ON THOSE DOGS.
THEY WON'T TURN BACK! THEY'RE JUST ORDINARY DOGS NOW!
...
Whinn
...
Whinn
...
I see.

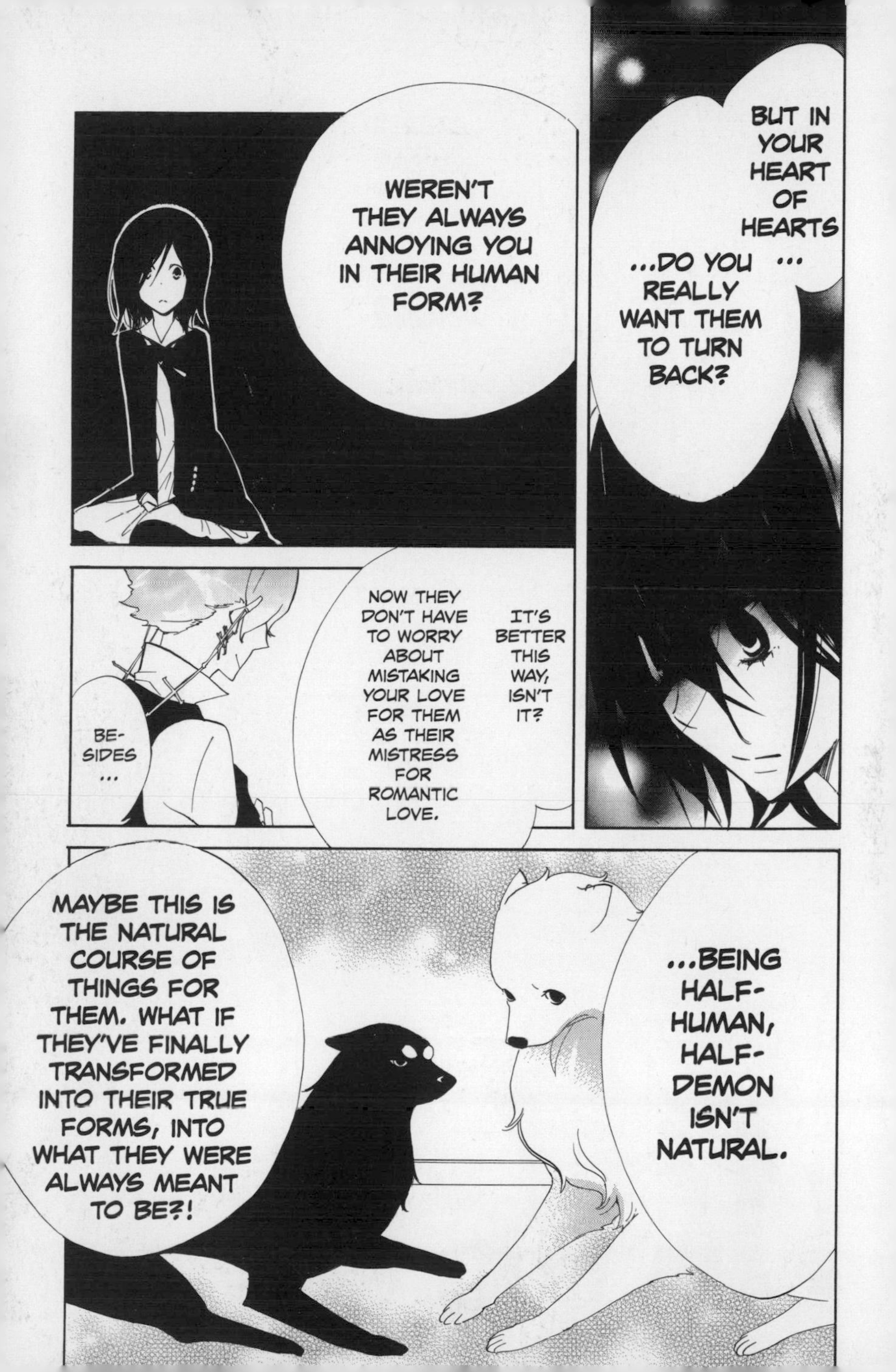
BUT IN YOUR HEART OF HEARTS ...
...DO YOU REALLY WANT THEM TO TURN BACK?
WEREN'T THEY ALWAYS ANNOYING YOU IN THEIR HUMAN FORM?
IT'S BETTER THIS WAY, ISN'T IT?
NOW THEY DON'T HAVE TO WORRY ABOUT MISTAKING YOUR LOVE FOR THEM AS THEIR MISTRESS FOR ROMANTIC LOVE.
BE-SIDES ...
...BEING HALF-HUMAN, HALF-DEMON ISN'T NATURAL.
MAYBE THIS IS THE NATURAL COURSE OF THINGS FOR THEM. WHAT IF THEY'VE FINALLY TRANSFORMED INTO THEIR TRUE FORMS, INTO WHAT THEY WERE ALWAYS MEANT TO BE?!

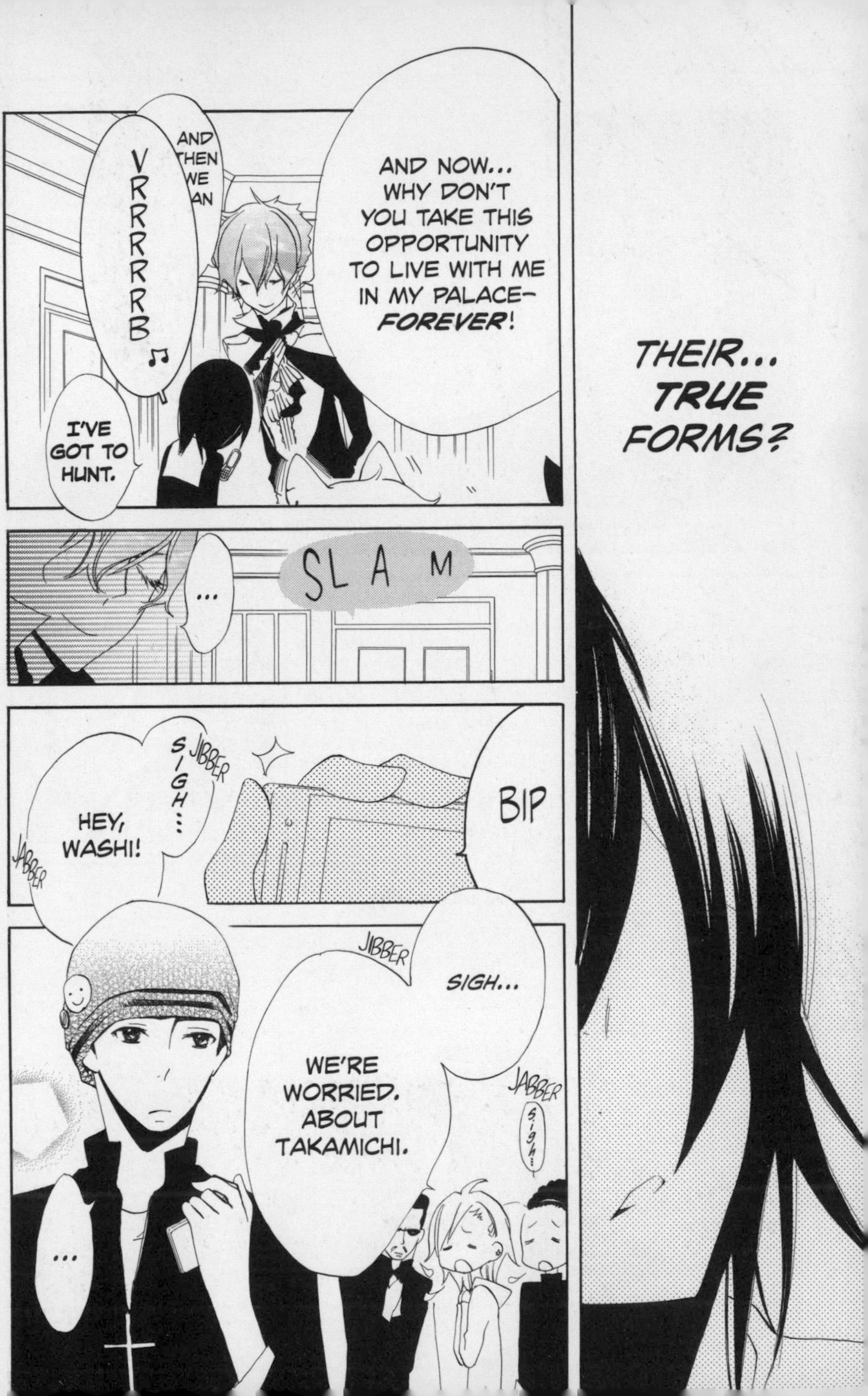
THEIR... TRUE FORMS?
AND NOW... WHY DON'T YOU TAKE THIS OPPORTUNITY TO LIVE WITH ME IN MY PALACE—FOREVER!
AND THEN WE AN
VRRRRRB ♪
I'VE GOT TO HUNT.
SLAM
...
BIP
SIGH...
JIBBER
HEY, WASHI!
JABBER
JIBBER
SIGH...
JABBER
SIGH...
WE'RE WORRIED. ABOUT TAKAMICHI.
...

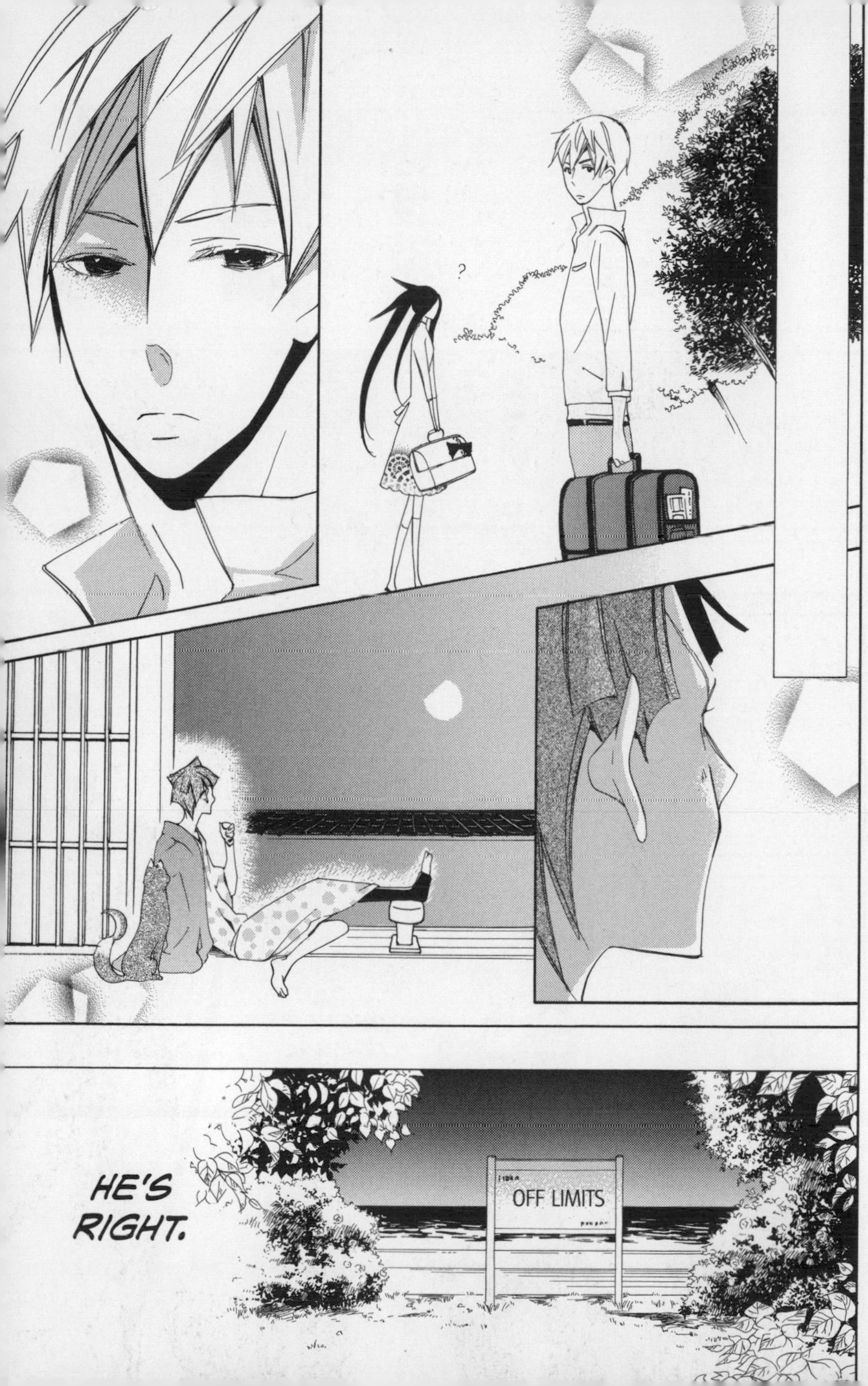
?
OFF LIMITS
HE'S RIGHT.

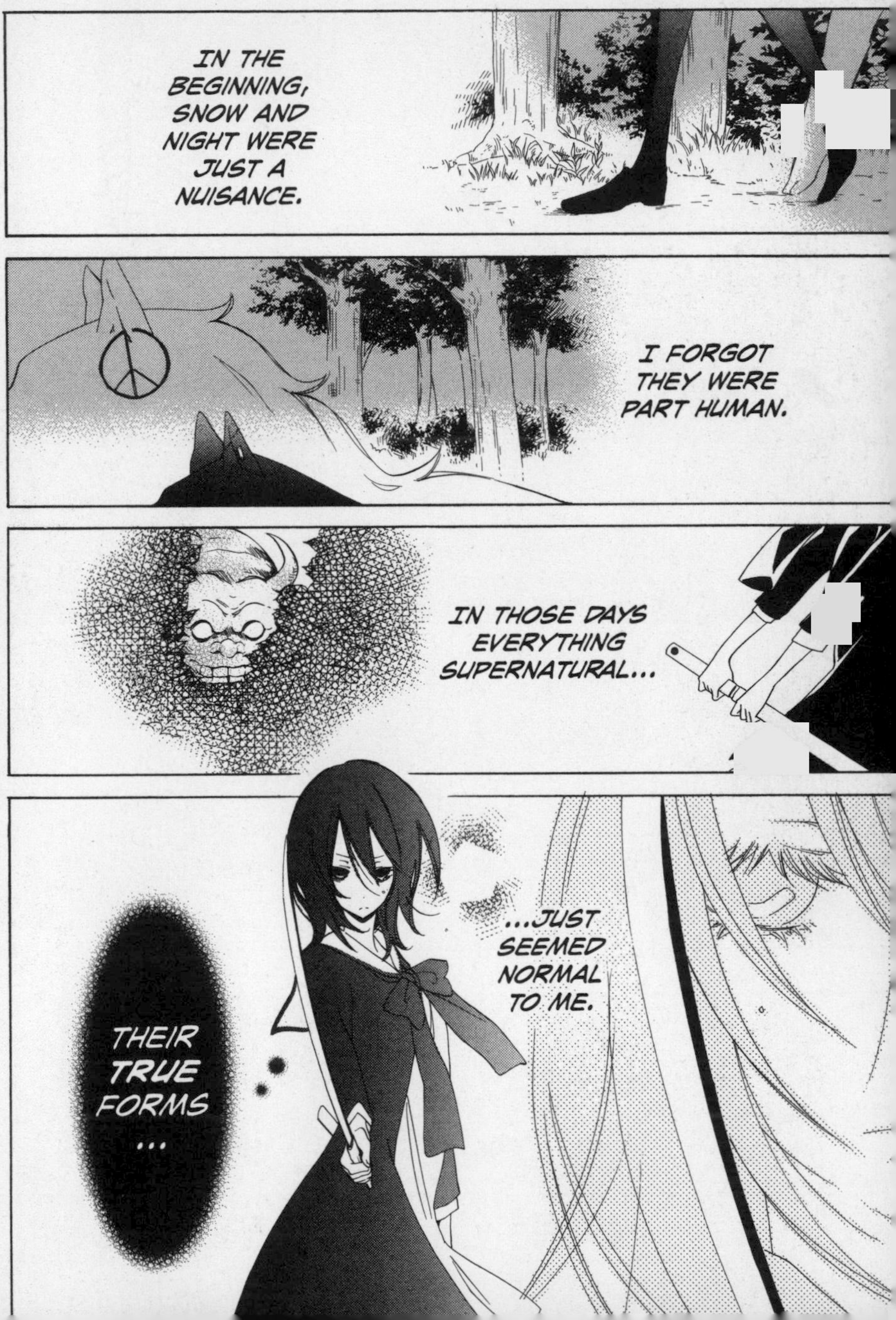

IN THE BEGINNING, SNOW AND NIGHT WERE JUST A NUISANCE.
I FORGOT THEY WERE PART HUMAN.
IN THOSE DAYS EVERYTHING SUPERNATURAL...
...JUST SEEMED NORMAL TO ME.
THEIR TRUE FORMS...

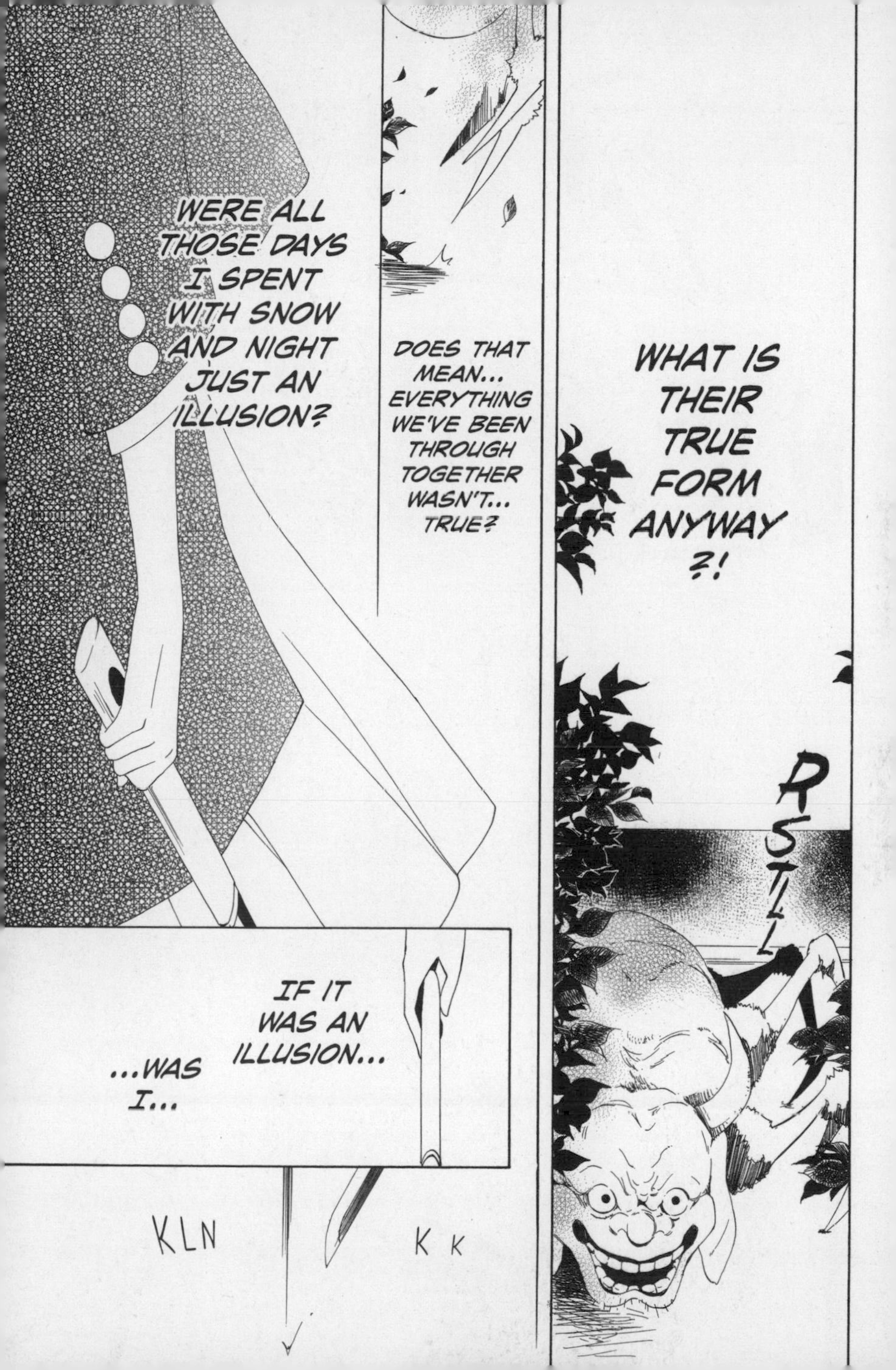
WHAT IS THEIR TRUE FORM ANYWAY?!
RSTL
DOES THAT MEAN... EVERYTHING WE'VE BEEN THROUGH TOGETHER WASN'T... TRUE?
WERE ALL THOSE DAYS I SPENT WITH SNOW AND NIGHT JUST AN ILLUSION?
IF IT WAS AN ILLUSION...
...WAS I...
KLN
K K

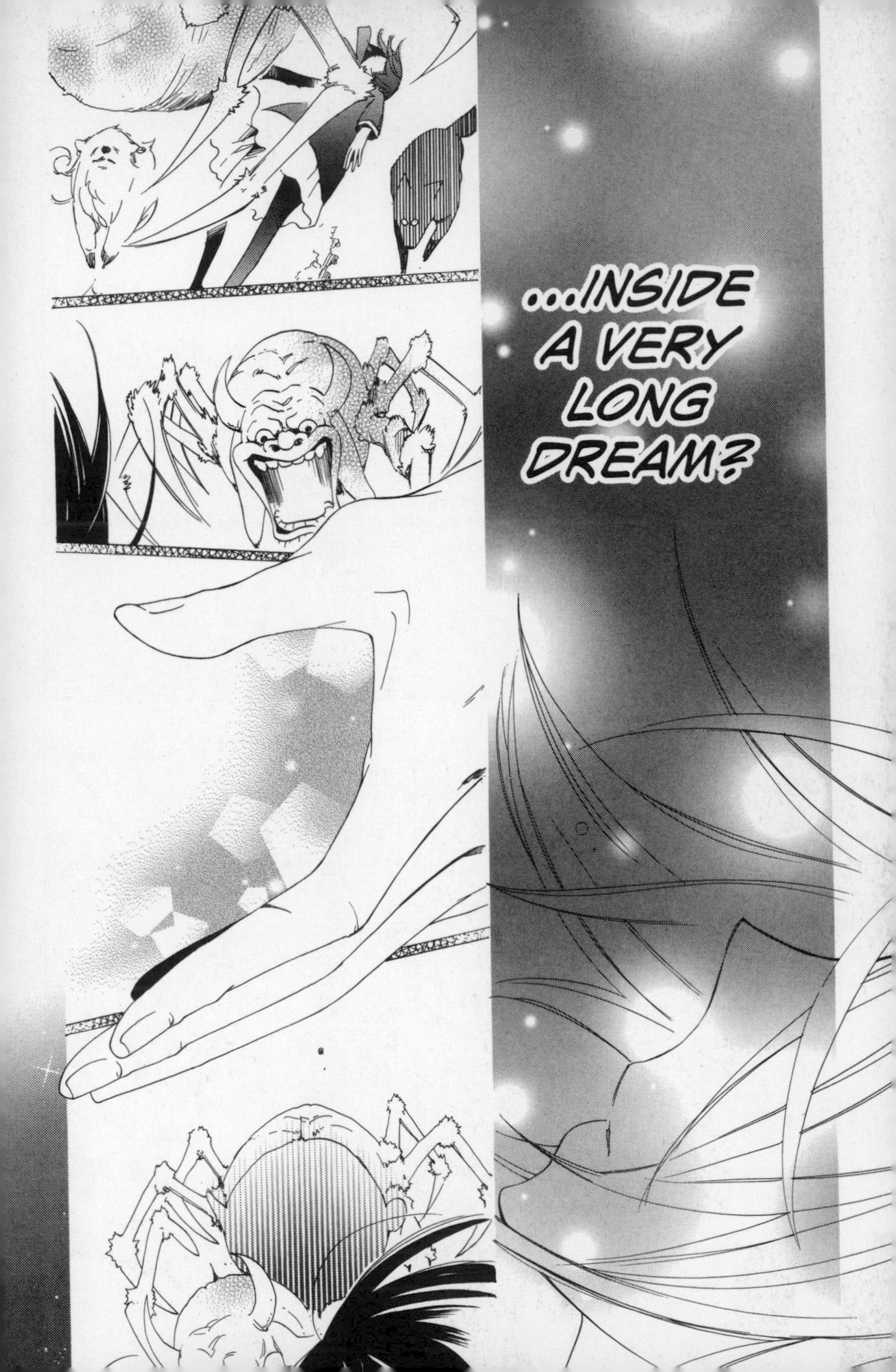
...INSIDE A VERY LONG DREAM?

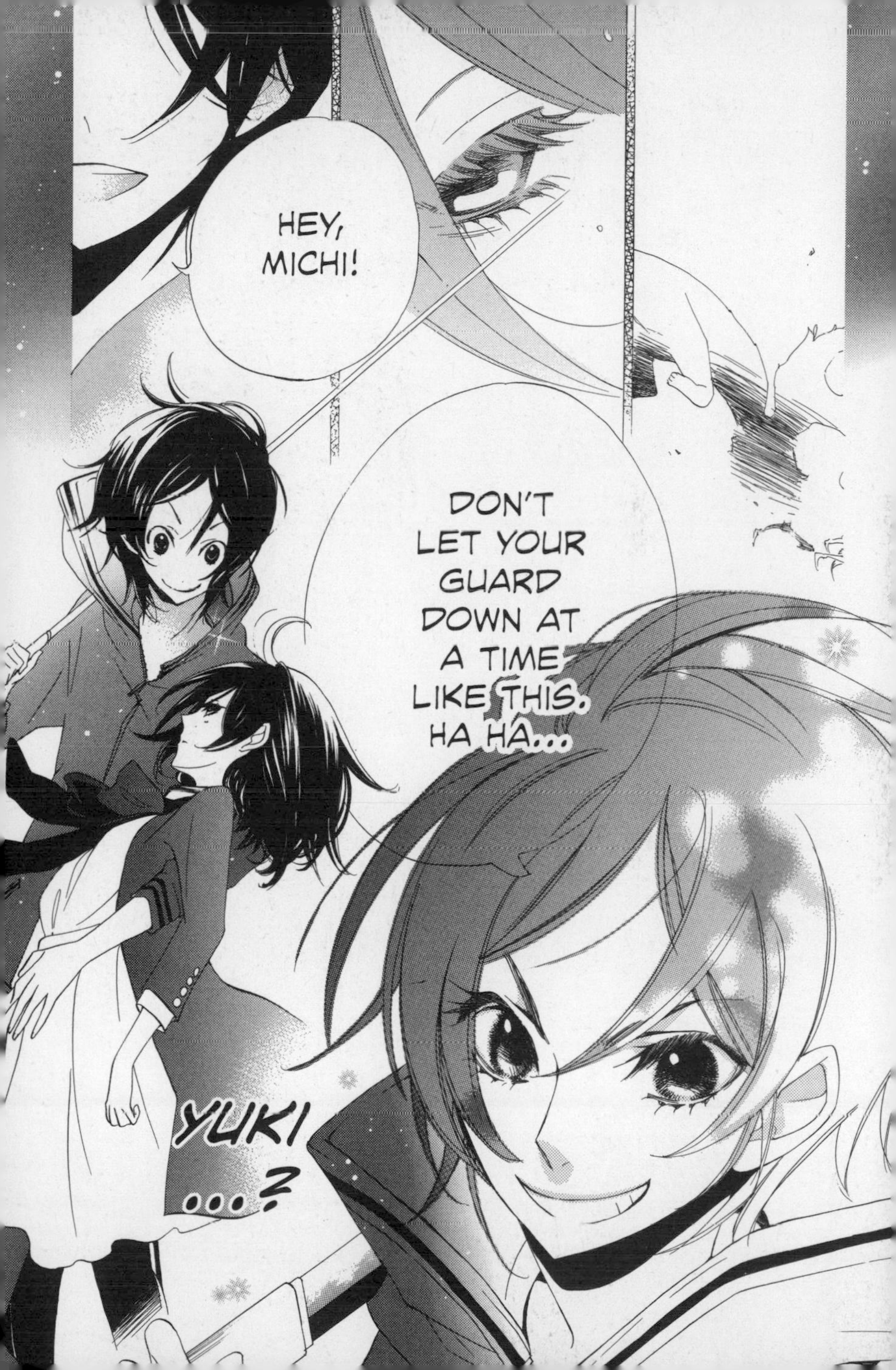
HEY, MICHI!
DON'T LET YOUR GUARD DOWN AT A TIME LIKE THIS. HA HA...
YUKI ...?

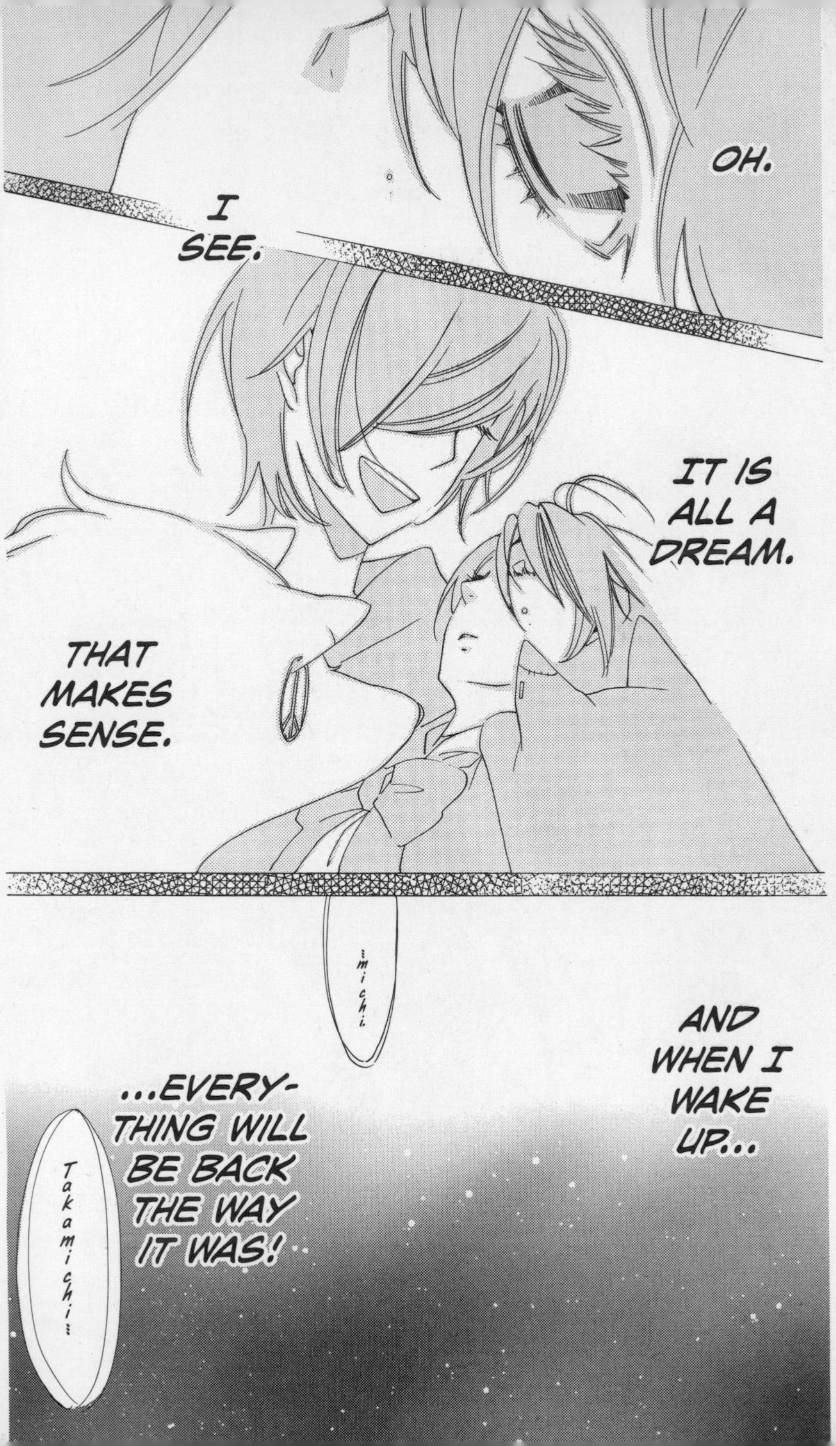
OH.
I SEE.
IT IS ALL A DREAM.
THAT MAKES SENSE.
...michi...
AND WHEN I WAKE UP...
...EVERY-THING WILL BE BACK THE WAY IT WAS!
Takamichi...

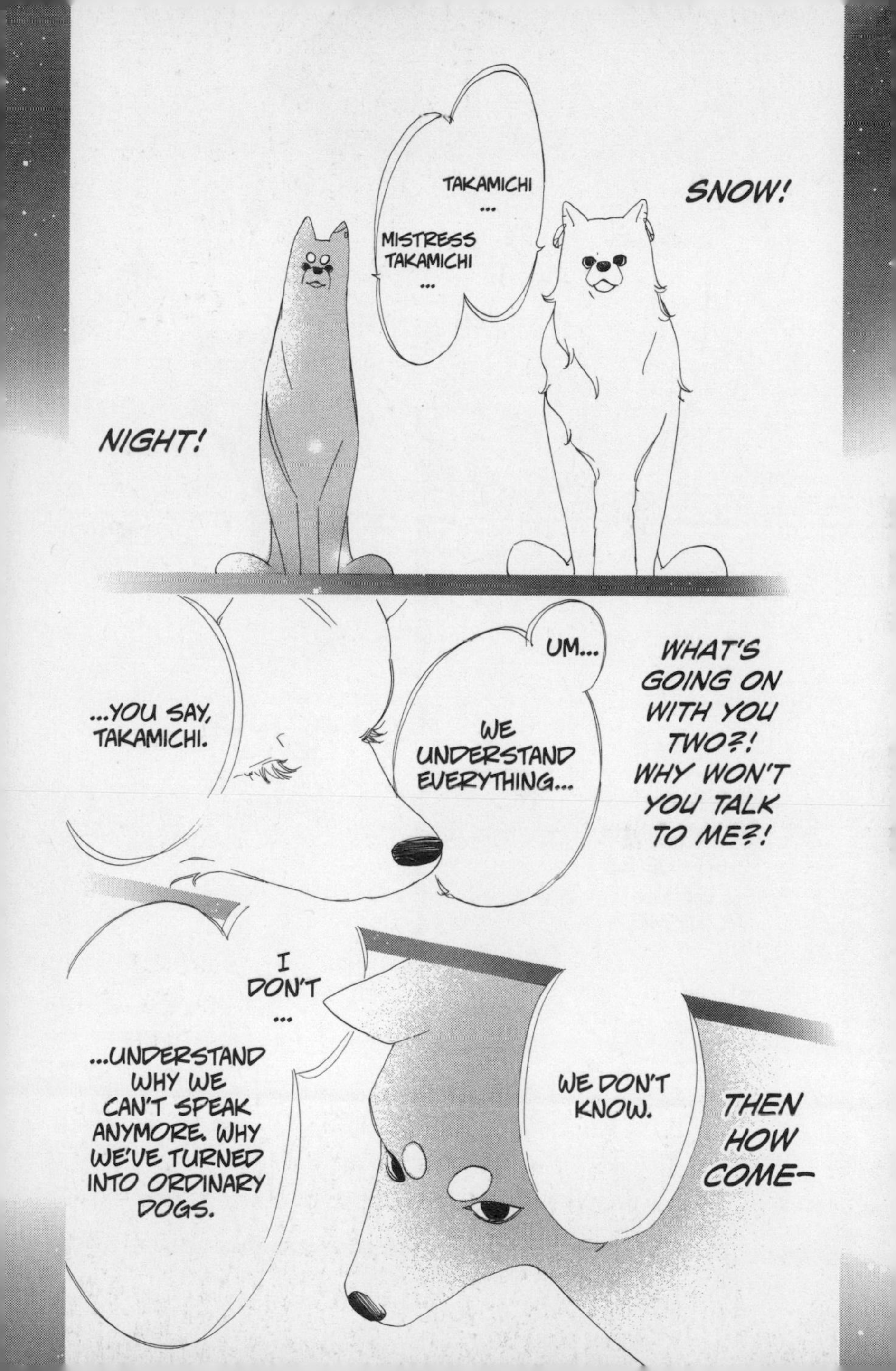
SNOW!
TAKAMICHI ... MISTRESS TAKAMICHI ...
NIGHT!
WHAT'S GOING ON WITH YOU TWO?! WHY WON'T YOU TALK TO ME?!
UM...
WE UNDERSTAND EVERYTHING...
...YOU SAY, TAKAMICHI.
THEN HOW COME—
WE DON'T KNOW.
I DON'T ...
...UNDERSTAND WHY WE CAN'T SPEAK ANYMORE. WHY WE'VE TURNED INTO ORDINARY DOGS.

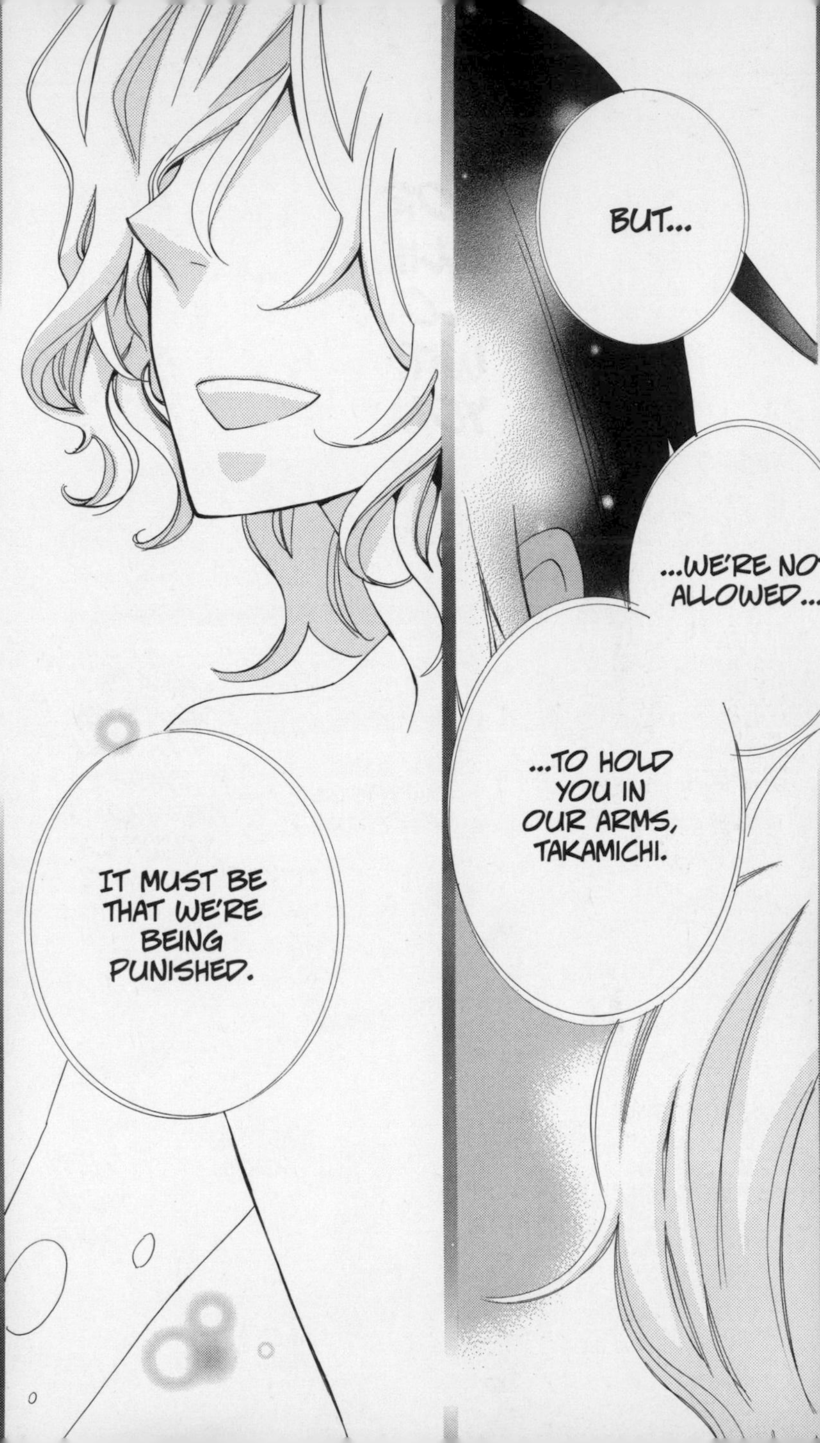
BUT...
...WE'RE NOT ALLOWED...
...TO HOLD YOU IN OUR ARMS, TAKAMICHI.
IT MUST BE THAT WE'RE BEING PUNISHED.

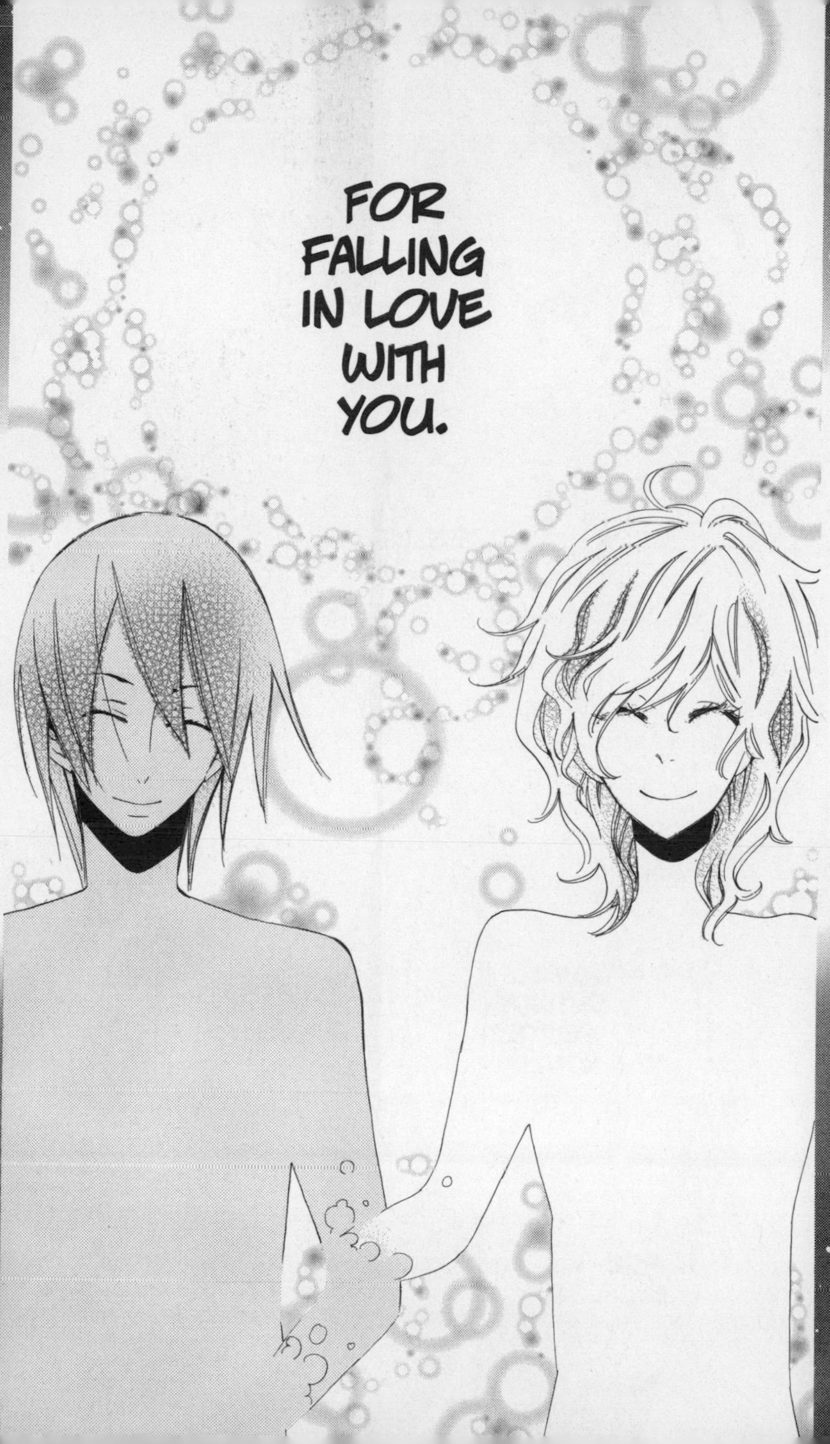
FOR FALLING IN LOVE WITH YOU.

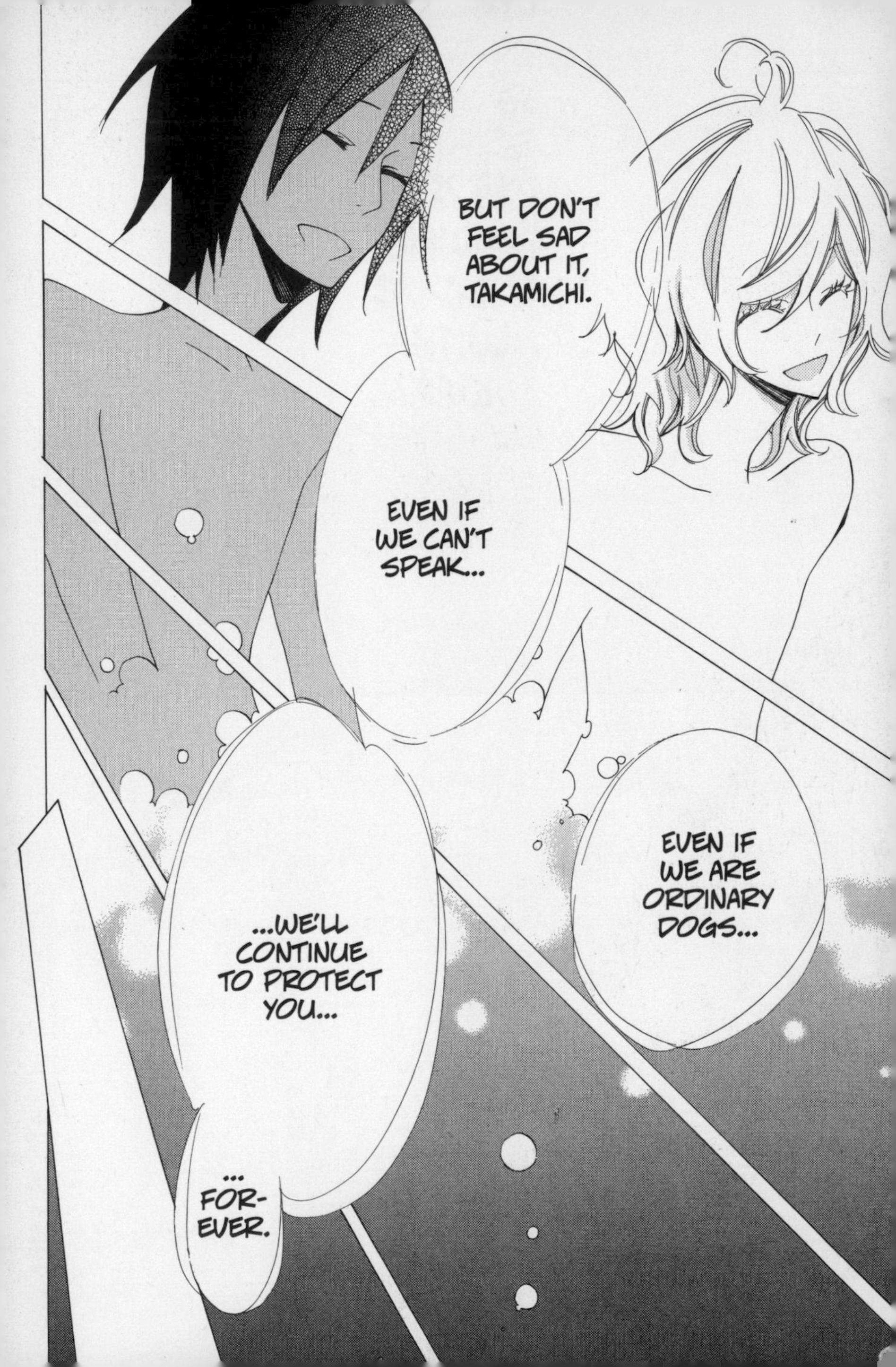
BUT DON'T FEEL SAD ABOUT IT, TAKAMICHI.
EVEN IF WE CAN'T SPEAK...
EVEN IF WE ARE ORDINARY DOGS...
...WE'LL CONTINUE TO PROTECT YOU...
...FOR-EVER.

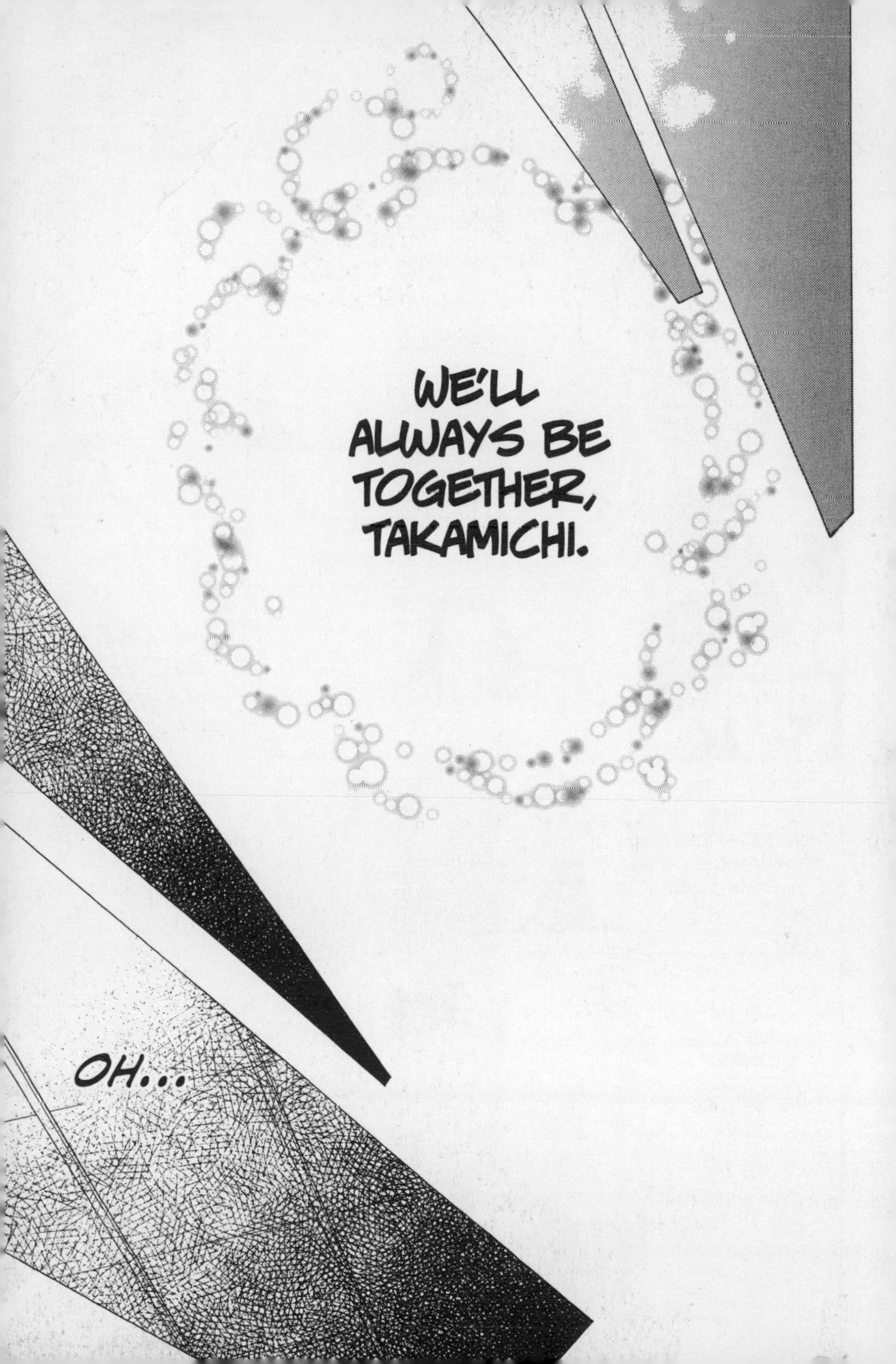
WE'LL ALWAYS BE TOGETHER, TAKAMICHI.
OH...

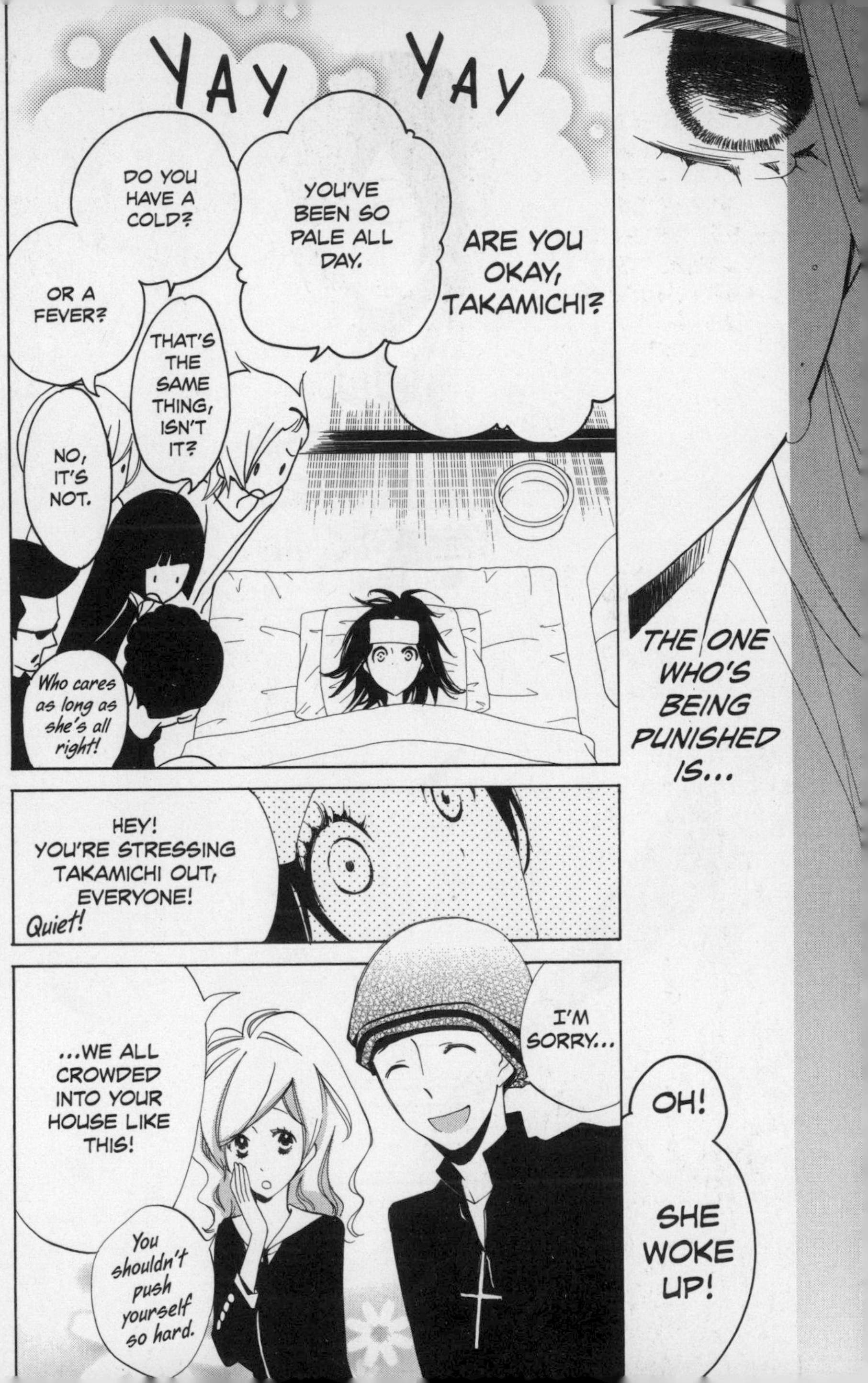
THE ONE WHO'S BEING PUNISHED IS...
YAY YAY
ARE YOU OKAY, TAKAMICHI?
YOU'VE BEEN SO PALE ALL DAY.
DO YOU HAVE A COLD?
OR A FEVER?
THAT'S THE SAME THING, ISN'T IT?
NO, IT'S NOT.
Who cares as long as she's all right!
HEY! YOU'RE STRESSING TAKAMICHI OUT, EVERYONE!
Quiet!
OH! SHE WOKE UP!
I'M SORRY...
...WE ALL CROWDED INTO YOUR HOUSE LIKE THIS!
You shouldn't push yourself so hard.

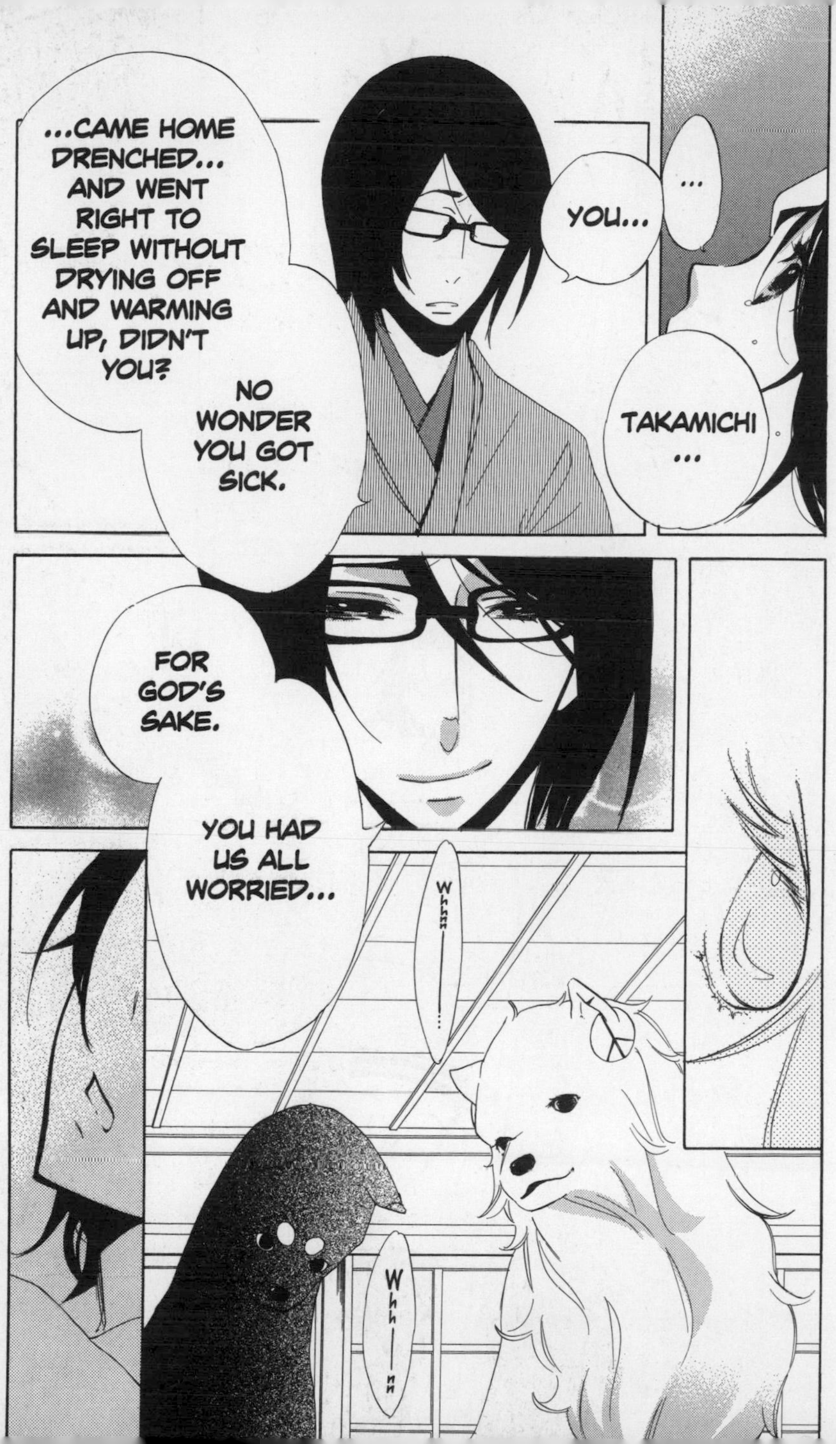
...
TAKAMICHI ...
YOU...
...CAME HOME DRENCHED... AND WENT RIGHT TO SLEEP WITHOUT DRYING OFF AND WARMING UP, DIDN'T YOU?
NO WONDER YOU GOT SICK.
FOR GOD'S SAKE.
YOU HAD US ALL WORRIED...
Whhn—......
Whh—nn

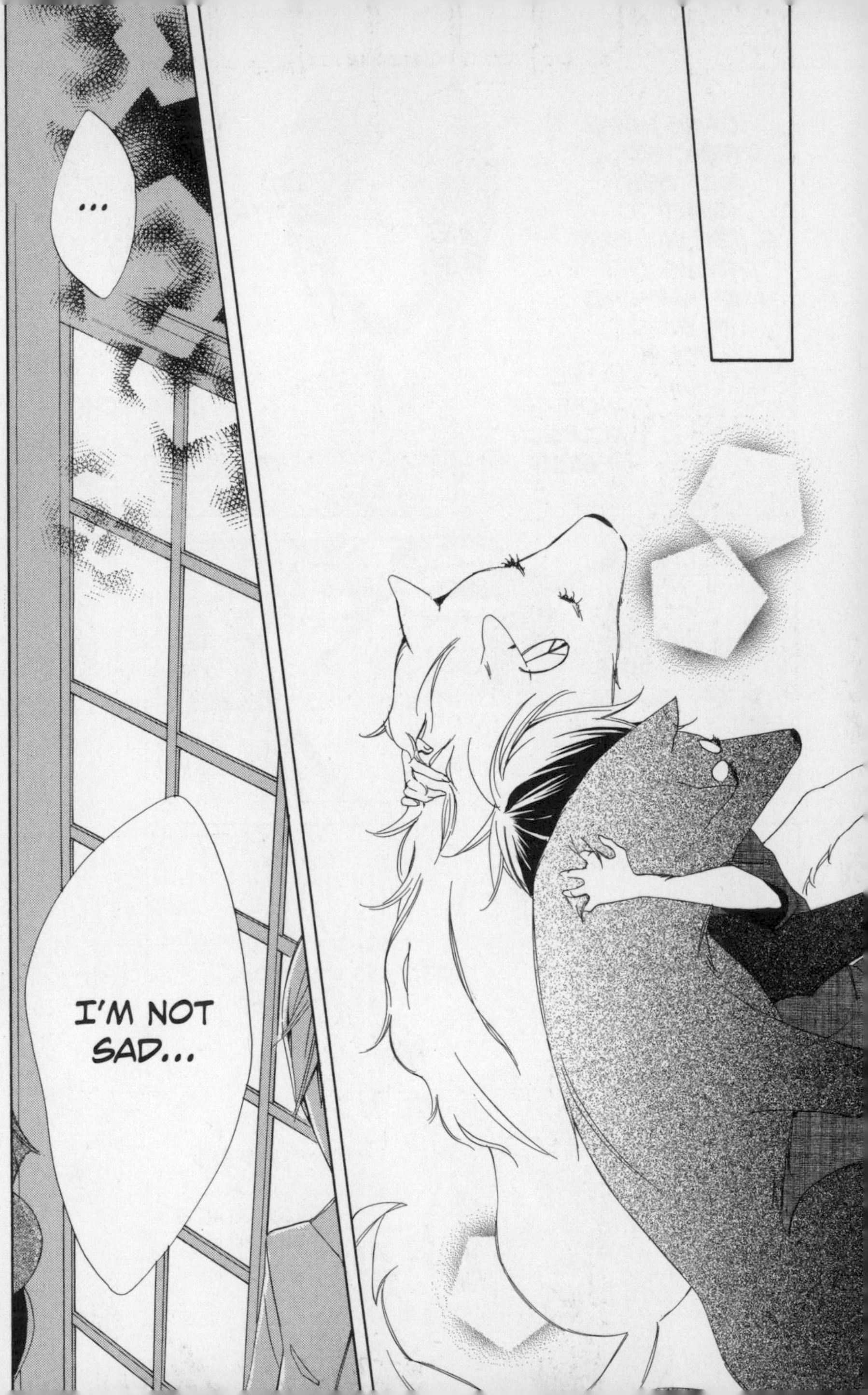
...
I'M NOT SAD...

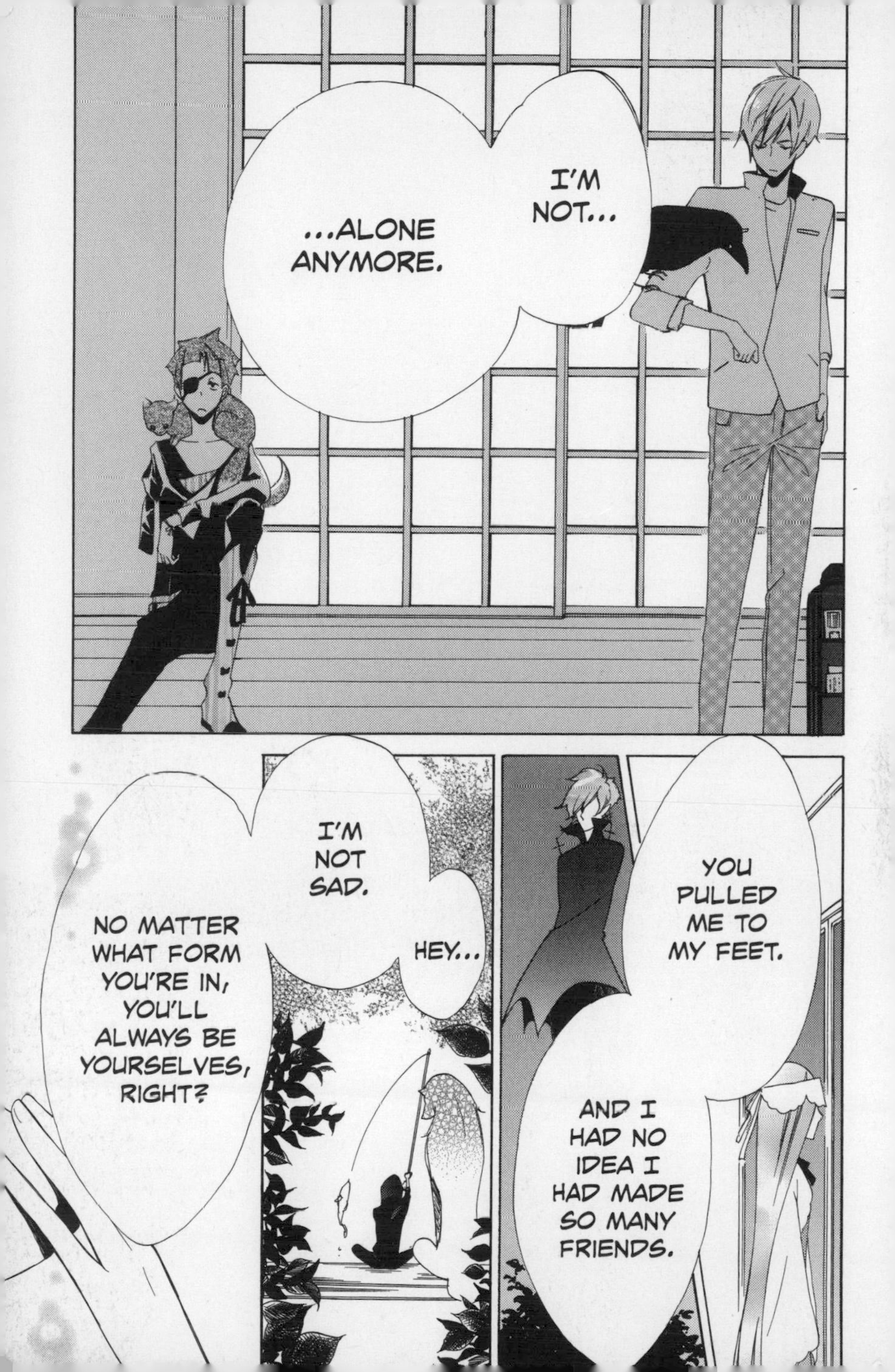
I'M NOT...
...ALONE ANYMORE.
YOU PULLED ME TO MY FEET.
AND I HAD NO IDEA I HAD MADE SO MANY FRIENDS.
I'M NOT SAD.
HEY...
NO MATTER WHAT FORM YOU'RE IN, YOU'LL ALWAYS BE YOURSELVES, RIGHT?

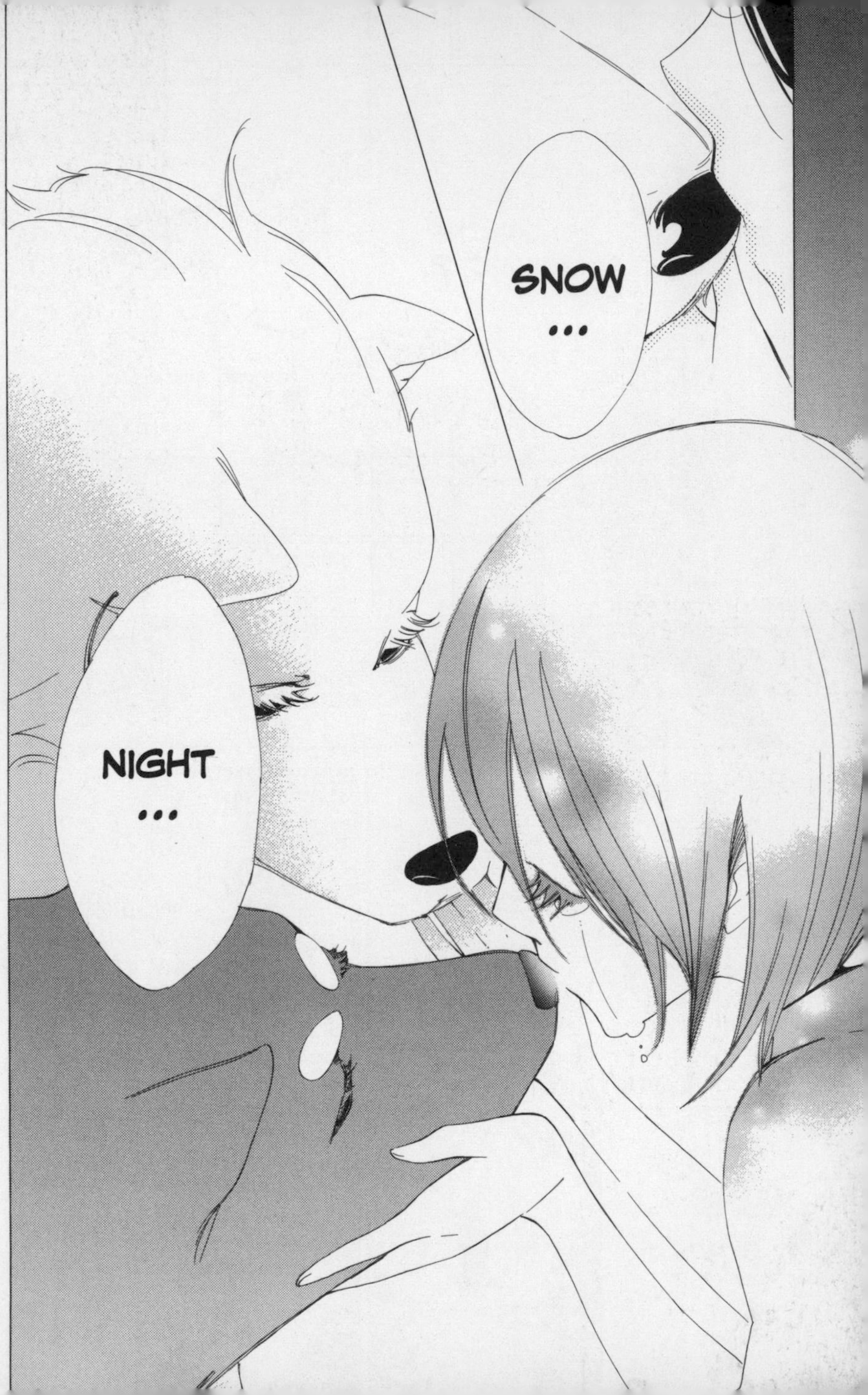
SNOW ...
NIGHT ...

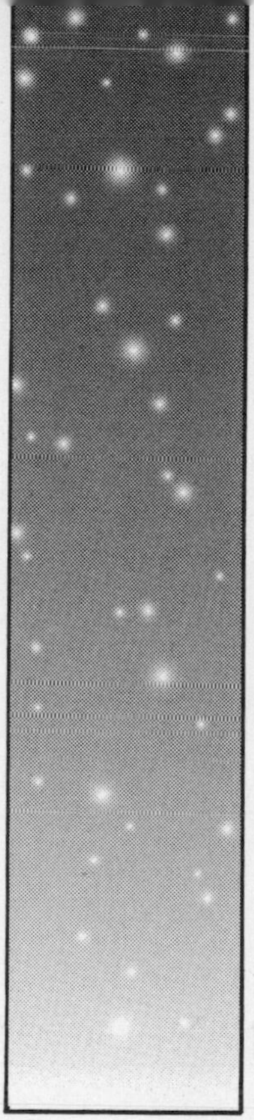

WE'LL ALWAYS BE TOGETHER.

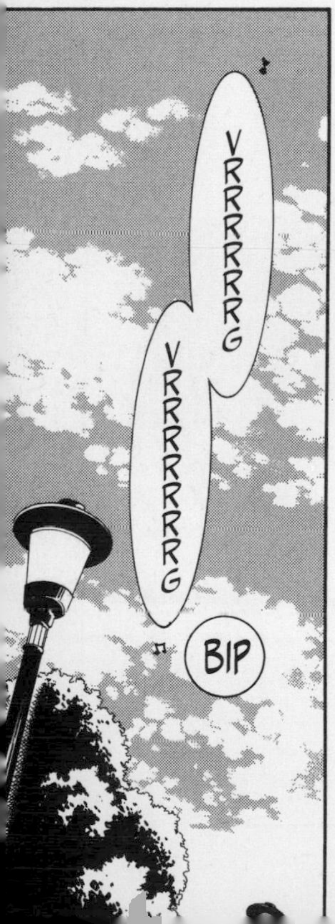
VRRRRRRG
VRRRRRRRRG
BIP

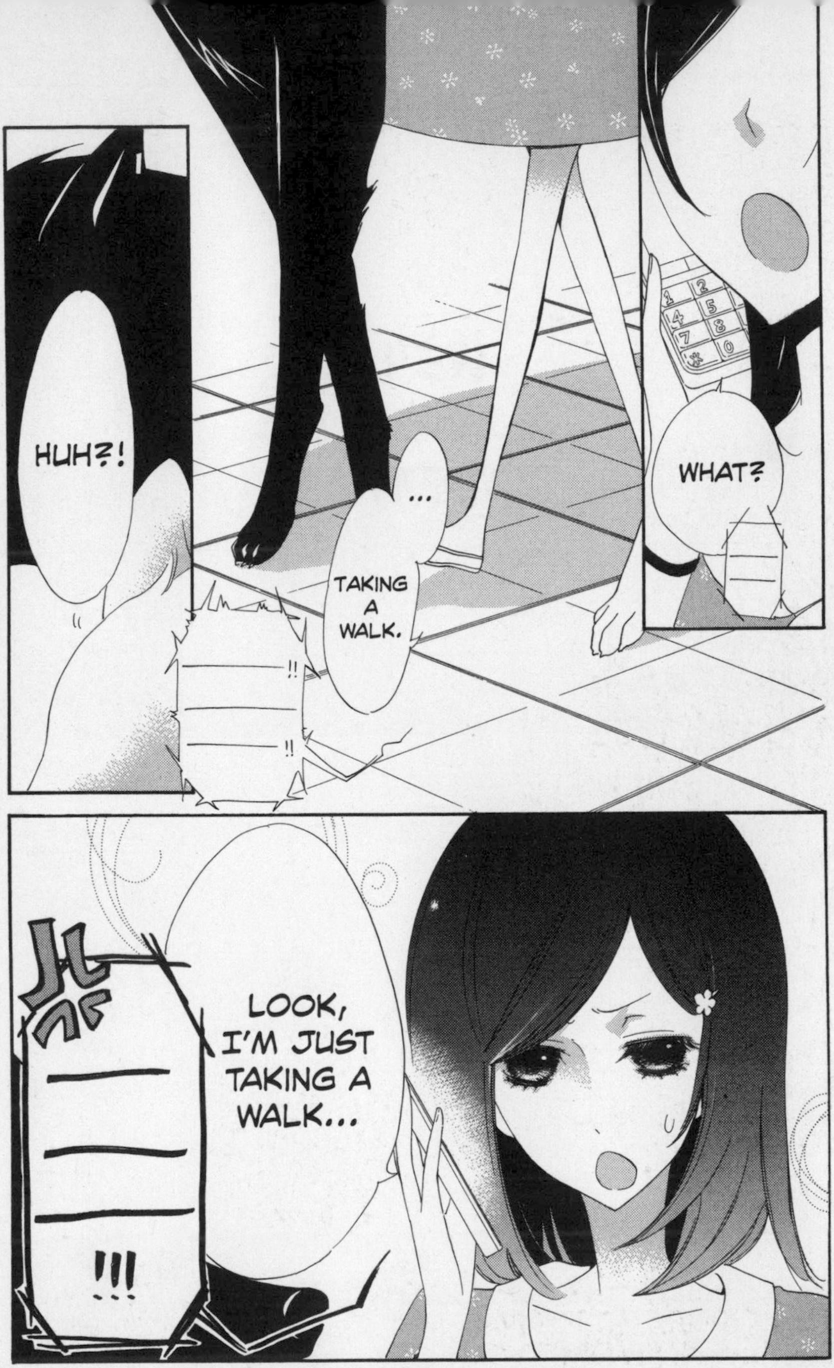
WHAT?
...
TAKING A WALK.
HUH?!
——!!
——!!
LOOK, I'M JUST TAKING A WALK...
———!!!

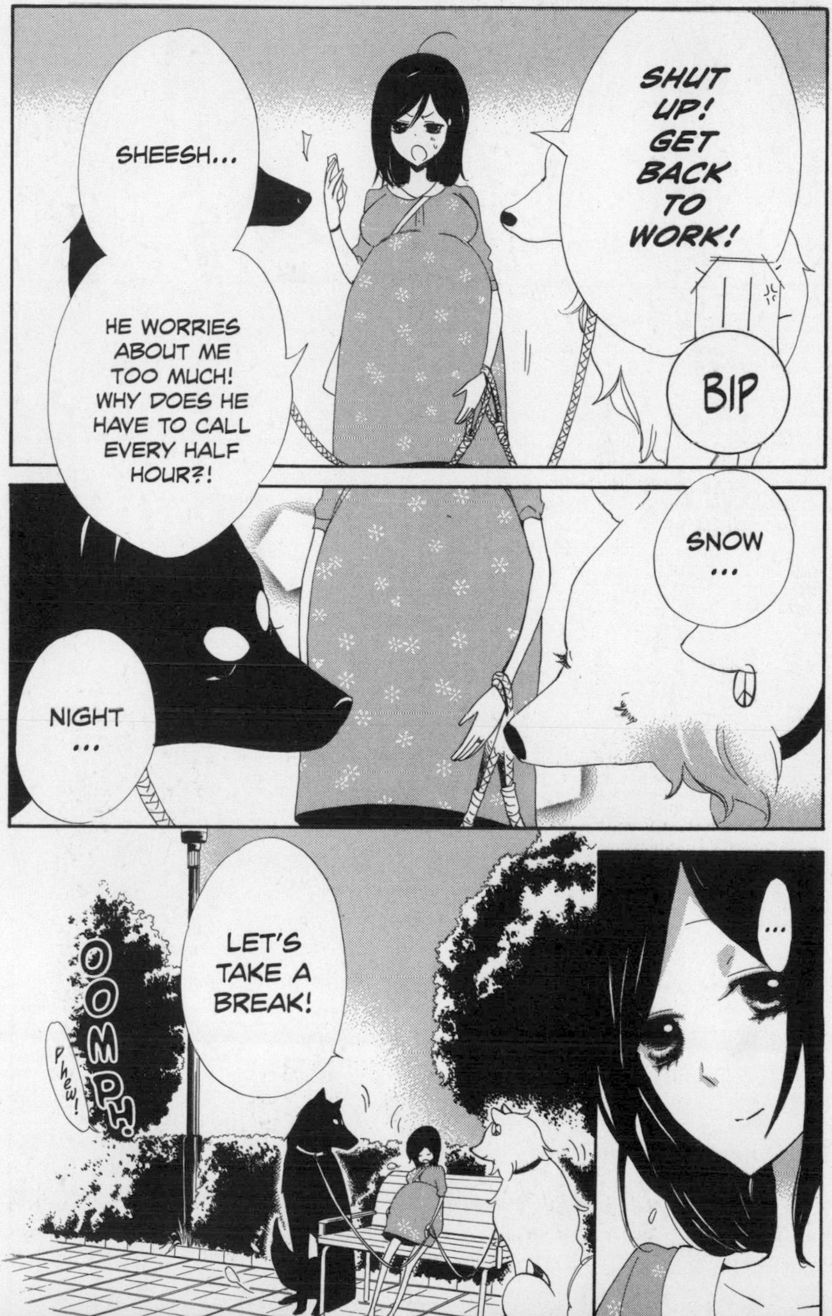

SHUT UP! GET BACK TO WORK!
BIP
SHEESH...
HE WORRIES ABOUT ME TOO MUCH! WHY DOES HE HAVE TO CALL EVERY HALF HOUR?!
SNOW ...
NIGHT ...
...
LET'S TAKE A BREAK!
OOMPH!
Phew!

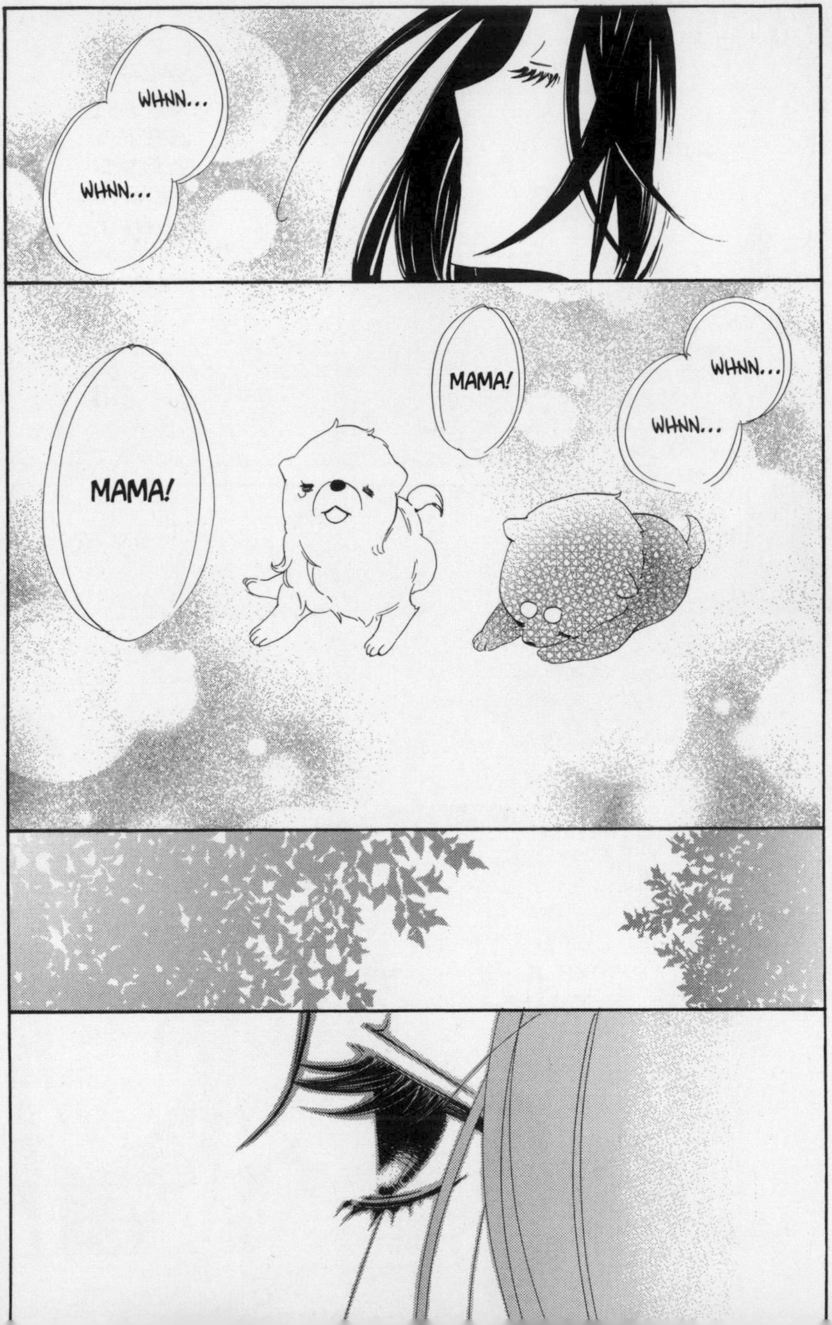
WHNN...
WHNN...
WHNN...
WHNN...
MAMA!
MAMA!

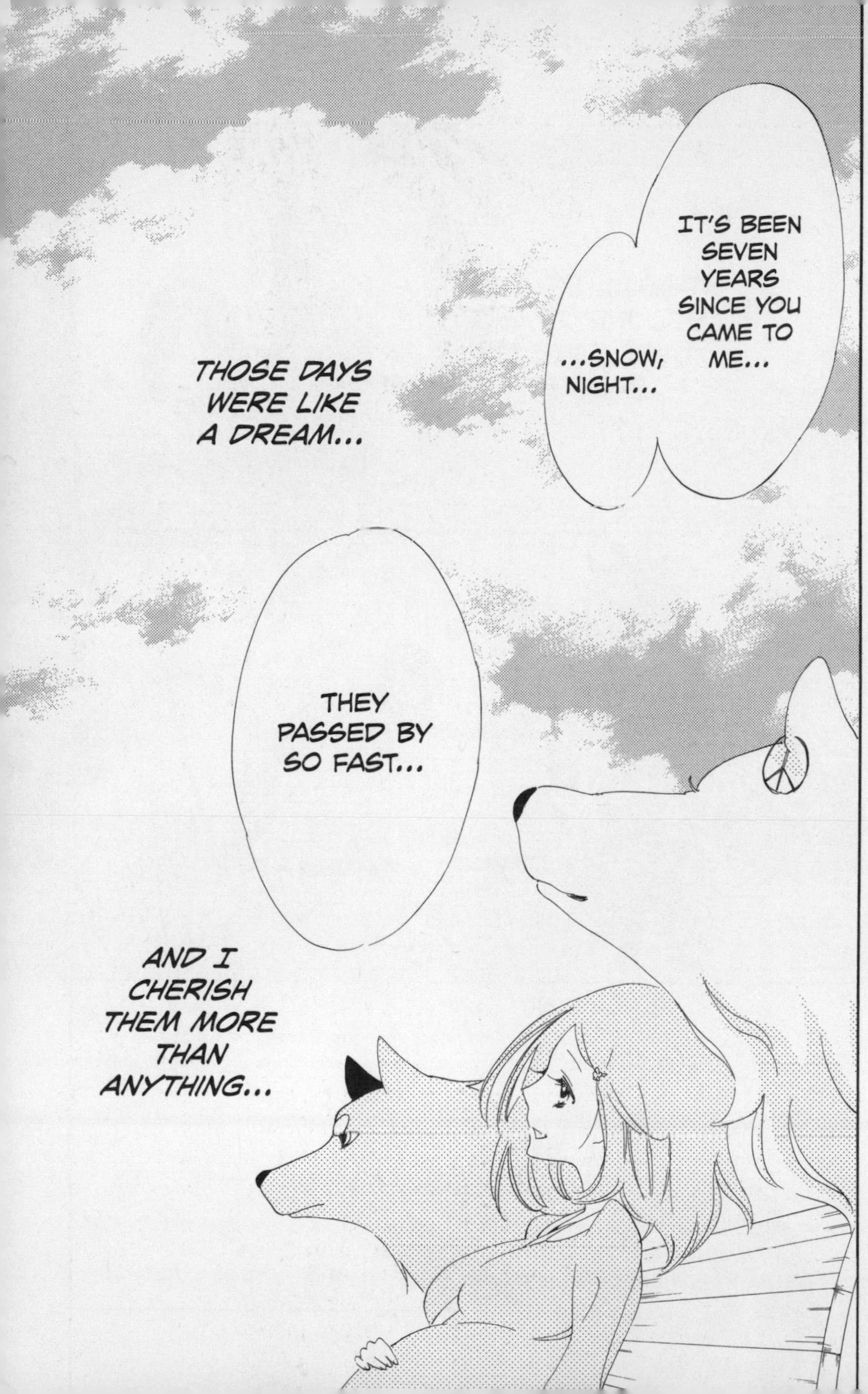
IT'S BEEN SEVEN YEARS SINCE YOU CAME TO ME...
...SNOW, NIGHT...
THOSE DAYS WERE LIKE A DREAM...
THEY PASSED BY SO FAST...
AND I CHERISH THEM MORE THAN ANYTHING...

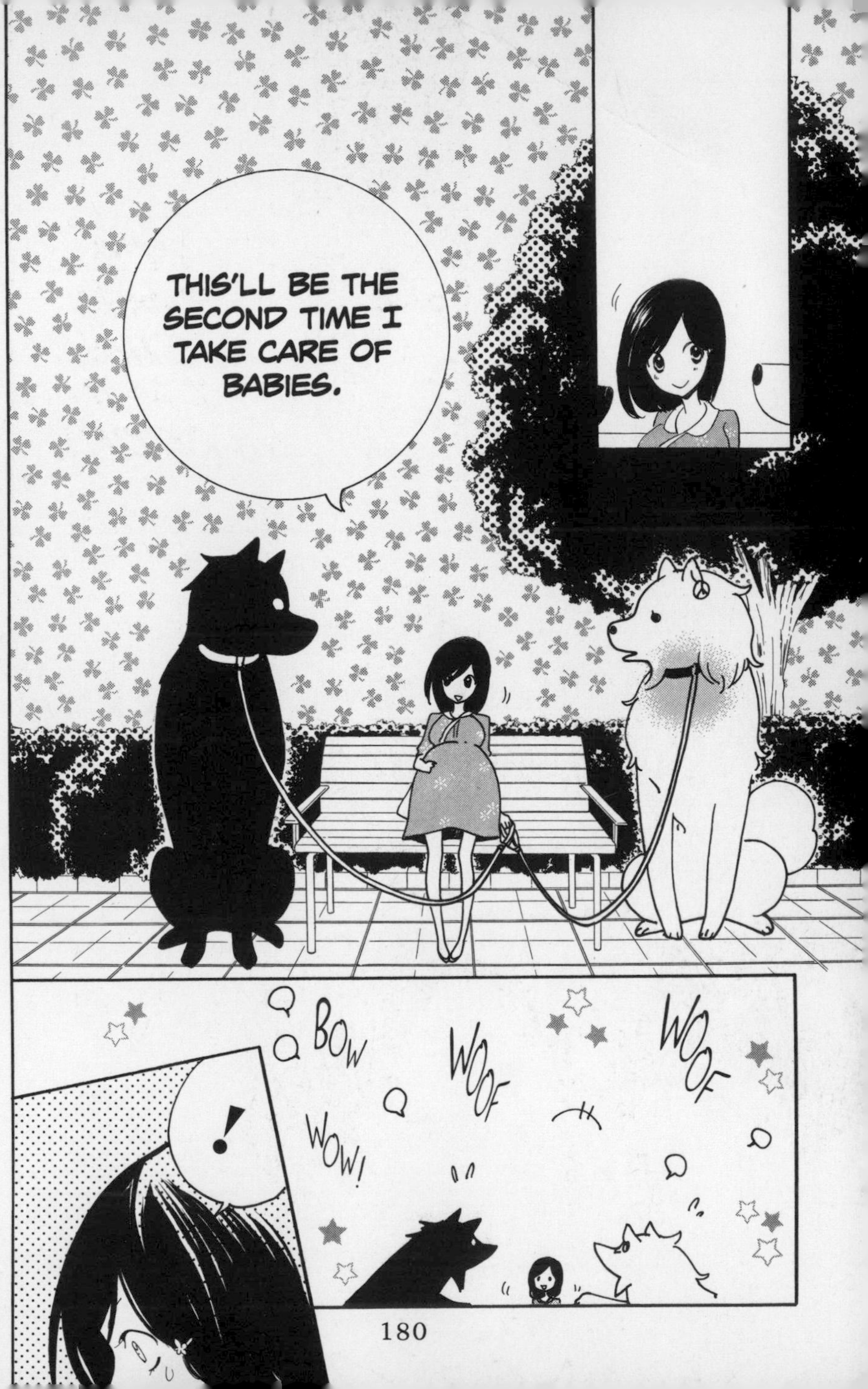
THIS'LL BE THE SECOND TIME I TAKE CARE OF BABIES.
BOW
WOW!
WOOF
WOOF
!

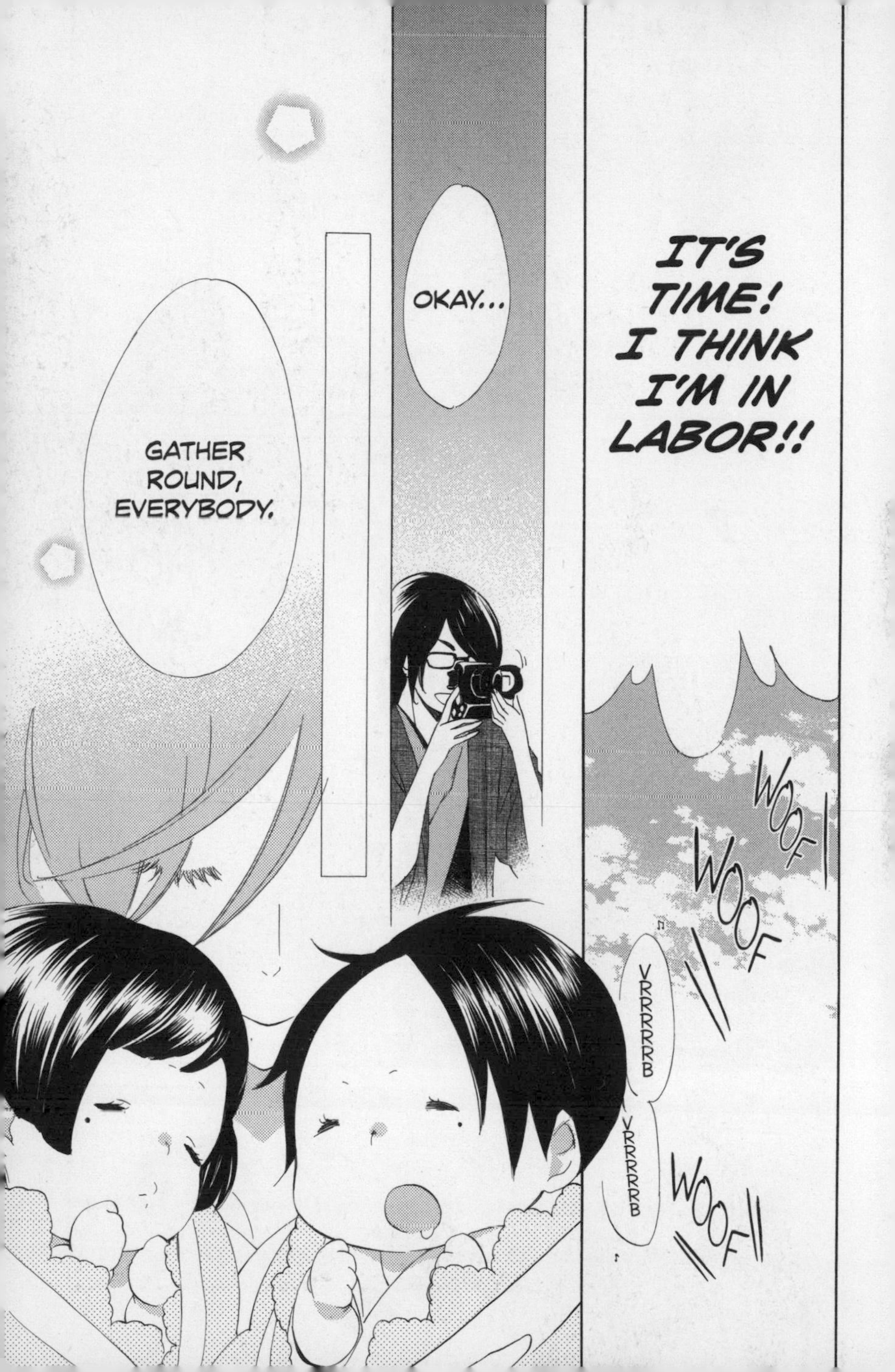
IT'S TIME! I THINK I'M IN LABOR!!
WOOF
WOOF
VRRRRRB
VRRRRRB
WOOF
OKAY...
GATHER ROUND, EVERYBODY.

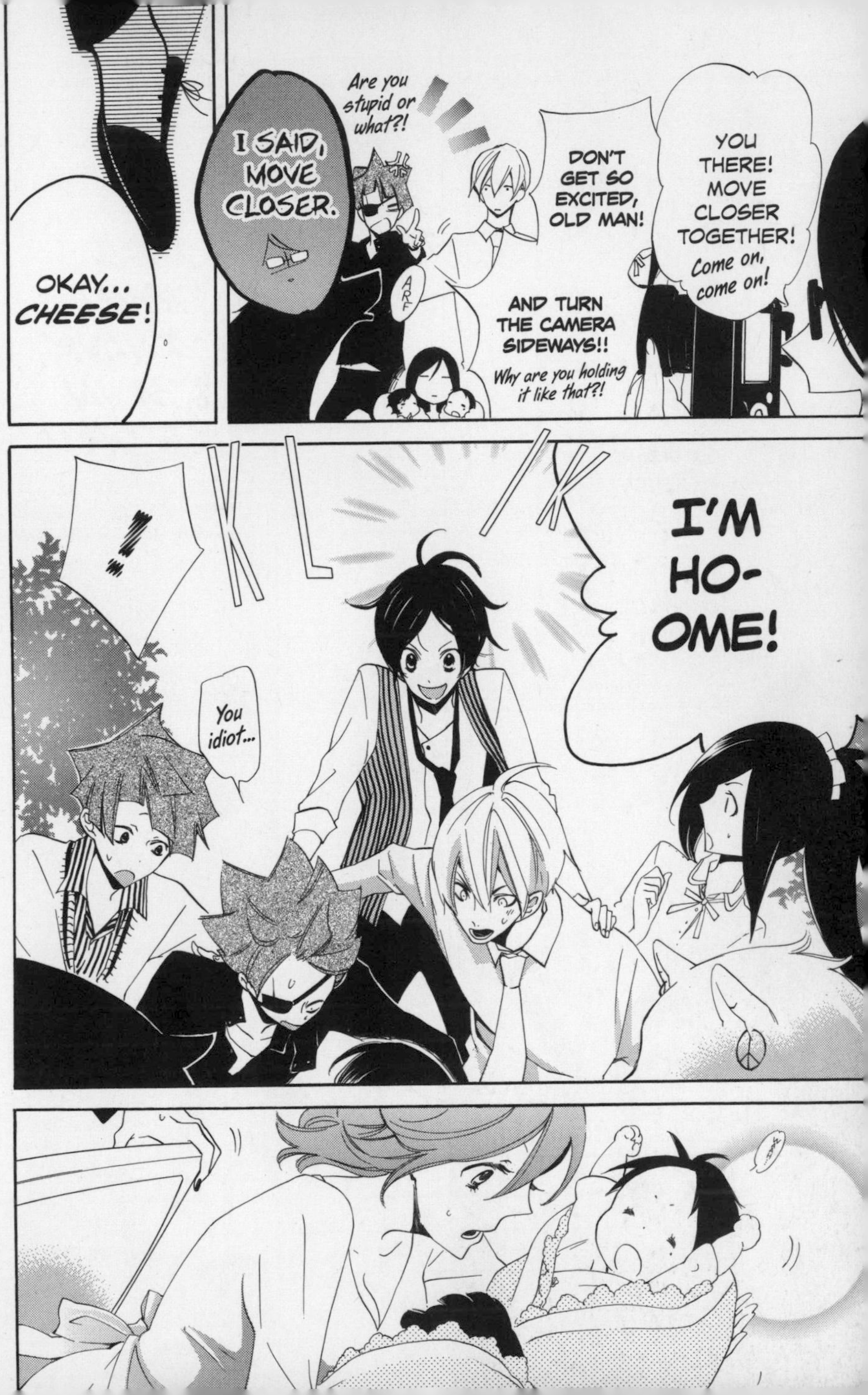
YOU THERE! MOVE CLOSER TOGETHER!
Come on, come on!
DON'T GET SO EXCITED, OLD MAN!
AND TURN THE CAMERA SIDEWAYS!!
Why are you holding it like that?!
Are you stupid or what?!
I SAID, MOVE CLOSER.
ARF
OKAY... CHEESE!
I'M HO-OME!
KLIK
!
You idiot...

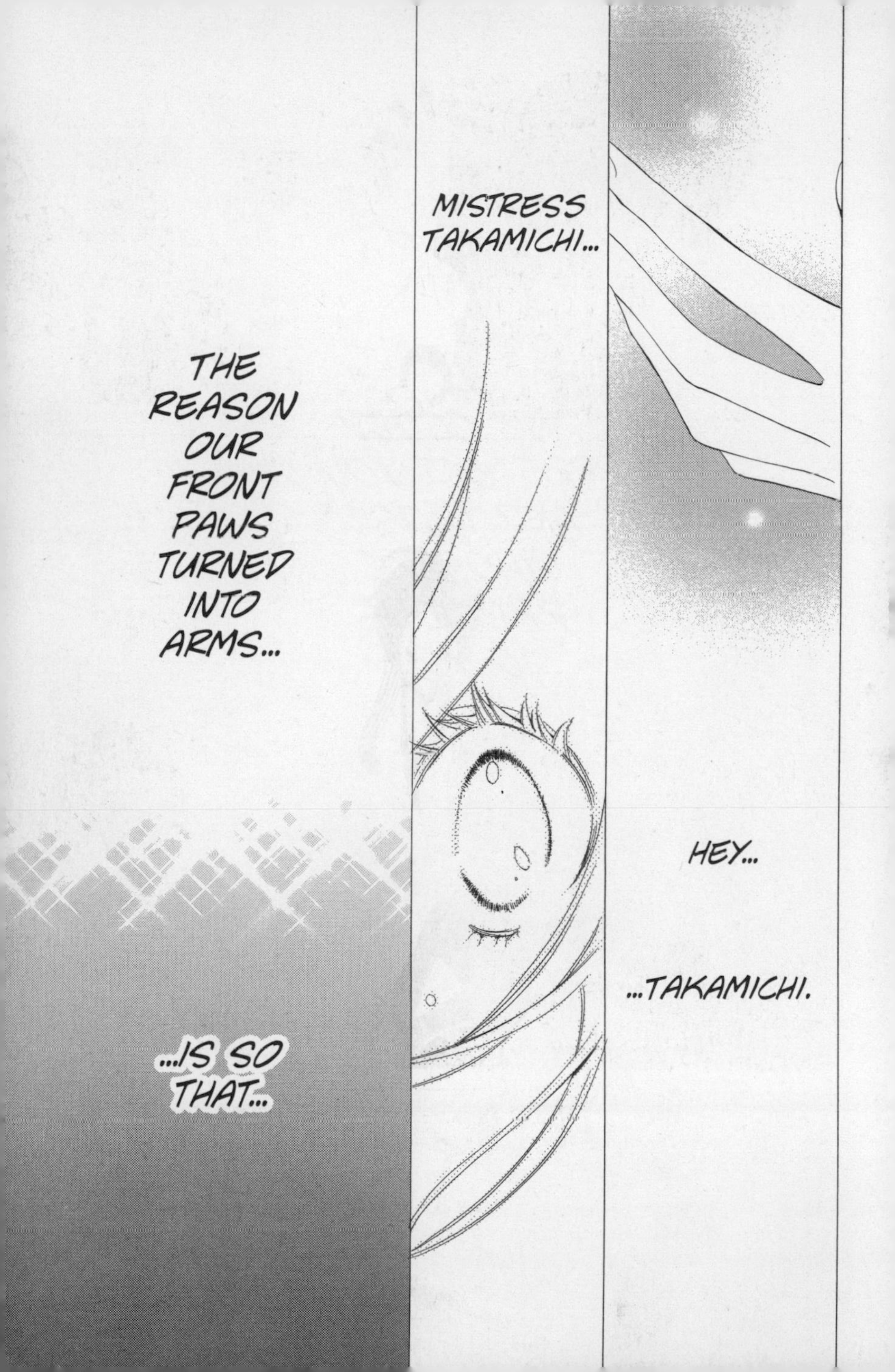
HEY...
...TAKAMICHI.
MISTRESS TAKAMICHI...
THE REASON OUR FRONT PAWS TURNED INTO ARMS...
...IS SO THAT...

...WE COULD
PROTECT YOU
AND THOSE
WHO ARE
PRECIOUS
TO YOU.

Thanks

Haruka Hodaka-sama
Mizuho Komata-sama
Nana Ginna-sama
Mirai Yamada-sama
Seico-sama
Pochi Takahashi-sama
Subaru Akino-sama
Hiitan-sama
Kino Hiragi-sama
Ryo Kikitsu-sama

Takeda-sama
Sakuma-sama
Ishigaki-sama
Nagashima-sama
Takemura-sama
Noro-sama

Everybody Involved
Nakamura Family

And most of all
to all of you
for reading this!

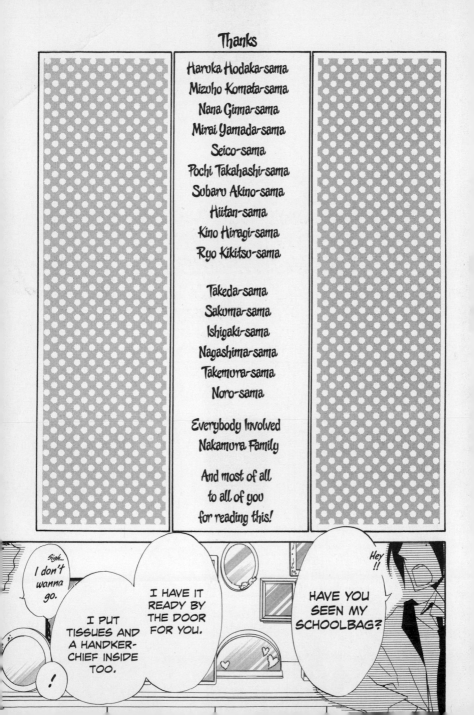

Hey!!
HAVE YOU SEEN MY SCHOOLBAG?
I HAVE IT READY BY THE DOOR FOR YOU.
I PUT TISSUES AND A HANDKERCHIEF INSIDE TOO.
!
Sigh... I don't wanna go.

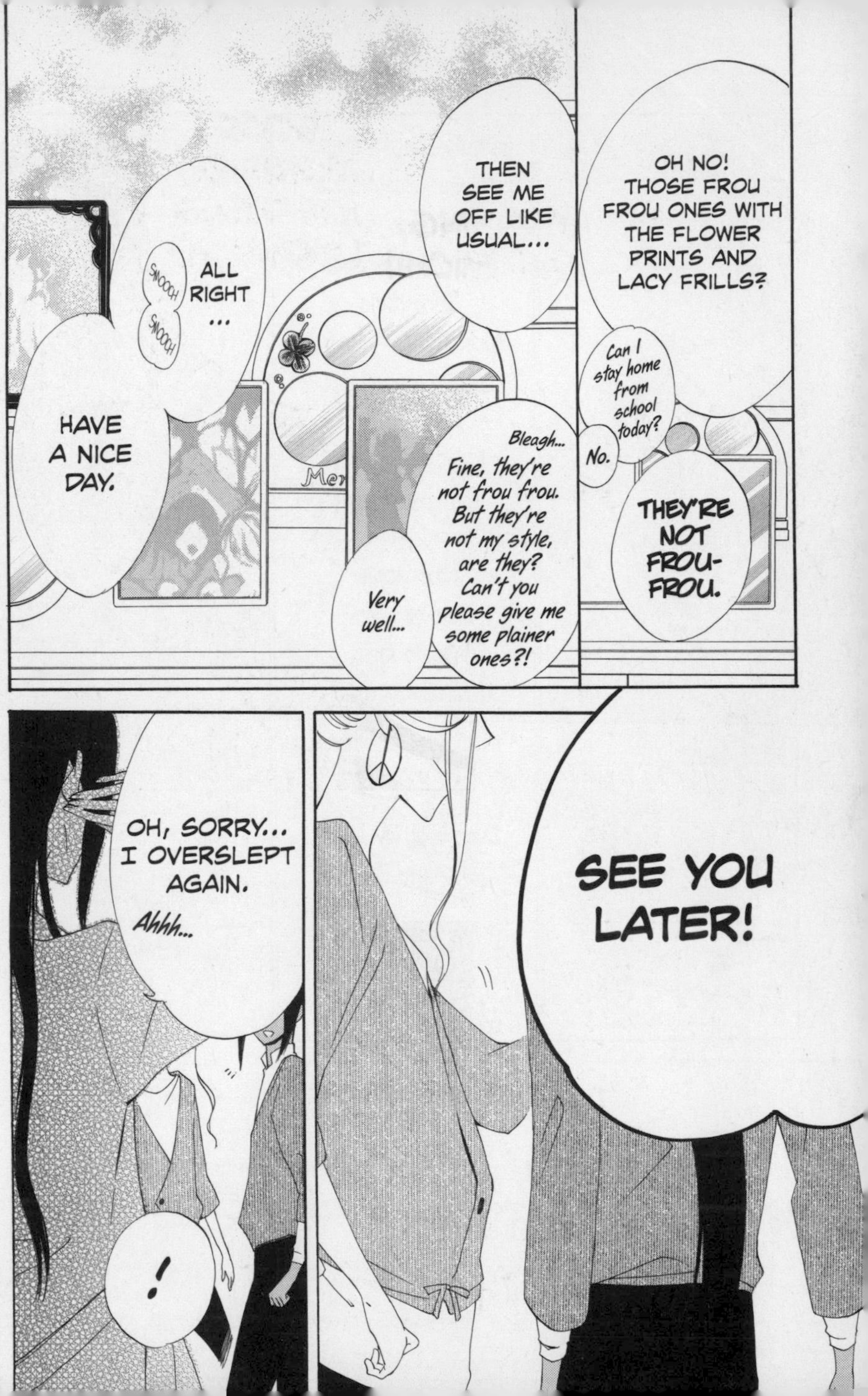
OH NO! THOSE FROU FROU ONES WITH THE FLOWER PRINTS AND LACY FRILLS?
Can I stay home from school today?
No.
THEY'RE NOT FROU-FROU.
THEN SEE ME OFF LIKE USUAL...
Bleagh... Fine, they're not frou frou. But they're not my style, are they? Can't you please give me some plainer ones?!
Very well...
ALL RIGHT...
SMOOCH
SMOOCH
HAVE A NICE DAY.
SEE YOU LATER!
OH, SORRY... I OVERSLEPT AGAIN.
Ahhh...
!

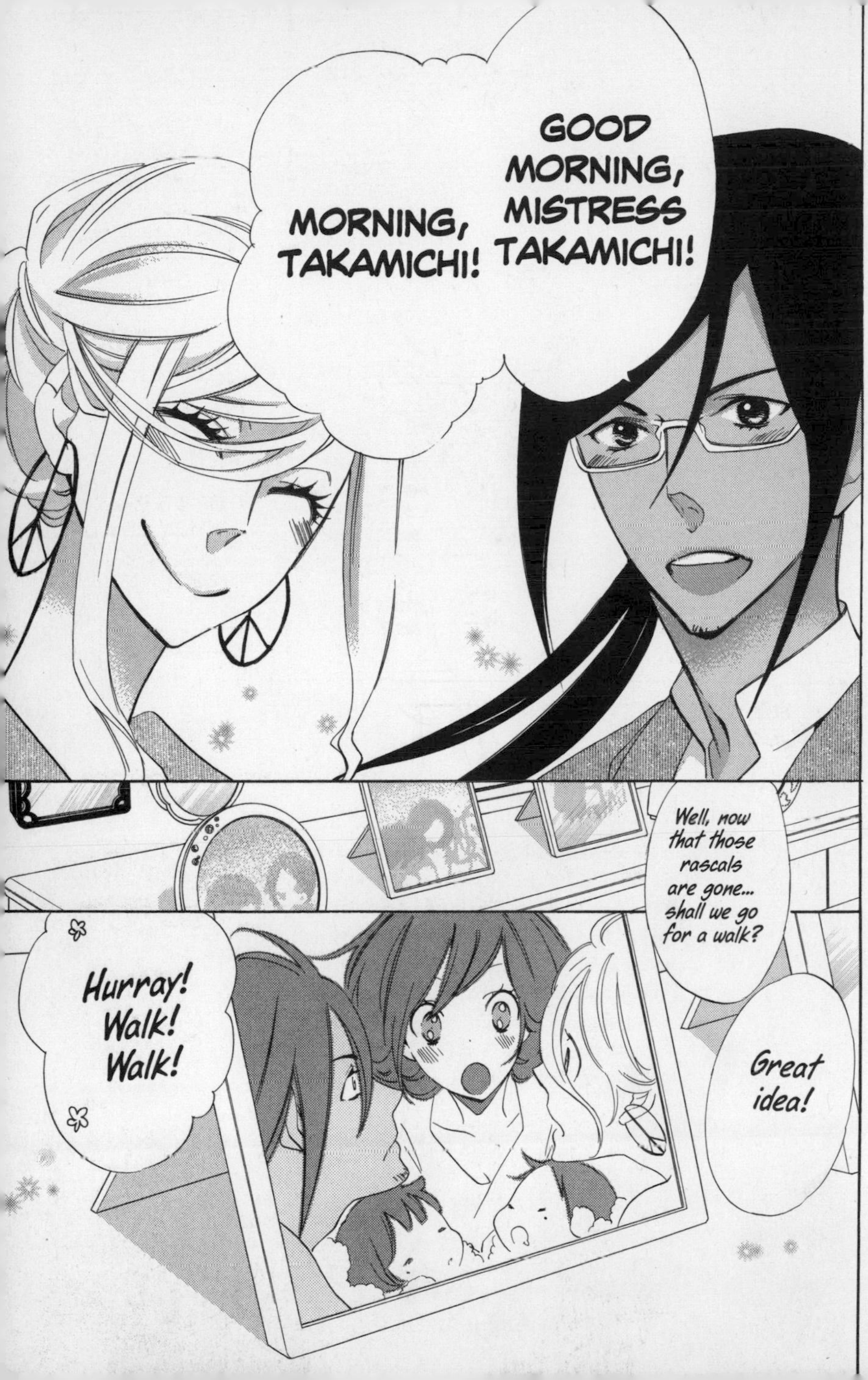
GOOD MORNING, MISTRESS TAKAMICHI!
MORNING, TAKAMICHI!
Well, now that those rascals are gone... shall we go for a walk?
Great idea!
Hurray! Walk! Walk!

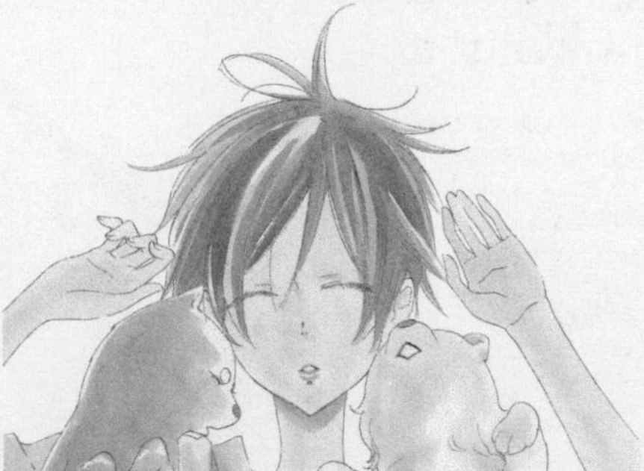

Touya Tobina is from Tokyo. Her birthday is May 23 and her blood type is O. In 2005, her series *Keppeki Shonen Kanzen Soubi* (Clean Freak Fully Equipped) won the grand prize in the 30th Hakusensha Athena Shinjin Taisho (Hakusensha Athena Newcomers Awards).

JIU JIU
VOL. 5
Shojo Beat Edition

STORY AND ART BY
Touya Tobina

English Translation/Tetsuichiro Miyaki
English Adaptation/Annette Roman
Touch-up Art & Lettering/James Gaubatz
Design/Shawn Carrico
Editor/Annette Roman

First published in Japan in 2012 by HAKUSENSHA, Inc., Tokyo.
English language translation rights arranged with HAKUSENSHA, Inc., Tokyo.

Printed in the U.S.A.

Published by VIZ Media, LLC
P.O. Box 77010
San Francisco, CA 94107

10 9 8 7 6 5 4 3 2 1
First printing, July 2013

www.viz.com
www.shojobeat.com

RATED T+ FOR OLDER TEEN

PARENTAL ADVISORY
JIU JIU is rated T+ for Older Teen and is recommended for ages 13 and up. This volume contains violence.
ratings.viz.com

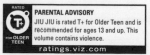

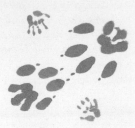

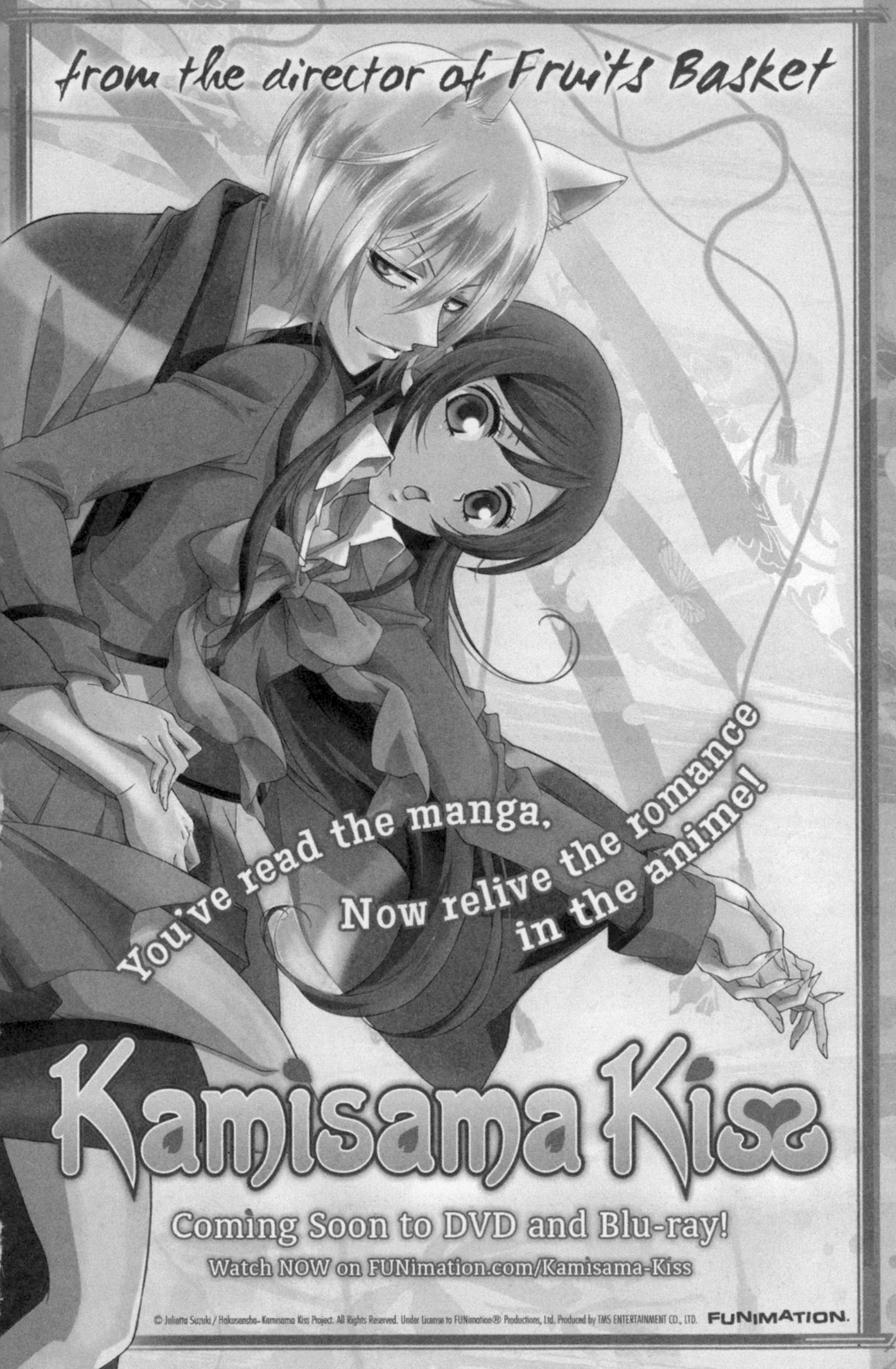
from the director of Fruits Basket
You've read the manga,
Now relive the romance
in the anime!
Kamisama Kiss
Coming Soon to DVD and Blu-ray!
Watch NOW on FUNimation.com/Kamisama-Kiss
© Julietta Suzuki / Hakusensha–Kamisama Kiss Project. All Rights Reserved. Under License to FUNimation® Productions, Ltd. Produced by TMS ENTERTAINMENT CO., LTD.
FUNIMATION.